rtial Ros
01962

Under Postcolonial Eyes:
Figuring the "jew"
in Contemporary British Writing

Under Postcolonial Eyes:
Figuring the "jew" in
Contemporary British Writing

Efraim Sicher and Linda Weinhouse

Published by the University of Nebraska Press, Lincoln and London, for the
Vidal Sassoon International Center for the Study of Antisemitism (SICSA)
The Hebrew University of Jerusalem

Manufactured and distributed for the Vidal Sassoon International Center for
the Study of Antisemitism (SICSA), the Hebrew University of Jerusalem, by
the University of Nebraska Press

Library of Congress Cataloging-in-Publication Data
Sicher, Efraim.
Under postcolonial eyes: figuring the "jew" in contemporary British writing/
Efraim Sicher and Linda Weinhouse.
p. cm.—(Studies in antisemitism)
Includes bibliographical references and index.
ISBN 978-0-8032-4503-7 (cloth : alk. paper) 1. English literature—History
and criticism. 2. Jews in literature. 3. Postcolonialism—Great Britain. 4.
Judaism and literature—Great Britain. 5. Postmodernism (Literature)—
Great Britain. I. Weinhouse, Linda. II. Title.
PR151.J5S54 2012
820.9'3529924—dc23   2012027878

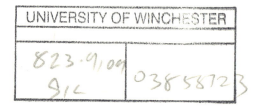
Editing and Typesetting: Alifa Saadya

Contents

List of Illustrations

Acknowledgments

Research for this project was undertaken for the Vidal Sassoon International Center for the Study of Antisemitism at the Hebrew University of Jerusalem. We are grateful to the Center's director, Robert S. Wistrich, for his support and encouragement. The following individuals shared advice, information, and insights:

> The Hon. A. E. Abrahamson, Reuven Amitai-Preiss, Anthony Bale, Clive Bennington, Stephen Clingman, Ivan Cohen, Tina Hamrin Dahl, Ruth Davis, Anita Desai, Shuly Eilat, Sander Gilman, Linda Grant, Andrew Griffiths, George Halasz, David Hirsh, Susie Jacobs, Anthony Julius, Ann Kershen, Lesley Aviva Klaff, Aaron Landau, David Newman, Howard Palmer, Melanie Phillips, Milton Shain, and Suseela Yesudian-Storfjell.

Efraim Sicher thanks his research assistants Hava Oz and Charlotte Guez Shitrit and gratefully acknowledges funding of research by the Israel Science Foundation Grant #233/06.

Linda Weinhouse thanks Wendy Sears, Interlibrary Loan Manager at the Community College of Baltimore County/Essex Campus, for her resourcefulness and super-efficiency.

Earlier versions of a few passages in the Introduction first appeared in Efraim Sicher, *Antisemitism, Multiculturalism, Globalization: The British Case* (Analysis of Current Trends in Antisemitism [ACTA], no. 32. Jerusalem: Vidal Sassoon Center for the Study of Antisemitism, Hebrew University of Jerusalem, 2009); and "The Image of Israel: A View from Britain," *Israel Studies* 16.1 (Spring 2011): 1–25.

Excerpts from chapters two and three first appeared in Efraim Sicher and Linda Weinhouse, "The Passage of the 'jew' to India: Desai, Rushdie, and Globalized Culture," *European Review of History/Revue européenne d'histoire* 18.1 (January 2011): 111–21; and Efraim Sicher, "Sir Salman Rushdie Sails for India and Rediscovers Spain: Postmodern Constructions of Sepharad," in *Sephardism: Spanish Jewish History in the Modern Literary*

Imagination, ed. Yael Wise-Halevi (Stanford: Stanford University Press, 2012) 256–73. We are grateful to the publishers for permission to use this material.

The reproduction of the woodcut in the Almanach of Peter Wagner, Nuremburg 1492, is taken from Heinz Schreckenberg, *The Jews in Christian Art: An Illustrated History* (London: SCM Press, 1996), © SCM Press, reproduced with kind permission.

The photograph of Morris Abrahamson's store in chapter one is reproduced with the kind permission of the Hon. A. E. Abrahamson. That of Fieldgate Synagogue in chapter five is reproduced with the kind permission of Clive Bennington. The photographs of the murals outside the Jewish Soup Kitchen in Brune Street are supplied by courtesy of the East End Celebration Society, with thanks to Philip Walker. The photographs of Brick Lane and the New Synagogue in chapter five are taken from *The Jewish East End,* edited by Aumie and Michael Shapiro (London: Springboard Education Trust, 1996), © Springboard Education Trust. The still from Rachel Garfield's installation *So You Think You Can Tell* is reproduced with the kind permission of the artist, © R. Garfield, 2000.

Preface

DISCOURSES OF THE "JEW"

Shylock, Fagin, and Svengali have long passed into common usage in the English language and can hardly be regarded as evidence of antisemitism, even if some Jews take offense at the term "shylocking," associated with underworld loan sharks and sharp business practice (more recently also with trafficking in body parts). The cosmopolitan subversive moneyed parvenu is easily recognized in *An Education* (2009), a British film which reworks the Pygmalion theme, familiar from Shaw's play and the popular *Educating Rita* (1967), to tell the story of an English schoolgirl seduced by a much older man about town, David Goldman, who introduces her to the adult world of shady deals and promiscuity. David Goldman's "jewishness" is not concealed or coded, since the assimilated Jew has become largely "invisible," but it is evident in archetypal character traits. As in Graham Greene's novel *Brighton Rock* (of which the 2010 movie remake was set, like *An Education,* in the hippie swinging sixties), an innocent woman is corrupted and her life destroyed, except that this is no religious morality tale of evil but a tragic story of an adolescent rebellion against parental control which opts for Paris and happiness instead of forced study for Oxford entrance. Shylock, Fagin, and Svengali are frequently invoked whenever a public figure is suspected of wrong-doing or it is suggested that he is not to be trusted. Fagin was "an indelible part of British culture," a TV adjudication body decided, when clearing the Channel 4 satire show *Bremner, Bird and Fortune* of racial defamation in depicting Lord Levy as the hook-nosed Fagin of the musical *Oliver!,* singing, "you've got to pick a pocket or two."[1] The revival of Lionel Bart's musical in 2009, with comic actor Rowan Aitkinson playing Fagin as a comic but sinister villain, with insinuations of sexual deviancy (bringing together the traditions of pantomime and the Stage Jew), aroused the wrath of Jewish playwright Julia Pascal,[2] but most critics could only see an uproarious Cockney knees-up that did little justice to Dickens.[3]

Shylock has often been read through Fagin, and it seems few could believe that the "jew" was not synonymous with dishonest and merciless money-making. The fact that Disraeli in his time was caricatured stereotypically as a Jew says something about the ubiquity of racial typing in politics.[4] When complaint is made, this is seen as proof of Jewish ownership of the press. As Princess Michael of Kent famously observed in an interview with a German newspaper when Prince Harry was criticized in early 2005 for wearing Nazi uniform at a party, "The press has a different sensibility because of its ownership structure."[5] Each incidence is surely not sufficient to warrant hysteria over a "tsunami" of antisemitism (to use British Chief Rabbi Lord Sacks' controversial phrase), but it certainly points to the recurrence of stereotyped language that may no longer be regarded as offensive in a postmodern spirit of free speech. However, there may be underlying anxieties and prejudices here, as well as political manipulation of ethnic sensibilities. In 2010, the TV soap opera *Eastenders,* which had a strong multicultural agenda, featured in its summer–fall 2010 series a Jewish character, Darren Miller, who was rejected by his girlfriend Jodie Gold for not being "Jewish" enough because he was not circumcised, and thus racially excluded from the clan. Familiar tropes of the intolerant, vengeful "jew" and Jewish wealth are reinforced when it turns out Jodie isn't really her father's daughter (and thus not even half-Jewish), which sets Harry, her dodgy, underworld father, on a vengeful mission against both daughter and gentile mother that makes Shylock appear meek in comparison. When Martin Amis in his novel *London Fields* (1989) describes a mother's pimping of her underage teenage daughter as "kosher," the reader understands what is meant, just as the front cover in January 2002 of the respected liberal magazine, the *New Statesman,* could ask whether there was a "kosher conspiracy" against the background of a gold Star of David piercing the British flag, insinuating suspicions of Jewish money undermining the British economy and politics.

At the same time, the "jew" has become an emblem of the quintessential postcolonial migrant, at home everywhere and nowhere, a product of the postmodern condition, an exemplary figure of the repressed and humiliated of the Third World for South Asian and Caribbean writers seeking an identity in early twenty-first-century Britain. Jewish historical experience has become the measure of Black suffering and a trope for genocidal slaughter, though this is hardly the first time that persecution of the Jews has been appropriated as the emblem of another nation's' suffering (for example, in the poetry of Polish patriot Adam Mickiewicz). In "A Far Cry from Africa" (1956), for example, Caribbean poet Derek Walcott (recipient of the 1992 Nobel Prize for Literature) bemoans the callous cruelty of colonial policy in its brutal exploitation of the "savages, expendable as Jews."

In multicultural societies, ethnic identity is no longer to be considered as marginal or defined in terms of center and periphery, but, instead, we should think in terms of "frontier" selves negotiating for ethnic space with other minorities and define difference as a subject position within and in a sense opposed to multiculturalism. As Sander Gilman has suggested in *Multiculturalism and the Jews,* the figure of the "jew" is a key to understanding the very nature of the multicultural society represented in cultural texts. Gilman's study looks at the question obliquely, as an issue in Jewish self-identification and cultural politics, beginning with enlightened German Jewish intellectuals in the nineteenth and early twentieth centuries and continuing through the debate over cultural pluralism versus a competitive difference in the diaspora in the early twenty-first century.[6] The Holocaust is seen in this scheme as a radical marker of difference, marking out the Jew as both victim and witness. We will see later in this study how that radical marker of extermination has given rise to the figure of the Vanishing Jew and how Jews have radically redefined themselves in a multicultural society, but let us note that the multicultural debate has often marginalized Jews and also brought with it a competition for victimhood.

In all these cases we are addressing *discourses* about the "jew," not the religion or historicity of characters. It is, as Bryan Cheyette has explained, a shifting and ambivalent signifier in the dominant social discourse about nation or empire that defines the Other, not to be understood outside the historical and ideological context, but also not a means to overdetermine authors as "antisemitic."[7] By "jew" we mean the cultural construction of a figure (as distinct from real Jews, with capitals, whether or not they have any capital). Such a construct tells us about the perception of the alien, who always plays a vital role in the formation of nationhood, and it reflects shifts in identity in the host society. In public discourse, the "jew" and, more recently, the "zionist" have been imaginary yet powerful constructs that serve as handles with which to divide the world politically and to conscript the support of an ideological constituency in a global solidarity. These constructs have entered the mainstream of public discourse in Europe, unlike the United States, where aggressive anti-Israel rhetoric is associated with militants on the political fringe such as David Duke or radicals like Noam Chomsky,[8] though antagonism to Jews and harassment of Zionists are on the rise on American as well as European campuses. There is little or no relation to the many and diverse beliefs and practices of real Jews or Zionists, though it can be said that the rhetorical positioning of much public discourse tends to misrepresent substantive issues or occlude any true understanding of the identities and views of opponents, whether as conscious manipulation or in a lazy, almost unconscious conformism to familiar clichés and received opinions, that may hide unthinking prejudices and bias. The reason for this is that media coverage and the circulation of cultural texts construct what we "know" about social types and determine the identity of the "Other" in any debate over the boundaries of social behavior, thus concealing or implicitly permitting exclusionary practices (hostile attitudes, boycotting, and other forms of outgrouping). As levers of political debate, such labels tend to be reductive and not usually available to rational analysis or empirical verification.

As a metonym for the entrenched particularism opposed to Enlightenment values and the universal principles of the French Revolution, the "jew" has circulated widely in European political thought, and was racialized in the twentieth century as a trope for the enemy within, devoid of roots in the nation, but has been revalorized in postmodern philosophy.[9] The use of the figural "jew" in the rhetoric of radical opposition to authoritarian forms of national identity, in fact, has become widespread since May 1968, when the barring of German Jewish student leader Daniel Cohn-Bendit gave rise to the slogan "nous sommes tous les juifs allemands." Like the French republican support for Dreyfus earlier in the century, the figure had little to do with real Jews, but was inspired by the spirit of *fraternité* and civil rights, yet here the French students were adopting the victim's identity as a "jew" in their own universal figural identity.[10] Later, the previously hostile figure of the "jew" as the rootless cosmopolitan became almost synonymous with the exiled intellectual and paradigmatic refugee fleeing persecution, opening up to appropriation that disidentified the "jew" from the Jewish people; echoing Derrida in "Circumfession" (1993), Edward Said once claimed for himself the title of the last Jewish intellectual, one of the dying breed of followers of Adorno, and a "Jewish Palestinian."[11] The ambivalence of this metaphorical identification, internalized in a post-Holocaust Jewish identity, was taken up by Alain Finkelkraut's celebrated *Le juif imaginaire* (1980; *The Imaginary Jew*, 1994), but Finkelkraut soon realized that on the Left the figure excluded Jews as Others and in the first decade of the twenty-first century it slid into a general equivalence of victims in the discourse of the "New Antisemitism."[12]

The figure of the "jew" has been further allegorized in French philosopher Jean-François Lyotard's *Heidegger and the "jews"* (1988), where he refers to the forgotten in European memory, as distinct from real Jews or Jews as a political or religious referent.[13] Daniel and Jonathan Boyarin have critiqued this use of an allegorical trope to refer to all Arabs, Blacks, and Others who have suffered persecution and genocide because it deprives real Jews of their ethnic and cultural difference, as well as their historical memory outside of a universalizing discourse.[14] However, the dichotomy between figurative and real Jews, which Steven Beller has held responsible for obscuring the study of the history of antisemitism,[15] can be useful in understanding normative and influential Western discourses about "jews" which relate to widely held beliefs and perceptions that make up a textual web of conventions projecting a Jewish collective in the Western imagination.[16] Indeed, the dissemination of facts about real Jews, the presence of real Jews, or even their murder and absence from society do not seem to shake the myth of the "jew." As Jonathan Judaken has noted in the case of the anti-antisemitism of the Frankfurt School, the construction of "the jew" both describes and inscribes a marker of difference based on religious, ideological, biological, or genetic concepts, whether hostilely, philosemitically, or as internalized self-image.[17] If we refer to real Jews living in a historical situation and affected by the impact of antisemitism in real life, we will drop the quotation marks; Jews, Zionists, Whites, and Others will all be treated as case sensitive.

THE "JEW" AND THE DISCOURSE OF NATION

The figure of the "jew" is instrumental in discourses about the nation which determine who are the outsiders and where the boundaries of membership in any national or ethnic group may lie at any one moment. We must therefore first coinsider the peculiarities of the historical context in Britain. The British Isles—to use a convenient geographical term, for "Britain" is a name that relates to a changing or unstable geographical and political entity—were invaded and settled by Romans, Jutes, Saxons, Vikings, Normans, and Celts, and at various times saw mass immigrations of Huguenots, Irish, Jews, Caribbean and African Blacks, Indians (from East Africa as well as South Asia), Pakistanis, Bangladeshis, Arabs, Iranians, and, more recently, Poles. Whether the English were descended from Celts or Saxons was always a matter of more than national pride—it bolstered the Protestant ethos and shaped the ethnicity of the English, which would exclude by definition immigrant aliens or Irish laborers corrupting the nation's culture and the body politic.[18] The ethno-class racialization of the Other was partly displaced in the postcolonial period by color and cultural biases, but in the age of hybridity and multiculturalism it is worth recalling that at the beginning of the eighteenth century Daniel Defoe was complaining in *The True-Born*

Englishman (1701) that dislike of foreigners was hardly appropriate for a nation of mongrels:

> Go back to elder times, and ages past,
> And nations into long oblivion cast;
> To elder Britain's youthful days retire,
> And there for true-born Englishmen inquire,
> Britannia freely will disown the name,
> And hardly knows herself from whence they came,
> Wonders that they of all men should pretend
> To birth, and blood, and for a name contend. . . .[19]

A multitude of nations had settled and become "true Englishmen," yet the descendants of the Normans had the audacity to pride themselves on their pure English ancestry.

> But grant the best. How came the change to pass,
> A true-born Englishman of Norman race?
> A Turkish horse can show more history,
> To prove his well-descended family.[20]

While England colonized Ireland, Wales, and Scotland, and built an empire stretching across the world, the unity of the nation was never certain. Before the fall of empire, Ireland was gaining independence, and at the end of the twentieth century Scotland and Wales asserted their political, cultural, and linguistic separateness. Two hundred years after the Union Act, the United Kingdom seemed caught up in a process of devolution and perceptible, if slow and ponderous, break-up, a floundering rather than a *Titanic* sinking, as Tom Nairn put it, which could only be understood by examining the character of Britain's historical development as a nation-state.[21]

The Industrial Revolution and rapid urbanization had, from 1750, transformed England from an agrarian economy into an industrialized nation that rapidly became a trading empire and superpower, a process that apparently leveled out regional differences, although these have not disappeared entirely and there are many English people who can trace their ancestry back hundreds of years to a place not far from where they presently live. Post-industrial Britain, on the other hand, is dependent on transatlantic alliances and economic integration into Europe. No longer self-sufficient, but a vulnerable island in a sea of global change and fiscal storms, the United Kingdom no longer seems a suitable case for the nation-state model, since it does not represent one national identity. Instead, it is a disunited kingdom comprising various regional and national identities, none of whom, however, seem ready to establish a separate entity. Britain of the late twentieth century was not only *not* the sum of its citizens but was beginning to look like an "archipelago" of ethnic and sexual minorities. Long overdue constitutional reform, therefore, floundered on the question of whom was being represented by the polity. It was no longer useful to talk in terms of "nation" or "state" when discussing the make-up of British society.[22] "The break-up of Britain in the present," the cultural historian Raphael Samuel wrote, "and the uncertainties of the future, necessarily makes us more aware of its contingent character in the past."[23] For this reason, memory of the past is contested, and this is particularly so when identity is in question.

National identity is never stable or static, and it is often multiple. It cannot be totally separated from the idea of statehood, and to a great extent it is based upon traditions handed down from generation to generation and perceived national or ethnic values, or affiliation of kinship.[24] Notably, the relations between different ethnic and geographical identities within Britain (e.g. Celtic/Scottish) have been unstable and shifting, yet they can be summoned to single identity by patriotic song or poetry.[25] Indeed, in modern times, cultural production, particularly literature, can be a unifying as well as excluding force in forging national identity. But it should not be forgotten that, alongside the narrowing ideological landscape of "Englishness" in the nineteenth century, there was always a strong regional voice that was absorbed in a romanticized nationalism that included Scots, Welsh, and Irish within an English literary canon. Notwithstanding the utilitarian trend toward centralization and the importance of London as a cultural marketplace, the refining, rather than redefining, of Englishness did not rule out an exploration of foreign tastes and peripheral voices (including travel literature, the Gothic, the picaresque, or the historical novel), and Edinburgh, as well as Dublin, flourished as *English* literary centers in *British* culture.[26] So we should not regard multiculturalism as "new" if we recall the somewhat contradictory make-up of British culture. At the beginning of the twenty-first century, Britain could no longer be easily defined in terms of Englishness, or the English language, which had become an international language bringing together writers from the Commonwealth and several developing nations.

Proponents of multiculturalism would claim national and ethnic differences are subordinate to human solidarity. As Lisa Jardine, Professor of Renaissance Studies at Queen Mary College London, sees it, national identities are decided by the historical moment:

who lives where on the face of the globe, is not much more than a historical snapshot. The location of communities in specific places and nations has almost always been the outcome of individual or mass migration, often enforced under pressure of politics or war."[27]

The 1707 Union Act could not wipe out the historical memory of the separate traditions of Wales and Scotland, but, as in Belgium, currently going through a crisis between Walloons and Flemish-speakers, migrations and wars have changed where people live and, in Jardine's opinion, there is no more sense in Scots going back to Scotland from London than for her to return to the Polish *shtetl* where her father (the scientist and broadcaster Jacob Bronowski) was born. That she is British does not change the fact that the "green and pleasant land" which Blake immortalized was England, just as old John of Gaunt in Act II of *Richard the Second* praises his native England, not (as the lines were rewritten in a TV commercial for tea), Britain,[28] though that lament of the imminent passing of this "sceptered isle" was itself a Shakespearean construction that would have sounded strange to the real John of Gaunt, who had multiple European identities and affiliations.[29] Britain has somehow eclipsed "England" and accommodates all comers and outsiders, including Jews. It is the meaning of being "British" that has changed and the relation of citizenship to nationality has become destabilized. Multicultural diversity has in some senses reinforced difference and strife rather than created a rainbow coalition of faiths. While an increasing number of Muslims would accept a hyphenated British identity (54% in a June 2002 poll), very few (3%) would substitute British for Muslim as their identity.[30] Indeed, "multiculturalism" does not necessarily mean racial diversity in the sense used by the media so much as a fraught striving by immigrants from non-European and non-White backgrounds for some certainty and status in an alien country, wavering between community and the host culture.[31]

The loss of empire and Britain's altered strategic and economic position after the Second World War, a partner in the NATO alliance and an offshore island in Europe, necessarily required a readjustment of national self-definition. The post-*Windrush* influx of colonial subjects led to a new generation of non-Whites born and bred in England, speaking English and enjoying British citizenship. Xenophobia in the form of "England for the English," which characterized the 1950s and 1960s, was an alienating and sometimes violent forcing tube into proud ethnic identity, which, with the advent of Malcolm X, many regained.[32] Discrimination continued, subtly and almost invisibly, but racism could no longer be acceptable social or political behavior when large ethnic minorities were themselves British and changing the meaning of being British. Yet South Asian communities and other British Muslims continued to complain of discrimination and ostracism, especially in the backlash following 9/11 and 7/7, and the 2001 Oldham riots gave cause for concern about the success of integration. While anxiety about an encroaching Muslim presence, as elsewhere in Europe, as well as adverse reaction to European unification and to massive immigration of non-White populations, suggested a spread of Islamophobia, antisemitism among both right-wing nationalists and radical Islamist militants questioned the viability of multiculturalism to sustain ethnic coexistence and social cohesion. The global wave of Islamist antisemitism draws on tropes from European discourses about the "jews," particularly the conspiracy theory, as well as the myth of superior Jewish intelligence and world domination, suggesting not a "new antisemitism," but a transformation of existing cultural functions of the "jew."[33] With an estimated 1.6–2 million Muslims resident in the UK, resentment and anger over events in the Middle East could easily spill over into hostility towards British Jews and even physical attacks, as was seen during and after the war in Gaza in January 2009. The British government attempted to contain the security threat after 7/7 and stem extremism among British Muslims, but could not disengage from a link between British foreign policy and race relations at home. For this reason, it was difficult to tackle an anti-racist discourse which claimed that accusations of antisemitism were a smokescreen for Islamophobia.[34]

Legislation on immigration and citizenship defined the "New Commonwealth" immigrants for purposes of exclusion, although anti-discrimination laws delineated some measure of tolerance for racial minorities, re-categorized in the 1980s as "Blacks" and "Asians." By the beginning of the twenty-first century Britain was facing contradictions and conflicts, as did France, in attempting to integrate large ethnic and racial minorities. The Jews largely fell outside these parameters as having successfully achieved a measure of assimilation, while the Black-White polarities of the debate did not take account of the instability of ethnic and racial boundaries (Muslims could be European, African, or Asian; not all south Asian immigrants were Muslim). Legally, it was not clear if Jews were an ethnic or racial group, and therefore it was unclear whether prosecution could be brought against neo-Nazis for incitement of racial hatred against Jews. Moreover, sociologists were very slow in recognizing Jews as a distinct ethnic group that had a history of its own within British society, despite the long lineage of antisemitic discourse in English culture.

Significantly, in both Britain and France a postmodern frame of cultural difference, not marked solely by skin color, replaced the former premise of racism on colonial discourse, and reflected the breakdown of integration through institutions, while universalism played off against embattled particularism.[35] "Ethnicity" has become a description of social practice around Europe, rather than a sociological term for cultural difference, and has been applied in an instrumental way that further isolates immigrant communities in the process of integrating them into a secular society, while alienating their religious sensibilities and need for common bonds, often expressed in identification with a remote homeland they may not have known and with radicalism which further isolates them (the absurdities to which these paradoxes lead are satirized in Zadie Smith's *White Teeth*).[36]

In this context, the Muslim takes center stage as the "Other," standing in for the religious, ethnic, language, and cultural difference of the new "jew." While qualifying the analogy, some sociologists and commentators have drawn parallels between how immigrant Jews were perceived at the turn of the twentieth century and how Muslims are perceived in contemporary Britain, their loyalties questioned and branded as a terrorist threat, as if antisemitism could help understand "Islamophobia," and the conflation of a Muslim collective with radical fundamentalism.[37] Anthropologist Paul Silverstein has proposed a model of racialization of Europe's new Muslim immigrants in the backlash of the War on Terror for the same reasons that Jewish refugees were once a suspect ethnic group and Gypsies (Roma) still are because of their mobility and extraterritorial loyalties which destabilize national entities and borders.[38] The headline "Muslims are the New Jews" catches attention when Muslims want to make a case against discriminatory practices and prejudiced thinking in contemporary Britain.[39] This is a significant attempt to substantiate the paradigm of an ethnic minority suffering cultural racism in a "conflict of civilizations," but it is misleading—for a start, Jewish "extremists" did not try to harm national security nor were they involved in a real plot to cause disruption and mayhem in Western countries, as Joe Bulman seemed to suggest in his 2009 Channel Four TV documentary, *The Enemy Within*, though some Russian revolutionaries did have ideas about destabilizing tsarist tyranny. Certainly, the anarchists involved in the siege of Sidney Street were by no means identified with the Jewish community or Jewish beliefs; they wore neither *streimels* nor *yarmulkes* and were, in fact, defiantly anti-religious.[40] The collective fear of

"Jewish Bolsheviks" cannot be compared with the treatment of the Muslim population because immigrant Jews were subject to legal discrimination as aliens, not as terrorists; moreover, they were encouraged to shed their religious and ethnic differences in order to become "English."

Anti-racism could attack both antisemitism and the "racist" Jews, while the successful assimilation of Jews in British society which supposedly made them "invisible" raised questions about just how they were perceived in terms of an equal citizenry. The use of stereotypes in representing Jews in the media still prevailed, a good example being Maureen Lipman's portrayal in the British Telecom TV campaign in the 1980s of a Jewish grandmother "Beattie" (to match the telephone company's acronym BT). If "Beattie" encouraged the middle classes to use the phone, as a model citizen representing Thatcherite self-help, less innocuous stereotypes of Jewish vulgarity (unwelcome social climbing and disrespect for social boundaries) and stinginess (trying to get something for free) were not far behind a comic figure of the Jewish mother who treats the telephone line as an umbilical cord to her family.[41] British children's historical fiction could present an ambivalent adoption of Jewish suffering in the middle ages and in the Holocaust to teach racial tolerance, but, for all the mandatory cultural sensitivity, without necessarily acknowledging the Jews' full religious equality in the present or challenging some older stereotypes.[42] There is much talk of integration which cites the Jews as a "good" example for Muslims, ignoring the fact that the "bad" inassimilable Jews who refuse intermarriage and maintain separate lifestyles from the rest of society are still being criticized, as they were prior to the Aliens Act of 1905, only this time in the name of multiculturalism. Hasidic Jews in Stamford Hill were perceived as beyond the pale of multiculturalism because they did not adopt the rules of "civility," wore strange clothes, and separated themselves socially and sexually from the rest of society out of obedience to a "fundamentalist" religious practice which one columnist in a liberal progressive newspaper likened to female genital mutilation, illegal in Britain but carried out on thousands of British girls each year; the "racist" Jews, she believed, were not integrating like the Caribbeans in such classic tales of immigration as Sam Selvon's *Lonely Londoners* (1956) or Zadie Smith's *White Teeth* (2000).[43] On the one hand, the public space of multiculturalism beckons with its promise of respect for difference; on the other hand Jewish difference is abhorred as "racist" or "inassimilable." Integration demands giving up religious "intolerance" of sexual freedom in its "fundamentalist" modesty, dress, and behavioral codes, as well as its "exclusionist" sexual practices or gender segregation.

FIGURING THE "JEW" IN MULTICULTURAL TEXTS

The promise of multiculturalism may be weighed against traditional Jewish separateness and clannishness, while in-marriage rules (despite rampant exogamy) have reinforced old stereotypes of the Jews as exclusionist racists, unwilling to overcome their ancient particularism. The class snobbery so characteristic of the English has remained an almost unthinking reaction that disparages Jews, or envies them (or both), while traditional working-class resentment of Jews as wealthy capitalists and/or alien immigrants also reinforces negative stereotypes. Moreover, in Britain acceptance of immigrants has, historically, been a process of accommodation that recognizes difference on condition difference is assimilated into national identity and values, something that is problematic when national identity and values are in dispute and different constructions of ethnicity and race are in play within liberal universalism.[44] The "jew" is caught doubly, as archetypal alien undermining society, and as agent of European colonialism. Moreover, whereas the Jews were suspect as cosmopolitans undermining Englishness and holding dual loyalty in right-wing antisemitism, the Jewish community is subject to political scrutiny in liberal progressive circles whenever Israel is portrayed as a perpetrator of war crimes and as morally guilty of its own inception. Israel has become identified as the world's number one enemy for both the far right and the far left, but in the eyes of many liberal intellectuals it has somehow become tainted with colonialism. We therefore open our discussion by showing how the narrative of the "jew" is embedded in English culture, but must be examined in both its local and global contexts in order to understand the complex transformation of the figure of the "jew" that changes in accordance with the needs of the moment, yet often reverts to familiar tropes.

The recurrence of blood libels and the revival of conspiracy theories in the early twentieth century, for example, can be explained by a complicated intertwining of biological race theory, economic causes, political crises, and anxieties arising from modernity. The demonization of Israel similarly revives familiar tropes, yet emerges from an ideologized *anti*-racist platform. The demonisation of Israel is reinforced by the recirculation of hostile images from Arab and anti-Zionist propaganda that originated in Western medieval and Nazi images of the world Jewish conspiracy and now imperceptibly reactivate latent narratives embedded in English culture with its shelf memory of blood libels and ubiquitous icons of Shylock and Fagin. The apparent contradiction of an anti-racist antisemitism can be partly explained, as we will see, by a tendency to exclude Jews in postcolonial discourse and to transfer the figure of the "jew" to Muslims, who come to be seen as neocolonialism's new "jews."[45]

Beyond sympathy for the anti-Zionist cause, which might conceivably project guilt for British imperialism, it is curious that colonialist attitudes sometimes persist even among writers known for progressive and liberal views. The perception of the "jew" has a complex relation to the color bar and to racial/ethnic prejudices, for example in the life and writing of Doris Lessing, to be considered in chapter one. For Lessing, the "jew" figures as a source of intellectual power, a cosmopolitan who is a middleman in the colonial equation, but also serves as a screen for other minorities. There may be a projection here of colonial anxieties caught between the historical situation in southern Africa and the autobiographical writing time of British postwar politics. The "jew" is the object of desire, yet also of dubious sexual and racial identity who is successfully assimilated, but not fully accepted into colonial society.

We move on in the next chapter to Anita Desai and an Indian view of the "jew" in *Baumgartner's Bombay*. Baumgartner is a Holocaust survivor who enters the Hindu-Muslim divide in India during the violence of partition and independence. *Baumgartner's Bombay* presents the dual mirror of the Jew in Europe and the Muslim in India. Each suffers exclusion and expulsion, and each is a stranger at home in a multicultural ocean of humanity. Baumgartner is the other's Other who, through his passage to India in Venice and later in the internment camp, grasps an identity that remains elusive, denied, and unclaimed, in a postcolonial paradigm of rootless hybridity. Desai, of course, passes over the real genealogy of Indian Jews, who include a number of eminent Indian writers such as Ruth Prawer Jhabvala (a German-Jewish refugee), Esther David, or Nissim Ezekiel,[46] and seems to be more interested in the figure of the "jew," for so long a site of anxiety about modernity and miscegenation in the Western imaginary. The "jew" is now the quintessential outsider and embodiment of migration across continents and cultures, and, as Anna Guttman contends, a literary figure that gives easy access to the Anglo-American market, with its middlebrow taste for Jewish and Holocaust themes.[47] The "jew," as Vijay Mishra has put it, is, in the "unfinished narrative of modernity," either a Romantic version of the Jew's beautiful daughter (such as Rebecca in *Ivanhoe*), or an exemplary figure of urban estrangement (Leopold Bloom, for example), and therefore fits into the transnational mobility of postcolonial writing. Amitav Ghosh's *In an Antique Land,* for example, is a novel which proposes an anthropological contiguity between medieval Jewish merchants trading between the Middle East and the Indian subcontinent and resistance to colonial erasure of such cross-cultural migrations.[48] There is in the "jew" both an affinity and an attraction for Indian writers such as Desai and Salman Rushdie who are preoccupied with themes of wandering, homelessness, and alienation, and who see in Jews fellow cosmopolitans. The Wandering Jew, after all, is the ultimate figure of the outsider at home everywhere and nowhere, typifying for modernity

> *l'homme moyen sensual,* . . .vainly trying to integrate himself into
> a culture to which he is essentially alien. And this predicament of
> the Jew is merely a magnification of the predicament of modern
> man himself, bewildered and homeless in a mechanical world of
> his own creation.[49]

To this we should add the historical experience of the Holocaust as an exemplary racial violence and traumatic uprooting, which Anna Guttman sees as a natural path for South Asian authors to explore when negotiating their global identities,[50] though Ruth Prawer Jhabvala, who fled Nazi Germany with her family to England before World War Two and later moved to India with her husband, seems to have erased her Jewishness in her construction of an imaginary "India" as a site of displacement and marginality seen though Jane Austen characters wearing masks of Englishness.[51]

Immigrants to Britain have, on the whole, wished to be seen to be more English than the English and to pass on to their children the perceived values of their adopted culture, in which, like the Jews before them, they were often upwardly mobile but not fully accepted. The postmodern and postcolonial situation encourages a mixing of religions, races, languages, and cultures. The resulting hybridity breeds a generation that enjoys multiple identities, but it does not necessarily comprise a workable "multiculturalism." Hybrid children may turn out to be monstrous animals, like the child in Peter Carey's *My Life as a Fake,* or the failed experiment in Zadie Smith's *White Teeth.* In his novel *Elizabeth Costello* (2003), J. M. Coetzee comments

> It is as hard to imagine the child of Red Peter as to imagine the
> child of Kafka himself. Hybrids are, or ought to be, sterile; and
> Kafka saw both himself and Red Peter as hybrids, as monstrous

thinking devices mounted inexplicably on suffering animal bodies. The stare that we meet in all the surviving photographs of Kafka is a stare of pure surprise; surprise, astonishment, alarm. Of all men Kafka is the most insecure in his humanity. *This*, he seems to say: *this* is the image of God?[52]

Hybridity bears a heavy price and may conceal family secrets, as we will see in the following chapter, "Hybridity's Children." Andrea Levy is herself of mixed Jewish and Caribbean descent. In her *Small Island* (2004), one of the four protagonists who tell the story is of Jewish descent, and the significant context is World War Two and racism. Racist England is encountered as an island as small minded as the small island of Jamaica, where ignorance and prejudice are rife. Zadie Smith's *White Teeth* brings the offspring of Pakistani immigrants into contact with a Jewish family in order to parody liberal fostering of "hybrids" as ideal multiracial objects for breeding. But the hybrids are not happy with their multiracial identity, and the children of Pakistani immigrants are split between assimilation to a latent English colonial identity and a confused fundamentalism. In Smith's *The Autograph Man* a hybrid Chinese/Jewish collector of autographs explores multiple identities, many of which are fake, like the autographs he collects, thus indicating that postmodern identity in Britain is often phony but life can never be reduced to essentialist labels, however much Alex tries to keep his identities (and also his women) separate. India is an interesting example of hybridity and multiple cultures in the writing of Salman Rushdie, whose novel *The Moor's Last Sigh* (1995) turns to the historical experience of Spain and the encounter of Jew and Moor, which serve to unpack the construct of hybridity as a slippery creature that undermines the very concepts of identity and our understanding of history.

In the next chapter, we show how Caryl Phillips rewrites Shakespeare from the perspective of Othello, thus writing back to racial stereotyping. In the end, however, the Jew-Black switch is turned around into a confrontation between European racism and an imagined Othello figure, a confrontation refracted in the humiliation and indignity inflicted on the Holocaust victim and on the Black Jewish Ethiopian in *The Nature of Blood*. Again, we will see how the trope of the "jew" is manipulated into a politicized postcolonial agenda, but here presented as a contiguity between the view of European racism seen by the former colonized subjects of the British Empire, and direct experience of "epidermic" racism as Black citizens of Europe. In pressing for a careful review of such contiguity, Paul Gilroy has cautioned against a

simplistic parallel between the Black and Jewish experiences, illustrated by
the irony of Black soldiers fighting fascism on behalf of a country that
discriminates against them. Gilroy reminds us of the shock of General
Patton's Black troops on liberating a concentration camp filled with corpses
and dying Jewish inmates, which brought home the ultimate logic of
colonialism and the complex irrational hatred which crosses color lines.[53] In
urging us to take note of the testimony of Primo Levi and Jean Améry, as
well as that of colonial prisoners-of-war, Gilroy wishes to alert us to the ever
present thinking behind modernity which leads to the complicity of
rationality in barbarism. In the postmodern era of loss of innocence, the
histories of the Jews and the Blacks in the West serve as counterweights.[54] In
Caryl Phillips' *The Nature of Blood,* the Black's view of European racism
works through the confused identities of the Other, as well as presenting the
subaltern's view of European antisemitism.

In the following chapter, the cultural reconstruction in postmodern texts of
the memory of London's East End is explored in order to interrogate the
ethnic boundaries of an imagined urban territory. In Monica Ali's *Brick Lane,*
a Jewish territory is vacated and occupied by Asian immigrants, in a parallel
immigrant experience that posits a multicultural existence which is doubtful
when matched against the historical record. The absence of the Jews haunts
the streets of the East End, giving rise to a search for the "Vanishing Jew,"
understood quite differently in the work of Iain Sinclair and Rachel
Lichtenstein. Rachel Lichtenstein and Iain Sinclair's *Rodinsky's Room*
(2000), and Lichtenstein's subsequent book entitled *On Brick Lane* are
preoccupied with reconstituting part of the urban palimpsest, but for
Lichtenstein this is also a personal search for her own identity and roots.
Jeremy Gavron's novel about Brick Lane, *An Acre of Barren Ground,* on the
other hand, posits different immigrant experiences as part of a polyphonic
and multiple ethnic identity that says a lot about the ambiguities and
contradictions of cultural identity in contemporary Britain. The figure of the
"Vanishing Jew" emerges as a post-Holocaust construct of a cultural absence,
a post-traumatic phantom that haunts the imagination but also inspires a
postmodern remolding of cultural identities that can be multiple and fluid.

Indeed, in postmodern fiction, as we will see in chapter six, the
"Postmodern Jew" has become an ambiguous figure of post-historical
sensibilities of invented or fake identities. The figure of the "jew" as
marginalized outsider re-emerges as a radical source of cynicism and healthy
subversion of middle-class complacency. Yet Jewish writers have also
increasingly written back to antisemitism, contributing to the general

postmodern debunking of history a revision of the imperialist past that uncovers deceits and betrayal, but also undoes the apparent invisibility of British Jews achieved by successful assimilation and model integration. They join other subalterns whose marginalized voices have become more central to the literatures of the former Empire and have helped to redefine both Britishness and the parameters of English literature.[55] In externalizing antisemitic stereotypes and showing how Jews seem unable to escape the "Auschwitz syndrome," Howard Jacobson throws off any taboos about the Holocaust in his comic novel *Kalooki Nights* (2007) and externalizes antisemitic stereotypes in offensive and obscene black humor. Jacobson would defend racial jokes such as Bernard Manning's stand-up comedy in Manchester clubs, which does not spare Blacks among the audience from racial insults, because he believes humor to be the lance that releases the pus and heals social tensions.[56] Perhaps there is a confusion of ethnic humor (particularly Jewish self-mocking humor that often relies on hostile stereotypes) with racial stereotyping, which is often demeaning and has a history in colonialist culture.[57] However, the exposure of prejudice among the host society and the out-group can, as in Zadie Smith's *White Teeth,* easily fit into a long tradition of British satire which ridicules through burlesque exposure and reduction to the absurd. The participation in postcolonial discourse of real Jews has complicated the racialization of the "jew," as will be seen in the final chapter, when secular radical Jews assert alternative cultural identities, alongside self-hating and antisemitic Jews. On the other hand, Jewish feminist artists have contributed their own gendered perspective to the exposure of racial stereotypes, often in an intervention in sexual politics and social discourse that transgresses boundaries.

   This book is timely as the study of postmodern and postcolonial fiction has been reconfigured in the transnational matrix of global migrations, suggesting, as Stephen Clingman has proposed, a new "grammar of identities" that cuts across paradigms of modern/postmodern, colonial/ postcolonial, as well as across time and space.[58] Migrancy not only changes the way we think about the human condition, but also the way we read literature across national and ethnic borders. Susheila Nasta, for example, has recast South Asian writers in Britain within a hundred and fifty years of Black presence and the contemporary debate over hybridity and diaspora.[59] At the same time, the usual Eurocentric view has been challenged by Edward Said and others, and Said has famously remarked on the resemblance of the history of antisemitism to the way the political and cultural discourse of the West has "Orientalized" Islam.[60] In fact, the mirroring of antisemitism and

Orientalism has attracted the attention of Aamar Mufti, who has attempted to shift the discussion of the "Jewish question" into a postcolonial axis that spans the Middle East and the Indian subcontinent.[61]

In the present reflection on the figure of the "jew" in postmodern and postcolonial fiction we hope to contribute to that debate by showing how the image of the Other, in this case the archetypal Other—the "jew"—affects changing national identities and the notion of identity itself, while transformations of familiar tropes and new directions in the sorry history of antisemitism point to both surprising as well as disturbing implications. In particular, the displacement of the "jew" by the Muslim can summon global solidarity with victimhood, but, while recognizing Jewish suffering in the Holocaust, postcolonial discourse has tended to erase real Jews from the mental and cultural landscape or to deny particularity to Jews as Jews. What happens when the Other is reimagined by transnational writers, especially when they engage with the figures of Shylock and Othello, as in the novels of Salman Rushdie and Caryl Phillips, and look at Jewish history from the perspective of, respectively, India and the "Black Atlantic"? What of real, as distinct from imagined, Jews who cross from marginality into multiethnic diversity and write against the antisemitism of Empire, revisioning history? These are some of the questions we will be addressing in our book, which cherishes the modest ambition of reexamining the parameters of British fiction from the standpoint of an Other who was scapegoated and excluded in the process of the shaping of Englishness, and is now, once more, central to the political and literary imagination of global diasporas.

NOTES

1. "Broadcast Bulletin Issue number 62-12|06|06," Office of Communications, http://www.ofcom.org.uk/tv/obb/prog_cb/pcb33. The lyrics of the original musical were changed to fit the sums of money for alleged purchase of peerages. See Simon Rocker, "Spot the difference between these men (Channel 4 can't)," *Jewish Chronicle,* 16 June 2006.

2. Julia Pascal, "Time to bury Fagin," *Guardian Comment is Free,* 17 Jan. 2009; accessed online.

3. Michael Billington, "Oliver!" *Guardian,* 15 Jan. 2009; accessed online.

4. In his book, *The Victorians* (New York: W. W. Norton, 2004), A. N. Wilson comments on the antisemitic reactions to Disraeli that these were a "flaw" more characteristic of the left than the right and that such remarks were muted after the Holocaust.

5. Luke Harding, "Princess Michael defends breeding, Botox—and Harry," *Guardian,* 17 Feb. 2005; accessed online. The scandal, it must be said, was more to do with the erratic and shameful behavior of the royals than antisemitic sentiments.

6. Sander L. Gilman, *Multiculturalism and the Jews* (New York: Routledge, 2006).

7.Bryan Cheyette, "Neither Excuse nor Accuse: T. S. Eliot's Semitic Discourse," *Modernism/modernity* 10.3 (2003): 433.

8. Robin Shepherd, *A State Beyond the Pale: Europe's Problem with Israel* (London: Weidenfeld & Nicolson, 2009), 51–52.

9. For a history of the postmodern trope of the "jew" from Dreyfus to Levinas and Derrida see Sarah Hammerschlag, *The Figural Jew: Politics and Identity in Postwar French Thought* (Chicago: University of Chicago Press, 2010); and see also Neil Davison, *Jewishness and Masculinity from the Modern to the Postmodern* (New York: Routledge, 2010).

10. Hammerschlag, *Figural Jew,* 3–4

11. Ibid., 23–24; Said, "My Right of Return," quoted in ibid., 1.

12. Ibid. Finkielkraut, cited in ibid., 5.

13. Jean-François Lyotard, *Heidegger and the "jews,"* trans. Andreas Michel and Mark S. Roberts (Minneapolis: Minnesota University Press, 1988), 3–4. For a detailed critique of this use see Geoffrey Bennington, "Lyotard and 'the 'Jews,'" in *Modernism, Culture, and 'the Jews,'* ed. Bryan Cheyette and Laura Marcus, 188–96; and Max Silverman, "Re-Figuring 'the Jew' in France," in ibid., 197–207.

14. Jonathan and Daniel Boyarin. "Diaspora: Generation and the Ground of Jewish Identity," *Critical Inquiry* 19, 4 (Summer 1993): 700–01. For a summary of critiques of Lyotard's use of the term see Hammerschlag, *Figural Jew,* 8–10.

15. Beller, *Antisemitism: A Very Short Introduction* (Oxford: Oxford University Press, 2007), 3–5.

16. See Sander Gilman, *Difference and Pathology: Stereotypes of Sexuality, Race, and Madness* (Ithaca, N.Y.: Cornell University Press, 1985), 27–29.

17. Jonathan Judaken, "Between Philosemitism and Antisemitism: The Frankfurt School's Anti-Antisemitism," in *Antisemitism and Philosemitism in the Twentieth and Twenty-first Centuries: Representing Jews, Jewishness, and Modern Culture,* ed. Phyllis Lassner and Lara Trubowitz (Newark: University of Delaware Press, 2008), 41, n. 6.

18. Robert J. C. Young, "Hybridism and the Ethnicity of the English," in *Cultural Readings of Imperialism: Edward Said and the Gravity of History,* ed. Keith Ansell-Pearson, Benita Parry, and Judith Squires (London: Lawrence & Wishart, 1997), 127–50.

19. Daniel Defoe, "The True-Born Englishman," *The Novels and Miscellaneous Works of Daniel De Foe* (London: George Bell & Sons, 1888), 5: 433.

20. Ibid., 438.

21. Tom Nairn, *The Break-Up of Britain: Crisis and Neo-Nationalism* (London: New Left Library, 1977), 12–13.

22. See "Who We Are and What We Ought to Be," *Guardian,* 8 May 1990, reproduced in *National Identities: The Constitution of the United Kingdom,* ed. Bernard Crick (Oxford: Blackwell, 1991), 168–71.

23. Raphael Samuel, *Theatres of Memory 2: Island Stories—Unravelling Britain,* ed. Alison Light with Sally Alexander and Gareth Stedman Jones (London: Verso, 1998), 22.

24. See Benedict Anderson, *Imagined Communities: Reflections on the Origin and Spread of Nationalism,* rev. ed. (London: Verso, 1991).

25. Margaret Canovan, "'Breathes there the man, with soul so dead…' Reflections on patriotic poetry and liberal principles," in *Literature and the Political Imagination,* ed. John Horton and Andrea T. Baumeister (London: Routledge, 1996), 170–97.

26. Katie Trumpener, *Bardic Nationalism: The Romantic Novel and the British Empire* (Princeton: Princeton University Press, 1997), 15–16.

27. Lisa Jardine, "A Point of View: Nation or State?" BBC Radio Four, 7 Dec. 2007; http://news.bbc.co.uk/1/hi/magazine/7133315.stm accessed 9 Dec. 2007.

28. Ibid.

29. Ania Loomba, *Shakespeare, Race, and Colonialism* (Oxford: Oxford University Press, 2002), 12.

30. According to a *Guardian* ICM opinion poll, quoted in Tariq Modood, *Multiculturalism: A Civic Idea* (Cambridge: Polity Press, 2007), 108.

31. Clive J. Christie, *Race and Nation: A Reader* (London: I. B. Tauris, 1998), 233.

32. For a stunning visual record of the passage of Black Britons from travelers to arrivals on the *Windrush* and from the Notting Hill riots to celebrity in entertainment and sport, see Paul Gilroy, *Black Britain: A Photographic History* (London: Saqi, 2007).

33. Gilman, *Multiculturalism and the Jews,* 225–42.

34. Efraim Sicher, *Antisemitism, Multiculturalism, Globalization: The British Case.* Analysis of Current Trends in Antisemitism #32 (Jerusalem: Vidal Sassoon Center for the Study of Antisemitism, Hebrew University of Jerusalem, 2009).

35. Max Silverman and Nira Yuval-Davis, "Jews, Arabs, and the Theorization of Racism in Britain and France," in *Thinking Identities: Ethnicity, Racism and Culture,* ed. Avtar Brah, Mary J. Hickman, and Máirtín Mac an Ghaill (Basingstoke: MacMillan, 1998), 25–43.

36. See Alice Bloch and John Solomos, eds., *Race and Ethnicity in the 21st Century* (Houndmills: Palgrave Macmillan, 2010); Salvador Cardús, "New Ways of Thinking About Identity in Europe," in *Ethnic Europe: Mobility, Identity, and Conflict in a Globalized World,* ed. Roland Hsu (Stanford: Stanford University Press, 2010), 63–79; Commission on Integration and Cohesion, UK, 2006, cited in Cardús, 75, n. 5.

37. Nasar Meer and Tehseen Noorani, "A Sociological Comparison of Anti-Semitism and Anti-Muslim Sentiment in Britain," *Sociological Review* 56.2 (2008):

195–218. See Maleiha Malik, "Muslims are now getting the same treatment Jews had a century ago," *Guardian,* 2 Feb. 2007. See chapters three and five below.

38. Paul Silverstein, "Immigrant Racialization and the New Savage Slot: Race, Migration, and Immigration in the New Europe," *Annual Review of Anthropology* 34 (2005): 366–67.

39. For example, India Knight, "Muslims are the new Jews," *Sunday Times,* 15 Oct. 2006.

40. David Cesarani, "Why Muslims are not the new Jews," http://www.thejc.com /comment/comment/21173/why-muslims-are-not-new-jews, 19 Oct. 2009. Cesarani is a professor of history at Royal Holloway, London University.

41. Linda Rozmovits, "'Now you see 'em, now you don't': Jewish Visibility and the Problem of Citizenship in the British Telecom 'Beattie' Campaign," *Media Culture Society* 22.6 (2000): 707–22.

42. Madelyn Travis, "'Heritage Anti-Semitism' in Modern Times?: Representations of Jews and Judaism in Twenty-first-century British Historical Fiction for Children," *European Judaism* 43.1 (Spring 2010): 78–92.

43. Christina Patterson, "Lessons from literature—and YouTube—in immigrant life," *Independent* 24 July 2010; "The limits of multi-culturalism," *Independent,* 28 July 2010; see her response to protests from Muslim and Jewish readers, "We need to talk about integration," *Independent,* 4 Aug. 2010. British journalist India Knight (of mixed race) also records her anxiety in response to the furor over wearing veils in public; walking in Golders Green, she is avoided by Hasidic men in black ("Muslims are the new Jews").

44. Tony Kushner, "Remembering to Forget: Racism and anti-Racism in Postwar Britain," in *Modernity, Culture, and 'the Jew,'* ed. Bryan Cheyette and Laura Marcus, 226–27.

45. Efraim Sicher, "The Image of Israel: A View from Britain," *Israel Studies* 16.1 (Spring 2011): 1–25.

46. See Shalva Weil, *India's Jewish Heritage: Ritual, Art, and Life-Cycle* (Mumbai: Marg, 2002). On American Asian writers who use the figure of the "jew" in constructing Indian identity see Jonathan Freedman, "'Who's Jewish?' Some Asian-American Writers and the Jewish-American Literary Canon," *Michigan Quarterly Review* 42.1 (2003): 230–54.

47. Anna Guttman, "Marketing the Figure of the Jew: Writing South Asia, Reading America," in *The Global Literary Field,* ed. Anna Guttman, Michel Hockx, and George Paizis (Newcastle-upon-Tyne, England: Cambridge Scholars Press, 2006), 60–79. The global literary economy is, of course, heavily Americanized, but in addressing marketing and its effect on reception, rather than engaging in textual analysis, Guttman ascribes to Desai the *intention* of writing for an American Jewish readership, thus downplaying the author's postcolonial concerns and the significance of her biographical background, which are, as we shall argue, all-important.

48. Vijay Mishra, *The Literature of the Indian Diaspora: Theorizing the Diasporic Imaginary* (London: Routledge, 2007), 10–11.

49. Joseph Frank, *The Idea of Spatial Form* (Brunswick: Rutgers University Press), 38.

50. Anna Guttman, "The Jew in the Archive: Textualizations of (Jewish?) History in Contemporary South Asian Literature," *Contemporary Literature* 51.3 (2010): 503–31.

51. Ronald Shepherd, *Ruth Prawer Jhabvala in India: The Jewish Connection* (Delhi: Chanakyu Publications, 1994), 1–3.

52. Coetzee, *Elizabeth Costello* (New York: Penguin, 2003), 75.

53. Paul Gilroy, *Against Race: Imagining Political Culture beyond the Color Line* (Cambridge, Mass.: Harvard University Press, 2000), 287–326; "Not Being Inhuman," in Cheyette and Marcus, *Modernity, Culture, and 'the Jew'* (Cambridge: Polity Press, 1998), 292–97.

54. Gilroy, *Against Race,* 82–96.

55. See Bill Ashcroft, Gareth Griffiths, and Helen Tiffin, eds., *The Empire Writes Back: Theory and Practice in Post-Colonial Literatures,* 2nd ed. (London: Routledge, 2002).

56. Michael L. Ross, *Race Riots: Comedy and Ethnicity in Modern British Fiction* (Montreal: McGill-Queen's University Press, 2006), 14; Ross cites Jacobson's *Seriously Funny* (1997).

57. Ibid., 7–14.

58. Clingman*, The Grammar of Identity: Transnational Fiction and the Nature of the Boundary* (Oxford: Oxford University Press, 2009).

59. Nasta,. *Home Truths: Fictions of the South Asian Diaspora in Britain* (Houndmills: Palgrave Macmillan, 2002).

60. Edward Said, *Orientalism,* 25th anniversary ed. (New York: Vintage, 1994), 27–28.

61. Aamar Mufti, *Enlightenment in the Colony: The Jewish Question and the Crisis of Postcolonial Culture.* (Princeton: Princeton University Press, 2007).

Introduction

OUTING THE OTHER:
FROM MEDIEVAL ANTI-JUDAISM TO MODERN ANTISEMITISM

This study is about representation of the "jew" in contemporary British writing, something that cannot be understood without first considering the embedding in English culture of an antisemitic discourse. Whether such discourse enjoys a continuum that outlasts the viability of the theological assumptions and original historical circumstances which gave rise to it is a debatable question. Certainly, we must examine the local context of any narrative and bear in mind its possible audiences, the gaps in the text, the transformations of myth, and influences across national or ethnic borders.

The literary scholar Bryan Cheyette has commented on how the "phony war" between liberal humanism and political correctness has obscured the racialization of the stereotype of the Jew in Western culture.[1] Cheyette has pioneered the study of the "jew" in modern English culture as a racialized stereotype and shown how "semitic discourse" emerged by the 1870s out of a cultural inclusivity and a racist exclusivity.[2] In what follows, we will show that, indeed, the figure of the "jew" cannot be understood outside the formation of "Englishness" as a national and cultural identity and that it must be read through the lens of ideological constructs in the imperialist project. It would be misleading to reduce representations of nationhood to a dip test that ranges from philosemitism to Judeophobia, and Zygmunt Bauman has suggested that allosemitism, the difference of the Jews as Jews is the better term, as it contains the fundamental ambivalence of the "jew" within Western society bequeathed by Christianity.[3] Such representations reflect longstanding constructions of a dominant masculinity and whiteness, against which the "jew" may be juxtaposed as feminized and dark, an alien presence of a diseased body.

In the early modern period, as James Shapiro has shown, after Jews were officially expelled and were absent from the realm, there seemed much confusion about color, race, and religion as definitions of national identity, and the construction of the "jew" was important in thinking through these issues; more confusion to the matrix of race, religion, and color is added by the apparent clandestine existence in England of Marranos (converts from Spain and Portugal who secretly practiced Judaism), while there were dissenting or Judaizing sects who were dubbed "Jews."[4] Clearly, one should be careful not to collapse constructions of the Other into a flat narrative of how these determined formation of national identity, and Ania Loomba has been careful to point out that at the critical moment of England's emergence into nationhood in the early modern period it was also negotiating real encounters with alien peoples in trade and colonization of the New World, which, for all the distortions of travel accounts and the "mirror" of the Shakespearean stage, provided a self-image and at the same time shook up conceptions of "race," gender, religion, and nation in the representation of the weird and wonderful world being discovered. On the one hand, anxieties about the thousands of strangers at home ignited violence at the time of the writing of *Othello,* while, on the other hand, courtesans and even royalty happily donned exotic dress and masks in playful impersonation of outsiders and foreigners. There could be fear of miscegenation and of Englishmen "turning Turk" or becoming savages, as well as welcoming of hybridity in the mixing of blood.[5]

Nevertheless, social affiliation and group membership are usually defined in parameters that are determined by the identity of the Other, a means of self-definition through what one is not: the alien, the hostile, the unknown, the foreign, the non-human, the outsider and outcast of society. The formation of national identity is always a long and confused story of foundation myths, political fictions, and geo-historical exigencies, but national self-definition always works by constructing an Other about whom one can safely say one is not that. The measures and policies undertaken by the state or by public institutions against the Other bolster the ethnic and sociopolitical identity of the collective in many subtle and not so subtle ways, from boycotting and stigmatizing to genocide and ethnic cleansing, which has a history of its own in England, dating to the beginning of the eleventh century when King Aethelred the Unready sanctioned the lawful killing of Danish persons living in England in language that chillingly echoes twentieth-century racism.[6] The Danes were identifiable alien invaders, and this does not explain the formation in the Middle Ages of a persecuting society which "othered" Jews, witches, heretics, or lepers who were demonized and marked out for legitimate ostracism and exclusion, as well as collective punishment and judicial killing. Here, as the historian Tony Kushner has remarked, context is crucial, for Christian anti-Judaism was conscripted to power struggles that enabled genocidal thinking in an irrational hatred that was later revived in modern antisemitism, but to trace back twentieth-century anti-Jewish racist violence to mediaeval constructions of the "jew" risks flattening out a complex history and invites misunderstanding of the causes of contemporary racism, as well as the "antisemitism of tolerance," that is, the anxiety about Jewish difference within assimilation.[7]

In the nineteenth century it was the Irish who were racialized, but even the poor were criminalized and considered contaminated: they were to be "policed" and regulated as a sick limb of the economic and political body.[8] Over the ages, hatred of aliens has been a rallying cry among the lower classes in the hands of opportunist politicians. "Generally speaking," declared Labour MP Josiah Wedgwood, speaking in a House of Commons committee in 1919 on a bill to limit immigration,

> aliens are always hated by the people of this country. . . . The Flemings were persecuted and hunted, and the Lombards were hunted down by the London mob. Then it was the turn of the French Protestants. . . . You always have a mob of entirely uneducated people who will hunt down foreigners, and you always have people who will make use of the passions of the mob in order to get their ends politically.[9]

Wedgewood urged that the proposed legislation be rejected in the name of an internationalist spirit of the working classes, but successive Labour governments did continue to control immigration and the working class did not always welcome foreigners, especially when there was competition for jobs.

Should we regard stereotyping as universal in human society, or do we need to look for historical and ideological causes for the persecution of the Jews, as distinct from other aliens and outsiders? Stereotypes do have a history, and are never innocent. Myths do kill. The execution of Jews in Lincoln and Bury St. Edmunds in the twelfth century followed ritual murder accusations; in the twentieth century, the German public was prepared for the extermination of six million Jews by indoctrination in the idea that the Jews were an evil, anti-social inferior race against whom Germany had to defend itself, a campaign accompanied by vicious medieval libels in *Der Stürmer*. The psychological factor in the human drive to ostracize and murder does not explain historical forces or the political and ideological context. This is because, as Michael Pickering has argued, if stereotypes are proportionate to the degree of alienation producing them, then they are not absolute or invariant and they always have a historical basis, which may change over time, so that the social dynamics must be understood, not just the psychological reasons behind the human instinct for prejudiced behavior:

> Stereotyping always operates in relation to what is culturally ambivalent and thematically contrary within everyday life, and does so as a common sense rhetorical strategy of naturalizing order and control. Stereotypes operate as socially exorcistic rituals in maintaining the boundaries of normality and legitimacy.[10]

The "jew" may be a projection of fears and anxieties which arise from instabilities in perception of the world: "The deep structure of the stereotype reappears in the adult as a response to anxiety, an anxiety having its roots in the potential disintegration of the mental representations the individual has created and internalized."[11] These anxieties are typically displaced onto the outcasts and discontents of society. Moreover, "they" bear the qualities and exhibit forbidden desires which "we" deny in ourselves and can therefore more readily be identified as the Other masquerading under fake identities and therefore invisible within the nation (otherwise there would be no need to mark the Jews with an emblematic badge or hat and impose segregation rules or promulgate expulsion orders). Stereotyping is a universal response to the inability to control the world or to a disintegration of perceived order.[12] However, this account of the dynamics of stereotyping and outcasting does not tell us why particular stereotypes about Jews developed in particular times and places. The function of the "jew" in the text is to enable the familiar, it is part of Englishness, Christianity, family, and home. It is what gives them meaning. The "jew" is a construct widely and diffusely available in English and European narratives, so that there is no need to examine the antisemitic intention of manuscript copyists (who may have been filled with zealous hatred for Jews) or to investigate motives of modern novelists who disseminated hostile images of the "jew," as if there was some reality in an imaginary textual figure.[13] Blood libels and other myths have no basis in fact and have no place in Jewish beliefs; rather, they can be profitably studied as part of Western cultural codes and narratives.

Transgressive or judicial violence is contained and justified by belief in collective guilt of the Other, yet the "jew" carried a particular set of meanings in Christian belief and in English lore and myth. Transformations of the economic, social, and cultural function of this figure recur with surprising frequency whenever national identity is in question. The ubiquity of the figure has little relation to the actual presence of Jews in England, as in the plays of Marlowe and Shakespeare which were written when there were, officially at least, no Jews resident in England. The figure of the "jew" grows out of mythical beliefs that are basic to a theological and ideological worldview which feeds on hostile images of Judaism in the Christian scriptures, but can survive the waning of those beliefs and resurface centuries later in an entirely different ideological context. Each society has its own demons, but the "jew" alone is central to the Christian theological worldview in which the divine savior is believed to be in conflict with the antichrist or Satan, with whom the "jew" has been associated in medieval constructions of universal evil, sexual perversion, political subversion, and that most inciting anti-social activity, usury.[14] Many of these tropes, as we will see, outlived their original context, but it is not always easy to maintain a watertight distinction between general prejudice or xenophobic attitudes and a programmatic antisemitism in the modern sense of genocidal hatred directed exclusively towards Jews as a biologically defined "racial" group.[15]

Besides heretics and lepers, there are other aliens on the medieval horizon, and their relation to the "jew" is instructive when it comes to understanding the construction of "otherness" and the limits of the human or the socially acceptable. As Sheila Delany shows in her study of the cultural matrix of Jews and Muslims in Chaucer's "The Prioress's Tale," the "jew" has long been a protean figure that is intricately tied to perceptions of Muslims as heathens and Orientalized aliens. According to Delany, "Asia," the setting of Chaucer's tale, is not some mythical far-off place, but the very real political geography of a world at the end of the fourteenth-century ruled by Muslims from the Iberian Peninsula to Asia Minor and Arabia.[16] Nevertheless, there are versions of the miracle of the boy singer that are set in other locations, including England, and the reference to the martyrdom of Hugh of Lincoln by Chaucer's Prioress makes explicit the referential setting of the narrative. All this suggests that the exemplary punishment of the Jews is meant to serve as a model for a truly Christian ruler; indeed, England's expulsion of the Jews, the first of its kind in Europe, was emulated in France and elsewhere. The Orientalized location serves to emphasize the foreignness of the situation and to imagine a place where assimilation is resisted.[17] Whatever irony may be read into the authorial framing of the Prioress's character and of her performance of a devotional narrative, the effect nevertheless is to unite the listeners in identification with a Christian community of belief which has put the Jews beyond the pale of human society: there can be for them neither mercy nor the possibility of conversion (as in other versions of this narrative).

From a Christian standpoint, the Muslim tolerance of Jews, albeit as *dhimmi,* second-class citizens protected by the ruler, was unforgivable and their free practice of usury was "hateful to Crist and all his compagnye." That Jews and Muslims were thought of being in league with each other can be seen over the centuries in political fears of Jewish allegiance with the dangerous forces of Islam—the Saracens, Turks and Tartars—and this is reflected in canon law, especially in cases of property and conversion. The edicts of the Fourth Lateran Council in 1215 designated clothing that ensured segregation of both Jews and Muslims from Christians. Indeed, in medieval English drama we find a confusion of Judaism and Islam: in the *Croxton Play of the Sacrament* Jewish characters pray to "Machomet" and in the Digby *Mary Magdalene* the High Priest swears by Mohamed. Both Jews and Muslims are to be seen as anti-Christ.[18] In medieval law and medieval imagination the Jew and the Muslim "were inextricably linked together in the consciousness of Christians"[19] and both were targeted as enemies of Christendom during the Crusades, a holy war which sought to liberate the Holy Land from Muslim rule and which served as pretext for the brutal massacre of Jews in many communities in Western Europe.

The Orientalization of the Jews further justified in retrospect their expulsion from England as aliens with links to the nation's enemies. In "The Prioress's Tale" the Jews are removed to Asia, but their defiling presence and their polluting acts—the kidnapping and ritual murder of a Christian boy and the disposal of the body in a latrine—are exclusively an outrage to Christendom with its theology of virginity and purity. The miracle is to be understood as further proof of the Jews' disbelief, while their vicious punishment vindicates their unacceptability as members of a Christian society. The reworking here of Marianic tales and the legends and ballads about Hugh of Lincoln place the story in an English cultural discourse and construct the Orientalized Jewish space as polluted, to be resisted by a pure and miraculously purifying Christian community. Hence the removal of the story to Asia effectively "colonizes" the "jew" by "translating Jews from time into space."[20] It thus inscribes the contested Orientalized territories of the East onto the bodies of the Jews punished for their inherent criminality and their threat, both to the body of the Christian and the Christian god, through the original crucifixion and its repetition in ritual murder or host desecration.

In passing, we might note that in the medieval discourses about the "jews," Jewish voices were usually silenced or went unheard. In response to the widespread anti-Jewish violence in the beginning of the eleventh century, in the wake of the Crusade of 1096, there was a real Jewish voice that found expression in liturgical lament in some of the finest Hebrew poetry of the period, such as the poems written by Kalonymous ben Judah to mourn the destruction of the communities of Worms, Speyer, and Mainz and those by Menachem ben Machir. The lamentations written by these and other poets explicitly counter Christian accusations against the Jews and eulogize the victims as pure unsullied martyrs whose blood will one day be avenged by God.[21] In England, referred to in these lamentations as the "Land of the Isle," Joseph of Chartres wrote an elegy in 1170 and Menachem ben Jacob wrote another for the Boppart and York martyrs of 1190. Both are included in canonical liturgical collections of lamentations for Tisha B'Av, the Fast of the Ninth of Av, and thus form part of the canon of commemoration of Destruction from the First and Second Temples to the present. But in English culture even Barakhiah ha-Nakdan (Benedictus le Pointeur of Oxford), author of the *Fox Fables,* or Rabbi Yom-Tov of Joigny, a well-known Tosaphist and one of the York martyrs.

Besides the drive behind stereotyping in the human psyche and the ideology of nation-forming, the cultural construction of the Other must be considered in relation to the political, socioeconomic, and gender hierarchy. In medieval England, for example, women and Jews shared a gendered inferiority in being perceived as theologically deficient and having bodies that were not male—the Jew's circumcised body was thought to be mutilated or castrated. Indeed, it was widely believed that male Jews menstruated like women, possibly because they were supposedly afflicted by hemorrhages in punishment for their part in the crucifixion after they declared that the blood of Jesus would be upon their heads and their children's. Moreover, like women, Jews were regarded as carnal—incomplete and empty of spirit, incapable of fully participating in the universality of a Christian salvation.[22] "The Hermeneutical woman and the Hermeneutical Jew both become associated with veiled knowledge, a clouded seeing, with carnality, and, of course, with the body itself. Both become figured as embodied particulars in relation to a universal that transcends embodiment."[23] In other words, salvation is facilitated through a normative male transcendence of the body, so that both the "jew" and women are genders that have to overcome their innate carnality in order to be redeemed by a paradoxical construction of a Christian "universal." The contrary and sometimes ambivalent representations of "jew" and women can be explained by a binary polarization of patriarch/deicide and virgin/whore that underlie the hermeneutic system of Christianity in Western Europe.[24]

In addition to the Jews' theological role as "witnesses" to the coming of the Christian messiah and the mythical role of the "jew" as anti-Christ (in host desecration tales and blood libels) or as scapegoats for the Plague, who allegedly poisoned wells, the figure of the "jew" was essential to the construction of Englishness itself. The American political scientist Ira Katznelson has argued that the reason for the expulsion of the Jews in 1290 lay not in the Jews' decreasing usefulness as the royal milk cow, squeezed of taxes and fines to the last drop, but may be explained by the shifting balance of power between King and barons. The Magna Carta itself supplies evidence of the concession of power by the monarchy in clauses that provided for relief from debt to the Jews, who were the property of the Crown, a price the king was prepared to pay for stability and survival. In summer 1290, the King was granted the tax he had requested from Parliament, whose founder, Simon de Montfort, began his career in Leicester by expelling the city's Jews.[25] It is not often remembered that one of the foundational moments in the history of liberal democracy happened to be a moment of extortion, persecution, and ethnic cleansing, a paradox that reveals a startling connection between the two historical processes.[26]

It might be easier to explain not why the Jews were expelled from England, but what prevented them from being expelled. Edward I was a deeply religious man who had associated himself with building not so long after the Expulsion, among other shrines, the one to little Hugh of Lincoln, martyred victim of the Jews. In doing so, the English monarch effectively reinforced the power dynamics in the reversed roles of victim and perpetrator.[27] Anglo-Jewish historian Colin Richmond sees Edward as a religious bigot who in 1278 had 268 Jews hung for alleged coin-clipping and confiscated their property to the tune of £16,000. Yet persecution of the Jews and their profitable exploitation was to be always remembered as a defense of Christendom and of Englishness. The loss of Normandy was, moreover, one act in the trend towards insularity and one that isolated the Jews from their brethren in mainland Europe, making them all the more vulnerable as outsiders in a sea of Englishness.[28] It must be said, however, that the Jews were identifiable as a people apart only after the Jew badge became statuary from 1253. They were largely tolerated until 1189, when a delegation of Jews to the coronation of Richard I was attacked, leading to anti-Jewish violence in London and elsewhere, followed the next year by the martyrdom of the Jews of York. Excluded from the guilds, many, but not all, Jews were moneylenders (an occupation barred to Christians), and their knowledge of Hebrew and other languages enhanced the efficacy and security levels of their business transactions, as well as ensuring the mysteriousness of their dealings. Despite discriminatory measures in the thirteenth century, such as the Jew badge, they were not confined to ghettos, and they mixed with the general population. However, the Jews became outsiders when towns grew and when the social hierarchy gradually changed as civil society became increasingly defined as English. When town burghers acquired more freedom, royal protection of the Jews relaxed, and changes in the fiscal system rendered the Jews less indispensable as the financiers of royal military campaigns.

Expulsion was, in a way, a consolidation of both the new power structure and the unity of the nation (a process to be seen two centuries later in the expulsion of the Jews from Spain, where the unity of one nation, religion, and language marked the final end of foreign rule and the opening of a new colonial era of conquest with the discovery of America). Sylvia Tomasch has gone further and claimed that just as the expulsion of 1290 served England's political needs, the virtual presence in English culture of the "jew" was necessary to define the nation in terms of its imagined Other. This "virtual jew" constituted an "internal colonization" that protected the religious, political, and geographical integrity of the host society.[29] The figure of the "jew" in medieval chronicles does not always reflect anti-Jewish violence, yet what these texts have in common is the symbolic presence of the "jew" in "the social and narrative fabric of England's past. The Jews are linked, implicitly, to the political and economic crises affecting England and so function as a kind of lens through which the nation is projected."[30] Underpinning the formation of a polity out of a community of ethnic and linguistic kinship is a synecdochal Other who embodies the anti-nation in collective memory.[31]

The image of the "jew" is ever mutable, and the disparities and disjunctions in its narrative transformations reveal much about the uses to which the image is put. For example, to display exemplary behavioral patterns of authority, ritual, piety, and language—as in "The Prioress's Tale"—the punishment meted out to Jews, or the miracles shown to Jews inspire devotional attitudes in the target audience but also offer a critical model of governance implied in the desirable or "proper" treatment of the Jews.[32] Paradoxically perhaps, Jews could be pitied for their exile after their long sojourn in England (in the Waverly Annals), but also the expulsion could be justified as fitting punishment for the Jews' sinfulness and blasphemy (in the Annals of Osney).[33]

Changing dogmas may have affected the "hermeneutical Jew" in Christian theology, besides the polemical tradition of the *Adversus Judaeos,* which deeply influenced Church teachings. Iconographical representation of Jews in illustrated manuscripts of the biblical and Christian scriptures or in church art could be contradictory and inconsistent.[34] Yet the figure of the "jew" continued to be prominent well into the fourteenth century, often conforming, though not consistently, to the common archetype of Biblical characters as positive and the Jews in the Christian scriptures as satanic deicides. The delusion of Jewish guilt for ritual murder found in normative medieval texts such as the "Prayer to St. Robert," a fifteenth-century contribution to the devotional cult of the child-martyr of Bury St. Edmunds, is dictated by a typology which prefigures the represented event in the crucifixion of Jesus but in which the Jews are "subject to their medieval role at the point of Jesus' incarnation."[35] Historical time and space are collapsed into the sacramental present, while political and devotional interests combine in the communal bonding of cult-followers or in the representation of the cultic myth (for example, in the visual icons of the liberty of Bury St. Edmunds and the typically English robin, whose red breast, according to legend, recalls the blood of the crucifixion).[36]

Here we see the workings of the medieval imagination in conjuring up a mythical figure that could be identified in local time and place with real Jews, but, as in other European Christian countries, could also be understood as outsiders in a transhistorical belief system. By emphasizing the refusal of the Jews to believe in the Christian messiah and by delineating the Christians' "New" Testament from the "Old" one of the Hebrew bible, the universalistic, spiritual faith of Christians was juxtaposed with the particularistic, literalist adherence to the Law of the Jews, who had forfeited the status of chosen people, later to be supplanted by the British in Protestant thinking. Having said this, we should bear in mind that the construction of the "jew" was always a "dual image," for, in his parable of the olive tree, the Christian apostle Paul required the regeneration and conversion of the Jews as

Title page of *Coryat's*
Crudities (1611) (detail)

witnesses to consummate Christian redemption in the second coming of their messiah.[37] The Church did not have a vested interest in the expulsion of Jews for they were necessary to vindicate its redemption theology and their presence was necessary for their conversion. When no longer present or visible on English soil, the "jew" was nevertheless still very much present as a hermeneutical and theological construction.

In the period of early modern discovery of unknown lands and non-White, non-Christian peoples, familiar images of the "jew" could be found alongside representations of strange alien bodies, often of grotesque naked natives, but also of noble savages (Montaigne, it will be remembered, mocked the xenophobic attitudes of the French court toward visiting cannibals). Thomas Coryat, for example, was chased out of the Venice ghetto after trying to convert the Jews there, but on the cover of his well-known travelogue, *Coryat's Crudities,* he includes a drawing of a turbaned Jew pursuing a Christian with raised knife ready to circumcise him. The blood lust of the "jew" is thus a projection of the dynamics of Jewish-Christian relations, except in a reversed direction (contempt for the Jews and the mission to convert them are projected into defense against Jewish threats). The specter of Jewish forced circumcision, so clearly linked to the Christian belief in the blood libel, did not go away and resurfaced at the time of the abortive attempt to emancipate England's Jews in 1753. The Stage Jew might now be represented as only too human, a real villain, like Barabas or Shylock, but he had not shed his mythological role or allegorical antecedents. However, the myth of the evil Jew and his beautiful daughter (*pace* Abigail or Jessica) both complicated the ambiguities of sincere conversion and offered an attractive legend for Romantics such as Sir Walter Scott, in *Ivanhoe.*

With Romanticism, particularly in the legend of the Wandering Jew, the "jew" acquired tragic overtones, a figure to be hated and feared, but also an object of pity and, after the rise of movements for national liberation in the nineteenth century, of renewed respect (for example, in *Daniel Deronda*). What Mark Gelber calls "literary anti-Semitism,"[38] that is, the dissemination of hostile stereotypes which promote anti-Jewish prejudice and provoke anti-Jewish violence, could still nevertheless draw on the older cultural and theological constructions to serve ideological ends. And yet, despite the English cultural heritage of narratives of the blood libel, host desecration, or coin-clipping, the argument was made that the representation of "bad" Jews is not antisemitic, but merely reflects objective facts (a "real" knowledge of the Jews). Charles Dickens, for example, claimed, rather unconvincingly, that his portrayal of the Jew Fagin was "true" because it represented the reality of London's underworld at the time—yet only wicked Jews are portrayed in *Oliver Twist,* whereas Christian characters are both good and villainous. "Fagin, in *Oliver Twist,*" wrote Charles Dickens in a letter of 10 July 1863 to Mrs. Eliza Davis, "is a Jew, because it unfortunately was true of the time to which that story refers, that that class of criminal invariably was a Jew."[39] This oft-quoted self-defense against a charge of antisemitism in the portrayal of Fagin claims as an objective truth not that all Jews are criminal, but that fences were "invariably" Jews. In the entry on Ikey Solomons, generally considered the prototype of Fagin, in the second volume of *The New Newgate Calendar,* there is not the slightest suggestion that fences were predominantly Jews at this time, even though Jews in the East End were connected with Dutch Jews who handled stolen bank-notes. Nor does Henry Mayhew in volume four of *London Labour and the London Poor* identify Jews with the training of pickpockets. The "fact" that fences were invariably Jews inscribed the racialization of crime found, for example, in Watts Phillips' *The Wild Tribes of London* and other mid-century guides to Victorian London's outcast population.[40] Dickens would have us regard Fagin not as "the Jew," as he was called throughout editions of the novel before 1867, but as a *bad* Jew because he is a fence. It is not, however, difficult to see in the figure of Fagin the bogey-man of modern capitalist society, a filthy reptile slinking through the offal of London's underworld, the satanic embodiment of a primeval regression to what was most threatening in modernity itself, the evil lurking

John Leech, "The Cheap Tailor and his Workmen," *Punch* (1845)

within the Victorian city which corrupted and depraved, and which could easily be recognized in the caricatures of ugly Jewish traders and money-lenders in magazines such as *The Illustrated London News* and *Punch*.

Political or "modern" antisemitism from the end of the nineteenth century singled out the "jew" as a biological and economic threat to society, while reinforcing the function of the "Other" in the identity of the nation-state. T. S. Eliot writes in "Gerontion":

> My house is a decayed house,
> And the jew squats on the window sill, the owner,
> Spawned in some estaminet of Antwerp,
> Blistered in Brussels, patched and peeled in London.

Delineation of the targeted group for discrimination, expulsion, or extermination actually creates the identity of the Other in collective consciousness; the legal expert Anthony Julius writes that "while German anti-Semitism killed Jews, English anti-Semitism helped create them."[41] However, whereas Jews were regarded with some ambivalence as cosmopolitan or international agents of modernity, they were also seen as enemies of modernity in their perverse resistance to full assimilation and their identification with capitalism.[42] In the postcolonial period, when one would have expected Jews to be identified as victims of racism and when they finally had a state of their own, the Jews are again attacked for clinging to their nationhood, as the nation-state comes under attack by anti-racists who hold it responsible for the oppression and persecution of the twentieth century. Moreover, intellectual and academic understanding of world affairs is heavily dominated by a multicultural agenda which has tended to exclude consideration of Jewish issues or antisemitism, while making "Palestine" the center of political consensus and redefining diaspora as a transnational scattering of migrants not tied to any ancestral homeland.[43]

POSTCOLONIAL DISCOURSES OF THE "JEW"

Liberal humanism was from the outset often ambivalent about the Jews, and there is little reason to believe this ambivalence has disappeared.[44] The new era of globalization and postcolonialism has, moreover, reinvented the "jew" as an ambiguous figure, to be feared as agent of oppression but at the same time welcomed as the ultimate victim. The reinvention of the "jew" in the context of "New Antisemitism" can be partly explained by ongoing political agendas and ideological discourse in gentile society. Walter Laqueur recognizes familiar archetypes in the contemporary "non-racist" antisemitism in Europe. Excessive "Jewish" influence is imagined everywhere in politics and the economy, serving conspiracy theories about corporate globalism, American imperialism, and dangers to democracy. Whereas previously Jews were denigrated for being impoverished and powerless, now they are resented for being affluent and all-powerful.[45]

Indeed, if we now turn to postcolonial theory and particularly to the discourse of cultural studies in Britain, we may see a tendency to displace the "jew" as a victim of racism in the view of the world Homi Bhabha describes in his essay "The Postcolonial and the Postmodern," which has replaced the old model of class conflict. Now there is a shift to the marginalized view of the formerly colonized world, which overturns the former historicity of canonic narratives and political discourses and which changes in complex ways social and political boundaries so that cultural value is located in a hybrid state, the "transnational as translational."[46] One might have thought that Jews would be candidates for consideration as benign subjects of such a view, at least as veteran diaspora globetrotters who have borne racism and entered their host cultures as migrants and outsiders. Antisemitism is increasingly recognized as a model of European racism arising from the promotion of the nation-state as a totalitarian ideology in the twentieth century. Yet it is this development which is introduced as an explanation of political Zionism, that, paradoxically, is depicted as itself guilty of "nationalism" and made responsible for the Arab refugee problem after the

Arabs rejected the UN Partition Plan and five Arab armies attacked the fledging Jewish state. The "ethnic cleansing" that is alleged to have occurred illustrates for scholars of race discourse the way Zionism turned from portraying Jews as outsiders in Europe to becoming itself a typically European "colonial project," characterized by "racial" superiority and territorial expansion that gave Jews the right to immigrate and settle the land.[47] That the tiny state of Israel should be considered a threat to radical Arab nationalism (a favorable ideology that grew out of a revolt against European colonialism) is an unstated irony in this view of the relation between race and nation.

Commenting on the silencing of Jews in postcolonial discourse, Jonathan Boyarin has posited the hypothesis that postcolonial theorists and authors have constructed a White Eurocentric knowledge that was responsible for Nazism and the exploitation of colonial and postcolonial peoples alike. When Henry Gates or Wole Soyinka talk of the "Euro-Judaic" civilization responsible for the evils of Apartheid, Jonathan Boyarin can only deduce that they are referring to the chauvinism of the Chosen People, in the old Christian paradigm of Jewish intransigence and arrogant racial superiority, or that they infer racism to be a product of the European Enlightenment.[48] The victims of colonialism are never Jews, while ex-colonial Jews like Cixous marginalize their Jewish identity.[49] It is unfortunate that postcolonial theorists such as Henry Gates and Edward Said (in *Culture and Imperialism,* 1993) have joined the fray against the White European "Judeo-Christian culture" which is held responsible for colonialism. Historically, Jews were not always included in such cultural acceptance, and the discourse of the Enlightenment tended to grant emancipation and civic equality to Jews on condition of their abandoning their "primitive" or "separatist" behavior, while fearing the Jews' supposed superior intelligence.[50] The Victorians generally found it quite difficult to contain Jews within the category of "White," let alone part of some "Judeo-Christian" superiority fit to rule the world.[51] Indeed, within English culture Jews themselves have been silent or silenced. Whether we are talking about Matthew Arnold's notion of "Hebraism" in *Culture and Anarchy,* which elided real Jews, or T. S. Eliot's *After Strange Gods,* which could find no place for too many free-thinking Jews, Jews have not been regarded as assimilable to constructions of English cultural identity. Nor does there seem to be room for them in Raymond Williams' class-based cultural community in *Culture and Society.* And yet the "jew," often in the form of

"Israel" or "Zionism," is lumped together with "Judeo-Christian" civilization as the scourge of the world's oppressed.

"Race" came late to cultural studies in Britain, contends Jon Stratton, and antisemitism was rarely acknowledged.[52] This is surprising, in view of the Orientalist view of the "jew" as the suspicious alien seeking admission to liberal democracy. And yet racialization of the "jew" has a history on the political left, as well as the right. In the twentieth century, the "jew" was hounded as the alien cosmopolitan in Stalinist Russia, while in the West the "jew" was the archetypal enemy of humanity embodying the evils of capitalism. Orientalism depends (in Edward Said's terms) on a "flexible *positional* superiority," which builds a cultural hegemony on a construction of the European colonizers' knowledge, views, and images of the Orient in a whole series of relationships which meet no resistance.[53] The "jew," is, according to Kalmar and Penslar in *Orientalism and the Jews,* seen, like all other Oriental subjects, as not only *not* hybrid, but as having an essence that is exclusive and unchanging. Nonetheless, Kalmar and Penslar maintain, it is strange that the Jews have been excluded from the literary discourses of postcolonialism and hybridity, for in truth, they occupy a position on the border between cultures and civilizations, Western "but not quite," a liminal position between Christian and Muslim.[54] And to those who object to discussing Jews within the context of Orientalism or of reading the discourses of Muslims and Jews together, they reaffirm Gil Anidjar's advice: "Read the incomparable, Shylock and Othello."[55]

Recently, the "zionist" has been "Occidentalized," that is, reduced to an object of political and cultural construction, but with the curious and quite perverse twist that the "zionist" has become the colonizer, not the fighter against imperialism, and bears the White Man's burden of responsibility for importation of the European project of Enlightenment into the Middle East and the Indian subcontinent. This indicates how important the "jew" is to the West's discourse about India and Islam. For Aamar Mufti, the Enlightenment project's handling of the "Jewish Question" is paradigmatic for the colonization of the Indian sub-continent. In effect, the "jew" is displaced into the Muslim as the figure for a marginalized minority, before disappearing from view.[56] Two thousand years of Jewish history are conflated in order to stigmatize the Jewish nation-state as a result of the European solution of the Jewish Question in the Holocaust, which is chronologically (but not causally) parallel with Partition in India:

The history of Zionism and Indian Muslim separatism unfolded over almost precisely the same period of time, that is, the first half of the twentieth century, and of course the establishment of the (European) Jewish state and the creation of the (Indian) Muslim state occurred less than a year apart in its fifth decade, both through massive transfers of population and the partitioning of territories in the process of their abandonment by the British Empire. . . . They are both signs of a crisis in the nation-state system at a specific moment in its history. They mark the inability of the modern system of nation-states to complete the nationalization of society except through its violent reorganization: breakdown of communities, massacres and transfer of populations, in the one instance, and, in the other, dispersal and industrialized genocide followed by resettlement in a distant and violently appropriated land and the displacement of its own indigenous inhabitants.[57]

The "jew," then, is in this view a necessary figure in a postcolonial discourse, even if the Jewish nation is de-legitimized in a revision of history.

John Hutnyk, Professor of Cultural Studies at Goldsmiths College, University of London, has decided that there is no Jewish nation but rather diverse Jewish peoples (in the plural) who were dispersed prior to the destruction of the First Temple in Jerusalem by the Babylonians—so that there could conceivably not be any common political or ethnic entity such as "the Jews" who (falsely) claim their forced exile justifies a return to Zion:

By the fourth century BC there were more Jews *outside* rather than inside the region of Jerusalem. Nevertheless, the association of the term "diaspora" with loss or exile or some sort of suffering has meant that the Jewish experience has come to be seen as the prototype diasporic experience. This description of a group is seductive as it allows people living all over the globe to articulate a connection with each other and to think themselves connected to a greater or lesser extent, with a piece of land (whether this be mythical or actual). Of course, we are aware that in the Jewish case this has also precipitated tragic consequences and injustice for the peoples of Palestine. Ironically, given the intimate connections between the exile of Jewish peoples and the concept of diaspora as trauma, this has not prevented the creation of another victim diaspora in the Palestinian people. This may have something to do with the Jewish diaspora occupying an ambivalent place in racial hierarchies.[58]

This redefinition of diaspora, naturally, has implications for the discourse of race and Otherness which are elaborated by Hutnyk in his assertion that "the dialectic between whiteness and Otherness [*sic!*] is succinctly expressed in the formation of the Israeli nation-state (created as a compensation for the Holocaust of the Second World War), but it has effectively become a representative of White supremacy with strong backing from the U.S. government and a sanctioned systematic oppression of displaced Palestinians."[59] In other words, the "zionist'" deceit that conceals their racism—American backed White supremacy!—is the primal sin against the real Others, the Jews' "jews," the Palestinian Arabs. The parallel being constructed here is with America, for the "Whites" have driven out "natives" from "their" land, a characteristic move in such reductive demagogy which imperceptibly robs Jews of their victim status and make them appear historically perpetrators with an "ambivalent" place in the racial hierarchy. Significantly, and this is commonplace dogma in Arab propaganda constructions of "Zionism," it is the Holocaust which is the moral standard of the injustice done to Others as "compensation" for the suffering of the Jews. In other words, Jews can be recognized as victims of the Holocaust and at the same time perpetrators because of the Holocaust, a remarkable act of double thinking which sees the Holocaust as precursor of Zionist aggression, not as the culmination of antisemitism.

Stuart Hall, a leading British scholar of race, has redefined diaspora as a metaphorical figure for heterogeneity, ruling out the Jewish historical experience as a false "backward-looking" diaspora bound to a sacred homeland which was regained by forcing out the Palestinians.[60] As Jonathan and Daniel Boyarin have noted, the disqualification of the Jewish experience as a paradigm of diaspora requires a bogus and bogey "zionist" diaspora that must be removed. In order for hybridity to emerge from a diasporic model it has to be purified of the "jew."[61] We might say, more precisely, that postcolonial discourse tends to think of diaspora in terms of a transnational community of global migration. This displaces the historical sense of diaspora as the dispersion of Jews in the Babylonian captivity and the Roman exile which would come to an end with the reestablishment of a Jewish state in the land of Israel.[62]

It has been pointed out that contemporary postcolonial discourse replicates Christian replacement theology, in particular Toynbee's neo-Pauline position that the Jews were a fossil of history, and that their racist exclusiveness had forfeited their claim to be the Chosen People in a global universal human identity. In his 1961 *Study of History,* Toynbee castigated Israeli "colonialism" as an anachronistic and racist nation building by "East European" Zionists, which is equated with the conquest of the Amerindians.[63] Similarly, postcolonial discourse operates within an attempt to think through globalized identities and their relation to the new gospel of human rights. The imperialist "myth" of land as nation is regarded as a cause of racism and war, antediluvian in a globalized world of transnationalism. Paul Gilroy, for instance, celebrates instantaneous global solidarity with the victims of "occupation" in a new cosmological sense of a shared, imperiled biosphere (he is thinking specifically of International Solidarity Movement activist Rachel Corrie).[64] Such globalization of local and national conflicts (such as the Arab-Israeli war) does not seem to contradict complaint about the opposite trend of world wide atomization of society, indifference, and failure of international cooperation, as seen in the fact that no outcry or solidarity prevented the atrocities in Srebrenica, Kosovo, or Darfur. Indeed, given the preoccupation of NGOs and "boutique" ideologies with regional issues or local effects of global problems, "human solidarity" cannot always be taken at face value as evidence of transnational or cosmopolitan identities.[65] Paul Gilroy calls for an interpretation of the failure of cosmopolitanism and the dream of humanism, which he believes must entail a re-definition of the legacy of European colonialism and the politics of racism. The postcolonial construct of "zionism" stands at the center of such reexamination.[66]

Why "zionism" should be so prominent in postcolonial discourse can be better understood if we recall that since the 1980s, as a political "philosophy," postcolonialism has turned the world upside down. As Robert J. C. Young explains, if we see things from a non-Western and non-White perspective, it may be possible to dissolve the barrier of difference and inequality between the first and Third Worlds which had been based on anthropological constructs of race and culture that legitimized exploitation in the nineteenth century of much of the globe by Europeans.[67] According to Young, to resist colonizing knowledge is to acknowledge the alleged Israeli destruction of Palestinian Arab refugee camps, which becomes in his account the archetypal image of repression of all uprooted and homeless people and of "deterritorialization" everywhere.[68] As for the "specter" of terrorism, this has, it is claimed, been created by the "neocolonialist" globalizing forces that share the planet's resources so unequally and who (even if we admit the possibility that capitalism is itself divided) occasionally foster dissent in order to subvert or control opposition.[69]

Not all cultural theorists put "Palestine" at the center of postcolonialism, but some are resistant to accepting that Jews might be a nation.[70] Nevertheless, since the publication of Edward Said's *The Question of Palestine* (1979) a number of postcolonial theorists have pleaded for theorizing the Israeli-Arab conflict as a means of identifying with the Palestinian campaign, especially during the second Intifada, arguing that it is now legitimate, without being accused of antisemitism, to criticize Israel, which is no longer to be considered an exceptional case as a nation threatened with extermination, and that this would lead to "decolonization" of Israel and a change in American foreign policy.[71]

The problem may be with the reductiveness of analogous thinking in a discourse that has tried very hard to break down conventional boundaries of race and ethnic difference. When distinguished cultural theorists such as Homi Bhabha dutifully voice their identification with the correct global causes, these risk being reduced to analogous cases, for example when Bhabha generalizes "blackness" into the marginal status of all outsiders who come late to White European modernity. In the conclusion of *The Location of Culture,* Bhabha thinks of Frantz Fanon's story of the "Dirty Nigger" in "The Fact of Blackness" whenever he hears angry words about, among others, "the Jew in the *estaminet* of Antwerp, or of. . .the Palestinian on the West Bank, or the Zairian student eking out a wretched existence. . .on the Left Bank."[72] This kind of rhetoric tends to flatten out different situations into "a chain of subalternity," and the Palestinian becomes an archetype of the "jew" in T. S. Eliot's poem, while the "Israeli" is denied a similar metonymic status.[73] In a revision of this view, that accords to the "jew" both a personal and paradigmatic place in postcolonial discourse, Bhabha has written that

> the "Jew" stands for that experience of a lethal modernity, shared by the histories of slavery and colonialism. . . . In the half century since the Shoah, we have had to stand too often with, or in place of, "the Jew," taking a stance against the spread of xenophobic nationalism. To stand today besides the Palestinians, the Bosnian Muslims, the Black South Africans, or the Indian Dalits, is to occupy a position from which the very discourse of modernity is

eviscerated and needs to be rewritten from a place other than its enlightened or "civilisational" origins."[74]

We will see in the following chapters to what extent reductive analogous thinking shapes the metaphoric figure of the "jew," erasing real Jews as colonized subjects, and how a more complex postcolonial construction of the "jew" has been incorporated into the work of Anita Desai and Caryl Phillips.

THE DEMONIZATION OF ISRAEL

When Israel is defamed in a smear campaign in the British press the archetypes latent in the old cultural narrative of the "jew" obsessed by bloodlust conspiring to kill virgin boys come to the surface. The prize-winning cartoon in *The Independent,* in 2003, showing a naked, monstrous Ariel Sharon, the Israeli Prime Minister, eating children, was ostensibly modeled on Goya's *Saturn Devouring his Children* (1819–23), as the caption "After Goya" spelled out, but the background of Israeli missiles hitting towns changed the meaning to an indiscriminate appetite for a monstrous devouring of children of the Other in order to win election votes, presumably from Israelis satisfied at these brutal atrocities in the name of their security.[75] The caricature's image can no longer be interpreted in terms of any allegorical reading of Goya's painting. Instead, it portrays an obsessive cannibalism that is more satanic than Saturnic, in the name of a nation's political survival, regardless of which children are sacrificed. The "eating" of Palestinian Arab children, presumably the victims of "reprisal raids" on Gaza City after terrorist atrocities in Israel, is a common trope in Arab propaganda; it has been pointed out[76] that Dave Brown's image resembles a cartoon in the Palestinian Arab newspaper *al-Quds* (17 May 2001) showing Sharon eating Palestinian Arab children for breakfast, and similar representations of the embodiment of Israeli evil in a bloodthirsty Sharon,[77] or Jewish bloodthirstiness allied with American imperialism, as when pro-Palestinian protestors on Holocaust Day in 2002 at San Diego University carried placards showing "canned Palestinian children meat, slaughtered according to Jewish rites under American license."[78] At first glance, there seems to be a line between personal caricature of a political leader and defamation which carries resonances of collective guilt in medieval blood libels. In fact, medieval portrayals of Saturn swallowing children in order to maintain power do occasionally identify this figure of evil and disaster with the contemporary Jew, in Jew hat and Jew badge (see image below).

Woodcut in the Almanach of Peter Wagner
(Nuremburg, 1492)[79]

Brown's cartoon was produced in the context of other hostile caricatures of Sharon as a blood lusting tyrant who was held indirectly responsible by an Israeli public inquiry for the Sabra and Shatilla massacres during the First Lebanon War. The stock-type was reproduced in the *Guardian*'s on-line cartoon gallery ironically entitled "Twice Promised Land," which reread cartoons from the thirties and forties (some sympathetic to the Zionist cause) as somehow portentous of the Jews' greed for land in "Palestine" and their intransigent, aggressive refusal to make peace.[80] The gallery included Brown's "After Goya" and Steven Bell's cartoon on the occasion of Sharon's 2001 election victory in the *Guardian,* 7 February 2001, which shows Sharon at the Western Wall with hands literally stained with blood. Here too we see a slippery ambiguity between political caricature and resonance of mythical archetypes that identify the Jews with Cain and the Jew as crucifier.[81]

In his study of medieval English images of the "jew," Anthony Bale urges us to read texts such as Brown's cartoon in their local cultural and political contexts and to remember that, as in medieval times, the narrative may contain ambivalences and be open to different readings. Bale contends that medieval narratives about Jews reveal discontinuities, elisions, and incoherencies. Nevertheless, whatever their origin, these stock images were not produced in a vacuum and cannot be removed from a history of virulent theological anti-Judaism.[82] The use of a mythical archetype may not generally be conscious or even intentional, but may be deeply embedded in cultural discourse and it freely circulates as ready reference to "jewish" behavior, such as wanton or ritual killing of innocent children.[83]

Political cartoons, even when they do not explicitly defame an ethnic group, do draw upon and speak to collective fears and preconceptions of the

Cartoon from the
Iranian newspaper *al-Vefagh*

Other. In doing so, they often incite responses from the offended group. In the case of the reactions to the Danish caricature of Mohammed in 2006, however, the response was to relate to the incident as an attack on all Muslims by the West, and particularly by the "Zionist" conspiracy, while the Danish press saw it as a fight for freedom of speech. Offense, of course, can be used politically in a local as well as international power struggle. What happened was that the cartoon controversy spun out of the orbit of debate over freedom of the press and was appropriated in a variety of agendas, among others by the British National Party, who pointed to Muslims demonstrating against the Danish cartoons as evidence of the threat to the nation. Various spokesmen of the global Jihad typically defended Muslims around the world against a perceived onslaught of Islamophobia organized by "Zionists," as in an Iranian response to the Danish cartoon, which neatly merges the Viking horns and spear with the satanic "jew" complete with Star of David armband. In the Iranian government response, an official competition invited Holocaust denial cartoons, since the outrage was inevitably linked to the Zionist "myth" of the Holocaust, which allegedly justified displacing Muslims.[84] In the wake of the controversy, the post-9/11 sensitivity to offending Muslims increased and hatred of Israel became all the more volatile.

Stereotypes, as the American Jewish comics artist Art Spiegelman has contended in his response to the Danish cartoon affair, can draw blood, and his cover for the issue of *Harper's* in which his essay appeared demonstrates the parodic effect of sexist, anti-Arab, and antisemitic caricatures.[85] Yet in Britain a number of British literary figures have made anti-Israel statements in language that draws on antisemitic stereotypes almost unthinkingly. Roald Dahl, the popular children's author who was a World War Two fighter pilot, claimed that the First Lebanon War made people hate Jews, though this was edited to "Israel" when published in a book review, yet he denied being antisemitic (there is a sympathetic portrait of a German Jewish refugee in his 1986 memoir *Going Solo*). Dahl defended himself by declaring there was a "trait in the Jewish character that does provoke animosity. . . . I mean there is always a reason why anti-anything crops up anywhere, even a stinker like Hitler didn't just pick on them for no reason."[86] And before his death in 1990 he told the *Independent*, "I am certainly anti-Israel and I have become anti-Semitic."[87] Peter Reading, a contemporary English poet, also drew fire for castigating the biblical pedigree of aggression by Israeli vermin in 1984, in words that echoed the Horst Wessel song.[88] A poem written by Oxford professor of poetry Tom Paulin published in a respectable Sunday newspaper took this anti-Zionist justification of antisemitism further and reinforced the "Zionism is Nazism" lie.[89] "Killed in Crossfire" could be taken as characteristically abusive polemics by a politically militant activist and a vociferous anti-Zionist, and it would be a pity to shame the name of poetry by elevating it to serious literary analysis. However, the device that Paulin employs to make his point about the victims of war in the Middle East is one that forces an equation of Israeli government policy with Nazism, since no other interpretation can be given to the letters SS, identified by the poet with the crossfire, which appear in the middle of that word and which explain that the innocent Palestinian Arab boy caught in "crossfire" is actually "gunned down by the Zionist SS," the victim of a deliberate genocidal killing.

We can see how myth does its libelous work by identifying an immediate source for the new version of an ancient blood libel involving a "child martyr": the widely disseminated image of the Palestinian Arab boy Mohammed Al-Dura hiding with his father behind a barrel in Gaza on September 30, 2000, at the outbreak of the Second Intifada. This was an iconic martyrdom reproduced endlessly as the symbol of the struggle against the "occupation," although the purported martyrdom seems never to have taken place, for it has been demonstrated that the boy could not have been struck by an Israeli bullet and that the scene was manipulated by French TV station France 2 in coverage of the incident.[90] This was an icon that easily fitted into a media narrative about the Middle East—that Israel was the aggressor in an unending cycle of violence and was not morally justified to remind Europeans of their part in the Holocaust.[91]

Catherine Nay, a well-known news anchor from the Europe1 network, declared in late 2000, "The death of Muhammad [al-Dura] cancels out, erases that of the Jewish child, his hands in the air from the SS in the Warsaw Ghetto."[92] In Paulin's poem, we are made to suspect that the innocent boy is victim of some greater evil, and we cannot but cast our minds back to the little clergeon of "The Prioress's Tale," similarly waylaid and killed by Jews for nefarious purposes.[93] The structuring plot is the same—an innocent boy martyr dies for a holy cause—but in Paulin's poem there is no miracle and the perpetrators are not punished. Nor is there any ironic framing of the narrative, as in the *Canterbury Tales*. However, like the Prioress, the poet "exposes" the deceit and villainy of the Jews, so this too may be viewed as an exemplary tale that conscripts devotion to a totalizing ideology and indoctrinates in hatred for its enemies. Our argument is that the trope is so much part of the culture that it should not be surprising when it reenters from another source that itself may be influenced by Christian archetypes (such as the sacrificial innocent victim) against a background of long-standing native hostility among society's upper echelons and intellectuals to Jews, Judaism, and Zionism.

The poet wishes to alert us to the deceit of Zionist propaganda which would see the incident as anything but the murder of the innocents, for "we don't—dumb goys— / clock in that weasel word *crossfire*." We should note that the phrase "dumb goys" is actually borrowed from an English translation of *Mein Kampf,* thus revealing the poem's underlying antisemitic discourse that perversely ascribes to Jews Hitler's view of them:

> For while the Zionists try to make the rest of the world believe that the national consciousness of the Jew finds its satisfaction in the creation of a Palestinian state, the Jews again slyly dupe the dumb *Goyim*. It doesn't even enter their heads to build up a Jewish state in Palestine for the purpose of living there; all they want is a central organization for their international world swindle, endowed with its own sovereign rights and removed from the intervention of other states: a haven for convicted scoundrels and a university for budding crooks.[94]

The tell-tale quotation from a passage in a chapter in *Mein Kampf* on "Nation and Race," where Hitler berates the emergence of a Jewish nationalism as a result of Jewish world domination, reveals the hidden agenda—to expose Zionism as an international conspiracy.[95] And if the Jew-Nazi trope is not sufficiently clear, the poem is prefaced with a quotation taken out of context from Victor Klemperer, writing in his diary in 1934, which compares the Zionists' zeal in returning to the Jewish homeland to the Nazis. In an interview with the Egyptian weekly, *Al-Ahram,* which featured the poem and

praised the poet for "breaking the conspiracy of silence," Paulin, who denies he is antisemitic, was unambiguous in his view of Jews: he declared that Jewish settlers from Brooklyn should be "shot dead" and he has "nothing but hatred" for them. As for critics of his poem, "These are the Hampstead liberal Zionists," he explains, "I have utter contempt for them. They use this card of anti-Semitism. They fill newspapers with hate letters. They are useless people." He continued to explain that Blair's government was a "Zionist government," because it was compromised by Lord Levy and its links with Israel, a state, he believed, that had no right to exist, and for whose creation the British bore much guilt.[96]

Considering these statements and the strong background of decades of Soviet and Arab propaganda which linked the Zionists and the Nazis, it is hardly surprising to find the Jew-Nazi motif in Paulin's poem, though puzzling to find the basis of his thinking in Nazism itself. In his defense, Paulin has claimed that criticism of his poem is tantamount to "being served the anti-Semitic card," to quote the title of a poem Paulin published in January 2003 in the *London Review of Books*. This was a familiar defense that accused supporters of Israel of dishonestly defaming their opponents with the charge of antisemitism every time that Israel was criticized. It was a claim that criticism of Israel could not be antisemitic, and was common on American and British campuses and in the press: the charge of antisemitism, it was claimed, was an apologia for Israel's supposedly indefensible actions.[97]

The sociologist David Hirsh has labeled this defense the *"Livingstone formulation,"*[98] after Ken Livingstone said memorably, in campaigning for reversal of his temporary suspension from office as Mayor of London for allegedly making an antisemitic remark to a reporter, that "For far too long the accusation of antisemitism has been used against anyone who is critical of the policies of the Israeli government, as I have been."[99] He went on to identify with Antony Lerman, then director of the Institute for Jewish Policy Research, who vigorously defends criticism of Israel as not being antisemitic, and cited the example of Daniel Barenboim, the Israeli conductor who has voiced criticism of his government's policies.[100] But criticism of Israel had nothing to do with the charge against Livingstone of antisemitism.

The "Livingstone formulation" has a history going back to the *Protocols of the Elders of Zion* which accused Jews of themselves inventing or being the cause of "antisemitism." The "Livingstone formulation" is a "straw man" against a charge of antisemitism, an ad hominem argument that conveniently deflects criticism by claiming such criticism is made in bad faith.[101] Moreover, such an argument makes it difficult for supporters of the peace process to engage in meaningful debate, for there is no rational answer to such an argument, and, indeed, it makes the Jewish community's attempts to defend itself against antisemitism seem almost illegitimate.

The formulation has been used in various wordings to legitimize the boycott campaigns, or to deflect suspicion of antisemitism, for example by Jenny Tonge, Liberal Democrat MP for Richmond Park from 1997 to 2005 (from 2005, Baroness Tonge), who vigorously defended Palestinian Arab suicide bombers and later decried the pro-Israel lobby's "grip" on politics and finances in terms that recall Jewish conspiracy theories. This last example in particular points to a broad spectrum of the political arena in which such remarks are made and indicate a trend for such views to enter mainstream opinion among the British intelligentsia. Chris Davies, Liberal Democrat leader in the European Parliament, was, like Tonge, also criticized and was forced to resign after an unfortunate comparison of Israeli policy in Gaza with Auschwitz. Through slippage, anti-Israel statements end up endorsing antisemitic conspiracy theories which have been around a long time but for which support is sought in the Walt-Mearsheim report, although the report explicitly discounts any conspiracy theory.[102] The accusation that the Israel lobby had helped instigate the war in Iraq is not made in that report, but it gained potency with revelations about the deceit by political leaders before the attack on Iraq, not to mention mounting media speculation that Israel might bomb Iran (both Iraq and Iran were bracketed with Palestine as victims of imperialist aggression in political demonstrations).

What is particularly disturbing is that similar anti-Zionist rhetoric is adopted by right wing extremists and Islamist fundamentalists. Those who see a continuity of antisemitism through the ages and a contiguity of terror attacks on the West and Israel see nothing new in the "New Antisemitism," except that the Jewish scapegoat has been replaced by the State of Israel and antisemitism has become politically correct in this ideological guise in North America and Europe, including among Jews and Israelis who have internalized the lies told about them.[103] We recall Martin Luther King's response to an anti-Zionist heckler: "When people criticize Zionists, they mean Jews. You're talking anti-Semitism."[104]

Cultural texts such as Tomlin's poem not only spread pernicious falsities; they, wittingly or unwittingly, reinforce the negative image of the "jew" which functions in public discourse as the outcast responsible for absolute evil, such as poisoning wells and the premeditated murder of little children, whom it is expedient to hold collectively responsible. For example, in his *Evening Standard* column the biographer and critic A. N. Wilson accused Israel of poisoning wells at the time of the purported Jenin "massacre" and claimed there was a cover-up of "genocide."[105]The medieval slander of poisoning wells was a staple of the anti-Israel campaign in the British press, popularized as it was by Suha Arafat during Hillary Clinton's visit to Ramallah in November 1999. For example, an op-ed for Israel's approaching sixtieth anniversary in the *Independent* alleged that sewage was deliberately being pumped into Palestinian Arab drinking water sources. The author, Johann Hari, recipient of the 2008 George Orwell prize, drew on the revisionist historian Ilan Pappé for allegations of ethnic cleansing in the establishment of the Jewish state in 1948.[106]

Not all criticism of Israel should be regarded as antisemitic in the modern sense of the word, the organized and politically motivated promotion of race hatred against the Jews. However, anti-Zionism may sometimes take on antisemitic form, or merge with an antisemitic discourse, for example when demonization of Israel or negation of the right to existence of a Jewish state become politically correct, creating a hostile environment in which Jews may be insulted or physically assaulted with little or no social censure. In his study *Anti-Zionism and Antisemitism* (2007), sociologist David Hirsh investigates the complex relationship of anti-Zionism and antisemitism in contemporary Britain and warns: "The danger is that antiracist anti-Zionism is creating commonsense discourses which construct antisemitism as thinkable and possible."[107] The media regularly use common cultural referents in their manipulation of public opinion, pushing the envelope of acceptability in the effort to sensationalize and provoke. Indeed, it has not been noticed how much these *topoi* in anti-Zionist discourse are rooted in the mentality and language of Nazi and Soviet propaganda, which is "historically linked to racist, eliminationist thinking and automatically carries that force with it. Intentional or not, the effect is the same."[108]

In fact, the casual use of Nazi slogans, tropes, and clichés is not limited to anti-Zionist critiques but can been found, for example in a Conservative campaign against British adoption of the Euro and the branding of Peter Mandelson as the "Goebbels" of the pro-Europeans.[109] Mandelson, a cabinet minister who was Tony Blair's "spin doctor" and the master-mind behind Labour's 1987 election victory, was widely described in the media as a Svengali-like manipulator. Like many words and phrases that have become part of the English language,[110] Svengali is a common cultural referent that is inextricable from the "jew's" sinister influence, brought about by mesmeric evil powers and accompanied by strong erotic associations. Svengali is often caricatured as a spider weaving a web, from Du Maurier's original drawing of Svengali to Steve Bell's 1997 cartoon of Mandelson.[111] The 2001 corruption scandal[112] was compared to the 1963 Profumo affair, which exposed sleaze in high places, but this time it did not have similar political repercussions[113] and Mandelson was brought back amid a global fiscal crisis as a minister for business affairs in Gordon Brown's cabinet reshuffle of October 2008. He was soon at the center of a new scandal involving allegations of corruption and attempts to implicate the Conservative Shadow Chancellor George Osborne in illegally soliciting donations by the magnate Nathaniel Rothschild. Mandelson was painted as a "money changer," the satanic arch-villain of the affair, with Svengali imagery of spider-webs, and, on his elevation to the House of Lords, comments were made about his being gay and a "quintessential Jew."[114] It became a touchstone for the general resentment against Blair's brand of New Labour and his support for American foreign policy. In an interview in *Vanity Fair*, Scottish MP Tam Dalyell, for example, spoke up against a "cabal of Jewish advisors," including Mandelson and Lord Levy, but denied these remarks were in any way antisemitic.[115]

That resurgence of an older racial discourse is the by-product of the open society is corroborated by columnist Petronella Wyatt, who was shocked to discover that since 11 September antisemitism and its open expression had become respectable once more. Not in Germany or Catholic central Europe— but at London dinner tables. "Too frequently to discount now, I hear remarks that the Jews are to blame for everything."[116]

The British journalist Barbara Amiel agreed, writing that people now said openly what they always felt about the Jews, and it was even chic to do so.[117] The French ambassador's offensive comment on the state of Israel was one incident that earned publicity because it outraged the Jewish community, but more importantly it showed that such attitudes were common among what is jocularly termed the "chattering classes."[118]

The oppression of "defenseless" victims of colonialism seemed such an obvious clear-cut case of a grievance to be fought, as perhaps one of the last great struggles after Vietnam, along with globalization and Venezuela, which could rouse intellectuals on the left who still identified with Che Guevara and Fidel Castro to action on behalf of "injustice." In fact, as Colin Shindler has concluded in his study of media coverage of Zionism in the liberal newspaper

The Guardian, there was a generational shift away from Old Labour that embraced Third World causes, foremost the Palestinians who represented a neo-Maoist struggle against "colonialism." Such identification was quite detached from any former sympathy among British intellectuals for Jews as Holocaust victims now that, in a multicultural society, Jews were no longer "oppressed" but themselves perpetrators of "injustice."[119] In her commissioned study, the London-based Israeli anti-Zionist journalist Daphna Baram clears the *Guardian* of any antisemitism or anti-Israel bias in editorial policy, but however much the paper wanted to "get the story right," journalists did occasionally use "unfortunate" (that is, defamatory) language about Jews and Israelis, hyperbole, and sensational comparisons; the editors seemed unable to perceive they had a problem with how the paper was viewed by the Jewish community or did not know what to do about it.[120] Nevertheless, Baram quotes former *Guardian* columnist Linda Grant who suggests that criticism of Israel cannot be detached from perceptions of Jews: "The approach stating that all the world's problems derive in Israel found a warm home in the *Guardian.*"[121] The incessant stories of Palestinian suffering, according to Linda Grant, found receptive ears among readers prone to prejudiced views of Jews, even if these articles did not promote such views, and inevitably reinforced antisemitism, while splitting the Jewish community between those who were wary of the effect of criticism of Israel on attitudes towards Jews and those who spoke openly against Israel.[122]

Caryl Churchill's hastily composed ten-minute play, *Seven Jewish Children: A Play for Gaza* (2009), written immediately after Operation Cast Lead to drum up support for aid to Gaza and performed at London's Royal Court Theatre, dramatizes the confusion of Jews with Israelis, and blurs criticism of Israel with maligning Jews. Apart from the defamatory propaganda statement that Israel indiscriminately and deliberately kills babies and breeds hatred in their children, Churchill is riding on a wave of political correctness that sweeps the ground from Israel and the Jewish people in any claim they may have to sympathy as victims of the Holocaust or of terrorism. Instead, she returns to the old charge that the Jews claim they are the Chosen People and use it to justify their acts of barbarity and injustice.[123] Her play does not target the Israeli government or the military, and its title singles out Jewish children and their parents who lie to them about the Holocaust, about the return to their homeland in Israel, and about the Arabs in Gaza, whom they hate and would like to kill just as they were hated and killed by the Nazis. The impression is of a people who are hardhearted and perfidious, mercilessly exploiting the usurped Palestinians, reminiscent of blood libels against Jews, even if there is a singular lack of clarity about the play's message.

To be fair, few British playwrights and novelists seemed to be concerned with Israel, which is quite surprising given the prominence of the Holy Land in British popular culture in the nineteenth and early twentieth centuries.[124] London's National Theatre did in the first decade of the century host a number of Israeli theater productions, some of which dealt with the Arab-Israeli conflict, but it was by no means a preoccupation on the British stage. Exceptionally, Jim Allen's *Perdition,* loosely based on the Kasztner affair, became a *cause célèbre* in 1987 when it was withdrawn at the Royal Court Theatre following protests at its dramatization of the by now commonplace fabricated accusation of Zionist collusion with the Nazis; it was revived in 2007 by the Palestine Solidarity Campaign in Edinburgh.[125] And Christopher Hampton's adaptation of George Steiner's *The Portage to San Cristóbal of A.H.* (1982), at the time of the First Lebanon War, won rapturous applause for Hitler's closing speech comparing Nazi ideology with Biblical Judaism and the Jewish "racist" idea of the chosen people.[126] Churchill's play is, however, not exceptional as political drama, which acts out ideological positions, as in her previous work, such as *Top Girls* (1982), which deals with women's roles in society (including a female Pope). Another example of political drama is David Hare's *Via Dolorosa,* first presented in 1998, also at the Royal Court Theatre, a meandering monologue by the author himself about his trip to Israel on his and Israel's 50th birthday. Hare, who describes himself as a convinced heathen, was looking for an inspiration of faith, a cause worth dying for, to escape the dull boredom of London. What is apparent from the start is his prejudgment, bordering on prejudice, expressed in inaccurate statements (to put it charitably), which portray Herzl as a president of a "World Jewish Congress" in a Biblical mission to conquer Palestine. Hare adopts a subaltern viewpoint, unable to resist the idea that the Jews have no right to this land. Everything that is Western in Israel is "nasty" or "dismal," and Europe has exported religious violence to the Middle East (a rather odd view, given the religious zeal of the Jihad against the West that is inspired by Islam). While Palestinian Arabs are invariably portrayed as positive characters living in a Third World "Bangladesh," the Jewish settlers in Judea and Samaria are described as White supremacists colonizing Arab territory with American-style bourgeois villas and (quite imaginary) four-lane highways, clinging to meaningless biblical laws and ridiculous ancient myths about their legal rights to the Land of Israel.[127] Yet in Orientalizing the "natives" as supposedly rightful owners of the land, despite his professed ignorance and incompetence, Hare betrays a familiar cultural superiority and strangely colonial attitudes not so distant from those of the imperialist rulers during the British Mandate.[128] Yet he can barely think of his own country as a "homeland" and is alarmed at the Jews' messianic yearning to return "home." Hare is openly an assimilationist, declaring he is married to a Jewish woman from Turkey, and regrets that his "fanatic" religious hosts cannot find place in their lives for multiculturalism. They are the inassimilable "jews" who, like Shylock, boast of Abraham's or David's business deals in purchasing land for shekels,[129] unlike the "good" left-wing Jews who blame extremism on their fellow-Jews.

The power of myth to shape beliefs and alter history should not be underestimated. What is particularly striking about the rhetorical attacks on Israel that claim not to be antisemitic is the irrefutable logic of typecasting which does not allow any other interpretation but black-and-white binary opposition of good and evil, underdogs and oppressors. It amounts to a Trotskyite insinuation that those not for us are against us, but also assumes that any argument opposed to politically correct statements must come from the devil, the Jew-anti-Christ, the Apartheid-Zionist, or whoever is the fashionable Enemy of the People. David Hirsh sees anti-Zionism as a political discourse that places anti-imperialism at the center of an absolutist ideology which divides the world into two camps, a position which may cause antisemitic rhetoric but might not in itself be antisemitic.[130] Hirsh is surely correct in stressing the complex overlapping of the different manifestations of anti-Zionism in a fragmented and confused state of affairs, but anti-Zionism should not be seen as a creature of a particular political moment without reference to its language and tropes shared by the political far-right and without reference to a cultural history that must be contextualized both locally and globally.

The danger of antisemitism is not coming from the workplace, the streets, or even the brick through the window, but from public discourse, and in particular from a smear campaign against Israel in the media, which mobilizes social forces to political action. A "pretty strong degree of anti-Semitism in Europe is at the root of the hostile coverage Israel receives in parts of the European media," Rupert Murdoch, the News Corporation global media chief, charged in an interview with the *Jerusalem Post* in May 2008.[131] Freedom of speech is open to both use and abuse, but it was only with the Arab Spring revolutions in 2011, which highlighted the distorted view of the

Middle East in the British media and exposed the hypocrisy of governmental and intellectual support for corrupt tyrants, that the media's obsession with Israel was questioned. It also showed how much the obsession with Israel had obscured crucial developments that had nothing to do with the Palestinian Arab cause, as the left-wing English journalist Nick Cohen commented.[132] And yet old familiar tropes were still displayed in coverage of Israel, such as Jewish arrogance and racist superiority in Louis Theroux's "The Ultra-Zionists" (broadcast BBC TV, February 2011), which showed Jewish settlers making Christians serve them, while zealously not allowing any non-Jew to touch their wine. Or the image of wealthy Jews in their swimming pools in the Channel Four historical drama TV series *The Promise* (2011), set during the British Mandate.

Individuals actively disseminating politicized views of Israel and of the Jews may have a far greater impact than their small number, especially when the information revolution allows instantaneous access around the globe to a world-view based on false deductions or partial truths, and this in a cyberspace environment that hosts a multitude of "truths" whose relative values are rendered equable or unquestionable. The space of public debate has also changed with an uncontrollable and sometimes unmediated freedom given to bloggers to air racist, homophobic, and bigoted views.[133] The Jew-hatred of the global Jihad is circulating freely around the world, while "Israel" or the "jews" are blamed for the wars and crises stemming from 9/11, which has also been alleged to be the work of the Mossad in a Jewish plot to destabilize the world and spark hatred of Muslims.[134] The war on terror was in fact to be seen as another example of imperialist aggression, for which the "Zionists" were somehow responsible. The resurgence of antisemitic imagery cannot be understood outside the global context of the Jihad against the West, in which the former colonial powers of Europe and America were slated to be defeated. The anti-imperialist platform of the Jihad aroused sympathy on the Left, which did not necessarily endorse or even properly understand the aims of a radical Islamist revolution that would offer "justice" only in terms of *sharia* (Islamic holy law). As it happened, the cause of Muslims against colonialism made an obvious alliance, for example in the "Stop the War" campaign, which could be expedient for Islamists, who generally had only loathing for communism and all secular ideologies.

The "antisemitism" of public discourse does not necessarily depend on the intention to cause harm to Jews as Jews, and there is little evidence of a popular movement to exclude Jews from public life, though an academic boycott would inevitably target Jews and the boycott campaigns have created a hostile atmosphere for many Jews. There have nevertheless been hate mails, desecration of cemeteries, and acts of violence against the background of "low level" racism. Yet it ought to disturb us that the discourse we have analyzed accrues its invective from ready-made and available stereotypes. When Jews have integrated into British society to the point of being mostly invisible as Others, it should not be surprising that there is a failure to perceive that stereotypes of the "jew" or the "jew-zionist" could be in any way antisemitic. Even among liberal circles, no harm is seen in criticism of Jews or Israel, and it is usually said that the Jews are ultra-sensitive or that they deflect criticism of Israel with the charge of antisemitism (as in Paulin's "Livingstone defense"). This climate of opinion, the British philosopher Bernard Harrison argues, is far from innocuous, but there is little that is new, apart from its resurgence, in the "New Antisemitism."[135] Moral indignation and sympathy with the oppressed are generally regarded as praiseworthy, but, when these are inscribed in a politically correct discourse that assigns sole and total blame to one group or nation, we approach a familiar form of antisemitism that transforms established paradigms and plots (both literary and criminal). What has happened is that in the championing of transnational identities the Muslims have become the archetypal Others, while the "jew" is again the perpetrator, not the victim, scapegoated for global disasters, as well as blamed for local social problems. The phenomenon of antisemitism in contemporary Europe thus cannot be reduced to a simplistic barometer of attitudes to Israel, however much events in the Middle East trigger an upsurge in antisemitic incidents.

It is not generally realized that collectively blaming the Jews or Israel may make racist incitement or assault thinkable and imperceptibly acceptable. British MP Denis MacShane has argued in *Globalising Hatred: The New Antisemitism* (2008) that radical Islamist ideology feeds on traditional antisemitic rhetoric and imagery on the right and left in Europe and has fed back into anti-Zionism on campuses and in politics, to which governments and leaders around the world have remained largely complacent or apologetic. Not only, he complains, has antisemitism not gone away after the Holocaust, but it has come back to serve local and global politics of hatred. Jonathan Judaken has reminded us of the "new antisemitism" that appeared after the Six Day War, the 1973 war, indeed after every Middle East war.[136] Indeed, the term "new antisemitism" was being used after the Six Day War when British Jews began to feel a new pride though still unsure of their identity and were confronted by racism on the right and expulsions of Jews in Poland in an anti-Zionist campaign on the left.[137]

Part of the impetus on the left may be explained by a lingering guilt for colonialism that is transferred to the Zionist "colonizers," but this discourse is also coming from the far right against the background of increased racial tensions and loss of empire. It is a discourse that conveniently reduces any moral debt for the abandonment of the Jews during the Holocaust (most notoriously at the Evian conference and in British immigration policy). The cultural climate has changed and the old genteel antisemitism native to the racial and class prejudice of the Foreign Office and the cultural elite has become acceptable in mainstream discourse, especially when pandering to pro-Arab sympathies, as when Sir Oliver Miles, former British Ambassador to Libya, wondered aloud at the inclusion of two Jewish historians (at least one of whom was pro-Zionist) in the public inquiry into the Iraq war in November 2009 which, he feared, would give the impression of bias.[138] In the next chapter we will see examples of vestiges of colonial discourse about the "jew" in representation of race and color in southern Africa in the work of the acclaimed British novelist Doris Lessing that raise unsettling questions about the ambivalence toward assimilated Jews among White Europeans and the persistence after the Holocaust of racial typing.

NOTES

1. Bryan Cheyette, "Preface," in *Between "Race" and Culture: Representations of "the Jew" in English and American Literature*, ed. Bryan Cheyette (Stanford: Stanford University Press, 1996), vii.

2. Bryan Cheyette, *Constructions of "the Jew" in English Literature and Society: Racial Representations, 1875–1945* (Cambridge: Cambridge University Press, 1993), 10–11; see also Jonathan Freedman, *The Temple of Culture: Assimilation and Anti-Semitism in Literary Anglo-America* (New York: Oxford University Press, 2000).

3. Zygmunt Bauman, "Allosemitism: Premodern, Modern, Postmodern," in *Modernity, Culture, and 'the Jew,'* ed. Bryan Cheyette and Laura Marcus (Cambridge: Polity Press, 1998), 143–57.

4. James Shapiro, *Shakespeare and the Jews* (New York, N.Y.: Columbia University Press, 1995), 20–42.

5. Ania Loomba, *Shakespeare, Race, and Colonialism* (Oxford: Oxford University Press, 2002), 6–19.

6. Michele Wates, "Massacre at St Frideswide's," *Oxford Today* 15.1 (2002): 26.

7. Tony Kushner, "Antisemitism," in *A Companion to Ethnic and Racial Studies*, ed. David Theo Goldberg and John Solomos (Oxford: Blackwell, 2002), 64–72.

8. See James Shuttleworth-Kay, *The Moral and Physical Condition of the Working Classes Employed in the Cotton Manufacture in Manchester* (1832) 2nd ed. (London: Frank Cass, 1970).

9. Quoted in Paul Foot, *Immigration and Race in British Politics* (Harmondsworth: Penguin Books, 1965), 106.

10. Michael Pickering, *Stereotyping: The Politics of Representation* (Houndmills, Basingstoke: Palgrave, 2001), 45. See Anthony Bale, *The Jew in the Medieval Book: English Antisemitisms, 1350–1500* (Cambridge: Cambridge University Press, 2006), 156.

11. Sander L. Gilman, *Difference and Pathology: Stereotypes of Sexuality, Race, and Madness* (Ithaca, N.Y.: Cornell University Press, 1985), 19.

12. Gilman, *Difference and Pathology,* 12, 18.

13. Bale, *Jew in the Medieval Book*, 166.

14. See Robert Wistrich, ed., *Demonizing the Other: Antisemitism, Racism, and Xenophobia* (Amsterdam: Harwood Academic Publishers, 1999); Joshua Trachtenberg, *The Devil and the Jews: The Medieval Conception of the Jew and its Relation to Modern Anti-Semitism* (New Haven: Yale University Press, 1943).

15. Gavin Langmuir delineates such a division in arguing against a transhistorical view of antisemitism in his *Toward a Definition of Antisemitism* (Berkeley: University of California Press, 1990), 310–52.

16. Sheila Delany, "Chaucer's Prioress, the Jews and the Muslims," in *Chaucer and the Jews,* ed. Sheila Delany (New York: Routledge, 2002), 43–57. See also Suzanne Conklin Akbari, "Placing the Jews in Late Medieval English Literature," in *Orientalism and the Jews,* ed. Ivan Davidson Kalmar and Derek J. Penslar (Waltham, Mass.: Brandeis University Press, 2005), 32–50.

17. Bale, *Jew in the Medieval Book,* 61–64.

18. Delany, "Chaucer's Prioress, the Jews and the Muslims," 49–50.

19. Michael Camille, *The Gothic Idol: Ideology and Image-Making in Medieval Art* (Cambridge: Cambridge University Press, 1989), 164; quoted in Christine M. Rose, "The Jewish Mother-in-Law: Synagoga and the Man of Law's Tale," in *Chaucer and the Jews,* ed. Sheila Delany (New York: Routledge, 2002), 7.

20. Kathleen Biddick, "The ABC of Ptolemy: Mapping the World with the Alphabet," cited in Sylvia Tomasch, "Postcolonial Chaucer and the Virtual Jew," in *Chaucer and the Jews,* 73.

21. Linda Weinhouse, "Faith and Fantasy: The Texts of the Jews," *Medieval Encounters* 5:3 (1999): 391–408. See also Louise O. Fradenberg, "Criticism, Anti-Semitism and the Prioress' Tale," *Exemplaria* 1 (1989): 69–115; Miri Rubin, *Gentile Tales: The Narrative Assault on Late Medieval Jews* (New Haven, Conn.: Yale University Press, 1999).

22. Lisa Lampert, *Gender and Jewish Difference from Paul to Shakespeare* (Philadelphia: University of Pennsylvania Press, 2004), 21–57.

23. Ibid., 29.

24. Ibid., 35.

25. Ira Katznelson, "'To Give Counsel and to Consent': Why the King (Edward I) Expelled His Jews (in 1290)," in *Preferences and Situations: Points of Intersection Between Historical and Rational Choice Institutionalism,* ed. Ira Katznelson and Barry Weingas (New York: Russell Sage Foundation, 2005), 88–126.

26. Ira Katznelson, "Why did the King Expel the Jews: Notes on Membership, Ethnic Cleansing, and the Liberal Political Tradition," Joe and Paulette Rose Annual Lecture, Ben-Gurion University of the Negev, 7 June 2007. Some contemporary attitudes toward the Jews reflected the extent that they were seen as furthering the monarch's centralization of power or were victims of royal policy, for example Matthew Paris in his chronicles (Sylvia Tomasch, "Postcolonial Chaucer and the Virtual Jew," in *Chaucer and the Jews,* 70). For an understanding of the complex motivations for the decree of expulsion, not least Edward's deep religious faith, see Robin R. Mundill, *England's Jewish Solution: Experiment and Expulsion, 1262–1290* (Cambridge: Cambridge University Press, 1998), 244–85. Certainly, Edward made no profit from the expulsion (Robin R. Mundill, *The King's Jews: Money, Massacre and Exodus in Medieval England* [London: Continuum, 2010], 145–66).

27. Bale, *Jew in the Medieval Book,* 137–38.

28. Colin Richmond, "Englishness and Medieval Jewry," in *Chaucer and the Jews,* 213–27.

29. Tomasch, "Postcolonial Chaucer and the Virtual Jew," 69–85.

30. Bale, *Jew in the Medieval Book,* 37.

31. Ibid., 37.

32. Ibid., 40.

33. Tomasch, "Postcolonial Chaucer and the Virtual Jew," 76.

34. For some examples of the complexity of representation of the "jew," see Denise L. Despres, "The Protean Jew in the Vernon Manuscript," in *Chaucer and the Jews,* 145–64. See also Bale, *Jew in the Medieval Book,* passim.

35. Bale, *Jew in the Medieval Book,* 125.

36. Ibid., 122–26.

37. Harold Fisch, *The Dual Image: The Jew in English and American Literature* (London: World Jewish Library, 1970), 14.

38. Mark Gelber, "What is Literary Anti-Semitism?" *Jewish Social Studies* 47.1 (1985): 1–20.

39. Charles Dickens, *The Letters of Charles Dickens, 1862–1864* (Oxford: Oxford University Press, 2002), 10:269–70.

40. See for examples of eighteenth-century stereotypes of the wealthy Jewish fence, Frank Felsenstein, *Anti-Semitic Stereotypes: Paradigms of Otherness in English Popular Culture, 1660–1830* (Baltimore: Johns Hopkins University Press, 1999), 216–18.

41. Anthony Julius, "Is there anything 'new' in the 'New antisemitism'?" in *A New Anti-Semitism?: Debating Judeophobia in 21st Century Britain,* ed. Paul Iganski and Barry Kosmin (London: Profile Books, 2003), 70.

42. See Gary M. Levine, *The Merchant of Modernism: The Economic Jew in Anglo-American Literature, 1864–1939* (New York: Routledge, 2003). Robert Wistrich considers, to the contrary, that Jews were unlikely to be portrayed negatively as bearers of modernity and capitalism (*Antisemitism: The Longest Hatred* [London: Thames Methuen, 1991], 104).

43. For a critique of the redefinition of "diaspora" in postcolonial studies in the United States, see Michael Galchinsky, "Scattered Seeds: A Dialogue of Diasporas," in *Insider/Outside: American Jews and Multiculturalism,* ed. David Biale, Michael Galchinsky, and Susannah Heschel (Berkeley: University of California Press, 1998), 185–93.

44. For the different positions on this issue see Bryan Cheyette, "Liberal Anti-Judaism and the Victims of Modernity," *American Literary History* (2001): 540–43.

45. Walter Laqueur, *The Changing Face of Anti-Semitism: From Ancient Times to the Present Day,* paperback ed. (Oxford: Oxford University Press, 2008), 1–20.

46. Homi K. Bhabha, *The Location of Culture* (London: Routledge, 1994), 171–97.

47. Clive J. Christie, *Race and Nation: A Reader* (London: I. B. Tauris, 1998), 175.

48. Jonathan Boyarin, *Storm from Paradise: The Politics of Jewish Memory* (Minneapolis: University of Minnesota Press, 1992), 103.

49. Ibid.

50. See Sander L. Gilman, *Smart Jews: The Construction of the Image of Jewish Superior Intelligence* (Lincoln, Neb.: University of Nebraska Press, 1997).

51. Bryan Cheyette, "Neither Black nor White: The Figure of the Jew in Imperial British Literature," in *The Jew in the Text,* ed. Tamar Garb and Linda Nochlin (London: Thames & Hudson, 1995), 31–32. For further comments on why postcolonial theorists have been so resistant to acknowledging Jews other than as part of a European colonial discourse, see Cheyette, "Venetian Spaces: Old-New Literatures and the Ambivalent Uses of Jewish History," *Essays and Studies* 53 (2000): 53–55.

52. Jon Stratton, "Speaking as a Jew in British Cultural Studies," in *Coming Out Jewish: Constructing Ambivalent Identities* (London: Routledge, 2000), 35–52.

53. Edward Said, *Orientalism* (New York: Vintage Books, 1979), 7.

54. Ivan Davidson Kalmar and Derek J. Penslar, *Orientalism and the Jews* (Waltham Mass.: Brandeis University Press, 2005), xx.

55. Quoted in Kalmar and Penslar, *Orientalism and the Jews,* xxii.

56. Aamir R. Mufti, *Enlightenment in the Colony: The Jewish Question and the Crisis of Postcolonial Culture.* (Princeton: Princeton University Press, 2007).

57. Ibid., 175.

58. John Hutnyk, "Home and Away: Social Configurations of Diaspora," in *Diaspora & Hybridity,* ed. John Hutnyk, Virinder S. Kalra, and Raminder Kaur (London: SAGE, 2005), 9–10.

59. John Hutnyk, "Journeys of Whiteness," in *Diaspora & Hybridity,* 119.

60. Stuart Hall, "Cultural Identity and Diaspora," in *Identity: Community, Culture, Difference,* ed. Jonathan Rutherford (London: Lawrence and Wishart, 1990), 235.

61. Jonathan and Daniel Boyarin, *Powers of Diaspora: Two Essays on the Relevance of Jewish Culture* (Minneapolis: University of Minnesota Press, 2002), 11–13.

62. For a reconsideration of these terms from a post-Zionist perspective, see Jon Stratton, "Historicising the Idea of Diaspora," in idem, *Coming Out Jewish: Constructing Ambivalent Identities* (London: Routledge, 2000), 145–63.

63. Shalom Lappin, *This Green and Pleasant Land: Britain and the Jews,* Yale Initiative for the Interdisciplinary Study of Antisemitism Working Paper no. 2, August 2008, 22.

64. Paul Gilroy, *After Empire: Melancholia or Convivial Culture?* (London: Routledge, 2004), 89–92. Gilroy dedicates his book to Corrie, who was allegedly crushed to death by an Israeli bulldozer, though the Israeli authorities have disputed this version of events (video footage of the incident also casts doubts on its accuracy).

65. Pheng Cheah, *Inhuman Conditions: On Cosmopolitanism and Human Rights* (Cambridge, Mass.: Harvard University Press, 2006), 34, 44.

66. Gilroy, *After Empire,* 89–92.

67. Robert J. C. Young, *Postcolonialism: A Very Short Introduction* (Oxford: Oxford University Press, 2002), 2–3. Young's dichotomy of the West versus the Rest does little credit to the dizzying array of critical practices and contesting theories that go by the name of "postcolonialism," and indeed the term came to mean so many different things to different people by the early twenty-first century that some wondered if it had any useful meaning (Bill Ashcroft, Gareth Griffiths and Helen Tiffin, *The Empire Writes Back: Theory and Practice in Postcolonial Literatures,* 2nd. ed. [London and New York: Routledge, 2002], 193–99). Moreover, Young's monolithic and linear presentation of colonialism must be set against local differences and particularities, though he would claim that these were a construct of imperialist knowledge (ibid., 211).

68. Ibid., 14–15.

69. Ibid., 137. Young comes close to Naomi Klein's "disaster capitalism" when he cites examples of Unilever and Ben & Jerry's Ice Cream funding of progressive anti-

capitalist conferences and American support for Bin Laden's insurgency, actually a resistance to the Soviet invasion of Afghanistan.

70. For example, Jane Hiddleston critiques Levinas's "fuzziness" in his position on Israel and Jews, suspecting him of being close to marginalizing Islam as an alien presence in Europe (*Understanding Postcolonialism* [Stocksfield: Acumen, 2009], 21–22). Ania Loomba, on the other hand, points to the persecution of both Moors and Jews in Spain as a cultural claim to biological identification of European nations that excludes Islam as incompatible. (*Colonialism/Postcolonialism*, 2nd ed. [London: Routledge, 2005], 217).

71. Rebecca Stein, "The Ballad of the Sad Cafés: Israeli Leisure, Palestinian Terror, and the Post/colonial Question," in *Postcolonial Studies and Beyond,* ed. Ania Loomba et al. (Durham, N.C.: Duke University Press, 2005), 331.

72. Bhabha, *Location of Culture,* 236.

73. Stein, "The Ballad of the Sad Cafés," 331. Stein is in fact arguing that the Palestinian Arabs lose out in this equation; her essay analyzes the "leisure discourse" of Israeli victims of terror, without a word about the murder of Israeli children or targeting of buses and schools.

74. Homi K. Bhabha, "Joking Aside: The Idea of a Self-Critical Community," in *Modernity, Culture, and 'the Jew,'* xv–xvi.

75. Dave Brown, "After Goya," *The Independent,* 27 Jan. 2003. An angry letter from the Israeli embassy in London complained that the publication of the cartoon on Britain's Holocaust Memorial Day recalled the worst excesses of *Der Stürmer;* Brown denied having in mind any such associations. On the official complaint and its rejection see Anthony Julius, "Anti-Semitism and the English Intelligentsia," in *Old Demons, New Debates,* ed. David I. Kertzer, (New York: Holmes & Meier, 2005), 74–75.

76. Winston Pickett, "Nasty or Nazi?: The Use of Anti-Semitic Topoi by the Left-Liberal Media," in *A New Anti-Semitism?: Debating Judeophobia in 21st Century Britain,* ed. Paul Iganski and Barry Kosmin (London: Profile Books, 2003), 160.

77. Reproduced in Reuven Ehrlich, ed., *Incitement and Propaganda against Israel, the Jewish People and the Western World, conducted in the Palestinian Authority, the Arab World and Iran.* Intelligence and Terrorism, Information Bulletin No. 1 (Tel Aviv: Center for Special Studies, January 2002); http://www.terrorism-info.org.il/malam_multimedia//ENGLISH/HATE-ARAB/PDF/JAN_02.PDF, downloaded 18 Feb. 2008. See also the cartoon in a Qatar newspaper of Sharon drinking the blood of Palestinian Arab children from a goblet "made in USA" (*Al Watan,* 24 July 2002). The demonization of Sharon was by no means limited to the Arab press: see the front cover of a 2002 issue of the Spanish magazine *El jueves* showing Sharon with a pig's face and the caption adorned by a swastika, "Sharon ese peazo animal."

78. Cynthia Yacowar-Sweeney, "Islamic Outposts in North America," INN news, 6 Nov. 2002, http://www.israelnationalnews.com/article.php3?id=1527.

79. Reproduced in Heinz Schreckenberg, *The Jews in Christian Art: An Illustrated History* (London, SCM Press, 1996), 331.

80. "Twice Promised Land," *Guardian Arts Unlimited*, arts.guardian.co.uk /gallery/image/0,8543,-10104962079,00.html, retrieved 13 Dec. 2007.

81. It must be said that Bell's use of Jewish symbols can be inconsistent if not puzzling, for example in giving both sides a star of David in "Defiant Iran tests missiles to show strength in face of US warnings," *Guardian*, 10 July 2008.

82. Anthony Bale, *Jew in the Medieval Book,* 7–9, 13. Tony Kushner, too, urges us to consider local circumstances, not just global trends and universal phenomena, when studying Jewish history (*Anglo-Jewry since 1066: Place, Locality and Memory* [Manchester: Manchester University Press, 2009]).

83. See Arieh Stav, *Peace, the Arabian Caricature: A Study of Anti-Semitic Imagery* (Jerusalem: Gefen, 1999); Reuven Ehrlich, ed., *"Hate Industry" Anti-Semitic, anti-Zionist and anti-Jewish publications in the Arab world and Iran* (Part 2) (Tel Aviv: Center for Special Studies, Information Bulletin No. 5, October 2002); PDF version: http://www.intelligence.org.il/eng/bu/oct/ocf.doc; Joël and Dan Kotek, *Au nom de l'antisionisme: L'image des Juifs et d'Israël dans la caricature depuis la seconde Intifada* (Brussels: Éditions Complexe, 2003).

84. See Manfred Gerstenfeld, "The Mohammed-Cartoon Controversy, Israel, and the Jews: A Case Study," *Jerusalem Center for Public Affairs* 43 (2 Apr. 2006) www.jcpa.org/phas/phas-043-gerstenfeld.htm; accessed 4 Jan. 2008.

85. Art Spiegelman, "Drawing Blood: Outrageous Cartoons and the Art of Outrage," *Harper's Magazine* (June 2006): 43–52; see also Deniz Göktürk, "Jokes and Butts: Can We Imagine Humor in a Global Public Sphere?" *PMLA* 123.5 (2008): 1707–11.

86. Jeremy Treglown, *Roald Dahl: An Autobiography* (New York: Farrar, Straus, Giroux, 1994), 255–56.

87. *Independent,* 21 Mar. 1990.

88. Peter Reading, "Cub," *Times Literary Supplement,* 23 Mar. 1984. See David Vital, "After the Catastrophe: Aspects of Contemporary Jewry," *Lessons and Legacies: The Meaning of the Holocaust in a Changing World,* ed. Peter Hayes (Evanston: Northwestern University Press, 1991), 135, 349–50, n. 10.

89. *Observer,* 18 Feb. 2001, http://www.guardian.co.uk/books/2001/feb/18/poetry .features1/, accessed online.

90. James Fallows, "Who Shot Mohammed al-Dura?" *Atlantic Monthly* (June 2003); www.theatlantic.com/doc/200306/fallows; accessed 13 Mar. 2007; "Report: 12-year-old Palestinian boy's martyrdom 'staged': French media complicit in perpetuating 'myth' of Mohammed al-Dura," WorldNewsNet, 5 Mar. 2003, www.worldnetdaily.com/news/article.asp?ARTICLE_ID=31363; accessed 13 Mar. 2007. See also Melanie Phillips, "The al Durah blood libel," *Spectator* blog, 14 Nov.

2007,   www.spectator.co.uk/melaniephillips/354621/the-al-durah-blood-libel.thtml;
accessed 13 Mar. 2007. Phillipe Karsenty, founder of a French on-line media
watchdog, lost the libel case brought against him by France 2, but appealed in 2007.
The appeal court ordered the release of uncut footage from the film of the incident,
which raised many questions about whether anyone on the scene was actually dying
or injured. A verdict on the appeal in favor of Karsenty was given on 21 May 2008.
See the video investigation of Boston professor, Richard Landes, "Birth of an Icon,"
http://www.youtube.com/watch?v=pOwZ8wgV7I4. This was not the only blood libel
during the second Intifada; for example, during the supposed "massacre" in Jenin in
April 2002, the "dead" were seen being helped back onto stretchers after falling off,
but Mohammed Bakri's film *Jenin! Jenin!* (2002) nevertheless helped perpetuate a
massacre that never took place.

91. Caroline Glick, "The media and enduring narrative," *Jerusalem Post,* 8 July
2008; http://www.jpost.com/servlet/Satellite?cid=1215330891500&pagename=Jpost
%2FJPArticle%2FshowFull.

92. Quoted in Glick, ibid.

93. This is the interpretation offered in Anthony Julius, *Trials of the Diaspora*: *A
History of English Anti-Semitism* (Oxford: Oxford University Press, 2010), 236–40.

94. Adolf Hitler, *Mein Kampf,* trans. Ralph Manheim (Boston: Houghton Mifflin,
1943), 324–25. Italics in the original.

95. Edward Alexander, "Tom Paulin: Poetaster of Murder," www.acpr.org.il
/ENGLISH-NATIV/03-issue/alexander-3.htm.

96. Omayma Abdel-Latif, "The Weasel Word," *Al-Ahram Weekly Online,* 4–10
Apr. 2002, accessed online. The phrase "useless people" is an old antisemitic label.

97. Alvin H. Rosenfeld, *Anti-Zionism in Great Britain and Beyond: A
"Respectable" Anti-Semitism?* (New York: American Jewish Committee, 2004);
accessed online www.ajc.org/atf/cf/%7B42D75369-D582-4380-8395-D25925B85
EAF%7D/AntiZionism.pdf.

98. Hirsh, *Anti-Zionism and Antisemitism,* 11, 54.

99. "An attack on voters' rights," *Guardian,* 1 Mar. 2006, http://society.guardian
.co.uk/localgovt/comment/0,,1720439,00.html. Downloaded 29 Nov. 2007.

100. See for example Antony Lerman, "Sense on Antisemitism," in *A New Anti-
Semitism?, 54–67.*

101. Hirsh, *Anti-Zionism and Antisemitism, 79.* On the ad hominem argument and
the charge that saying this is itself an ad hominem argument, see 13–14. See also
Hirsh, "Accusations of malicious intent in debates about the Palestine-Israel conflict
and about anti-Semitism: The Livingstone Formulation, 'Playing the Antisemitism
Card' and Contesting the Boundaries of Antiracist Discourse," *Transversal* 1 (2010):
42–77.

102. John J. Mearsheimer and Stephen M. Walt, *The Israel Lobby and U.S.
Foreign Policy* (New York: Farrar, Straus and Giroux, 2006), 111–50. Walt and
Mearsheimer are, however, quite vague about the identity of the "Israel lobby" which

they criticize. See for example, Robert Fisk, "United States of Israel?," *Independent*, 27 Apr. 2006, http://www.independent.co.uk/news/fisk/robert-fisk-united-states-of-israel-475811.html.

103. See Phyllis Chesler, *The New Anti-Semitism: The Current Crisis and What We Must Do About It* (San Francisco: Jossey-Bass, 2003); Abraham H. Foxman, *Never Again?: The Threat of the New Anti-Semitism* (San Francisco: HarperSanFrancisco, 2003).

104. Seymour Martin Lipset; "The Socialism of Fools: The Left, the Jews and Israel," *Encounter* (Dec. 1969): 24; quoted in Chesler, *New Anti-Semitism*, 4.

105. *Evening Standard*, 15 Apr. 2002. See also Wilson, "Tragic Reality of Israel," *Evening Standard*, 22 Oct. 2001, and idem, "Israel's record speaks for itself," *Evening Standard*, 2 Feb. 2003; the use in this article of White Supremacist views and Holocaust denial is traced in Pickett, "Nasty or Nazi?," 160–62. A. N. Wilson is the author of a fantasy novel which humanizes Hitler and excuses complicity with Nazism (*Winnie and Wolf*, 2007). For more examples of Wilson's hostile views on Jews and Judaism and his defense of the antisemitism of Hilaire Belloc, see Anthony Julius, "Anti-Semitism and the English Intelligentsia," in *Old Demons, New Debates: Anti-Semitism in the West*, ed. David I. Kertzer (New York: Holmes & Meier, 2005), 70–71; Robert S. Wistrich, *A Lethal Obsession Anti-Semitism from Antiquity to the Global Jiha*d (New York: Random House, 2010), 390–91.

106. Johann Hari, "Israel is suppressing a secret it must face," *Independent*, 28 Apr. 2008, http://www.independent.co.uk/opinion/commentators/johann-hari/johann-hari-israel-is-suppressing-a-secret-it-must-face-816661.html; accessed online). See http://www.honestreporting.com/articles/45884734/critiques/new/The_Stench_Spreads_Johann_Haris_Stinking_Op-Ed.asp. Hari had to give back the Orwell Prize in September 2011 after admitting to unethical conduct and plagiarism.

107. Hirsh, *Anti-Zionism and Antisemitism*, 5.

108. Pickett, "Nasty or Nazi?," 163.

109. Ibid., 158; Pickett adds that the *Guardian* report of the subsequent controversy described Mandelson as "of Jewish blood," a racist term not used of any other ethnic group.

110. See Jonathon Green, *Words Apart: The Language of Prejudice* (London: Kyle Cathie, 1996).

111. Daniel Pick, *Svengali's Web: The Alien Enchanter in Modern Culture* (New Haven: Yale University Press, 2000), 7–8.

112. "Sultan v. Svengali: How the storm blew up (Special report: Mandelson)," *Guardian*, 10 Mar. 2001, accessed online 13 Dec. 2007.

113. Peter Stanford, "Another time, another Mandy," *New Statesman*, 5 Feb. 2001; www.newstatesman.com/200102050010, accessed 13 Dec. 2007.

114. Alice Miles, "Peter Mandelson is too naive to be a Machiavelli," *Times* 15 Oct. 2008; Peter Wilby, "All plots lead to Mandelson," *Guardian,* 27 Oct. 2008; David Aaronovitch, "Corfu, and the nature of hate," *Jewish Chronicle,* 30 Oct. 2008, accessed online 4 Nov. 2008.

115. BBC News, 4 May 2003, http://news.bbc.co.uk/go/pr/fr/-/1/hi/uk_politics /2999219.stm; accessed 6 Jan. 2008. See on the political context, Bernard Harrison, *The Resurgence of Anti-Semitism: Jews, Israel and Liberal Opinion* (Boston: Rowman & Littlefield, 2006), 187; and see comments on the affair in Anthony Julius, "Anti-Semitism and the English Intelligentsia," in *Old Demons, New Debates: Anti-Semitism in the West,* ed. David Kertzer (New York: Holmes & Meier, 2005), 70–71.

116. Petronella Wyatt, "Poisonous prejudice," *Spectator,* 8 Dec. 2001.

117. Barbara Amiel, "Islamists overplay their hand but London salons don't see it," *Daily Telegraph,* 17 Dec. 2001, 13.

118. Ambassador Daniel Bernard made the remark about "that shitty little country Israel" at a party attended by top figures in the world of journalism, hosted by Lord Black, and they were reported by Barbara Amiel, Lord Black's wife, in her *Daily Telegraph* column ("Islamists overplay their hand but London salons don't see it").

119. Colin Shindler, "Reading *The Guardian*: Jews, Israel-Palestine and the Origins of Irritation," in *Jews, Muslims and Mass Media,* ed. Tudor Parfitt and Y. Egorova (London: Routledge Curzon, 2003), 157–77. In 2003, columnist Julie Burchill, a Christian feminist, castigated the rampant hatred of Jews cloaked by anti-Zionism and anti-Americanism and left the *Guardian* in disgust ("Good, bad and ugly," *Guardian,* 29 Nov. 2003; accessed online). Peter Tatchell was a lone voice who did, however, speak up against liberal support of the Hamas terrorists, whose use of violence and torture was criticized in an Amnesty report ("The left and the anti-war movement have double standards when it comes to Hamas," Comment is Free, *Guardian,* 21 Feb. 2009; accessed online).

120. Daphna Baram, *Disenchantment: The Guardian and Israel* (London: Guardian Books, 2004).

121. Grant, quoted in Baram, *Disenchantment,* 206.

122. Ibid., 221–22. A small majority of British Jews did believe they had the right to critcize Israel (David Graham and Jonathan Boyd, *Committed, Concerned, and Conciliatory: The Attitudes of British Jews towards Israel: Initial Findings from the 2010 Israel Survey* [London: Institute of Jewish Policy Research, 2010]).

123. Caryl Churchill, *Seven Jewish Children: A Play for Gaza* (London: Nick Hern Books, 2009). The script calls for nine actors, but in the performance distributed on the internet one actress performs the play, thus excluding any possibility of ambiguity (http://www.guardian.co.uk/stage/video/2009/apr/25/seven-jewish-children-caryl-churchill). See the leading critic Michael Billington's enthusiastic review, "Royal Court Theatre gets behind the Gaza headlines," *Guardian,* 11 Feb. 2009; accessed online. Billington openly conflates the Jews and Israel, an identification only implicit in the play. See Howard Jacobson's riposte to Caryl Churchill's play, "Let's see the

'criticism' of Israel for what it really is," *Independent,* 18 Feb. 2009, accessed online; and Churchill's reply, "Letters: Jacobson on Gaza," *Guardian,* 21 Feb. 2009, accessed online. Churchill denied she was antisemitic in being critical of Israel, but added two further defamatory statements that Israelis danced for joy at the destruction in Gaza and that Rabbi Shlomo Aviner, a leading spiritual leader, had distributed seditious leaflets among Israeli troops.

124. See Eitan Bar-Yosef, *The Holy Land in English Culture, 1799–1917: Palestine and the Question of Orientalism* (Oxford: Oxford University Press, 2005).

125. See the analysis of the play in Julius, *Trials of the Diaspora,* 512–16.

126. See Robert Wistrich, who was in the audience, *A Lethal Obsession,* 526.

127. David Hare, *Via Dolorosa and When Shall We Live?* (London: Faber, 1998), 13.

128. See Eitan Bar-Yosef, "I'm Just a Pen: Travel, Performance, and Orientalism in David Hare's *Via Dolorosa* and *Acting Up*," *Theatre Journal* 59.2 (2007): 259–77.

129. David Hare, *Via Dolorosa,* 16.

130. Hirsh, "Anti-Zionism and Antisemitism: Cosmopolitan Reflections." Yale Initiative for the Interdisciplinary Study of Antisemitism Working Paper Series #1, 2007. http://www.yale.edu/yiisa/workingpaper/hirsh/David%20Hirsh%20YIISA%20Working%20Paper.pdf, p. 8.

131. David Horowitz, "Anti-Semitism is at root of European media hostility to Israel, Murdoch tells Post," *Jerusalem Post,* 16 May 2008, 1, 23.

132. Nick Cohen, "The Middle East meant only Israel to many. Now the lives of millions of Arabs have been brought to Europe's attention," Comment Is Free, *Observer,* 27 Feb. 2011; accessed online.

133. The *Guardian*'s Comment is Free site, for example, has given racist antisemitic opinions a liberal leftist platform, something that was both predictable and unstoppable according to *Guardian* columnist Linda Grant (conversation with Efraim Sicher and Linda Weinhouse, July 2006).

134. On the response of British Muslims to 9/11 see Robert Wistrich, "Muslims, Jews, and September 11: The British case," in *A New Anti-Semitism?,* ed. Iganski and Kosmin, 169–91. The *Interparliamentary Report on Antisemitism* contained evidence that prominent Muslims in the Yorkshire area believed that 9/11 was a Mossad operation to discredit Islam (*Report of the All-Party Parliamentary Inquiry into Antisemitism, September 2006* [London: The Stationery Office, 2006], 27). It was commonly claimed that Muslims were not sophisticated enough to stage the attack on the Twin Towers and the Pentagon; only Israelis could have done it (Ed Husain, *The Islamist: Why I Joined Radical Islam in Britain, What I Saw Inside and Why I Left* [London: Penguin Books, 2007], 206; Wistrich, "Muslims, Jews, and September," 187). Another example of such conspiracy thinking was the rumor that Jews working in the World Trade Center had been forewarned and came to work late that day

(examples of such reports in Wistrich, *Muslim Anti-Semitism: A Clear and Present Danger* [New York: American Jewish Congress, 2002], http://www.ajc.org/atf/cf/%7B42D75369-D582-4380-8395-D25925B85EAF%7D/WistrichAntisemitism.pdf; downloaded 19 Feb. 2008, pp. 19–20).

135. Bernard Harrison, *Resurgence of Anti-Semitism*, 3–4.

136. Jonathan Judaken, "So what's new? Rethinking the 'new antisemitism' in a global age," *Patterns of Prejudice* 42.4–5 (Sept. 2008): 531–60.

137. Haggai Asher, "'Antishemiyut khadashah ve'tsiyonut khadashah' beangliya" [New antisemitism and "new Zionism" in England], *Dvar*, 10 May 1968, 5.

138. Oliver Miles, "The key question—is Blair a war criminal?" *Independent*, 22 Nov. 2009; http://www.independent.co.uk/opinion/commentators/oliver-miles-the-key-question-ndash-is-blair-a-war-criminal-1825374.html. For such examples of "genteel" antisemitism see Julius, *Trials of the Diaspora*, and for a comparison of colonial antisemitism after the Second World War with postcolonialist attitudes toward Israel, see Wistrich, *A Lethal Obsession*, 364–98.

CHAPTER ONE

Under Colonial Eyes:
Doris Lessing and the Jews

The recipient of the 2007 Nobel Prize for Literature, Doris Lessing, born Doris May Taylor in Persia (now Iran), grew up in Zimbabwe (then Southern Rhodesia) and described her experience on a farm there in the first part of her autobiography, *Under My Skin,* written in 1994. In 1945, she married her second husband, Gottfried Lessing, an immigrant from Germany whom she met at a Marxist group, and, after their divorce, moved to London in 1949. She was barred from returning to Rhodesia, and until 1995 she was banned from entering South Africa. The Nobel committee described Lessing as "that epicist of the female experience, who with scepticism, fire and visionary power has subjected a divided civilization to scrutiny."[1] Lessing's early novels expose exclusionary practices of colonial society that created White privilege, racial hierarchies, and cultural and ethnic difference. However, little attention has been paid to paradoxes and ambiguities in her representation of the relation of Jews to racial and color lines. As a former member of the communist party in colonial Rhodesia and in Britain, Lessing has spoken publicly about the Left's romance with revolution and with violence in view of the disastrous effects of communism in Europe. In an interview following the publication of her autobiography, she described herself arriving in postwar London, where she became known as a "kaffir-lover" and a Red, and spoke of how so many once believed that:

> the future was socialist or communist. We were going to have justice, equality, fair pay for women, cripples, blacks–everything, in a very short time.[2]

Yet when we examine the representation of the "jew" under Lessing's eyes we find colonial prejudices and stereotypes that do not fit so easily with such idealism.

Before going on to look at postcolonial representations of the "jew," this chapter looks at one example of the colonial view of Jews that works through anxieties about sexuality and hybridity in constructions of personal and ethnic identity. In the writing of Doris Lessing, Jewish characters or hybrid Jewish characters—that is, characters who are partially Jewish or who display recognizably Jewish traits—serve as screens or models that reveal the ambivalent desire and fear of the racial and sexual Other. These are often male objects of desire in the female gaze, even if they are sometimes described as physically ugly. They are invariably intellectuals, refugees, or some form of outcasts from English and colonial society. As almost Western but not quite (to paraphrase Homi Bhabha),[3] they are surrogates for other subaltern groups about whom it was not yet easy to speak. In the creation of the Jewish characters in her novels, especially the early volumes of *Children of Violence,* Lessing often appropriates literary and cultural antisemitic stereotypes while at the same time referencing a core of real social antisemitism in colonial Rhodesian society. In the fourth volume of the *Children of Violence* series, *Landlocked* (1958), the Jew becomes emblematic of everything that must be excluded in a postcolonial future.

In order to explore these issues, we shall compare Lessing's novels of the early *Children of Violence* series (particularly the first novel *Martha Quest*) with Lessing's autobiography and with a biography of The Hon. A. E. (Abe) Abrahamson, the story of a Jewish politician in the Rhodesian parliament (born in Bulawayo in 1922, he served as a Cabinet minister from 1958 to 1962).[4] In her autobiography she claims that there were no Jews in rural Southern Rhodesia despite compelling evidence to the contrary. In her fiction she projects colonial views of Jews onto her Jewish characters who then become a screen for the racism in colonial society. Thus, the figure of the "jew" is for Lessing a fake identity, a substitute for other pariahs in society.

Historians and literary critics who have studied the stereotypes of Jews in the culture of southern Africa provide an essential context for understanding the images of Jews in Doris Lessing's fiction. They emphasize the paradox that the Jews are a minority who suffered discrimination, but are classed as White and, thus, they are identified with the dominant group in a racially divided society. For example, in *The Roots of Antisemitism in South Africa,* Milton Shain endeavors to show that antisemitism in South Africa in the 1930s and 1940s was not an aberration and traces the prejudice and stereo-types that were prevalent in South African culture through cartoons, newspaper articles, and political propaganda. Among the common stereotypes are the Eastern European Jews, who were often traveling peddlers of the early colonial years, characterized as unkempt vendors, so-called

"Peruvians" who preyed upon farmers.[5] There was also definitely a difference in the way early Jewish settlers from the Italian-ruled island of Rhodes, England, and other parts of the British Empire were received in the colony versus the perception of later refugees fleeing antisemitism in Lithuania, Poland, and Latvia. The editor of *The Rhodesia Herald* in 1927 put it bluntly:

> In the main the South-east European is not the type of man to whom one looks to build up a country. It cannot be claimed that the South-east European possesses anything like the same degree of stability or colonizing ability as does the man from North or West Europe.[6]

In 1930, the Afrikaner-dominated South African government moved against the mainly Jewish immigration from Eastern Europe by introducing the Immigration Quota Act. As Barry Kosmin writes, this issue of immigration affected the Jewish community in Rhodesia as well; "For the first time a 'Jewish question' was raised and the incorporation of Jews within the European settler population was questioned in some quarters."[7] This was a time when English newspapers were carrying editorials against immigration,[8] and it "was a direct offshoot of the crisis in Central Europe whereby the evil doctrines of Fascism and Nazism began to reach out to Africa and poison the minds among the ruling oligarchy."[9] Abrahamson testifies, "There was difficulty on immigration from time to time especially during the 1930s when economic conditions were bad and there was White unemployment and tremendous resistance to the entry of 'aliens' which frightened the government of the day." In the postwar years, when rural poverty was rife among Afrikaner farmers, there was "further reinforcement of that other stereotypical Jew, the cosmopolitan financier."[10] In South Africa, that type of the wealthy Jewish financier was called "Hoggenheimer," after a stage character in Owen Hall's London West End musical comedy *The Girl from Kays* (1902).[11] Another stereotype of the Jew to emerge at this time was that of the Jew as Bolshevik agitator (quite common at that time in Europe).[12] Yet

> antisemitism was only one dimension, and a limited one at that, of South African prejudice and bigotry. A cardinal divide in South African society has always been one of color. Despite some observers' equating Jews with the much-maligned Indians, who similarly challenged the mercantile establishment, the white

status of the Jew was never seriously questioned or threatened. Thus could Indians be progressively excluded from, and Jews gradually integrated into society.[13]

The history of Jews of southern Africa, both in South Africa and in Rhodesia, can be seen to resemble those of the Jews of other New World Jewish communities, but they are unique in that they were part of the privileged White class in a system of racial discrimination in which the lives of the Black majority were rigidly controlled by a White minority. They were thus placed in a situation documented by Gideon Shimoni and others of extreme moral ambiguity. In South Africa, for example, in order to protect themselves from a government with a history of antisemitism, their leaders counseled and practiced caution in opposing the official policies, though a few prominent Jews actively fought Apartheid.[14] In her study of South African English writing in the period 1880–1992,[15] Marcia Leveson, like Shain, notes the persistence of antisemitic stereotypes, but with the following caveat: though "the dominant issue in South African politics had become the relationship between Blacks and Whites, and the Jews were finally fully accepted as members of the white group,"[16] the main stereotypes of Jews persisted, such as the IDB (illegal diamond buyer), the *smous* or peddler, and the shopkeeper, "that alien Other who appeared to be insinuating his way into South African society and economy and threatening the livelihood of local inhabitants" that "laid the foundations for most later negative images."[17] These same characters appear later "as the prosperous merchant and his wife, the 'kugel,' the professional or the leftist."[18]

In her fiction, Lessing uses a number of these antisemitic stereotypes in the early volumes of the *Children of Violence* series, which follows the development of the heroine Martha Quest through five volumes; *Martha Quest,* 1952; *A Proper Marriage,* 1954; *A Ripple from the Storm, Landlocked,* 1965, and *The Four-Gated City,* 1969. From the very first pages of *Martha Quest,* Lessing relates Martha's encounters with the sons of the local Jewish storekeeper, Joss and Solly, who regularly lend her books and with whom she maintains a friendship despite the obvious disapproval of her mother. What the Cohens and the books Martha borrows from them give her, is the ability to see herself objectively, from the outside:

> She was adolescent, and therefore bound to be unhappy; British and therefore uneasy and defensive; in the fourth decade of the

twentieth century, and therefore inescapably beset with problems of race and class; female, and obliged to repudiate the shackled women of the past.[19]

Thus, the function of these "others," the Cohens, though "there were moments when she hated them" is to allow Martha to begin to develop her own identity separate from her English parents and her Afrikaans neighbors, to become consciously aware of the racial and gender assumptions should be widely taken for granted.

Store owned by A. E. Abrahamson's father, Morris, ca. 1920

Lessing's description of the Cohens' store makes it look like an exact replica of the store owned by Abe Abrahamson's father. Admittedly, neither fictional nor biographical storekeepers are surprising since the prevalence of first generation Jews in commerce has been well documented by historians of the Jewish community in Zimbabwe,[20] and the stereotypes of Jews to which this concentration in commerce gave rise became quite familiar.[21] For instance, in *Martha Quest,* Lessing describes Joss and Solly's father, whom she makes the owner of the native or *kaffir* store at the station, as a "short, squat man" with "close-growing" hair and "pallid, unhealthy" skin.

> He had, she thought secretly, the look of a toad, or something confined and light-shunning; and in fact he was hardly ever away from his counter; but the commercial look of the small shopkeeper was tempered in him by purpose and dignity, which was not only because of his ancient culture, but because this penniless immigrant from Central Europe had chosen such a barren place, such exile, for the sake of his brilliant sons.[22]

The author implicitly repudiates the young protagonist for not being able to overcome her social awkwardness around this man and his Jewish body, but this Orientalized figure of the Jew as less than human—the man has a look of a toad—is left unexamined.[23] This association of the Jew with a toad has actually been internalized by South African Jewish writers, most notably Nadine Gordimer, who see themselves in the "distorting mirror" of the majority culture and incorporate negative images of Jews in their own writing. For example, Sarah Gertrude Millin is as ambivalent in her descriptions of her fellow Jews as she is notoriously of those classified as "coloured" in her novel *God's Stepchildren*. She refers to the Jew "by nature as climber" and to the first generation Jewish immigrant to South Africa as "the down-trodden, under-sized, underdeveloped fugitive from the ghetto."[24] Leveson quotes from Gordimer's short story "The Defeated," in which a Jewish woman is described as "ugly with the blunt ugliness of a toad. . . ." and remarks, "Jewish and animal ugliness are conflated in the image of the toad—the symbol of disgust identical to that found in the work of antisemitic colonial writers, which continued to be used as a mode of disparagement of Jews throughout the century."[25] Gordimer's recent biographer, Ronald Suresh Roberts attempts to discredit Leveson's entire thesis by claiming that she confuses the narrator with the author. Nonetheless he provides his own examples of Gordimer's ambivalence towards Eastern European Jewish immigrant Jews like her father, and seems to accept that the subject in Gordimer's *New Yorker* magazine article "My Father Leaves Home" is her own father.[26] When the man in that essay and his wife quarrel she scorns his people as "ignorant and dirty," people who "slept like animals around a stove stinking of garlic."[27]

Like the "Jewish American Princess," the South African stereotype for the Jewish woman that began to appear in mid-twentieth-century popular South African literature, newspapers, and magazine articles at about the time Jews became more affluent is a sexist term, "kugel," named after the heavy sweet puddings eaten by East European Jews. These are usually upwardly mobile, materialistic, young Jewish women, flashily dressed, often with big breasts and a distinctive whine that draws attention to their foreign accents.[28] In *Martha Quest,* when Martha goes to work for Mr. Cohen's more prosperous relations in town, this is how Martha views the wife of her first employer:

> Conventionally, she might be called tall, slim and elegant; Martha preferred to describe her as bony, brassy-haired and over-dressed. She wore a clinging white crepe afternoon suit, a white cap with dangling black plumes, and a great deal of jewellery. The jewellery was sound, but colourful. When Mr. Cohen came out, in answer to Mrs. Buss's call, Martha was still able to feel sorry for him but she was at once forced to examine this emotion when she understood that all the women around her were feeling the same thing.[29]

Here again, the narrator asks us to stand aside and examine with the protagonist the colonial assumptions regarding marriage and the relationships between Jewish men and their wives. Yet, when the narrator describes Martha's wedding, she reveals not only colonial insecurities, but also colonial stereotypes of Jews as cosmopolitans, sophisticated Europeans who stand out in the colonial backwater, towards whom she feels a certain degree of envy. She comments that Stella, who is Jewish, "wore sleek black, and a hat streaming with bright green feathers, and supplied a cosmopolitan smartness to the dowdy colonial gathering. Martha was atrociously dressed, and knew it, but had decided it was of no importance."[30]

Stereotypes of diamond thieves and whiskey merchants were not based on the law-abiding, bourgeois Jewish diamond merchants, but on the successes of the few, flamboyant characters who had more colorful careers in the diamond fields like the eccentric Barney Barnato.[31] Alcohol had an enormous influence on the development of the Transvaal and Jews were most commonly the bourgeois traders directly involved with the Black consumers and the objects of their hatred when they felt exploited.[32] Yet, however much Jews were shown as inferior in literature, there was real discrimination in

Rhodesian society. In *Martha Quest,* the Sports Club set to which Martha belongs, do everything in their power to break up her relationship with Adolph King the Jewish bandleader, who only comes to the club as an entertainer; it is clear that as a Jew he could not join the club or be a member of the civil service like the rest of Martha's set. The social ostracism of Martha's first lover accurately reflects the status of Jews in Rhodesian society. Though there were no legal restrictions on Jews entering the civil service, until the 1950s they were effectively barred from it. For example, when in 1925 H. U. Moffat, Minister of Mines and Public Works, was faced with a

> complaint from the Revd M. I. Cohen that a Jewish matriculant had not had his application to the civil service dealt with, Moffat denied that Jews were barred from it. But he told Leggate, the Colonial Secretary. . .young Levine is of the "aggressively Jewish" type. Leggate replied that inability to offer strict observance of Jewish religious festivals would be a good excuse for refusal. . . .[33]

When specifically questioned about the accuracy of the social antisemitism that Lessing describes in *Martha Quest,* Abe Abrahamson testified that "there was no bar to Jews in any legislation," though "there were restrictive convenants in respect to title of deeds to property in certain areas not extensive. Social anti-Semitism did exist in Rhodesia in many places, particularly in Clubs."[34] Jews in southern Africa were thus what Jacob Katz calls in his study of the process of Jewish emancipation, "social hybrids," "recognized by law as citizens but still excluded from the essential benefits entailed in this status."[35] As Katz explains, even when Jews achieved full legal emancipation, they were excluded from many voluntary social associations and from employment by state agencies and state-controlled institutions. Mufti quotes Katz in order to support his claim that the figure of the "jew" in works of the early modern period is characterized by rootlessness, dislocation and cosmopolitanism.[36] Apparently, this social hybridity persisted well beyond Lessing's departure from the colony in 1949. In his biography of Abrahamson, Clingman relates the following incident which reveals much about Jews as social hybrids:

> Harold Macmillan threw a cocktail party one evening during the negotiations for the 1961 constitution. A tall gaunt civil servant

came over to Abe, who happened to be talking to Joshua Nkomo. . .the Englishman said, "Mr. Abrahamson, you and Mr. Nkomo have to come to London to speak to each other—you couldn't be speaking to each other in the Bulawayo Club. . . ." Abe replied, "for two reasons. Neither Mr. Nkomo nor I would be welcome at the Bulawayo Club."[37]

During the colonial period Jews were among those excluded by British social clubs because they did not meet the standards of the race bar. Today, in Zimbabwe, as Paul Clingman notes, in these same clubs "men and women of all colours, backgrounds and religions appear free to gather, speak and mix in whatever company they choose, whenever they feel like it, and dressed in whatever attire makes them feel culturally comfortable."[38]

Thus, Lessing's early fiction seems to accurately reflect prevailing colonial perceptions of Jews. Nonetheless, it also reveals a disturbing tendency of its own to stereotype Jewish characters which may be further understood by examining Lessing's statements about Jews in her autobiography. In the middle of *Under My Skin: Volume One of My Autobiography, to 1949* (1994), Lessing relates how a South African author attempted to write a television script of *Martha Quest* that never came to fruition. There were two things in particular about the trial script that displeased her, the South African flavor and the way in which she felt it exaggerated the role of the Cohens. Her remarks below suggest why she was particularly sensitive to the latter point:

> When I wrote *Martha Quest* I had already had a decade or so of being asked, how is it that a girl isolated in the bush had all those clever ideas about life and race relations? My explanation that she had been soaked for years in the best that has been said and written was not considered adequate. I therefore put in the Cohen family, as storekeepers in Banket, but intellectuals, and politically minded. There were no Jewish shopkeepers in Banket, and probably not anywhere in the rural districts. . . . If the series was simply a story—why not?[39]

According to Lessing, the reason why in 1952, so soon after the Holocaust, she took hostile European stereotypes of the Jew and transported them into a colonial context was because it was simply easier than explaining how else she came to have knowledge and insight about her surroundings or how she came to be different from the other colonials around her. Yet Lessing was no doubt acquainted with the British antisemitic discourse that blamed the Jews for war profiteering and controlling the economy. The Jewish-controlled press was blamed for the jingoism of the Boer War (1899–1902), a "piratical imperialism" stirred up by "cosmopolitan" Jew-bankers and diamond merchants who manipulated the Balfour-Chamberlain clique into a "Jew war in the Transvaal."[40]

Lessing's claims in her autobiography that there were no Jews in Banket further complicates matters. When questioned about the discrepancy between Lessing's fictional representation of Jews at the station in the rural neighborhood in *Martha Quest* and her denial in her autobiography that there were any Jews in Banket or in any of the rural neighborhoods, Abe Abrahamson responded that "Her fiction is more real than her autobiography. There were Jews in Banket who owned stores and who sold to Blacks."[41] Jewish settlers in the rural areas would often begin as itinerant peddlers, then gradually become storekeepers or hotel owners and, if well established and successful, would eventually go on to become landowners. One of the rural areas where this happened is Banket. Harry Jacobson, a British Jew, who had originally started as a storekeeper in Selukwe,

> opened a store and hotel at Banket Junction when the railways reached there. In 1912 he applied for land when he had acquired 1,000 savings. He sold the hotel and by 1920 owned 10,000 acres at Banket for which he paid 5s. an acre and a further 30,000 acres at Gutu.[42]

From this historical record, it would seem as if Lessing is either denying or obscuring the truth in her autobiography. This is how she concludes that crucial passage in *Under My Skin* in which she describes the imaginary source of the Cohen family:

> Truth. Facts. All that. I was caught on my own cowardice. Over and over again in my life I've been sorry when I softened or changed truth for some reason to satisfy outside pressure, or make things easier.[43]

The Jewish characters that do appear in the novel are described using the stereotypes, often antisemitic, that were common in the popular culture and literature of the time. These characters are seen through the eyes of a character that is portrayed as free of the racist attitudes of her contemporaries, and yet these descriptions of Jews are not repudiated by the author. Lessing says she placed the Cohen family in Banket to satisfy outside pressure, to make things easier because of cowardice, and that this is something she regrets. This is the only element in an otherwise autobiographical novel that she expressly denies had a factual basis, yet there is evidence that there were Jews in Banket. Why is it so important for Lessing to deny that the Jewish characters in *Martha Quest* are based on real characters and to claim that there were no Jews at all in the rural district where she grew up, when the latter is a claim easily disproved? Doris Lessing unfortunately sheds little light on this mystery, but in a reply to the present authors she lets slip a surprising view of Jewish power in the colonies:

> People complained that they didn't see why Martha was so clever,
>
> And I said, But she was reading all those books. To save trouble, I put Jews into the station, in Banket, because in fact I did owe a lot to Jews later in Salisbury, who seemed to run everything from orchestras to political clubs. . . .[44]

The explanation we offer is that Jews function in Lessing's work as substitutes for the "Others" in colonial society. Let us start with a critical remark regarding race and hybridity in the autobiography. Lessing's Jewish obstetrician in *Under My Skin,* Dr. Rosen, is reviled in antisemitic epithets by one of his young female patients as she emerges from chloroform. Her second husband, Gottfried Lessing, has one Jewish grandfather, and, since he is eligible to fight for Hitler under the Nuremberg Laws, he immigrates to Rhodesia. Among their friends in Rhodesia during the war there are Jewish refugees such as Simon Pines who intends, he says, to immigrate to Israel, and a man named Kurt who may be Jewish. It is the ambiguous description of Kurt that we want to explore. Lessing describes him as a "bronze man, . . . heavy face. . .flattish thick nose. . .small dark eyes below heavy ridges. . .hair cropped short and clumsy modeling of the skull. . .ugly man. . . . Doctor of Philosophy. . . . and very intellectual. . . ."[45] After this not particularly flattering introduction, Lessing adds a revealing phrase:

> it was agreed that. . .he must have Mongol ancestors. In those days people said, "So-and-so must have Mongol blood," or did if they were not progressive.[46]

Kurt is from Vienna, and his wife is English. According to Lessing, if you were trying to find two complete opposites it would be those two, "anyone seeing them together must exclaim at the incomprehensible choices of nature." As if to underscore the hybridity of this couple, she says that Esther is constantly at work creating an English garden around their Rhodesian home. Esther would muse:

> 'But when you think of how many centuries the Mongols were invading your part of the world, of course there must be a lot of Mongol blood. Like us and the Vikings.'
> 'Esther, I beg you, not that word *blood*.'
> 'But why ever not?'
> 'Hitler,' he groaned. . . .[47]

Where does the notion of "Mongol blood" come from? As a member of the Communist Party in England—from which she later made a torturous withdrawal—Lessing was acquainted with Arthur Koestler, whom she mentions more than once in the second volume of her autobiography.[48] Lessing would have therefore been acquainted with Koestler's thesis in *The Thirteenth Tribe* which traces the supposed Mongol origins of Askenazic Jews to the Khazars. Indeed, in speaking of the steppe region of what is now southern Ukraine and European Russia,

> it may well be that some Jews mixed with some Turkish or Mongolian speakers. The Tatars of modern Russia (in the Volga region and the Crimea), an amalgam of Turks and Mongols speaking a Turkish language, would have been perhaps the last wave of such a contact.[49]

In her autobiography, Lessing describes a friend who is a Viennese refugee from Hitler's racial laws as a Mongol (a term Hitler used for the Jew-Bolshevik hordes threatening Germany, who were stopped by the Nazi invasion of Russia in 1941), a bronze man with short cropped hair, which is how she describes Joss and Saul's father in *Martha Quest*. In *Colonial Desire: Hybridity in Theory, Culture and Race,* Robert Young writes: "The identification of racial with sexual degeneracy was clearly always overdetermined in those whose subversive bronzed bodies bore witness to a transgressive act of perverse desire."[50] This suggests a fixation with the

Jewish body and raises anxieties about both race and sexuality that recall colonialist prejudices.

In *Martha Quest* Lessing wanted to write a *Bildungsroman* about growing up in rural Southern Rhodesia and then coming to the town with its gradations of social standing, and she used the Cohens, who would be recognizable types to her English readers, because it was an easy way of making them understand the intellectual and social climate she wanted to describe. By evoking these Jewish shopkeepers and lawyers—these middlemen—she articulates her attraction to people marked by gender difference or of mixed race. In the very first scene of *Martha Quest* we are told that Martha has borrowed a book on sex psychologists Epstein and Havelock Ellis from the Cohen boys, and so Lessing signals to the reader that her protagonist is acquainted with Havelock Ellis and books of this nature. However, in her autobiography Lessing denies her exposure to such writers came from Jewish intellectuals like the Cohen brothers, for she claims that there were no Jews in Banket.[51] Since we know this to be untrue, we may ask, whom is she shielding? Are the Jews in the novel signifiers of difference ("jews"), but not actually Jews?

In *Under My Skin,* as Doris Lessing begins the process of maturation, she travels around Southern Rhodesia, spending months in the homes of acquaintances of her family. In one place, "two large and authoritative" women took charge of her. Lessing says that she later understood that they were lesbians, and the man who lived with them was like a guest in the house. The description points to the source and nature of this knowledge in the perverse sexuality of the "jew":

> Each hut was completely lined with carefully fitted bookshelves, a carpetting feat since the huts were round: the walls seemed to be made of books. I took one look at them and lost my head and my heart.[52]

Lessing then spends two pages listing some of the books that she read in that house. In *Martha Quest* her intellectual mentors, both while she is still on the farm and when she moves to Salisbury, are Solly and Joss Cohen, and they are the ones who supply her with books. In *Under My Skin,* Lessing claims that she created them because she was a coward. According to Lessing, when she had to give an account of how a girl isolated in the bush had learned all sorts of clever ideas, she attributed them to the tutelage of two intellectual

Jewish boys rather than give a true accounting of her intellectual mentors. "I was caught," says Lessing, "on my own cowardice."[53] It is possible that in a novel written in 1952, she could not speak of her lesbian mentors and so Lessing introduced these stereotypical feminized Jewish youths as a way of projecting queer identity.

This suggests the Jew may function as a screen for an even more unacceptable relationship with the Black or colored Other. If we compare Lessing's description of her first lover in *Under My Skin* to the relationship between Adolph and Martha in *Martha Quest,* we see that she describes her first love as Oriental in appearance, someone who is rumored to be a man of color in this community so fiercely divided by the color bar.

> He was tall, he was dark, he was handsome. His skin was Mediterranean olive. They said on the verandahs that he had a touch of the tar-brush. Everything they found disturbing about this aloof, saturnine man found expression in the whispers. "Take a look at his eyes. . .at his hair. . .at his nails." Needless to say this aroused a passion of protectiveness in me and I loved him even more. . . . I was in an amorous trance. . . . My letter was unforgivable. I said I did not care about his tinge of colour, everyone was stupid and prejudiced. His reply was cool, correct; he probably did not know the District had so finally diagnosed him as not one of them. For years I writhed with shame, but what is the use of that. If it is felt I was writhing with shame a lot then yes, I did.[54]

This episode is certainly reminiscent of Martha Quest who is denounced by her friends as a lover of "Jews and Niggers."[55] At first she is willing to "fight the world" on behalf of Adolph whom they accuse of "seducing an innocent English girl."[56] She "pours scorn on Stella and Donovan. . .for being Philistines. . . ." and she too feels that "she was off down that slippery slope of compelled confession that was like a moment of madness. . . ."[57] The fact that Adolph's sexuality is seen as threatening strongly suggests that the Jew is a screen here for the Black man. This is how Frantz Fanon describes the perception of Jews as twinned with the sexual danger of Blacks in the White imagination: "The government and the civil service are at the mercy of the Jews. Our women are at the mercy of the Negroes."[58] He explains:

The Jew is attacked in his religious identity, in his history, in his race, in his relations with his ancestors and with his posterity. . . . The Jew menace is replaced by the fear of the sexual potency of the Negro. . . . When it is a question of the Jew the problem is clear: he is suspect because he wants to own the wealth or take over the positions of power. But the Negro is fixated at the genital. The Negro symbolizes the biological danger; the Jew, the intellectual danger.[59]

In this light, it is significant that Adolph is characterized in the novel as an *Ostjude,* a Jew of lower caste associated with a dangerous sexuality and a Jew who has tried to hide his identity by changing his name to the innocuous "King." Even Stella who has married a non-Jew and been accepted into the colonial set, is shown as a "kugel," wielding a more precocious sexuality and a loud and conspicuous taste in clothes than the other colonial women though she knows how to manipulate her sexuality and to suddenly act the part of "responsible, womanly dignity."[60] Lessing describes Adolph's "scrutinizing eyes" that make Martha "conscious of every joint and muscle in her body."[61] Furthermore, she shows that Martha believes he uses his pariah status as a tool of seduction, and nowhere does she contradict this impression. Lessing writes that for Martha, he "had this dubious fantastic quality," and she is practically mesmerized by him (something which may recall overtones of Svengali). The first time they make love, which is the first time ever for Martha, is described as follows:

> Recklessly she walked across to him, feeling that again, as usual, she was being pulled down a current which she did not understand, and she stood beside him laughing. He half violently, half doubtfully pulled her to the bed. . . .[62]

After the act of love, Martha feels the same sense of protectiveness towards Adolph that Lessing describes in *Under My Skin* towards her first lover, who was scorned by his community. Martha's reactions to her lover's difference are revealing:

> She remained silent, looked at his smooth, dark-skinned body; he was not fat or plump, but the flesh lay close and even over the small bones, like a warm and darkened wax, the dark tendrils of hair on his chest glistened, and she played with them, after an

initial reluctance—the thought had flashed through her mind that this man's body was wrong for her, that she was having her first love affair with a man she was not the slightest in love with. She suppressed it at once. . . .[63]

The stereotypes of racial otherness and sexual danger that are introduced here as a screen for that early lover are derived from images of the Black Jew that, according to Sander Gilman, are not only as old as the racist tracts of the late nineteenth century, but are found as far back as the association of Jews with blackness in medieval iconography.[64] Hybridization raises fears of sexual contamination and racial pollution through miscegenation. In nineteenth and twentieth century racist ideology Jews were often characterized as the least pure race, and, like the colored man of *Under My Skin,* suspect precisely because their racial identity could not always be identified with certainty. Houston Stewart Chamberlain, the son-in-law of Richard Wagner, categorized the Jews in 1899 as "a mongrel race," and considered the Jews to be the proof of the harmful results of interbreeding; the worst example of "hybridization" was the "admixture of Negro blood with Jewish" in the diaspora of Alexandria.[65] Hybridization threatens a colonial society haunted by the specter of miscegenation and obsessed with the color bar.

As mentioned earlier, Millin expressed an antipathy towards Jewish passing that was not very far from her attitudes towards miscegenation. Roberts shows that in her earliest fiction, Gordimer too can be read within the colonial tradition of Millin and Paton. He cites an early story "Babe" in which a "coloured" woman is punished for attempting to pass as White, and he mentions that in the 1940s, Gordimer spoke of the inner cities as a "squalid degenerate meeting-place of Black and White blood."[66] It is clear from Lessing's description of the man who might have been colored in *Under My Skin,* that the White community was not above examining the hair and nails of an individual they suspected might be of mixed race. In such a climate, the antipathy towards a Jew who changes his name might indeed be a screen for the fear of the Other's hybrid identities.

We do not need to look far for other examples of such color sensitivity masking racial fears in the figure of the "jew," but at the same time Lessing identifies the figure of the "jew" with the Jewish nationalism that arises against the historical background of the Holocaust and the Jewish struggle in British Mandate Palestine against the British, who are keeping out thousands of refugees from Europe. In 1958, after she had spent nearly a decade in

England, Lessing published the third volume of *Children of Violence,* entitled *Landlocked,* a novel in which, as she tells us in *Under My Skin,* she abandoned autobiographical writing altogether. In *Landlocked,* Lessing creates the first of the tortured refugee and/or Jewish lovers with whom her heroines inevitably fall disastrously in love. These include Jan Brod, in *Retreat to Innocence,* and Michael, in *The Golden Notebook,* whose families and friends are killed in Europe by the fascists and the communists. Martha Quest describes her Jewish lover, Thomas Stern, who is a refugee in Southern Rhodesia from Poland, as a Jewish Polish peasant, while Martha is described as "thin," "neurotic," and "tense," a typical "Western woman." He is consistently described as a *brown* strong man with *brown* strong hands,[67] though Lessing makes a point of describing his wife's *white* skin.[68] He too is an "Ostjude," one of the Eastern European Jews considered so undesirable not only by non-Jews in the colony, as Kosmin has shown,[69] but also by other Jews who internalized racial and social hierarchies until the rise of Hitler changed everything. In a painful scene, Lessing depicts the way in which Thomas's educated wife and his daughter reject him. His attraction to Martha fits the stereotype of all the colonized for the superior "White." He describes how as a boy in the village all the clever young men would go to town to see the American films and look at the women:

> We knew what was wrong with them. We understood Western women absolutely. We used to make jokes. . . . Just like Africans now. They look at white women in exactly the same way we used to look at women in the films or in the magazines.[70]

It is also Thomas that Lessing has take up arms against the British Empire, for he leaves Rhodesia and goes to British Mandate Palestine, or Israel, as he insists on calling the yet undeclared state, to fight on behalf of the Jewish refugees from Hitler. Since this novel engages with Zionism at the conclusion, one might be tempted to interpret it in a similar manner to Louise Bethlehem's analysis of Manfred Nathan's novel *Sarie Marais: A Romance of the Anglo-Boer War* which compares Nathan's Afrikaner nationalism with his activism in the Jewish community of South Africa and his Zionism.[71] Bethlehem claims that, to a certain extent, Manfred Nathan's Afrikaner nationalism was a symptom of his "deflected" Jewish nationalism: he still believed that Jews were entitled to their own homeland both because they had been oppressed elsewhere and because Palestine had once been the center of

Jewish tradition regardless of who was living in that territory at the present time. However, in Lessing's novel, Thomas is questioned how he can be both a Marxist and a Zionist, and he claims that he is a Zionist because his people have been victimized as Jews.

> A Marxist is not a Zionist. But I am a Marxist. And with every day I become more of a Zionist. I see British soldiers allowing refugees from Europe to drown rather than land in Israel, and I am a Zionist.[72]

Yet, for Lessing, Thomas is neither Fanon's intellectual who fights because of the fact that he is alienated from Western values, nor is he the man of color who picks up a gun to fight because he has been victimized on the basis of race "by a given branch of humanity. . .that pretends to superiority."[73] After Thomas returns from pre-state Israel, he takes off to help the Africans in the bush, which he characterizes as an attempt to escape from turning into a successful Jewish businessman, the same kind of middleman he would have been in Poland. Whereas in Bethlehem's study, it is the Jews' anxieties that act to screen Others within White colonial society, in Lessing's work, as I have shown, the Jews inhabit a liminal position in which they are Westernized colonials; they remain "storekeepers. . .but intellectuals, and politically minded."

By allowing the character of Martha in *Landlocked* to be the repository of Thomas's final testimony, Lessing makes it likely that the real meaning of his battle against the British Empire—his "Zionism"—is to be read as Lessing's own intended message. According to Martha, Thomas went to kill British soldiers in Israel as a surrogate for killing Sergeant Tresell in Rhodesia. Sergeant Tresell was Thomas's immediate superior in the army whose carelessness and mindless cruelty caused the deaths of a number of the Africans under his charge. Tresell is also antisemitic, but his antisemitism is presented as simply a natural by-product of his entrenched conviction of White supremacy. In claiming that Thomas goes to Israel just so that he can cast a blow against Sergeant Tresell, it seems Lessing is suggesting that Thomas's Zionism is a blow against the economy of colonialism only tangentially bound up at all with the history or even the suffering of the Jews.

Thomas ultimately dies in the bush, but manages to send back a document written in a delirium that is given to Martha to edit. The document concerns the state of the natives, and over it are written the words "vermin, vermin,

vermin." This document juxtaposes a chronicle of the lives and the tribulations of the natives with his life and the plight of the Jews in Eastern Europe. Martha compiles two versions: one version contains the biographies and obituaries, as well as recipes and charms, of the African natives, but the other she types over on flimsy paper, literally a screen, on which she includes all the "nonsense," the Jewish jokes, the memories of Europe, the talk of death, blood, vermin, murderers, vultures, and lice. In the end, she is advised to destroy the entire manuscript, for certainly the well-meaning officers of the Foundation that sent Thomas out to the aid of the Africans will not consider this document the work of a sane person. Thus Thomas's multilayered "last testament" is hidden away out of sight with its tales of Poland interspersed with tales of the natives: "Vermin, vermin. . .the world is a lump of filth crawling with vermin. . . . Death here. Death there too."[74] Martha's concealment of Thomas's African manuscript from the eyes of the Foundation cannot but recall Marlowe's censoring of Kurtz's report on the "Suppression of Savage Customs" for the Company that sent him into Africa in *Heart of Darkness.* The allusion here evokes a disturbing connection between the postscriptum "exterminate the brutes" that Marlowe tears off Kurtz's report and the unreadable and inassimilable tales of natives and Jews referred to in Thomas's document.

As the novel *Landlocked* progresses, the "jew" becomes progressively more of an Orientalized object, a metaphoric figure of myth. In a dream with an ahistorical setting; it might be the Second World War or the middle ages, Martha sees a wooden scaffold and Thomas is being led out be to be hanged by various officials, one of whom is holding a silver cross and reading from a small black book. Thomas, she writes:

> looked different. He looked more Semitic or Eastern. He was darker, thinner, And his brown hair had darkened and was curly. Chips of wood and straw were tangled in his hair.[75]

Though this is presented as only a dream in the novel, amazingly, once Thomas is dead and his testimonial is rejected, the problems faced by all the European characters in the novel suddenly find their resolution. Martha, the daughter of English parents who had been denied citizenship upon marrying a German immigrant and her husband Anton, a German, are granted British citizenship, and Martha finds a berth on a ship going to England. The colonists are reunited with the Motherland. It is as if, as Aamir Mufti claims, once the "jew" has been removed, the disparate European elements can easily be reabsorbed into the community. Mufti's reading of such canonical English works as *Ivanhoe* and *Daniel Deronda* is consistent with this view: "The Jewish Question can be evicted from the European home to be solved elsewhere – a strategy made possible by European global power itself."[76]

As Martha Quest drives off with a suitcase and a car load of books, leaving her first husband and daughter to begin a new life at the end of *A Ripple from the Storm* (the second volume of *Children of Violence),* she encounters Mr. Maynard, a representative of the colonial establishment, who remarks:

> I suppose with the French Revolution for a father and the Russian Revolution for a mother, you can very well dispense with a family.[77]

In imagining the Cohen brothers the midwives of modernity for her questing daughter of modernity and Thomas its martyr, Lessing is surely not alone. Many others on both the extreme Left and Right have held the Jews collectively responsible for single-handedly ushering in modernity and destroying the once harmonious consensus of pre-modern times. According to Mufti, the persistence of the "Jewish Question" in Europe posed such a threat to European national culture, as to make it "imperative to solve the problem by displacing it onto non-European spaces."[78] As we shall see in the next chapter, Anita Desai's novel *Baumgartner's Bombay* is the story of one Jew's attempt to escape his European fate by traveling to a non-European space, only to have it catch up with him in a series of ironic episodes that mimic the European experience.

NOTES

1. Swedish Academy, Nobel Prize committee press release, 11 Oct. 2007, http://nobelprize.org/nobel_prizes/literature/laureates/2007/press.html.

2. "A Notorious Life: The Salon Interview: Doris Lessing, November 11, 1997," http://dir.salon.com/story/books/feature/1997/11/11/lessing; accessed online.

3. Homi K. Bhabha uses the term "almost the same but not quite" in his essay "Of Mimicry and Man," *The Location of Culture* (London: Routledge, 1994), 122–23, and this phrase is taken up by Ivan Davidson Kalmar and Derek J. Penslar in their "Introduction," in *Orientalism and the Jews,* ed. Ivan Davidson Kalmar and Derek J. Penslar (Waltham, Mass.: Brandeis University Press, 2005), *xx.*

4. Paul Clingman, *The Moon Can Wait: A Biography of the Hon AE Abrahamson* (London: Penguin Books, 2004).

5. Milton Shain, *The Roots of Antisemitism in South Africa* (Charlottesville: University Press of Virginia, 1994), 27.

6. Quoted Kosmin, *Majuta: A History of the Jewish Community of Zimbabwe* (Salisbury: Mambo Press, 1980), 67.

7. Ibid., 67.

8. Ibid.

9. Ibid.

10. A. E. Abrahamson, email interview with Linda Weinhouse, 29 Sept. 2005.

11. Shain, *Roots of Antisemitism,* 62.

12. Ibid., 78.

13. Ibid., 152.

14. Gideon Shimoni, *Community and Conscience: The Jews in Apartheid South Africa* (Waltham, Mass.: Brandeis University Press, 2003). See also idem, *Jews and Zionism: The South African Experience, 1910–1967* (Cape Town: Oxford University Press, 1980).

15. Marcia Leveson, *People of the Book: Images of the Jew in South African English Fiction 1880–1992* (Johannesburg: Witwatersrand University Press, 1996).

16. Ibid., 27.

17. Ibid., 221.

18. Ibid., 222.

19. Doris Lessing, *Martha Quest* (New York: New American Library, 1952), 8.

20. In 1897 when they totaled 46 persons, 14 were storekeepers, 2 merchants, 2 tobacconists (Kosmin, *Majuta,* 11). In addition, the Jews were a higher proportion of the White population in Rhodesia than in South Africa—6% in 1897 compared to 1.0% in the Cape Colony.

21. See the illustrations in Shain, *Roots of Antisemitism,* following p. 77.

22. Lessing, *Martha Quest,* 40.

23. On the antisemitic perception of the unhealthy Jewish body see Sander Gilman, *The Jew's Body* (New York: Routledge, 1991).

24. Quoted in Leveson, *People of the Book,* 83.

25. Ibid., 180.

26. Ronald Suresh Roberts, *No Cold Kitchen* (Johannesburg: STE, 2005), 34.

27. Gordimer, "My Father Leaves Home," *New Yorker,* 7 May 1990, 42.

28. Leveson, *People of the Book,* 162–63.

29. Lessing, *Martha Quest,* 88–89.

30. Lessing, *Martha Quest,* 246.

31. Leveson, *People of the Book,* 32.

32. Charles Van Onselen, "Randlords and Rotgut 1886–1903," *History Workshop Journal* 2.1 (1976): 33–89.

33. Kosmin, *Majuta,* 55.

34. A. E. Abrahamson, email interview with Linda Weinhouse, 29 Sept. 2005.

35. Katz, "The Jewish Diaspora: Minority Position and Majority Aspirations," *Jerusalem Quarterly* 25 (Fall 1982): 76.

36. Aamir R. Mufti, *Enlightenment in the Colony: The Jewish Question and the Crisis of Postcolonial Culture* (Princeton: Princeton University Press, 2007), 51.

37. Clingman, *The Moon Can Wait,* 242.

38. Ibid., 243.

39. Lessing, *Under My Skin: Volume One of My Autobiography to 1949* (New York: Harper, 1994), 161.

40. Robert Wistrich, *Antisemitism: The Longest Hatred* (London: Thames Methuen, 1991), 105–6.

41. Abrahamson, email interview, 29 Sept. 2005.

42. Kosmin, *Majuta,* 36–37.

43. Lessing, *Under My Skin,* 161.

44. Doris Lessing to Linda Weinhouse, 16 June 2006. When asked for her views on race and color in postwar London, she displayed an equally surprising blindness towards immigrant groups: "You won't find from me any information about how immigrant groups act in London. Most of what I know comes from fiction."

45. Lessing, *Under My Skin,* 330.

46. Ibid., 330.

47. Ibid., 330.

48. Doris Lessing, *Walking in the Shade* (New York: Harper Collins, 1997), 58–59, 122.

49. Reuven Amitai to Linda Weinhouse, email, 1 Jan. 2008.

50. Robert J. C. Young, *Colonial Desire: Hybridity in Theory, Culture and Race* (London: Routledge, 1995), 26.

51. Lessing, *Under My Skin,* 161.

52. Ibid., 140.

53. Ibid., 161.

54. Lessing, *Under My Skin,* 193.

55. Lessing, *Martha Quest,* 208.

56. Ibid., 194.

57. Ibid., 182.

58. Frantz Fanon, *Black Skin, White Masks* (New York: Grove Press, 1967), 157.

59. Ibid., 162–65.

60. Lessing, *Martha Quest,* 181.

61. Ibid., 178–79.

62. Ibid., 183.

63. Ibid., 184.

64. Sander Gilman, *Jewish Self-Hatred: Anti-Semitism and the Hidden Language of the Jews* (Baltimore: Johns Hopkins University Press, 1986), 7.

65. Sander Gilman, *The Jew's Body* (London: Routledge, 1991), 174.

66. Roberts, *No Cold Kitchen,* 65–66.

67. Lessing, *Martha Quest,* 116, 161.

68. Ibid., 161.

69. Kosmin, *Majuta,* 69.

70. Lessing, *Martha Quest,* 80.

71. Louise Bethlehem, "Membership, Dismemberment and the Boundaries of the Nation—Manfred Nathan's *Sarie Marais: A Romance of the Anglo-Boer War,*" *African Studies* 63.1 (2004): 95–117.

72. Lessing, *Martha Quest,* 161.

73. Fanon, *Black Skin, White Masks*, 224.

74. Lessing, *Martha Quest,* 271.

75. Lessing, *Landlocked* (New York: New American Library, 1958), 202.

76. Mufti, *Enlightenment in the Colony,* 110.

77. Lessing, *A Ripple from the Storm* (New York: New American Library, 1958), 345.

78. Mufti, *Enlightenment in the Colony,* 110.

CHAPTER TWO

Under Postcolonial Eyes:
Baumgartner's Bombay

THE "JEW'S" PASSAGE TO INDIA

In *Baumgartner's Bombay* (1988), by the internationally acclaimed Indian novelist Anita Desai, a Jewish refugee flees Nazi persecution in Germany and finds himself embroiled in the sectarian violence in India following Partition. Through flashbacks, we are told of the childhood of the eponymous hero who grows up in Berlin, where his father's once flourishing furniture business is ransacked by the Nazis. His father, after being imprisoned briefly in Dachau, commits suicide; his mother sells the business, and her son Hugo sets off for Calcutta where they have business connections. But she refuses to accompany him, and he will never see her again. In India, the British imprison Hugo Baumgartner in an internment camp as an enemy alien alongside German Nazi sympathizers. Baumgartner is ostracized both in Hitler's Germany and in India where he is considered a "firanghi," a foreigner, a Parsi word common among Muslims and non-Muslims in India that does not usually denote disrespect (it is used by Northerners of South-erners, for example), but that here is being internalized in Baumgartner's sense of being always the outsider.[1] After the war, his only remaining companions are his cats and another lonely expatriate named Lotte. Baumgartner is murdered at the end of the novel by a blond German hippie who robs him in order to support his drug habit. This chapter shows the ways in which Anita Desai connects two pivotal experiences, her encounter with an Austrian Jew on the streets of Bombay and with the letters he left behind and her memory of a photograph of her non-Jewish mother leaving Germany for India to join her Bengali husband a decade before the war. Desai uses these two disparate memories, her knowledge of the history of Germany's Jews, and the stories her mother told her about Germany and the fate of her friends to show the ways in which Germans and Jews are inextricably linked by nationality and history. Her novel explores the postcolonial ramifications of that history for an understanding of pluralism in India's multicultural society.

Much has been said about Baumgartner as a figure of universal isolation[2] and Desai has confirmed that this is the reason she made her central protagonist Jewish:

> Yes. I began with this character who wandered about on the streets of Bombay and started building up a story around him. The trouble with that story was that it was too localized, particular to a place and time which meant something to me, but I couldn't see that it would mean anything to the readers of this book. So I had to find a way to generalize his isolation and one way of doing it was to make him a Jew.[3]

Desai speaks of meeting an Austrian Jew in Bombay who left a packet of letters when he died which his friend brought to her. She found that they were just affectionate, unimportant notes, but later she realized that these letters carried the number of a concentration camp inmate. In the novel, Desai describes Lotte fleeing from the "blood-spattered scene" of Hugo Baumgartner's murder clutching postcards found in his room covered by faint writing that forms a "skein or web on the yellowed paper," all dated from 1939, '40, and '41. These censored letters contain words of reassurance, "Sugary, treacly, warm, oozing love, childhood love, little mice and bunny rabbits of love—sweet, warm, choking, childish love."[4] They are written in repetitious, baby language "Are you well my rabbit? Do not worry yourself. I am well. I have enough. But have you enough, my mouse, my darling?"(5). These letters, sent by Hugo's mother when she was incarcerated in a concentration camp in Germany, become "emblematic" of a stifling European world "linked to destructive illusion, and the tragic facts of recent history."[5]

Yet, at the same time, Desai has reiterated that the novel also originated in her own family history. Paradoxically, according to Desai, her encounter with a slovenly Austrian Jew and his cats on the streets of Bombay, in addition to the letters he left behind, provided her with the key she needed in order to fulfill her desire to fictionalize her own German background and work though her ambivalent feelings about her German mother. The figure of the "jew" in Desai's novel is linked with the figure of the German as a Janus headed figure.[6] The widespread overvaluation of Baumgartner's ethnicity as a marker for the outsider tends to obscure the fact that Baumgartner is not the only European, the only German, or even the only German Jew in the novel.

And Baumgartner's choice of isolation, his determination to eschew other Jews and other Germans, rather than being indicative of the eternal nature of the Jewish outsider, represents his attempt to shed his identification with Europe and Germany and to deal with his survivor guilt in the aftermath of the European Holocaust that destroyed his family, as well as the Germany he once knew and to which he can never return. In particular, Desai imagines the memories of her German mother's generation in order to exorcise the racist demons of Germany's past and mourn the future which the German Jewish experience presages for pluralistic India.

POSTMEMORY AND MULTICULTURALISM

In *Baumgartner's Bombay,* Desai postulates a German-Jewish symbiosis and then recasts it in a text that probes the limits of memory and the act of writing in the aftermath of exile and war. Using the letters of an Austrian Jew in India and the photograph and stories of her German mother, Anita Desai creates what Marianne Hirsch describes as a "postmemory" of the trauma of isolation, disruption, and war.[7] According to Marianne Hirsch, the study of the genocides and catastrophes at the end of the twentieth century and the beginning of the twenty-first requires new methods in which we often find,

> the *language* of family can literally reactivate and reembody a "cultural/archival" image. . . . This "adoption of public anonymous images into the family photo album finds its counterpart in the pervasive use of private familial images and objects in institutions of public display—museums and memorials. . . .[8]

Desai uses the concentration camp letters and her mother's photograph to activate and embody the historical events in her novel. According to Hirsch, the most powerful image in the trauma of the Second World War is that of the "lost mother and her recovery,"[9] and at the genesis of *Baumgartner's Bombay* lies a maternal trope. Desai has stated that the inspiration for Hugo Baumgartner's journey to India came from a very early childhood memory of a gray sepia photo of her mother on her way to India from Europe, a full decade before Hugo's fictional departure from Venice, standing in the Piazza St. Marco feeding the pigeons; Desai was to revisit this memory spot fifty years later, in a soft November drizzle, and, though Venice showed none of its golden splendor, decided she would write about this place.[10] Her mother had stopped in Venice on a Grand Tour of Europe with her Indian husband, but actually left Europe from Marseille.[11] In fact, any boats leaving Italy for India in the years before the war would have left from Trieste, not from Venice.[12] Desai admits that she altered the memory of her mother's departure from Germany in the belief that "our parents' memories are always part of who we are."[13] Baumgartner was the vehicle through which Desai was able to recreate the "strange lives" and "strange histories" of her German mother and her large circle of German friends in India about whom, she says, she could not directly write, "they were too personal, they were too close to me—they were the aunties and uncles of my childhood."[14] Indeed, in an interview with Corinne Demas Bliss in Amherst in 1988, following the British publication of *Baumgartner's Bombay,* Desai expressed her view that the Europeans in India were "strangely eccentric, obviously outsiders."[15]

> I began to think a great deal about it and felt the need to supply them with a history, so I invented a history for this figure whom I had seen but not known. In doing that I was able to use all my mother's memories of prewar Germany which had been told me as a child. It used to be our bedtime story. . . . So I was able to put into the book and use the German language again, which gave me a wonderful feeling of liberating a part of my mind, of myself, which I had to keep silenced for all those years.[16]

Moreover, as Hirsch notes, pictorial images in particular can both perpetuate and revise existing hegemonic codes.[17] For example, in the photograph of Toni Niame, Desai caught her on the grand tour before she joined her Bengali husband in 1927 in India, where she learned to wear a sari, cook Indian food, and speak Bengali at a time when it was not "comfortable" to have a European wife.[18] The war brought increased hostility towards Europeans in India from the British and "Mrs. Desai was aware that her nationality was against her."[19] Later Desai learned that during the war her older brother and sister asked their mother never to wear dresses or speak to them in German in the street, and though she was only eight, she does remember the look of sadness and intense relief on her mother's face when the war ended. Desai confesses: "I don't think any of us in the family were able to give her the sort of support she needed. Perhaps only other Germans in her circle of friends could have done that."[20]

Baumgartner's imprisonment in an internment camp is perhaps the most compelling example in the novel of his outsider status. However, Desai had very little information regarding the internment camps in India. As she has said in an interview with Lalita Pandit, "All I had to go on was the material about the detention camps in the West. . . ."[21] The major literary source available to Desai was Heinrich Harrar's *Seven Years in Tibet* (1953), the first two chapters of which are devoted to his confinement and escape from one of these camps.[22] In the first chapters, Harrar relates his internment and escape from the camp to Tibet, but never mentions Jews. Hans Kopp in *Himalaya Shuttlecock* (London: Hutchinson, 1957) also fails to mention any Jews in his account of the British internment camp not far from Dehra Dun. Desai downplayed the brutality of the English military administration, the camp's ethnic diversity, and Harrar's many references to Indian guards in the camp, all in order to create an ahistorical environment which would enable Baumgartner "to escape the notice of history."[23] It seems that Desai is creating a postmemory of a world divided into Jews and Germans. This creates a polarized view of history, and Desai's concern is always for how that history might affect the hybridity and plurality that characterizes India.

Drawing on the bedtime stories of her German mother about whom she had long kept silent, Desai painstakingly develops Hugo's German childhood through German language nursery rhymes and references to canonical German texts; she evokes Jewish life in Germany during the Weimar years and creates an imagined German-Jewish childhood for Hugo Baumgartner as a son of successful, assimilated, emancipated, bourgeois Jews who had many reasons to be complacent about their future until 1933. As the historian Peter Pulzer writes, Jewish leaders and citizens during the Weimar years thought they were experienced in dealing with the adversities of diaspora existence; there was no precedence for the Nazi plan for the extermination of the Jews.[24] Historians have recounted the progression of the relationship between Germans and Jews which rather than leading relentlessly towards the Holocaust, followed a pattern of integration from the eighteenth century onwards despite the occasional scapegoating of foreigners.[25] Through authentic German children's songs, references to Goethe, and even detailed portrayals of the Baumgartners' clothing and household furnishings, Desai imaginatively recreates the domestic life of German Jews between the two wars when Berlin was said to compete with Paris as a cultural center.[26] Along with the confident materialism of Hugo's father, Desai evokes the Orientalist culture of Hugo's mother as she reads Tagore's *Gitanjali* with her poetic Jewish friends in the country, after Hugo's father has been imprisoned in Dachau and then released, a broken man. Later, when Hugo tries to convince her to accompany him to India he reminds her of her interest in Tagore, but she would rather read the "verses of our own dear Friedmanns" (56). However, at this point when she and Hugo return to Berlin from the country, they find that Hugo's father has committed suicide, and their status in Germany soon becomes clear as internal Orientals, as racial Others.

The terrible fate of these German Jews is evident in Desai's motif of the spun sugar in Hugo's mother's voice, the same sugar that nearly chokes Lotte years later, the sweetness that one night "shatters into splinters of glass," a clear reference to *Kristallnacht* (the Night of Broken Glass), in November 1938.[27] This sugar is not only connected with the love Mrs. Baumgartner has for Germany which includes her fashionable Orientalizing, but also with Hugo's first encounter with the "east" when he arrives in Venice. He breathes in the smell of Venetian chocolates, "he had known only as a small child. Then he felt himself to be inside a chocolate box, surfeited with sweetness and richness, and tore away to breathe freely" (60). This association of the East, danger, and sugar recalls the proposal of Johann David Michaelis, who, in his essay *Orientalische und exegetische Bibliothek* (Oriental and exegetical library, 1782), entered into the debate on Jewish emancipation initiated by Wilhelm Dohm in his book *Ueber die burgerliche Verbesserrung der Juden* (On the civic improvement of the Jews, 1781). Dohm had argued that the state could rehabilitate the Jews by sending them to the sugar islands to become productive in a climate "analogous to their place of origin where they might become colonial subjects promoting the wealth of the European fatherland."[28] The irony of these early German schemes to relocate their "Oriental" Jewish citizens in some Caribbean island soon becomes apparent when Desai depicts the ultimate failure of the German experiment in the emancipation of its Jewish citizens. For when Baumgartner escapes this fate, he is imprisoned as a German in an internment camp where he labors in the sugar cane fields.

When Baumgartner arrives in India he is attracted to its plurality, "the crowds of Indians, Britons, Americans, Gurkhas. . . ." (83). He sees that "India was two worlds or ten" (85). He is exposed to India's mixture of flavors, "the sweet, the astringent and the perfumed. . . ." (87), unlike the overly sweet, sugary flavor of his childhood. He enjoys meeting the showgirls Lola and Gisela, precisely because of their ethnic backgrounds. Lola / Lotte says she was Lulu in Germany, though Hugo knows that Lulu is not German. Later, when she lives alone in Bombay, she argues with her neighbors in a mixture of Konkani and Yiddish (67). Gisela tells everyone in Calcutta she is from Russia, though she advertises herself as Lily in Shanghai, and later in the novel even when she becomes a respectable matron and calls herself Gala von Roth and snubs him, Hugo is more delighted than appalled.

Baumgartner is confronted with the multiple discourses of India's indigenous native and expatriate communities:

> Languages sprouted around him like tropical foliage and he picked words from it without knowing if they were English or Hindi or Bengali—they were simply words he needed: *chai, khana, baraf, lao, jaldi, joota, chota, peg, pani, karma, soda, garee*. . .what was this language he was wrestling out of the air, wrenching around to his own purposes? He suspected it was not Indian, but India's, the India he was marking out for himself. (92)

Critics tend to see Baumgartner's linguistic confusion as one more signifier of his alienation in Indian society.[29] However, from Desai's own comments, it seems more likely that she saw this plethora of languages and Baumgartner's creation of his own hybrid tongue as a positive aspect of the Indian experience. For, according to Desai, Baumgartner does not lack a language; he creates a new language.[30] Desai's use of German, French, Portuguese, Bengali, Hindi, and Hebrew without translation in the text has been read as a direct appeal to a certain kind of readership, one of "sophisticated cosmopolitanism," a kind of "colonialism in reverse," one that orientalizes India, and makes of it a European invention in which India is "not modern, not developed, not civilized, not Western."[31] It seems, however, that this reluctance to translate originates from quite opposite motives, from the desire to replicate and retain a sense of India's linguistic and hitherto ethnic diversity far superior in its hybridity to just such Manichean formulations.

Desai valued the diversity of the India she knew when she was growing up in the pluralism of old Delhi, for, as she told Lalita Pandit, "probably the most traumatic event of my childhood was the 15th of August 1947, when the British and Muslim populations disappeared overnight, bringing about the transformation of the old city I knew into the new city of the postpartition era."[32] She compares her mother's exile from the land of her birth with her father's predicament after partition, when having chosen to live in Delhi and not in Dhaka, he could no longer even visit his relatives in East Pakistan, which became Bangladesh. Desai says: "It became the ultimate exile for both of them; cut off from their lands so totally."[33] Nonetheless, in the novel Baumgartner has only limited insight into the religious conflict that rages in Calcutta, despite his sympathy for his Muslim employer who must flee for safety in East Bengal, and, on the other hand, his boss does not understand why he cannot return to Germany now that the European war is over. An episode in the novel demonstrates Baumgartner's inability to assimilate into Indian society. While travelling for business, Baumgartner explores what appears to be a sacred cave, and then inexplicably has the impression that "whatever possessed or inhabited that temple. . .had spat him out. *Raus.* Baumgartner, out. . . . Shabby, dirty white man, firanghi, unwanted. Raus, Baumgartner, raus" (190). The irony here is that in Germany Baumgartner was too dark, and in India his fairness causes him to be rejected as a *firanghi.*[34] Indeed, as Sander Gilman notes, after the Holocaust, Western Diaspora Jews become White and thus "lumped with the forces of patriarchy and oppression by the new forces of multiculturalism."[35] As Anita Desai herself has noted, this episode echoes the Malabar Cave episode in E. M. Forster's novel *Passage to India,* a novel fascinated with the mystique of India. Yet in Forster's novel, this incident and the subsequent unraveling of the incipient relationships between British and Indian characters indicate the difficulty of establishing any true friendship and its repercussions represent a crisis in that attempt to reconcile colonizer and colonized. In Desai's novel, written when Rushdie was inverting the Orientalizing view of India, Baumgartner goes to visit the cave outside a small township in the course of a business trip undertaken on behalf of his Hindu employer, Chimanlal, a man who does invite him to his home and treat him as a valued employee and even a friend, though Baumgartner can never understand why, since he lacks the prestige of an "erstwhile ruler" (183). At first, Baumgartner believes that Chimanlal might like him because he made his first fortune dealing with a Jewish jeweler from Russia, but he discovers that Chimanlal has only the vaguest idea of this man's nationality or religion. Despite this personal connection with Chimanlal, Baumgartner's attempt to achieve some sort of spiritual connection with his adopted homeland is a failure. The mysterious god in the cave rejects him and immediately afterwards, when independence comes to India, Desai writes that Baumgartner is once again on the fringe. Desai's cave episode, in contrast to Forster's, is one more example in this novel of the limitations of imposing European concepts and history onto an Indian or postcolonial reality. The "jew," as the stranger, is the image of that which is inassimilable in the European and the Indian context. Even Forster, in a jarring passage at the end of *Passage to India,* hints at this insight when he has his British functionary, Heaslop, write to Fielding that after being in India through incident after incident, he has decided what is the connecting thread: "it's the Jews."[36]

POSTCOLONIAL POST-HOLOCAUST

For Aamir Mufti, in *Enlightenment in the Colony,* the Enlightenment project's handling of the "Jewish Question" is paradigmatic for the colonization of the Indian sub-continent, yet the Jewish nation is often critiqued in postcolonial discourse as racist in its exclusiveness or colonialist in its displacement of Muslims, thus bearing the sin of Europe's imperialism, so that the very definition of diaspora or the notion of hybridity may exclude Jewish identity.[37] What happens in Desai's novel is that the historical connection between the Holocaust and postcolonialism is explored in ways that draw parallels between German and Indian history, for Hitler's "imagination was caught by the example of the British in India. Their model of imperial rule, such as he conceived it, struck him as admirable. . .for him the Ukraine was 'that new Indian Empire.'"[38] Hugo Baumgartner is released from an internment camp inside India, just as the post-partition riots are peaking in Calcutta, and, in a foreshadowing of his own fate, dreams that the blood being spilt is the blood of his mother, murdered by the Nazis: "Yet his mother—so small, weak—could not have spilt so much blood. Or had she? The blood, ran, ran over the floor and down the stairs, soaking his feet which stood in it helplessly" (179). Hugo recognizes that this conflict is not identical to the genocide which murdered his mother, his family, and his people. That had been a "global war," a "colonial war," and the war into which he is now plunged, in which Muslims kill Hindus and Hindus kill Muslims, is "a religious war. Endless war. Eternal war" (180). Desai comments:

People kill for politics. People kill for religion. Perhaps there is
some kind of affinity between India and Germany. That helped
me bring these two together in the book.[39]

Nonetheless, she has Baumgartner killed by a German and not by an Indian.
The crisis which ultimately leads to Hugo's death begins with Farrokh's
urgent desire to have the German youth who wouldn't pay his bill removed
from his restaurant as quickly as possible, preferably by Baumgartner, whom
the Indian restaurateur identifies as a fellow countryman and therefore as
somehow responsible for him. Indeed, Farrokh sees all those of an inferior
race to him as "mleccha," meat-eating Muslims.

Baumgartner had come to Bombay following the post-partition riots and is
now living a lonely existence after his Hindu partner's son summarily boots
him out of the business upon his father's death. Baumgartner feels
immediately responsible for freeing Farrokh of this unwanted German,
however:

Farrokh had told him nothing—No one had mentioned
Germany—and had not needed to. In the camp, they had looked
at each other covertly, and not only was German-ness stamped
like a number on each, but further information as well—that one
was a Jew, another Aryan. The looks they had exchanged had
been the blades of knives slid quickly and quietly between the
ribs, with the silence of guilt. (21)

As soon as he sees the boy slumped and sleeping in the corner of Farrokh's
café, Baumgartner has a vision of "marching boots," "Wandervogels Lied,"
the songs of the German youth group:

The campfire and the beer. The beer and the yodeling. The
yodeling and the marching. The marching and the shooting. The
shooting and the killing. The killing and the killing and the
killing. (21)

Just as the German nursery rhymes had evoked the memory of the false
security of his early boyhood, so here music, this time yodeling, creates
postmemories of the killing he personally escaped. In fact, the Wandervogels
were misused by the Nazis who appropriated their movement for political
ends and changed their songbooks in order to transmit Nazi ideology.[40]
Despite the visions the German evokes, Baumgartner, seemingly against his

will, agrees to take this youth, Kurt, home with him. Why, he asks himself, "ask your blood why it is so, only the blood knows" (152).

This mysterious tie of blood that Baumgartner undeniably feels between him and his mortal enemy ultimately leads to his death. When this blood tie is recognized between Germans and German Jews, it is usually acknowledged as a tie that binds the perpetrators of the Holocaust to their victims rather than the reverse. Karl Jaspers wrote in one of the earliest treatises on German guilt, "because of our consanguinity, the German—that is, the German-speaking individual" is "co-responsible for the deeds of our con-temporaries. . . . We have to bear the guilt of our fathers."[41] To underscore these inexorable connections Desai drenches her text in references to blood. Lotte's body "thickens and clots" as she returns to her home after Hugo's death; when Baumgartner arrives in Bombay the driver screams until "blood ran from his mouth" (84); the walls of the hotel seem to be streaked with "blood from a gun battle" (84). India is described laughing "that blood-stained laugh" (86). Moreover, in Delhi Kurt had seen hundreds of animals sacrificed and stood with his "feet in blood, his hands in blood, all of him covered in blood" (159). Most of all, Hugo Baumgartner's death seems excessively bloody: "yes, that pale mound of yellow tallow was oozing with something dark, liquid. It was not like blood, it was like a diarrhea of blood" (220). This blood tie between Hugo and Kurt is a direct consequence of their inheritance as sons of perpetrators and victims. And as Hirsch has stated, postmemory "is a consequence of traumatic recall. . .at a generational remove."[42]

At this return to death and blood, we are reminded that the novel began with Lotte fleeing the "blood-spattered scene" on her "high red heels" (1). Indeed, as the opening quotation from "East Coker" proclaims, "In my beginning is my end" (*vii*). Hugo's beginning lies truly in his end. He left the violence of Berlin for India. Then, during the partition riots in Calcutta, Habibullah told him, "Go to Bombay. In Bombay you can do business and not be stabbed in the back when you are going home at night" (169). He goes to Bombay, which becomes by magic the Berlin of thirty years before (194), yet in Bombay he is stabbed by a young German. This is the only death that Desai could envision for him.[43] Baumgartner recognizes when he leaves Calcutta:

His war was not their war. And they had their own war. War within war. Everyone engaged in a separate war, and each war opposed to another war. If they could be kept separate, chaos could be averted. Or so they seemed to think, ignoring the fact that chaos was already upon them. (173)

This view, though geographically removed from the horrors of Germany, explores the legacy of violence the German/Jewish bond of victim and perpetrator represents for the postcolonial world within the nightmare of history. As Eliot writes later on in "East Coker": "The dripping blood our only drink, / The bloody flesh our only food,"[44] but he gestures there towards a Christian redemption that does not exist for Baumgartner or any of the characters in Desai's novel. They are caught in what Hugo calls, "A great web in which each one was trapped, a nightmare from which one could not emerge" (173).

Desai has commented in an interview with Feroza Jussawalla that she wrote two different endings for the novel. In the alternative version, Baumgartner is killed by the beggar who lives outside the door of his apartment building and who, in the final version, is mistakenly arrested for the murder. Desai notes that murder by the beggar, "had no meaning and Baumgartner was left incomplete or unfulfilled in a certain sense, because all through he has a sense of having escaped death in Germany. His mother was killed, but he escaped. The reason for his sadness through the book is the death that he escaped. . . . I had to have it catch up with him in the end and it seemed right and justified in the Greek sense if that death would be by a Nazi, by a German." Desai responded to Feroza Jussawalla's remark that Kurt could be read as a representative of the Germans, that all Germans are interchangeable with German Nazis, so although Kurt did not "see himself as a Nazi, he's too young to have been a Nazi. . . . one shares one's nation's history. The Germans now, even the younger generation, are aware that they haven't escaped the consequences" and this is true even for someone like Kurt in the novel who has destroyed his memory with drugs.[45] According to Desai, as a German, he doesn't have to have personal memories to share in the guilt and responsibility for the past. She declared that in his death Baumgartner must have felt relieved of his guilt over failing to bring his mother to join him in the safety of India. Indeed, although Desai makes associations between postcolonial and Holocaust traumas, between India and Germany, she seems to be saying in conclusion that one is bound by "one's nation's history."

CONCLUSION: ON NOT ARRIVING

In *Baumgartner's Bombay* postmemory of a historical and personal trauma bridges the echoes of Desai's own autobiographical concerns and an epistemological concern with hybridity and cultural identity in the aftermath of catastrophe. Leslie Morris writes in *Unlikely History: The Changing German-Jewish Symbiosis, 1945–2000*:

> as the memory of the Holocaust circulates beyond the actual bounds of lived, remembered experience (and beyond the geographical where the "real" took place), it seeps into the imaginary of other cultures (and other geographical spaces) as postmemory and as postmemoir. Thus the German-Jewish symbiosis is recast as the newly refigured presence of Germans and Jews in texts that probe the contours of memory and the contours of the act of writing and most significantly, in texts that move beyond the contours of Germany.[46]

The "post" according to Morris "is the space conceptualized by post-Holocaust art," art that comprises "in one way or another, hybrid forms of memoir, some false memoirs, some even exposed as fakes. . . ." that circulate "in the present as representation, as melancholia, as elegiac repetition."[47] *Baumgartner's Bombay* is certainly a hybrid novel, compiled of nursery rhymes, the memoirs of the Himalayan mountain climbers, Holocaust memoir, travelogue, and *Bildungsroman*. Yet, according to Desai, her novel began with the memory of the photograph of her German mother's departure for India, and that memory became transfigured in fiction in the image of a young Jewish man leaving his mother behind in Germany and departing from Venice on his way to India in the 1930s. Even in his old age, Baumgartner remembers the week he spent in Venice as something wonderful. He tells the German youth, *"Es war prima."* However, the depiction of Baumgartner's stay in Venice is a "false" memory. He ran away from the surfeit of sweetness he felt there. Significantly, Desai describes his (rather improbable) encounter with a Jewish woman who is reading a newspaper written in Hebrew, which entices him to find the Jewish ghetto in the labyrinth of Venice's streets, a space in which the outsider is always lost, a space that offers a trope for the postcolonial state of homelessness and exile, in fact for a preference for "being not quite right and out of place" (as Edward Said has put it)[48] over being rooted in one spot to a solid self. Baumgartner's failure to find the Ghetto begs explanation. When questioned on this point, Desai answered that in life there must always be something left undone, something that remains to be fulfilled.[49] Indeed, till the end of his life, Hugo remembers Venice as a hybrid mixture of East and West where he fancies he might have felt at home. As he tells Lotte in their old age when she says "there is no home for us,"

> If I could go, if I could leave, then I would go to Venice. . . . Once I was there. . . . It was so strange—it was both East and West, both Europe and Asia. I thought—maybe, in such a place, I could be at home. (81)

Kurt informs him that Venice is "only drains," and Lotte reminds him he could only live in Venice "if he were a duke or a count. . .a millionaire, maybe in your dreams" (81). Desai is not merely rewriting E. M. Forster's *A Passage to India* (as Bryan Cheyette has contended) in mutually exclusive distorted images of Europe and India,[50] but showing that the Orientalist view of India and the Indian view of Europe are equally false images that come together in the construction of "Venice" as an illusory site of strangeness and not belonging (quite different from Rushdie's "imaginary homeland" which we will visit in the next chapter). Thus, we see that Desai's postcolonial "postmemory" of the relationship between German and Jew refigures the historical memory and the metaphorical construction linking the two in a "Venice" to which they have not yet arrived and will never arrive.

NOTES

1. Farrokh, the Parsi owner of the Café Paris, where Baumgartner obtains scraps for his cats, uses the term more disparagingly of Kurt, the German junkie, whom he regards as another White like Baumgartner; see Lies Feryn. "Entangled Memories of the Holocaust and Partition in Anita Desai's *Baumgartner's Bombay*," (master's thesis, University of Ghent, May 2009; http://lib.ugent.be/fulltxt/RUG01/001/414 /388/RUG01-001414388_2010_0001_AC.pdf ; pp. 75-76.

2. Mrinalini Solanki, "Baumgartner's Bombay: An Attempt to Survive," in *Indian Women Novelists,* ed. R. K. Dhawan (New Delhi: Prestige Books, 1995), 2: 1–13; Corinne Liotard, "Otherness in Anita Desai's *Baumgartner's Bombay,"* in *Flight from Certainty,* ed. Anne Luyat and Francine Tolron (Amsterdam: Rodopi, 2001), 112–22; Peter De Voogd, "Anita Desai's Baumgartner," in *Shades of Empire in Colonial and Postcolonial Literatures,* ed. C. C. Barfoot and Theo D'haen (Atlanta: Rodopi, l993), 33–89; Usha Bande, "Baumgartner's Bombay: An Assessment," *Panjab University*

Research Bulletin 20.2 (1 Oct. 1989): 131–33; P. M. Nayak and S. P. Swain, "The Outsider in Desai's Baumgartner's Bombay," *Commonwealth Novel in English* 6 (1993): 112–20. Paul West, "The Man Who Didn't Belong," *New York Times,* 9 Apr. 1989.

3. Corinne Demas Bliss, "Against the Current; A Conversation with Anita Desai," *Massachusetts Review* 29.3 (1988): 522.

4. Anita Desai, *Baumgartner's Bombay* (New York: Houghton, 2000), 5. References to Desai will be to this edition and will be given in parenthesis.

5. Judie Newman, *The Ballistic Bard: Postcolonial Fictions* (London: Arnold, 1995), 53.

6. Another example of the ambiguous connection between Jews and Germans can also be found in Desai's more recent novel set in Mexico, *Zigzag* (2004). The fascinating Dona Vera (who was a dance hall performer like Lotte in *Baumgartner's Bombay*) reinvents herself as an expert on Huichol culture after a frantic escape from Nazi Germany in 1939. Ambiguity surrounds her identity—she might be Jewish (her father was beaten up by the Nazis), but she may have been a collaborator. The novel concludes with another example of the "jew" as universal outsider: in his search for a grandmother's grave in the ruins of a Cornish mine in Mexico. Desai's young English protagonist discovers she is buried on "Jews' Hill," the burial place of anyone "not of their faith" (*Zigzag* [Boston: Houghton, 2004], 155).

7. Marianne Hirsch, *Family Frames: Photography, Narrative and Postmemory* (Cambridge, Mass.: Harvard University Press, 1997), 22.

8. Marianne Hirsch, "The Generation of Postmemory," *Poetics Today* 29.1 (2008): 112–13.

9. Ibid., 120.

10. Public address on receiving the Ca' Foscari Prize at the EACLALS triennial conference, Venice, 25 Mar. 2008, published as "Footsteps on Water," *Wasafiri* 24.1 (2009): 54.

11. Ibid.

12. Shaul Bassi, conversation with the authors, Venice, 26 Mar. 2008.

13. Anita Desai, conversation with the authors. Venice, 26 Mar. 2008.

14. Feroza Jussawalla and Reed Way Dasenbrock, eds., *Interviews with Writers of the Post Colonial World* (Jackson: University Press of Mississippi, 1992), 174.

15. Bliss, "Against the Current," 521.

16. Jussawalla and Dasenbrock, *Interviews with Writers,* 175.

17. Ibid., 15.

18. John Cunningham, "Interview with Anita Desai: 'View from the Outside,'" *Guardian,* 29 June 1988.

19. Ibid.

20. Ibid.

21. Lalita Pandit, "A Sense of Detail and A Sense of Order: Anita Desai Interviewed by Lalita Pandit," in *Literary India: Comparative Studies in Aesthetics, Colonialism and Culture,* ed. Patrick Colm Hogan and Lalita Pandit (Albany: State University of New York Press, l995), 170.

22. Heinrich Harrar, *Seven Years in Tibet* (New York: Tarcher, 1997). See Katherine Capshaw Smith, "Narrating History: The Reality of the Internment Camps in Anita Desai's *Baumgartner's Bombay,*" *Ariel: A Review of International English Literature* 28.2 (l997): 143–57.

23. Smith, "Narrating History," 156.

24. Peter Pulzer, "Emancipation & its Discontents: The German-Jewish Dilemma," Centre for German-Jewish Studies, University of Sussex (1997), http://www.sussex.ac.uk/cgjs/1-2-10-1.html.

25. Eggerz Solveig, "The German-Jewish Epoch of 1743–1933: Tragedy or Success Story?" (2007), http: www.acjna.org/acjna/articles_detail.aspx?id.

26. Axel Stähler has argued that anyone familiar with the German nursery rhymes quoted in the novel would realize their sinister import after the Holocaust ("The Holocaust in the Nursery: Anita Desai's *Baumgartner's Bombay.*" *Journal of Postcolonial Writing* 46. 1 [2010]: 82–84).

27. Stähler, "Holocaust in the Nursery," 80.

28. Quoted in Jonathan Hess, "Sugar Island Jews? Jewish Colonialism and the Rhetoric of 'Civic Improvement' in Eighteenth Century Germany," *Eighteenth Century Studies* 32.1 (Fall 1998): 93.

29. Elaine Y. L. Ho, "The Languages of Identity in Anita Desai's *Baumgartner's Bombay,*" *World Literature Written in English* 32.1 (1992): 101. See also Paul West, "The Man Who Didn't Belong."

30. Anita Desai in conversation with the authors. Venice, Italy, 24 Mar. 2008.

31. Tony Simoes Da Silva, "Whose Bombay is it Anyway? Anita Desai's "Baumgartner's Bombay," *Ariel: A Review of International English Literature* 28.3 (l997): 66, 68.

32. Pandit, "A Sense of Detail," 153.

33. Cunningham, "Interview with Anita Desai."

34. Liotard, "Otherness in Anita Desai's *Baumgartner's Bombay,*" 115.

35. Sander L. Gilman, *Multiculturalism and the Jews* (New York: Routledge, 2006),180.

36. E. M. Forester, *Passage to India.*(San Diego: Harcourt, l984), 345.

37. Aamir R. Mufti, *Enlightenment in the Colony: The Jewish Question and the Crisis of Postcolonial Culture* (Princeton: Princeton University Press, 2007).

38. Mark Mazower quoted in Robert Eaglestone, "'You Would Not Add to My Suffering If you Knew What I have Seen': Holocaust Testimony and Contemporary African Trauma Literature," *Studies in the Novel* 40.1–2 (2008): 73.

39. Cunningham, "Interview with Anita Desai."

40. Bart Plantenga, *Yodel-Ay-Ee-0000* (New York: Routledge, 2004), 62.

41. Karl Jaspers, *The Question of German Guilt* (New York: Fordham University Press, 2000), 73.

42. Hirsch, "Generation of Postmemory," 106.

43. Anita Desai, "Interview with Feroza Jussawalla and Reed Way Dasenbrock," in *Interviews with Writers of the Post-colonial World,* 176.

44. Eliot, *The Complete Poems and Plays, 1909–1950* (New York: Harcourt, 1980), 128.

45. Ibid.

46. Leslie Morris, *Unlikely History: The Changing German-Jewish Symbiosis, 1945–2000* (New York: Palgrave, 2002), 291–92.

47. Ibid., 292–93.

48. Edward Said, *Out of Place: A Memoir* (London: Granta Books, 1999), 295.

49. Anita Desai, in conversation with the authors. Venice, Italy, 26 Mar. 2008. She also admitted she had not visited the ghetto prior to writing the novel, so that she too had to leave something undone.

50. Bryan Cheyette, "Venetian Spaces: Old-New Literatures and the Ambivalent Uses of Jewish History." *Essays and Studies* 53 (2000): 68–71 Cheyette cites a contemporary study by Alex Aronson, *Rabindranath Through Western Eyes* (Calcutta: RDDHI, 1943) as testimony to the sort of German Orientalism in which Baumgartner's mother indulged but fails to note the tragically ironic context in which it is introduced in Desai's novel.

CHAPTER THREE

Hybridity's Children:
Andrea Levy, Zadie Smith, and Salman Rushdie

DIVERSITY OR HYBRIDITY?

In this chapter, we wish to show some of the ways in which the figure of the "jew" in the work of Asian and Caribbean writers in contemporary Britain relates to the self-image of the immigrant and the construction of the Other in a multiethnic society. To what extent does hybridity present a viable identity, and how does this relate to multiculturalism? This is a question that bears directly on perception of the "jew," a figure that is often used to work through the contradictions and tensions of multiple identities—at times absurd and comic—among children of immigrants in Britain. We argue that the figure of the "jew" has been appropriated in postcolonial and postmodern fiction in order to test culturally ascribed, attributed, or "fake" identities which are negotiated in literary texts within a confused debate over cultural diversity.

The English are themselves of hybrid origin, in the original sense of the word, a crossbreed of a domestic and a wild creature, since they trace their history to a coming together of Greco-Roman civilization and primitive savages converted to Christianity. Added to this mix is a series of invasions, occupations, colonization, and immigration. The United Kingdom is itself a forced union of different nationalities: Irish, Scots, Welsh, Cornish, and Manx. The recent revival of the question of whether the English are descended from Celts or Saxons, decided nowadays by genetics rather than philology or physiology, harks back to a racialized discourse which has reemerged against the background of a perceived dissolution of national identity after loss of Empire and integration into Europe. Robert Young has shown that debates over hybridity in Britain in some ways mirror debates in nineteenth-century racial discourse, for hybridity is a concept embedded in cultural construction of nationhood and a racialized reading of history.

Today the notion is often proposed of a new cultural hybridity in Britain, a transmutation of British culture into a compounded composite mode. The condition of that transformation is held out to be the preservation of a degree of cultural and ethnic difference.[1]

Hybridity, for Robert Young, is the articulation of difference between ethnic and racial groups, rather than the fusion of cultural difference in some multicultural homogeneity. In what Young calls "double hybridity," postcolonial minority writing forms a resistance to the representation of ethnic minorities as marginal (Young cites Black film practice).[2] This is a definition of hybridity as a raceless chaos of radical heterogeneity, but we should notice that the sexual anxieties underlying nineteenth-century racial theories have not disappeared altogether, and at the same time we should be aware of the dangers of imposing on race discourse metaphorical uses of hybridity.[3] Susheila Nasta has commented, with reference to Young's study on the proliferation of uses of "hybridity" and its politicization in postcolonial theories, that often hybridity in South Asian writing in Britain strives through creolization to fuse formerly antagonistic identities. Such a fusion, she urges, would avoid determinism and essentialism in order to give expression to what Kureishi sees as the principal trope of the twentieth century, the immigrant.[4]

In fact, social anthropologist Pnina Werbner has argued that recent immigrant diaspora cultures tend themselves to be hybrid, and that postcolonial British fiction by South Asian writers has taken the place of transgressive rituals in their original communities which traditionally satirize sacred forms and restrictive practices in a carnivalesque parody. Werbner is referring here to Homi Bhabha's assertion that cultures are not unitary, and that cultural knowledge is never transparent.[5] Caribbean and South Asian immigrants have traditionally identified themselves as characteristically hybrid in a host society they regard as their mother country which is whole, pure and "real," an attitude they may bring with them from the former colonies. Ralph Singh expresses his rejection of colonial existence in V. S. Naipaul's *The Mimic Men* (1967) when he states,

> To be born on an island like Isabella, an obscure New World transplantation, second-hand and barbarous, was to be born to disorder. From an early age, almost from my first lesson at school about the weight of the king's crown, I had sensed this.[6]

When placed within the historical context of the encounter with modernity, a complex picture emerges of a dynamic response to multi-culturalism from within immigrant communities in contemporary Britain, while at the same time race discourse has become politicized. As Hanif Kureishi's novel *Something to Tell You* (2008) reveals, politics is still responsible for defining the identity of Others in England:

> When I was with my grandfather, I more or less passed for white. Sometimes people asked if I were "Mediterranean"; otherwise, there were few Asian people were we lived. Most whites considered Asians to be "inferior," less intelligent, less everything good. Not that we were called Asian then. Officially, as it were we were called "immigrants," I think. Later, for political reasons, we were "blacks." But we always considered ourselves to be Indians. In Britain we are still called Asians, though we're no more Asian than the English are European. It was a long time before we became known as Muslims, a new imprimatur, and then for political reasons.[7]

The ambiguity of the identity of the British-born children of immigrants from South Asia is compounded here by their self-perception, which is molded in the image of ethnic minorities created by the host society.

It's rather like what happens in Salman Rushdie's *Satanic Verses* (1988), the novel which earned the author a *fatwa* from the authorities in Teheran, when Saladin Chamcha finds himself arrested as an illegal immigrant and becomes demonized into the image which the English have formed of him. He has learnt to wear White masks at public school, and his profession is actual mimicry, yet his cherished and hard-won Englishness receives hard blows (not least when he is beaten by policemen or when his English wife throws him out). In *The Satanic Verses,* the lascivious Zeeny upbraids Chamcha for faking an English identity and making his living by impersonating voices on the radio together with his archetypal Jewish counterpart Mimi Mamoulian. But Zeeny and her pseudo-Bollywood crowd are no more authentic. Chamcha, in fact, flees India in horror at the grotesque scenario of Zeeny colluding with his father's bizarre and ghoulish domestic arrangements. Mamoulian, a tiny neurotic Jewish-Armenian woman, ab-surdly claims to be speculating in improbable property deals as therapy for her traumatic history.[8] Mimi's voice talking on the phone to the battered and goatish Chamcha from New York is what Bhabha calls the "siren song" of postmodern urban migrants and minorities.[9] She tells Chamcha she knows postmodern critiques of Western society talk of pastiche that flattens out individuals, but she consciously becomes the bubble bath she is paid to advertise: she willingly embraces her fake identity.

> Don't teach me about exploitation. We had exploitation when you-plural were running round in skins. Try being Jewish, female and ugly sometime. You'll beg to be black. Excuse my French: brown.[10]

For cash, Mimi is quite willing to be flattened into nobody, just as Chamcha has created a simulacrum out of his love and his life. Unfortunately, Mimi does not listen to Chamcha's warning about exploitation, lets herself be taken in by a con-artist, and lands up in jail. Perhaps it is appropriate that Chamcha, after literally falling from the sky and being arrested as an illegal immigrant, has been transformed into the very devil, as if to say that immigrants and other outcasts eventually turn into the demons and monsters they have been described as. Surfing TV channels, Chamcha is treated to an array of hybridity and crossbreeding, including mutant aliens on the popular children's TV series *Doctor Who* called "Mutilasians," the high priests of mutilated and mechanized bodies on the Coca-Cocalized postmodern planet. At least these monstrosities and particularly the mundane grafting of garden trees bring him down to prosaic reality, and he begins to shed his own mutant/mutilated attributes of horns and hooves.[11] The joke is that Chamcha disparages any identification with "his" people and prides himself on being British; certainly, in the English imagination a Jewish consort to Satan would be quite familiar and, in truth, the English imagination has projected its fears of aliens (from Jews to extraterrestrials) into monstrous and mutant forms.

In Rushdie's send-up of hybridity, dark supernatural forces lock English and Asians alike in witchcraft, voodoo practices, and satanic worship, leaving Hind to regret her husband has brought her to this "country full of jews and strangers."[12] Chamcha vents his demonic fire on the Thatcher effigy which stands for discrimination and repression, but also vents his fire at his double/antagonist, Gibreel Farishta, reincarnated as an archangel, who beds down with another fugitive from fake identities, Alleluia Cone, a famed mountaineer who suffers from flat feet. Alleluia is daughter of Otto, a Holocaust survivor who passed as English gentry. His wife, Alicija, a former

Polish Jewish concentration camp inmate, throws off the false identity forced on her and returns to the family's original name, Cohen, as well as to Chanuka, synagogue, and soup dumplings in Bloom's (when it was still in Whitechapel). Ignorant of the finer points of Paki-bashing a mere block away, her daughter climbs Everest and flings herself into a passionate affair with the revenant Indian film-star Gibreel Farishta resurrected as a schizophrenic failing/fallen archangel who at first resists his Blakean visions from *The Marriage of Heaven and Hell* and is identified by Alicija as a *dybbuk* from the Singer brothers.

In the continual metamorphosis of postmodern identities, amplified by a continual seeping of dreams and myths into reality, migrancy itself is a potent metaphor for the oscillating metamorphoses of postmodernity,[13] where there is no inside or outside the dream, no fixing transnationalism on the map or choosing between the many doublings of the novel, yet hybrid and alternating identities provide no protection against tyranny, fanaticism, and genocide. Moreover, Chamcha's mimicry results in his having no self to fall back on when he does return to India to tend to his dying father and redeem the magic lantern, yet he does find some peace in accepting his mutability (Ovidian malleability) and accepting death, unlike Gibreel who has disastrously attempted to move beyond the boundaries of Lucretian fixities.[14]

As Homi Bhabha has described hybridity in colonial India, it is fundamentally ambivalent, resisting the originary claims of Englishness and Christianity, while mimicking in mottled camouflage the discourse of colonial power and subverting its discursive attempt to elide difference into transparency. In this ambivalent relationship, the colonial subject mimics the colonizer but always with a difference, thus producing both a resemblance and a menace.[15] Homi Bhabha's by now celebrated insight into colonial mimicry of Englishness explains the formation of cultural hybridity in ways that may be carried over into the post-colonial era. The opening of V. S. Naipaul's *The Mimic Men* has been called the "ur-text" of postcolonial mimicry,[16] and provides an excellent example of how the archetypal "jew" transmutes into a metaphorical otherness that can be used to negotiate Anglicization. In the words of the Anglophile Ralph Singh in his initial excitement at being in London, in Mr. Shylock's Kensington boarding-house:

> I paid Mr Shylock three guineas a week for a tall, multi-mirrored, book-shaped room with a coffin-like wardrobe. And for Mr Shylock, the recipient each week of fifteen times three guineas,

the possessor of a mistress and of suits made of cloth so fine I felt
I could eat it, I had nothing but admiration. I was not used to the
social modes of London or to the physiognomy and complexions
of the North, and I thought Mr Shylock looked distinguished, like
a lawyer or businessman or politician. He had the habit of
stroking the lobe of his ear and inclining his head to listen. I
thought the gesture was attractive; I copied it. I knew of recent
events in Europe; they tormented me; and although I was trying
to live on seven pounds a week I offered Mr Shylock my fullest,
silent compassion.[17]

Here we have English tropes of the "jew" as the usurious, greedy landlord,
whose material and sexual extravagance can only impress the naïve
newcomer, unfamiliar with the "social modes" of London, which he takes to
be the norm, rather than antisemitic caricature, unused as he is to the
"physiognomy and complexions of the North," which in this context might
well be North London, that is, the Jewish territory of Golders Green,
mistaken for the usual faces and skin colors one would expect to meet in
Northern Europe. This amusing play on the ambiguity of the "jew's" identity
ironically places the Indian in identification with the archetypal Orientalized
Other in the split-consciousness of the narrative, while his ready sympathy
for the Jews' suffering in the Holocaust makes him complicit with his own
exploitation. In his desire to mimic English social modes, the Indian with
brown skin "in a white mask" (to paraphrase Fanon),[18] unwittingly mis-
perceives the model of mimicry and in this "multi-mirrored" coffin of a room
mirrors instead the antisemitic image of the Other and foreshadows his own
disappointments and failures.

ANDREA LEVY'S SMALL ISLANDS

The hybridity which Bhabha discerns in the act of mimicry in colonial India
can be seen in the new immigrant's mimicry of English ways before the end
of colonialism and may literally give birth to a real, non-metaphorical
hybridity. Andrea Levy, herself of mixed Jewish and Caribbean descent,
chooses in her novel, *Small Island* (2004)[19] to place her characters within a
particular postcolonial moment at the end of the Second World War, in a
Britain struggling to confront its imperial past and to come to terms with the
reality of its post-imperial multi-racial present. Each of her central four

characters, Queenie and Bernard Bligh, who are White English, and Gilbert and Hortense Joseph, who are Black Jamaican, take on a critical political stance in postwar England, a country which Levy reveals to be as small-minded as the small island of Jamaica. The two couples symbolically represent White and Black England, and their interaction demonstrates the way in which the colonized Others who flocked to England became the force against which British society, since the mid-twentieth century, defined and constituted its identity.

Hybrid identity is a dominant theme in the novels of the West Indies, where the great majority of the population are descendants of people who came as slaves or under duress from somewhere else, and the Jew is a "handy means of exploring the problem of identity."[20] In *Small Island,* the immigrant couple contains a hybrid member, Gilbert, whose father was a Jew. In a culture in which every gradation of color matters, Levy describes Gilbert's father as having "black curling hair and pale olive skin, 'a circumcised member of the Jewish faith'"(108). Yet, he is always telling his nine children how he saved them from being Jews by finding Jesus on the battlefield at Ypres and converting to Christianity. He claims that the community cast him out upon his conversion, and this is what Levy says happened to her own father who was born Jewish and converted.[21] Gilbert's father tells them about his Bar Mitzvah ceremony and the Jewish holidays, yet he drags them off to the Anglican Church, where they are barely tolerated by the Whites. After surveying Caribbean novels in which Jewish characters appear, Sue Greene concludes that the Jewish characters not only highlight the West Indian problem of identity, but they also stand apart from the culture and function as its conscience. In fact, a character who takes on the role of the political activist or moral compass in these Caribbean novels is often mistaken for a Jew—has a Jewish name, or is a refugee—is, so to speak, a "fake Jew." By the same token, despite the identification of Jews with the oppressed, Jewish characters can easily become, especially outside the islands, the oppressive "Shylock" landlord who appears, for example, in the opening of Naipaul's *The Mimic Man.*[22]

In *Small Island,* when Gilbert sees pictures in the papers of Jews humiliated in Germany, he recalls his father's rejection as a Jew in Jamaica. He enlists in the RAF to fight Hitler because he understands what it means to be the archetypal victim, or as he says, in words that curiously reverse Frantz Fanon's statement of identification with the Jew: "my father was a Jew and my brother is a black man."[23] Though Levy makes it clear that being a Jew is not the same as being White, Gilbert is nonetheless rejected by his cousin Elwood when he leaves for London after the war. Elwood declares: "You may look like one of us but no'in'gon' change the fact your daddy is a white man" (173). As a Jew and a Black man, Gilbert is constructed by Levy as both doubly colonized and belonging nowhere. Perhaps it is not only for autobiographical reasons, but also to indicate this double oppression that she gives Gilbert a twin brother like her own father.

Levy brings the two couples together in 1948 in that over-used trope of a traditional English home to work out the condition of England. The White woman, Queenie Bligh, was raised to look at a map of the world and believe she had "the whole world at [her] feet" (6). She marries above her to a man who is sent overseas to India during the Second World War, where he looks at every Indian as a coolie or a wog. Bernard Bligh, spurred on by a comrade in arms to prove his manhood, abuses a child prostitute; his fear of having caught syphilis makes him delay his return to England, and when he returns home, he finds it has been transformed by Blacks. The threat is racial and sexual, but he cannot see that he himself might be sexually and morally tainted.

The Jamaican, Gilbert Joseph, serves in the RAF as a commonwealth volunteer and he cannot understand the Geordie villagers, nor can they make sense of his blackness. The colonial attitudes of the British army thwart his ambitions to become an engineer and he is relegated to the duties of a truck driver. As such, he discovers the active racism of the Americans stationed in Britain who practice the segregation still in force in the States. As a British soldier he should not be subject to segregation, but as a Black he cannot be treated as an equal. In a series of misfortunes, his commanding officer has his revenge on the arrogant Americans by sending a colored man to collect a delivery, but he is mocked into his subaltern status. Later, in a racial brawl between American servicemen, Queenie's father-in-law dies as an accidental bystander, and this incident shows how far the color line could be taken on British soil.

Gilbert later returns to England on the legendary *Windrush,* and finds lodgings with Queenie, who is waiting for her husband to return from overseas. He is joined six months later by his educated Jamaican wife, Hortense, who describes her skin as "the color of warm honey" (59) and is shocked to find that no English school will employ her as a teacher. The mother country does not want to recognize its own children, and Hortense is shunned when Queenie takes her shopping, a lone Black woman on a White street that tries to keep up its class pretensions (as we see during the Blitz, when Queenie finds there is resistance to billeting a working-class woman and her children). But little prepares us for Queenie giving birth to a Black man's child, a classic scenario of the dark alien usurping the serviceman's marital bed, a double shock to Bernard who returns after the war to find Blacks in his house and himself cuckolded by a Black. Ineffectually struggling to prove himself master of the house. Bernard Bligh comes back from India to a changed England that appears to have shrunk into a very small island. Levy does not conclude with a multicultural paradise, and Queenie's child, unlike Helen Schlegel's in *Howard's End,* does not inherit the ancestral home. The Jamaican couple does find a home of their own, but it is into their arms that Queenie hands her baby, while she throws in her lot with Bernard and life in the suburbs. Moreover, when Gilbert attempts to persuade the Englishman of the rightness of this new multicultural age in moving rhetoric and stirring language, arguing that they have both fought for the same country (435), his wife is impressed with his nobility of character. However, Bernard's only response is "I'm sorry. . .but I just can't understand a single word you're saying" (435). To the White Englishman, the subaltern cannot speak, his language is still "damaged," still a salient marker of difference.

Gilbert Joseph is the son of a Jewish father, and as such, Levy implies, he knows what it means to be the ultimate victim. In all her novels up to and including *Small Island,* Levy explores the story of first and second generation Jamaican immigrants in Britain. Levy's novels show Jamaica's legacy of slavery, in a common English, Scottish, Indian, or Spanish ancestry, so that Jamaicans must deal not only with the racism around them, but also come to terms with their own hybrid identities. In Levy's novels those with Jewish ancestry, however, even when they have converted to Christianity, are shown to be excluded from both the Jewish and Black communities; to be part Jewish, apparently, is not just to be part White. In *Small Island,* Gilbert's father tells Elwood, the boy he raises until his mother shows up when he is ten, that now that his mother has appeared, "he could rest easy because he was certainly not Jewish" (164).

Levy's construction of Caribbean Jewishness assumes an importance larger than the small number of two hundred Jews left in Jamaica, mostly intermarried and interracial. In Levy's work Jewishness appears to be an exclusionary marker of identity within Jamaican hybridity, and it is mentioned in nearly all of Levy's novels. Her first semi-autobiographical novel, *Every Light in the House Burnin,* for example, traces the inadequate care the father Winston Jacobs receives in the NHS hospital, where he is being treated for cancer. Though he is not Jewish, he "passes" as one because of his name, so that instead of calling a Church of England priest when he dies, the hospital personnel call a Rabbi.[24] In that novel being mistaken for a Jew is the final humiliation in Jacobs' long and degrading hospital stay.

The achievement of a unified identity is the goal of Levy's Jamaican-British heroine in her third novel, *The Fruit of the Lemon,* Faith Jackson. She is born in Britain, the daughter of Black parents, but she lives and works with White colleagues and friends. Her alterity is emphasized by a number of racial incidents that lead to her nervous breakdown. Her parents send her back to the "homeland" she has never seen in order to resolve her identity issues. There, in the second half of the novel, she finds out the stories of her relatives and her mixed heritage and, again, Jewishness is singled out as inassimilable; it seems that one of her relatives turned down a young man because "half of him was Jewish."[25]

Small Island describes a Britain struggling to confront its imperial past and to come to terms with the reality of its post-imperial, multi-racial present. Small islands are what Jamaicans call the other islands in the Caribbean, but when Gilbert returns to Jamaica after his stint in the RAF he realizes that his island too is small. Hortense describes how she was sent to live with cousins who could offer her more opportunities for education and advancement because, as the illegitimate daughter of a White father, it was felt that she was entitled to more privileges than her own mother could offer her. These distinctions, as Levy describes them, are not recognized at all by White English people. Hortense belongs to the class of Jamaicans that Levy describes as the class of her own family. As Levy has said in an interview:

> My parents came from a class in Jamaica called "the coloured class." There are white Jamaicans, black Jamaicans and coloured Jamaicans. My parents' skin was light. They were mixed race, effectively. They came to Britain with a kind of notion that pigmentation represented class. They didn't necessarily have more money or education, but because they were somehow closer to being white, this was seen as a badge of pride. . . . My parents

arrived here and were surprised to discover that they were considered black. They thought that people would look at them as white. That sounds very funny now, but it can set up quite a conflict in a family. I was growing up knowing that things were so completely different. I didn't have any subtleties of shade. If someone didn't want to be my friend because I was black, that was it.[26]

Like Hortense, Levy's parents came to England dressing and speaking in a way they thought proper, but were confronted by notices in the windows saying "no dogs, niggers or Irish" and a country turned upside down by war. Levy thinks of herself as English "born and bred," even though her color raises eyebrows when she says this.[27] Empire for her family may have been the great mother, but it was a divisive one.

In *Small Island,* as critics have noted, Levy defiantly writes back to empire. Queenie, the Englishwoman, was raised to believe that she had "the whole world at [her] feet" (6). Yet, from the moment she shakes hands with the African man at the Empire Exposition as a child, until the climactic moment when she bears a Black child whom she conceived with a Jamaican RAF officer during the war, she becomes more and more identified with those characters who possess bodies that are marginalized and rejected by the society her husband Bernard represents: the Black, the Jew, the poor, and the disabled. Their Jewish neighbor is interned as a German national, and Bernard comments: "These Jews are more trouble than they're worth" (221). Bernard enlists, and Queenie is left with his father who is unable to speak due to the trauma of the last war. To make ends meet, she takes in West Indian tenants and is stigmatized in the neighborhood for flouting colonial, patriarchal roles of behavior. The last chapter belongs to Hortense, and in it Queenie's voice is effectively silenced. The Jamaican couple is moving into their new home and their life in England seems to be looking up. Only Gilbert's Jewishness seems to present a darker element, and though this is a work of fiction it may be that it derives from perceptions of Jewish separateness, as well as stories Levy heard about her grandfather's own banishment from and abandonment of his family. According to Levy her father

was born Jewish. His family had been in Jamaica for generations, but originated from North Africa. My grandfather had "married out," to a woman of Indian/African/Spanish descent and had taken the Christian faith while fighting in the war. His Jewish family disowned him and all his issue.[28]

These biblical sounding words, "and all his issue," resound against the promise of hybridity and the possibility of raising a child in an interracial household.

ZADIE SMITH'S HYBRID COMEDY

In a zanier take on hybridity, Zadie Smith's *White Teeth* (2000)[29] also writes back to Empire, as Phyllis Lassner has shown.[30] *White Teeth* brings the offspring of Asian and Caribbean immigrants into contact with a Jewish family only to resist the discourse of successful multiculturalism and ethnic diversity and to respond with a more complex narrative that pits ambiguities and accommodation with mixed identities against technology.[31] Joyce and Marcus Chalfen represent an elitist intellectual position devoid of communal ties: Joyce forcefully applies a horticultural Darwinism to human relations and Marcus experiments with a new transgenic breed of FutureMouse©— ironically, his mentor is a Nazi doctor whom Archie failed to kill during the war. Marcus, who is himself descended from immigrants, is the stereotypical liberal Jewish intellectual, still lustfully in love with his English wife's white flesh and pear-shaped body. Both Marcus and Joyce are fatally fascinated by the beautiful brown creatures they have adopted, whom they wish, like the colonialists before them, to educate.

The subjects of their social experiment in cultural cross-fertilization are Millat Iqbal and Irie Jones. Irie does not see anything problematic in Marcus' conversion from Judaism to therapy (as Smith jokes about the Jews' new secular faith in Freud and psychoanalysis); she only sees order and purity, above all freedom from the fears and conflicts in her own home (327–28). Most of all, she wishes for a neutral space and freedom from the anxieties of her roots and the pressures of ethnic identity. Each side harbors misconceptions of the other, lured by a multiculturalism that conceals, in the Chalfens' social and scientific determinism, a large measure of intervention and self-interest. The parents of Millat and Irie fear their children are being taken away from them, away from their ethnic roots, and away from their cultural values—not that Samad is a fervent Muslim, and his losing battle with the self-restraint so much admired by English women provides a laugh through the novel's sitcom scenes.

The melodramatic showdown at the climactic end of the novel suggests that when the promiscuous corrupt West is pitted against radical Islamism, animal rights militants, or Witnesses expecting the millennial apocalypse, there is little to defend besides inebriated, doped hedonism. The British display a moral cowardice in facing the evil of Nazism, as well as a general failure to face the "fundamentals" of life. Marcus Chalfens himself represents a parody of humanistic liberalism that threatens ethnic minorities because the Chalfens' patronizing championing actually severs their adopted subjects from their cultural roots. Though the object of envy for second-generation immigrants like Irie, they embody what fundamentalists like the KEVIN group (an unfortunate acronym) see as the evil infidel West, and what fanatics like the animal rights activists whom their son Joshua joins regard as the enemy of mankind. In fact, Smith treats fundamentalism itself to a satirical deconstruction, inviting us to get back to "fundamentals" and live life as it is, but also asking us to understand the complexities behind our ready stereotypes.[32]

The Autograph Man (2002)[33] similarly constructs anti-essentialist identities in a mixed heritage, Chinese and Jewish. Yet here the mix produces a confusion of no-identities: "hybridity" dissolves in a heterogeneity in which everyone is performing a role in a movie. Alex-Li Tandem has slit-eyes and shortly before his Bar Mitzvah, he thinks of the Jewish thing as something one is landed with, not by choice. Later, he starts to write a book (inspired by *The Essential Lenny Bruce*)[34] that divides the world arbitrarily into Jewish and Goyish, an attempt to define what is indefinable and culturally given, which says something about the comic absurdity of maintaining any one single identity. His friend Rabbi Mark Rubinfine tells him he is wasting his life, while another friend, the Black Hebrew Adam, doubts his sanity. Adam Jacobs, the primal and authentic Jew, seeks enlightenment in kabbala, but Alex cannot fathom unity in nothingness, perhaps because he cannot connect with anything or anyone, including his mother. Anything might substitute for anything, there might be a tree of the ten *sefirot* of Elvis Presley, for culture is whatever you plug in, as long as you know the in-jokes and the international sign language—there is something for everyone. The novel's take on Judaism is esoteric, seeing it as a cultural artifact not to be taken too seriously in the flood of unconnected trivia and films or novels being parodied as Alex periodically loses control and does damage to his car or to his girlfriend Esther.

The Autograph Man is a collector of famous people's names, cultural artifacts or collectibles, many faked. He imagines that he is the savior of objects that would otherwise be lost. Collectibles are what stand—in their false reassurance—between the self and death. This is a parody of Multiculturalism the Movie, starring a man with no faith or community, with nothing to cling to except marijuana and sexual fantasies, in a broken world of sick, damaged people who are like players on a mah-jongg board (119). At one point, Alex makes a note that life is *not* a movie. The main thing, Alex feels, is not to let the interface have power over him. Yet the interface of "kabbala" and "Zen" remains the irresolvable puzzle of the two halves of the novel. They are the *ying* and *yang* of the same bagel—London and New York—and of the puzzle of Alex-Li Tandem.

Alex cannot believe in redemption, and spirituality simply does not work for him, but at the end, he finds some kind of fulfillment when he inadvertently rescues Kitty Alexander from oblivion and brings her from cinematic myth to the fictional reality of his flat in Mountjoy in north London (the thinly disguised Willesden of Smith's own childhood). The concluding Kaddish which he says for his non-Jewish father is neither a culminating joy nor resolution, but it does perform a gesture to his friends and his lover Esther Jacobs, a gesture that amounts to no commitment beyond a temporary improvisation or donning of a mask.[35] Outwardly fulfilling his filial duty to a non-Jewish father, he cannot help noticing that all the characters who have come together in the synagogue are cynically preoccupied with their own selves and bodies. He remains egocentrically self-enclosed, childishly dependent on their love, waiting on line for the next scene in life-to-go. If anything comes together in the little boxes he has been trying to keep separate (not to mention the women he has been trying to keep separate), it is in this qualified acceptance of an imperfect world of multiple identities and multiple possibilities. This is heterogeneity amid a postmodern complexity, not some new hybrid development.

Multiculturalism can give writers from ethnic minorities a feeling of having a voice, but it can also place that voice as regional or as minority. If Monica Ali or Zadie Smith have entered the mainstream of British fiction, this may partly have to do with an ethnic tag that is placed on their work and may not necessarily characterize them as writers. Monica Ali's second novel, for example, is set in Portugal, and Zadie Smith's next novel, *Beauty,* deals with personal relationships among academics in New England. Smith's first two novels, as we have seen, do not vindicate a hybridity that sits easily with cultural or ethnic identity, nor do they resolve the tensions between deracination and a dangerous search for roots that leads to fundamentalism. Moreover, let us not forget that Smith, like Salman Rushdie, and Hanif Kureishi, is writing for a wider English readership, as well as an intellectual elite among second-generation Asian immigrants.[36] The satire of the absurdities of integrating as Asians into Englishness represents at best the view of a minority in Britain's South Asian community, while Andrea Levy and Zadie Smith have entered a mainstream British multicultural tradition, far from the concerns on the ground of immigrant communities.

RUSHDIE'S IMAGINED HOMELANDS

Salman Rushdie is often said to embrace hybridity, but what he actually writes in his 1982 essay "Imaginary Homelands" presents a somewhat less simple picture. Rushdie straddles two continents and only the English language can help him establish an international, extraterritorial voice. Typically, Rushdie grew up in middle-class Bombay with an admiration for a "dream-England" of cricket and fair play; but he knows that his easy acceptance results from "my social class, freak fair skin and my 'English' English accent"[37]; we might add his schooling at Rugby. India is an entirely imagined homeland, but the "stain" of racism makes England feel less of a homeland than an imagined India, misremembered in *Midnight's Children,* as if to show that all memory is phony to some extent, but that it is this unstable re/deconstruction of the past on which we build our identities.

Rushdie's vision of Britain is stereoscopic, divided by the color line, as Rushdie remarks in "The New Empire within Britain" (1984).[38] Hybridity has to be understood in the context of the postwar creation of a new empire of immigrant workers from the former colonies who were imported into Britain in the 1950s as cheap labor and treated as colonials in their own country. Multiculturalism, Rushdie declared in the Thatcherite and Orwellian year of 1984, is a sham, a catchword like racial harmony. The official policy of integration is intended to encourage the forced assimilation and policing of the Black population.[39] Homeland, then, can only be imagined, and hybridity is nothing more than a loose summing up of the multiple identities and cultures that constitute the fluid transnational and crosscultural contradictions of postmodernity.

Certainly, in Rushdie's *The Moor's Last Sigh* (1995), hybridity is a slippery creature that is as much a construct as some imaginary pure racial origin. Indeed, all constructions, including Aurora's hybrid art and the hybrid plot of the novel, stand on crumbling mythic foundations. However, stand they do. Rushdie's house of fiction is a "jamboree of creative confusion" built on shifting sands, "a compromised construction whose undoing is written into its being from the start."[40]

As with all stories, people tell different versions. There is no more hegemony over history and all master narratives are suspect. And the Jewish story of diaspora—the mother of all diasporas—is the paradigm for such crumbling of the myths that hold together nations and families. This realization enables a revisioning of India as seen through the *Western* yet marginalized eyes of Spanish Jews and Portuguese Christians that offers a postcolonial fiction of modernity.[41] After Abraham Zogoiby has discovered the doubted and perhaps doubtful story of his ancestry, he questions

> his mother with old papers bound up 'twixt twine and hide. 'Who is the author?' he asked, and, as she remained silent, answered himself: 'A woman.' And, continuing with this catechism: 'What was her name?—Not given.—What was she?—A Jew; who took shelter beneath the roof of the exiled Sultan; beneath his roof, and then between his sheets. Miscegenation,' Abraham baldly stated, 'occurred.' And though it would have been easy enough to feel compassion for this pair, the dispossessed Spanish Arab and the ejected Spanish Jew—two powerless lovers making common cause against the power of the Catholic Kings—still it was the Moor alone for whom Abraham demanded pity. 'His courtiers sold his lands, and his lover stole his crown.' After years by his side, this anonymous ancestor crept away from crumbling Boabdil, and took ship for India, with a great treasure in her bag, and a male child in her belly; from whom, after many begats, came Abraham himself. *My mother who insists on the purity of our race, what say you to your forefather the Moor?*[42]

If he is descended from miscegenation between a legendary Moorish prince, Boabdil *el zogoibi* (the unfortunate), and a runaway Jewess, he should disbelieve his mother's claim to purity of race. Moreover, the story of racial hybridity itself tempts us to substitute fiction for history. In fact, the Jew as emblem of hybridity is destined for extinction, as evidenced by the diminishing number of unmarried elderly Jews in Cochin. This is an extinction furthered by Abraham's own elopement with Aurora, the heiress of a wealthy Christian family of Indian spice traders. Unlike the biblical patriarch, Abraham manages not to sacrifice his son to his mother's desire to return him to the Jewish God. The bond is forfeit, yet he proves a Shylock of dubious moral qualities, living up to antisemitic stereotypes of the "jew" when he becomes involved in prostitution and shady business deals,[43] but also demonstrating "the destructive effects of rapacious globalism in India" with his mock-Satanic plan to eradicate any trace of local character in Bombay.[44] When Abraham gets involved in terrorism, his son puts his foot down and reminds his father, the divine creator of his world and his body, a wrathful and jealous anti-God, that he is a Jew. The father has only scorn for Cochin Jews and scoffs at his son's new-found Jewish identity, which is more a moral plea than an ethnic stance.

But then Abraham's betrayals and deceits, his drug trafficking and corruption, merely reflect the larger state of the nation and the world, where Black and White cannot be sifted apart:

> The city itself, perhaps the whole country was a palimpsest, Under World beneath Over World, black market beneath white; when the whole of life was like this, when invisible reality moved phantomwise beneath a visible fiction, subverting all its meanings, how then could Abraham's career have been any different? (184).

Because, continues the narrator with his explanation of life's mystery, none of us leads an authentic life, we are all trapped by the "fakery of the real," by its "weeping-Arab kitsch of the superficial," so how could "we have penetrated to the full, sensual truth of the lost mother below?" (184–85). It is not just that Abraham has created something *ex nihilio,* an invisible city reclaimed from the sea, but life itself is really a sleight of hand, a fake, and real identities are actually palimpsests of stories and images.

The mythic narratives are defeated, and hybridity seems untrustworthy as an anchor of identity. Yet hybridity does not totally dissolve, but remains as an empty signifier of postmodern multiple identities, themselves representations, like the hybrid fortress of the Moor in Aurora's paintings of her son, the Moor series, which look more strongly autobiographical than life, as if interpretative representations could shape reality as well as history. Aurora's art is based on a palimpsest, or Palimpstine, as she calls it (226), in which worlds and dreams flow into each other, collide, and wash away. In the "Aurorised" (un-authorized) version of the Boabdil legend, Spain and India merge in "Mooristan" so that imaginary homelands and imagined histories coexist, mingle, and contradict each other. In her evolving vision of the "Black Moor," Aurora reflects the troubled mother-son relationship by portraying herself as the stabbed Desdemona and her prematurely aging son as Othello, a characteristic transformation of the intertextuality that dogs and undermines the novel and tangles the relation of art and life, fantasy and fact, into a twisted conundrum, never to be unraveled, constantly rereading itself and reviewing if not revising history, a romp through Western culture that writes against empire in a playful postmodern way.[45]

The Othello connection, as Jonathan Greenberg observes, is a hidden undercurrent that has unexpected significance for Rushdie's use of the palimpsest to delve into ethnic difference, as well as to demonstrate how literature over the centuries accrues diverse meanings through overlayering, through ambiguities, and through textual confusions, though the reference to the base Indian/Jew in the last sigh of Shakespeare's Moor, in Othello's last speech (rather than Desdemona's sigh), is arcane and elided.[46] Othello dies testifying to the impossible split between black face and European mask, between his roles as insider and outsider, defender of the state and rebel.[47] The Moor's death in Rushdie's novel marks not the continuity of racial difference (as we will see in Caryl Phillips' *The Nature of Blood* in the next chapter), but the effacement of racial and cultural difference in India's turn toward nationalism;[48] Rushdie's Aurora is an anti-Portia, who does not dismiss the Moor, but reclaims the multiracial terms of love and justice as she herself is "near the height of her very Indian beauty" (an allusion to Bassanio's line in *The Merchant of Venice*, III, 2).[49] Jew and Moor share common space as vulnerable wanderers in a story of murders most foul.[50]

The hybrid pluralist nation is represented in Aurora's paintings as a multiple crowd in fancy-dress balls in a golden age of all ages and religions, a "patchwork quilt of man" (227), an Andalusian multiculturalism that one critic sees as setting up parallels between Moorish Spain and Mughal India in Rushdie's novel,[51] although factually Jewish participation in Moorish culture and politics was only part of a complex story of Jewish-Muslim coexistence in the Iberian peninsula over several centuries, which included persecution (Maimonides had to flee to Egypt) and segregation (intermarriage was discouraged by both groups).[52] In any case, in Rushdie's novel, hybridity gradually turns from being an ideal unity of opposites, with the Moor as a standard-bearer of the pluralism that is India, into a Baudelairean flower of evil with the Moor as a figure of decay, a motherless "creature of shadows, degraded in tableaux of debauchery and crime" (303). This transformation of the Moor's hybridity is, moreover, reflected in his physical deformity, a gift that is self-destructive, like his magic realist premature aging (which Gilman has diagnosed as Werner's syndrome). [53] Typically for Rushdie's writing, this metonym of the break-up of the nation's body is also symptomatic of the pathological disappearance of the ancient legendary Jew in the present. His deformed fist is a source of light and miracle in Aurora's eroticized imagination, yet it is also at once a source of brute power and of his downfall, as when it fatally attracts Uma and murders Mainduck. Rushdie means this to represent the violence that is rife and hyperbolic in India, but also the violence that is "in us too."[54]

If the Diaspora Jew is to be seen as an emblem of hybridity in his descent from a Marrano who has stolen the Moor's treasure and seed, we should immediately be suspicious. After all, the Marrano hides under various names and his enigmatic cloak covers the most slippery of identities, secretly Jew and publicly Christian, yet in some ways neither—and for this reason, Peter Berek claims that the Marranno emerges as the quintessential "Renaissance Man." He is the stranger on whom are projected anxieties about change and innovation, and, in the context of changing notions of race and nation; the secret Jews, the Marranos who came to England from the late fourteenth to seventeenth centuries were apt representations in drama of the period of the idea that identity was unstable and could be determined by individuals.[55] That fluidity of identity (so suited to the postmodern imagination) came with the freer movement across seas and continents of goods, as well as people, some of whom did not fit existing preconceptions of color, religion, race, and nation.

Far from celebrating hybrid identity as an ideal, Rushdie sounds a warning that identity is always multiple and suspect, never pure or "native," but hybrid in Bhabha's model of hybridity. The space which Bhabha creates between West and East is filled here by the hybrid "jew." Although European

Jews were not, strictly speaking, colonial subjects, Jon Stratton has argued that they were, in a sense, internally colonized; they were expected to be the same but were not ultimately assimilable. Their mimicry, like that of the Indians, resisted the colonizing culture because the excess mimicry (the signs of desired assimilation of the assimilating Jew) signaled a difference which became all the more threatening when genocide showed the impossibility of total assimilation.[56] After the Holocaust, the desired integration can only be illusionary, a false promise of a discredited enlightenment, so the Jews will always be "white but not quite."[57]

Abraham's son Moraes Zogoiby is raised as neither a Catholic nor a Jew.

> I was both, and nothing: a jewholic-anonymous, a cathjew nut, a stewpot, a mongrel cur. I was—what's the word these days?—*atomised.* Yessir: a real Bombay mix (104).

This playful salute to hybridity (with a nod to Joyce's "cathjew," Leopold Bloom) effectively exposes invented identities that are ultimately fake, in apparently mocking contradiction of Bhabha's understanding of the postcolonial condition—though we should be aware that nothing should be taken too seriously in Rushdie's subversive and parodic *mise-en-abyme,* least of all postcolonial theory.[58] Rushdie's parody of globalized hybridity effectively deconstructs any essentialized identity, just as it deconstructs the Moor's bastardy ("baas-turd").

Bombay is itself "central, had been so from the moment of its creation, the bastard child of a Portuguese-English wedding, and yet the most Indian of Indian cities" (350). Yet the Bombay that Rushdie celebrates here and in *Midnight's Children* is the multiethnic city of the fifties, when the various cultural groups shared and interacted in a dynamic and tolerant intersection of Gujarati and Marathi neighborhoods, as well as Hindu, Jewish, and Muslim communities, that enjoyed the spoils of the colonial past, the mixed heritage of British and Indian culture, before it became the Indian city dominated by Shiv Sena, the Hindu fundamentalist movement castigated in *The Moor's Last Sigh* as "Mumbai's Axis."[59] Like Anita Desai, Rushdie mourned the loss of a multiculturalism that has greatly diminished in India, together with liberal secularism.

Hybridity is for Rushdie the postcolonial condition of invented, thus to a large extent fake, identities, and the ensuing complexes of passing curiously recall the Marrano as "Renaissance Man." In Rushdie's later novel, *Shalimar the Clown* (2006), passing can be the key to survival for a Jew in Occupied France, but then the identities which Max Ophuls forges are literal, as well as literary, fakes that allow himself and others to escape thanks to his multidexterous humanist talents (at one point we are invited to see him as a real life version of Saint Exupery's Little Prince). Ophuls is the archetypal Jew who is the would be humanist of a former age, both printer and scientist, aviator and amorous adventurer, the Mole who stings a Panther and marries a Rat, but who comes undone in the snare of his own fantasies. Hybridity for both the Moor and for Max is a mixture of identities borrowed from fiction or from myth. As such, it is always indebted and inventive, unlike the real hybridity of Caribbean cross-breeding or Bhabha's postcolonial model. Language itself breathes and breeds an elusive hybridity, a Joycean pidgin English as spoken in India, as if jostling the joss sticks of the multiple gods and languages of the subcontinent, except that polysemy is taken to an extreme of endless possibilities of meaning, not just multiple meanings—anything and everything at the same time. Meaning might depend on a whim, and thus destabilizes any surety of a firm identity.[60] Moor is so called because his siblings are named in nursery-rhyme fashion Ina, Minnie, Mynah—and "moo" is his first cry—but he is also Moor because this suggests meaning is always *more* than what it appears (a Shakespearean pun on the pregnant Moor in *The Merchant of Venice*), excessively, insatiably *more,* and *more* than the sum of his inherited contradictions: willful arbitrariness is given as a birthright and fate. The Moor might well joke, "What's in a name?" (84). And his full name Moraes embodies the mix that deconstructs historical stereotypes, but also exposes a suspect hybidity that goes back to Muslim Spain.

The Moor seems to be forced back upon his forgotten Jewish identity by the confrontation with his father as a god of vengeance wreaking awe on his powerful empire (336–37) and by his father's rejection of him for not begetting a son. He goes back to Spain and tries to imagine himself as a Jew, but Maimonides' ghost laughs at him. Nor is he convincing as a Catholicised Córdoba mosque. "I was a nobody from nowhere, like no-one, belonging to nothing. . . . I had reached an anti-Jerusalem: not a home, but an away. A place that did not bind, but dissolved" (388). Here we have a statement—or what sounds to Moor more of a truth—about the "jew's" identity. This is not a yearning for an imaginary homeland, but a sense of not belonging anywhere. Instead of a pilgrimage to a point of origin, Moor finds himself in a vortex of history's repetition compulsion. After a surreal plane journey from India, with erotic fantasies that presage his strange encounters, Moor finds himself in a remote village in a room that curiously mirrors the Cochin synagogue, complete with oracular Delft tiles. And as equally false. On arrival in Spain in search of his roots he cannot say who he is, not even the product of that romantic and exotic crossbreeding of Jew and Moor which lives on secretly in the genes of the Spanish nation.

The imagined reconstruction of the Andalusian symbiosis of Jew, Moor, and Christian proves to be a trap set by the vengeful and mad painter Miranda Vasco, Aurora's former lover, who has stolen her paintings, including *The Moor's Last Sigh*. The latter-day Moor finds himself imprisoned in a simulacrum of the Alhambra under threat of death. His fellow-prisoner is a Japanese woman, whose name is comprised entirely of vowels, the opposite extreme, perhaps, of India's polyglossia, suggesting that language and identity have become amorphous and shapeless. Aoi Uë has in fact been stolen from *The Tale of Genji,* an eleventh-century novel attributed to the Japanese noblewoman Murasaki Shikibu, where Genji, like the Moor, is responsible for Aoi's death.[61] In Rushdie's novel, Aoi convinces the Moor that though love leads to betrayal and destruction, it is worth seeking, a conclusion that would be banal if the reader were not being teased with allusions to Cervantes in a postmodern parody of allusion and delusion that deconstructs all mythologies.

This is small comfort when history, in imitation of art and myth, repeats itself. When Vasco shoots his Japanese prisoner, Moor relives Boabdil's story, and he must bear him repeating the words of Boabdil's mother after the loss of Granada to Ferdinand, which completed the *Reconquista* in the year 1492, the year of Columbus' discovery of America and the expulsion of Spain's Jews: "*well may you weep like a woman. . .for what you could not defend like a man*" (432; italics in the original). The spot from which Boabdil looked for the last time on the lost city is known as "the last sigh of the Moor" (*el último suspiro del Moro*). And it is this last sigh/*soupir*/supper that is deconstructed in punning jokes through the novel and is reenacted at the end as Rushdie's Moor, Boabdil's putative hybrid offspring, expires. The novel ends not with redemption or return, but with defeat, with the Moor's final last sigh as he awaits death.

Rushdie explains how the Andalusian symbiosis of Jew and Muslim was relevant to his project:

> Although the Muslim sultans were the rulers, there were
> Christians and Jews and Muslims living side by side for hundreds
> of years, and their cultures affected each other. So the Muslims
> were no longer completely Muslim and likewise the others. . . .
> Now it seemed to me that the world I come from, India, the world
> this book comes out of, is also a composite culture.[62]

Historical accuracy aside, Moor embodies a "mélange," and the *masala* brew
of identities that melt into each other is seen by Rushdie as threatened by
single and thus false truths, by the Hinduism of the majority, by fundamentalism. The hybrid "jew" is therefore a necessary minority that challenges
majority rule and opinion, and it is from a minority perspective of a descen-
dant of Jewish and Portuguese settlers that Rushdie looks at India where
Partition has made the Muslims a minority. The figure of the "jew" introduces the complex cosmopolitan history of the Spanish-Jewish exiles. Indeed,
Aamir Mufti reads *The Moor's Last Sigh* as a "cosmopolitical" novel in the
Indian and Anglo-Indian tradition.[63]

The displacement of the Jew by the Muslim as the new "jew" would seem
to reaffirm Mufti's thesis of an analogy between Europe's treatment of the
Jews and colonialization of India. "MUSLIMS ARE THE JEWS OF ASIA," reads
one slogan painted on walls during the Partition riots in *Midnight's
Children*.[64] Indeed, Jews and Indians have coexisted in close proximity in the
Western and the Jewish imagination for centuries, and Homi Bhabha reminds
us that the Parsis were long known as the "Jews of the East," not least for
their performance of self-critical humor and for their imitation of Western
professionalism in business.[65] In a memoir of an uncle who married a
German Jewess and settled in North London, *Two Lives* (2005), Vikram Seth
gives another dimension to this trope of the Indians as Jews in his recognition
of the affinity of middle-class family values and social rituals, as well as the
multiplicity of identity in exile, but acknowledges that the Jewish presence in
India was minimal and has now diminished, almost unnoticeable in Indian
consciousness, nor was the Jewish history of persecution and battle for
survival replicated in India; yet European racism served an important lesson
in inhumanity, which Uncle Shanti witnessed under the Nazis as an honorary
"Aryan," allowed to study but not to practice dentistry.[66] At the same time,
Seth, who looks (like Rushdie) through Indian eyes at European history,
castigates all forms of nationalism, including Zionism, identifying Herzl with
Hitler, and implies Jewish complicity in South African Apartheid.[67]

Rushdie's "minority" tale (a tale of a minority hybrid figure as well as a minority voice in a majority culture) rather idealistically resists fundamentalism through Aurora's aesthetics and embraces mutation and difference, through the attraction of lurid beauty. Like Bombur Yambarzal banging with his spoons in *Shalimar the Clown* on the mosque doors of the "iron mullah,"[68] playful polysemy breaks the spell of indoctrination with its deceptive magic of multiplicity, but it cannot defeat fundamentalism alone, even if *The Moor's Last Sigh* is itself a resistance to the *fatwa* and the book-burning in Bradford that placed Rushdie's own art under threat. Indeed, it was as a liberal secularist and purveyor of modernism that Rushdie was condemned by the ayatollahs: not for misinterpretation of the Koran, but for the *cultural* heresy of treating the sacred in *The Satanic Verses* as profane literature which makes space for hybridity as irresolvable and borderline.[69] Vijay Mishray portrays Rushdie nailing the "theses" of *The Moor's Last Sigh* to the gates of literature in defense of magical realism and hedonist freedom against Hindu fundamentalism and argues that the novel is a manifesto of the diasporic imaginary because of its hybridization of Moor, Jew, Christian, and Goan.[70] Significantly, the last performance of the Pachigam *bhands* in *Shalimar the Clown* takes place as violence breaks out in Kashmir, and the coexistence of Muslims, Sikhs, and Jews comes to an end with the repression of un-Islamic traditions by the Islamist insurgents and the Indian Army's own "crackdown." After many have fled south, the son of the old dancing master Habib Joo tells Abdulah Noman, "we don't think it's a good idea to be Jewish when the Islamists come to town again."[71] The pun is fully intended.

Dohra Ahmad reads fundamentalism in *The Moor's Last Sigh* as an opposing mode of belief and of historiography to hybridity, but each comes to be the distorted mirror image of the Other. In this view, Jews and Muslims share an expulsion from Spain in the formative memory of their Indian-ness (though it might be pointed out that the ancestry of Muslims and Jews are very different), and Ahmad argues that they could be thought of as parallel ethnic minorities in Bombay's teeming and conflicted multitudes.[72] We have seen such a displacement of "jew" into Muslim in Desai's depiction of Bombay in chapter two, and one wonders if this metaphorical displacement relates to any historical reality among the disparate castes of Bombay's Jews (who suffered little persecution and whose upper echelons of wealthy merchants hailed from Baghdad, not Spain).[73] There is no significant depiction of Muslims in Rushdie's novel, and Hillel Halkin complains that all evil is off-loaded onto the latter-day Shylock, Abraham Zogoiby, as a cowardly projection of Rushdie's failure to win Muslim support for his cause and a buttress for a neo-Enlightenment attack on religion (*The Moor's Last Sigh* was the first novel Rushdie produced after the *fatwa* and was read as his stance on fundamentalism).[74] What Ahmad seems to have done is to conscript the "jew" to a critical discourse that would divide Islam from fundamentalism and present Muslims in India as "jews" who define Indian-ness by difference, in defiance of an authoritarian and dishonest Hinduism, and who are defined by migration and survival, just as Jews and Muslims are joined by Abrahamic monotheism.[75] This, it seems to us, is to ignore the complex realities of Bombay, Partition, and the language riots of 1957, and it misreads hybridity, imposing on it a homogeneity through the Western perspective of India as a Third World country.[76]

Hybridity is thought of as the liminal condition of the postmodern migrant, yet Mahatma Gandhi's own brand of eclectic syncretism drew on different religious traditions, as well as Western political models, to oppose Hindu nationalism. Such cultural and religious hybridity, rooted yet open to available resources, draws suspicion of Western ways of thinking when it is practiced in contemporary Indian writing, but it is nevertheless native to India.[77] Nehru, for example, once declared, "I have become a queer mixture of East and West, out of place everywhere, at home nowhere."[78] Indeed, it is Nehru's vision of a hybrid India that Rushdie parodies in *The Moor's Last Sigh,*[79] and Nehru's use of the palimpsest as an expression of transcultural exchanges, compounded by the image of the family of Mother India, may have been in Rushdie's mind when he constructed an allegory of nation through a series of metaphorical substitutions which work towards a pluralistic unity that adapts Western cultural and political models.[80] Yet the Moor's journey provides an anti-itinerary that goes back into history and undoes family ties and national identities in ways that contest the premises of postcolonial theory (the Moor is himself a scion of colonizers).[81] According to Anna Guttman, Rushdie has adjusted his perception of Nehru's model of the Indian nation since *Midnight's Children,* sensing a danger in both a false master narrative of national unity (exemplified by the *Reconquista* in Spain) and the chaotic disorder of pluralism, in which no identity holds and there is no coherent view of history (as in Western multiculturalism, in which Rushdie's novels are marketed as a taste of exotic hybridity). Unlike that earlier novel, *The Moor's Last Sigh* ends with corruption, decay, and dissolution.[82]

Actually, there is a more obvious preoccupation in Rushdie's work with defining not just Indian identity in Nehru's trope of the body of the nation, but the sense of a corruptive, crumbling decay of the body, a coming apart of ethnic and national ties in an imaginative inhabiting of other lives across genders, religions, languages, and ethnic groups in order to explore what is truly human. What Saleem describes in *Midnight's Children* as the Indian disease of trying to encapsulate all of reality is in fact a universal failure to arrive at a coherent narrative of all the voices in the writer's head.[83] The narrative of the "jew" could be seen as a paradigm of that failure to contain all of fractious, multi-sectarian India, or all of the autobiographical or writing self, and of the failure of any one identity to contain all of what is essentially human ("self" is never singular, but always multiple and protean for Rushdie). The "jew" is to be understood not as metaphor, but as metamorphosis.

It turns out to be impossible to escape the nightmare of history, and difficult to trace the course of one's own destruction. In *Midnight's Children,* Saleem, a pickler or conserver of stories, finds that memory is fluid. Paradoxically, in Rushdie's self-deconstructing "shaggy-dog yarns" of a "Moor's tale" (4), history seems an unreliable narrative, debunked along with all other myths and stories, that nevertheless lives out its myths in an interactive and self-questioning art that defies its own determinism and eschews the certainties of cause and effect.[84] Any narrative that traces hybridity to some pure origin must therefore be suspect, and national identity turns out to be based on myths.

Although *Midnight's Children* has been claimed as a watershed in post-Emergency Indian writing that turns polarities into art and heresies into prophesies and its author has been variously hailed or criticized as a diasporic and expatriate writer,[85] Rushdie should not be read solely in an Indian context. *The Moor's Last Sigh* wickedly satirizes Indian politics[86] and has been interpreted as an allegorical recuperation of India's premodern history in the context of the demolition in December 1992 of the Babri Masjid mosque, which sparked riots between Hindus and Muslims in a contest over the control and interpretation of Indian history and national identity.[87] However, *The Moor's Last Sigh* has also been read as a contribution to "critical cosmopolitanism" and the tradition of transnational writing in

English that includes Conrad and Joyce,[88] as an attempt to fashion a British novel out of Indian materials, rather than to create something made in India (where it met a hostile reception and was partially banned because of its subversive portrayal of Thackeray/Fielding and Hindu nationalism).[89] It presents a test of the heterogeneity of multiculturalism: do Asian and Black Britons share in the same heritage as their White English fellow citizens? It tests whether Enoch Powell is to be proven wrong and Thatcher mistaken in thinking of Black Britain as something separate from Englishness.[90] However, we should be wary of making Rushdie a champion of the multiculturalism that has been deemed a guarantee of global culture in postcolonial discourse or a representative of transnationalism (indeed, Rushdie, like Homi Bhaba and Zadie Smith, benefited from an elitist education within the established study of English literature).[91] Rushdie shows that multiculturalism should not be flattened into a collection of monocultures or an indifferent equality of opposing and incompatible identities, but like other grand schemes and projects it should not be trusted. As in Zadie Smith's *The Autograph Man,* identity is built on contradictions, not synthesis, and the figure of the "jew" is a demonstration of Rushdie's postmodern play with the inconsistencies and instabilities of human identity.

The "jew," as we have seen, is for Rushdie, as Bloom was for Joyce, the emblematic exile who is universally human in his *not* belonging to one place or nation, the marginal figure who is exemplary of the human. The global migrant is an everyday Ulysses or Zogoiby who is the eternal refugee with multiple cultural baggage. Like the writer striving in his art for an "imaginary homeland," the hybrid "jew" offers Rushdie an exemplary story in which he finds himself between two continents and, as we noted, at home only in his imagination, in the "Indias of the mind."[92] Rushdie shows how "voluntary exile from identity is the only means to redefine that identity as an unfixed constantly evolving notion. . . . Exile is identity in Rushdie's world, but the most productive sort of identity. . .mental, intellectual exile from fixed and constraining truths."[93] The hybrid "jew" is a migrant amongst a motley crowd of Others, as in "Uccello"'s imagination in *The Enchantress of Florence* (2008), where, impossibly, Jews, Chinamen, Dagos, and Englishmen, as well as lecherous Franciscan monks, share the bed of Hawkins' Portuguese mistress in Oporto's Ribeira fishermen's district.[94] But then "Uccello di Firenze" is a stowaway con-man and conjurer riding the seas under a false name, who knows, like his author, how to use his wit when a sword is at his throat. In one of many intertextual allusions and metafictional sleights of hand, he beats a Venetian Jewish diamond merchant, the bearded and ringleted Shalakh Cormorano, at cards and wins a particolored coat made at the famous tailor's shop *Il Moro Invidiosi* (the green-eyed Moor of Venice) that allows him to conceal his tricks and pilfered treasures in its many secret pockets,[95] references that conjure up *The Moor's Last Sigh,* invoke Shylock as a bird of prey, and send us to *Othello* in a counterhistorical tale of incest, fake identity, and colonialism, in which nothing is what it is believed to be and everything is make-believe. Real Jews, by contrast, are not conscripted into the Janassaries, because their faith cannot be broken, which makes them exceptions among those who turn Turk. In any case, these are small details in a magical story that fantasizes multicultural and erotic encounters between Persian kings, Italian adventurers (among them a fictionalized Machiavelli), and brutal pirates who deliver the postmodern message that peace is to be found nowhere and home is a delusion.

THE MULTICULTURAL LITMUS TEST: "WE ARE NOT JEWS"

For Rushdie, in his essay "The New Empire within Britain," insurmountable prejudice and hypocritical or discriminatory government policy was the White problem that stopped him feeling thoroughly British. Hanif Kureishi, too, cannot be quite at home in Britain, despite the fact that he is English-born and responds patriotically to anti-British remarks on a visit to Pakistan. The illiberalism of Pakistan and discouragement of the arts prevented him making his home there, and yet a diaspora identity of an exiled writer could not be acceptable, however much he was treated as a foreigner in his native country. He will always be a "Paki," yet being born of an English mother he cannot accept the separatist agenda of Malcolm X and Black supremacy. The tragic irony is that educated Pakistanis ape British ways in a country becoming increasingly anti-Western and Islamic. Yet Pakistan offers close bonding and acceptance compared with the frigid lives of bourgeois bohemia in London suburbs.[96] Following Fanon, Kureishi warns Britain of the consequence of increasing intolerance, but the colonial subjects in England have been deeply affected by English ways as well as by the hatred directed at them, yet they cannot return "home" to Pakistan easily, as Kureishi shows in *My Beautiful Laundrette*:

PAPA: This damn country has done us in. That's why I am like this. We should be there. Home.
NASSER: But that country has been sodomized by religion. It is beginning to interfere with the making of money. Compared with everywhere, it is a little heaven here.[97]

The picture of growing up amid racial hatred in the 1960s in East London in Kureishi's short story "We're Not Jews" (1997) seems pretty desperate, the only escape being an unknown fate in an unknown Pakistan or the reality of apartheid in South Africa. Azhar has been taunted and abused at school because his father is Pakistani. When the boy's mother defends the family by saying "We're not Jews," the father of the boy's schoolmate, their neighbor Big Billy, insults her with the sexual slur of "going with a Paki," for preferring a "darkie" to his English body.[98] Sander Gilman has cited this example to support his claim that the Jewish experience is a key to understanding identity in the work of South Asian writers and a litmus paper of multiculturalism.[99] Here antisemitism—specifically the Holocaust—exemplifies the genocidal hatred of neighbors (there had been gassing and the evil had not died), as well as exclusion from a full belonging to Englishness.

However, the Jews are merely a reference point, a definition of not being English from which Azhar's mother disassociates herself. There is no multicultural exchange here, and Azhar will presumably grow up unable to understand his Urdu- or Punjabi-speaking relatives or extricate himself from an immigrant experience that is not his. He can neither protect his mother from ostracism nor his father from the self-delusion that he will become a successful writer. Unlike Kureishi, Azhar's father failed to follow the Jewish immigrant pattern of upward mobility, which is often touted as the model for the new wave of South Asian immigrants and their children in London's East End, as we will see in chapter five. Yet it is the Jewish experience of antisemitism that Kureishi uses as a measure of the child's awareness of his identity, a mode of thinking to which we will turn in the next chapter, which examines a view of antisemitism as a vicarious expression of the Black experience in Europe.

NOTES

1. Robert J. C. Young, *Colonial Desire: Hybridity in Theory, Culture and Race* (London: Routledge, 1995), 23.

2. Ibid., 24.

3. Lola Young, "Hybridity's Discontents: Rereading, Science, and 'Race,'" in *Hybridity and its Discontents: Politics, Science, Culture,* ed. Avtar Brah and Annie E. Coombes (London: Routledge, 2000), 156–57.

4. Susheila Nasta,. *Home Truths: Fictions of the South Asian Diaspora in Britain* (Houndmills: Palgrave Macmillan, 2002), 178–80.

5. Pnina Werbner, "The Limits of Cultural Hybridity: On Ritual Monsters, Poetic License, and Contested Postcolonial Purifications," *Journal of the Royal Anthropology Institute* 7.1 (2001): 133–52; Homi Bhabha, *The Location of Culture* (London: Routledge, 1994), 35–36.

6. V. S. Naipaul. *The Mimic Men* (New York:Vintage, 2001), 141.

7. Hanif Kureishi, *Something toTell You* (London: Faber, 2008), 40.

8. Salman Rushdie, *The Satanic Verses* (London: Viking, 1988), 60–61.

9. Bhabha, *Location of Culture,* 320.

10. Rushdie, *Satanic Verses,* 261.

11. Ibid., 405. Some scholars have failed to notice that these characters are Rushdie's own invention, a parody of racist stereotypes (mutant or mutilated Asians). See Stephen Clingman, *The Grammar of Identity: Transnational Fiction and the Nature of the Boundary* (Oxford: Oxford University Press, 2009) 125; Martin Corner, "Beyond Revisions: Rushdie, Newness and Authenticity," in *The Revision of Englishness,* ed. David Rogers and John McLeod (Manchester: Manchester University Press, 2004), 165–66.

12. Rushdie, *Satanic Verses,* 289. Lower case in the original.

13. See Stephen Clingman's incisive reading of the sources of metamorphosis in *Grammar of Identity,* 126–28.

14. Ibid., 131–32.

15. Bhabha, *Location of Culture,* 102–23.

16. Shaul Bassi, "Mooristan and Palimpstine: Jews, Moors, Christians in Amitav Ghosh and Salman Rushdie," unpublished paper.

17. V. S. Naipaul, *The Mimic Men* (Harmondsworth: Penguin Books, 1987), 5.5.7

18. Susheila Nasta, *Home Truths,* 107–08.

19. Andrea Levy, *Small Island* (New York: Picador, 2004). Further references will be to this edition and will be given in parenthesis.

20. Sue Greene, "Use of the Jew in West Indian Novels," *World Literature Written in English* 26.1 (1986): 151.

21. Andrea Levy, "This Is My England," *Guardian,* 19 Feb. 2000, http://books.guardian.co.uk/departments/politicsphilosophyandsociety/story/0,,138282,00.html.

22. Greene, "Use of the Jew in West Indian Novels," 156.

23. Frantz Fanon, *Black Skin, White Masks,* trans. Charles Lam Markmann (New York: Grove Press, 1967), 110.

24. Andrea Levy, *Every Light in the House Burnin'* (London: Headline, 1994), 247.

25. Idem, *Fruit of the Lemon* (London: Headline, 1999), 308.

26. Interview with Bonnie Greer, "Empire's Child," *Guardian,* 31 Jan. 2004, http://books.guardian.co.uk/departments/generalfiction/story/0,,1134242,00.html.

27. Ibid.

28. Levy, "This Is My England."

29. Zadie Smith, *White Teeth* (London: Penguin, 2000). All further references will be to this edition and will be given in parenthesis.

30. Phyllis Lassner, *Colonial Strangers: Women Writing the End of the British Empire* (New Brunswick, N.J.: Rutgers University Press, 2004), 193–201.

31. See Dominic Head, "Zadie Smith's White Teeth" in *Contemporary British Fiction,* ed. Richard J. Lane, Rod Mengham, and Philip Tew (Cambridge: Polity, 2003), 106–19.

32. The novel was written before the 7/7 bombings in London, which brought home just how much British Islamist fundamentalist groups did pose a serious threat. The satirical point that it was not easy for Muslims, however strict, to overcome evils of the West such as drinking, drugs, and women and that fundamentalists mimicked Western heroes such as Rambo suggests either a deluded idealism or a failure of imagination.

33. Zadie Smith, *The Autograph Man* (London: Penguin, 2002). All further references will be to this edition and will be given in parenthesis.

34. On Bruce's jocular division of the world into "goyish" and "Jewish" as an example of his use of Jewishness and Yiddish to undo the civility to which Jews were meant to assimilate, see Jon Stratton, *Coming Out Jewish: Constructing Ambivalent Identities* (London: Routledge, 2000), 299. Here, of course, Smith's Autograph Man is parodying the Jewish/goyish divide to foreground a desired hybridity.

35. Jonathan P. A. Sell, "Chance and Gesture in Zadie Smith's *White Teeth* and *The Autograph Man*: A Model for Multicultural Identity?" *Journal of Commonwealth Literature* 41.3 (2006): 27–44. Sell perhaps attributes too much philosophical purpose to this comedy of paradoxes, while Andrew Furman has actually co-opted Zadie Smith to a Jewish literature that examines identity ("The Jewishness of the Contemporary Gentile Writer: Zadie Smith's *The Autograph Man,*" *MELUS* 30.1 [Spring 2005]: 3–17).

36. Pnina Werbner, "Theorizing Complex Diasporas: Purity and Hybridity in the South Asian Public Sphere in Britain," *Journal of Ethnic and Migration Studies* 30.5 (2004): 895–911.

37. Salman Rushdie, *Imaginary Homelands: Essays and Criticism, 1981–1991* (London: Granta Books, 1991), 18.

38. Rushdie, *Imaginary Homelands,* 129–38.

39. Ibid., 137–38.

40. Madelena Gonzalez, *Fiction after the Fatwa: Salman Rushdie and the Charm of Catastrophe* (Amsterdam: Rodopi, 2005), 114.

41. Timothy Weiss, "At the End of East/West," in idem, *Translating Orients* (Toronto: University of Toronto Press, 2004) 47; Stephen Morton, *Salman Rushdie: Fictions of Postcolonial Modernity* (Houndmills: Palgrave Macmillan, 2008).

42. Salman Rushdie, *The Moor's Last Sigh* (London: Vintage, 1996), 82. Italics in the original. All further references to this edition will be given in parenthesis.

43. Bindu Malieckal, "Shakespeare's Shylock, Rushdie's Abraham Zogoiby, and the Jewish Pepper Merchants of Precolonial India," *Upstart Crow* 21 (2001): 154–69. Malieckal enumerates the references to Shylock in the novel (163).

44. Andrew Teverson, *Salman Rushdie* (Manchester: Manchester University Press, 2007), 176.

45. Stephen Baker speaks of Rushdie as the neo-colonialist of capitalism because of the raiding of a free-fall commodity culture in this novel ("'You must remember this': Salman Rushdie's *The Moor's Last Sigh,*" *Journal of Commonwealth Literature* 35.1 [2000]: 43–54).

46. Jonathan Greenberg, "'The Base Indian' or 'the Base Judean'? Othello and the Metaphor of the Palimpsest in Salman Rushdie's *The Moor's Last Sigh,*" *Modern Language Studies* 29.2 (1999): 104–6.

47. Ania Loomba, *Colonialism / Postcolonialism,* 2nd ed. (London: Routledge, 2005), 175.

48. Ania Loomba, "Local Manufacture Made-in-India Othello Fellows," in *Post-Colonial Shakespeares,* ed. Ania Loomba (New York and London: Routledge, 1998), 153–55.

49. Ania Loomba, *Shakespeare, Race, and Colonialism* (Oxford: Oxford University Press, 2002), 135–36.

50. Vijay Mishra, *The Literature of the Indian Diaspora: Theorizing the Diasporic Imaginary* (London: Routledge, 2007), 219–20.

51. Paul A. Cantor, "Tales of the Alhambra: Rushdie's Use of Spanish History in *The Moor's Last Sigh,*" *Studies in the Novel* 29.3 (1997): 323–41.

52. On the appropriation of Spanish Jewish history in postmodern fiction, see Efraim Sicher, "Sir Salman Rushdie Sails for India and Rediscovers Spain: Postmodern Constructions of Sepharad," in *Sephardism: Spanish Jewish History in the Modern Literary Imagination,* ed. Yael Wise-Halevi (Stanford: Stanford University Press, 2012), 256–73.

53. Sander Gilman, *Multiculturalism and the Jews* (New York: Routledge, 2006), 163.

54. Rushdie quoted in Gonzalez, *Fiction after the Fatwa,* 108, n. 8.

55. Peter Berek, "The Jew as Renaissance Man," *Renaissance Quarterly* 51.1 (1998): 128–62. As a well-known refuge, sixteenth–seventeenth-century England was rife with accusations of Judaizing, which also served Protestant and Catholic polemics, so the term "Jew" was applied not only to secret Jews masquerading as Christians. See James Shapiro, *Shakespeare and the Jews* (New York: Columbia University Press, 1995), 13–43.

56. Stratton, *Coming Out Jewish: Constructing Ambivalent Identities* (London: Routledge, 2000), 61.

57. For a discussion of why Jews are thought of as "not White" or "the same but not quite" in terms of Bhabha's mimcry and excess, Stratton, *Coming Out Jewish,* 57–61. The term "white but not quite" has circulated among scholars of American Jewry; see Davida Bloom, "White, But Not Quite: The Jewish Character and Anti-Semitism--Negotiating a Location in the Gray Zone Between Other and Not," *Journal of Religion and Theatre* 1.1 (Fall 2002), http://www.rtjournal.org/vol_1/no_1/bloom.html. See also Katya Gibel Azoulay, *Black, Jewish, and Interracial: It's Not the Color of Your Skin, but the Race of Your Kin, and Other Myths of Identity* (Durham, N.C.: Duke University Press, 1997) and Karen Brodkin, *How Jews Became White Folks And What That Says About Race In America* (New Brunswick, N.J.: Rutgers University Press, 1998).

58. Gonzalez, *Fiction after the Fatwa,* 120. In a description of criticism of Aurora's paintings in the novel, Gonzalez identifies a parody of Homi Bhabha's critique of *The Satanic Verses* to which we have referred above.

59. Rachel Trousdale, "'City of mongrel joy': Bombay and the Shiv Sena in *Midnight's Children* and *The Moor's Last Sigh*," *Journal of Commonwealth Literature* 39.2 (2004): 95–110.

60. Gonzalez, *Fiction after the Fatwa,* 102.

61. Anna Guttman, *The Nation of India in Contemporary Indian Literature* (Houndmills and New York: Palgrave Macmillan, 2007), 86.

62. Rushdie, quoted in Gonzalez, *Fiction after the Fatwa,* 102–3, n. 3.

63. Aamir Mufti, *Enlightenment in the Colony: The Jewish Question and the Crisis of Postcolonial Culture* (Princeton: Princeton University Press, 2007), 247.

64. Rushdie, *Midnight's Children* (New York: Vintage, 1995), 72. Capitals in the original.

65. Homi K. Bhabha, "Joking Aside: The Idea of a Self-Critical Community," in *Modernity, Culture and "the Jew,"* ed. Bryan Cheyette and Laura Marcus (Cambridge: Polity Press, 1998), *xv.*

66. Vikram Seth, *Two Lives: A Memoir* (New York: HarperCollins, 2006), 388–89, 393–95, 400, 403.

67. Ibid., 319.

68. Salman Rushdie, *Shalimar the Clown* (London: Vintage Books, 2006), 114–15. This incident prevents a jihad being launched on the neighboring village of Pachigam (whose village council includes three Hindus and one Jew), but it does not prevent the revengeful rape of Boonyi's surrogate victim, which sets off a local version of the 1965 India-Pakistan war.

69. Bhabha, *Location of Culture*, 225–56

70. Mishra, *Literature of the Indian Diaspora*, 221–22.

71. Rushdie, *Shalimar the Clown*, 302.

72. Dohra Ahmad, "'This fundo stuff is really something new': Fundamentalism and hybridity in *The Moor's Last Sigh*," *Yale Journal of Criticism* 18.1 (Spring 2005): 1–20.

73. On Rushdie's use of the complex history of the Cochin and Bombay Jewish communities see Milieckal, "Shakespeare's Shylock." Milieckal points out that antisemitism really only began in India with the coming of the Portuguese and that their encounter with Indian Jews colored (literally and metaphorically) the Orientalized image of the "jew" in European depictions. Flory Zogoiby's citing of historical facts, of course, is both selective and faulty.

74. Hillel Halkin, "Salman Rushdie Surrenders," *Commentary* (July 1996): 55–59.

75. Ahmad, "'This fundo stuff is really something new,'" 5.

76. As John Hutnyk comments on the Western perception of Calcutta (*The Rumour of Calcutta: Tourism, Charity and the Poverty of Representation* [London: Zed Books, 1996], 127).

77. Robert J. C. Young, *Postcolonialism: An Historical Introduction* (Oxford: Blackwell, 2001), 345–47. Young is discussing how postcolonial theory in the work of Bhabha and Nandy is similarly eclectic and hybrid.

78. Quoted in Young, *Postcolonialism*, 348.

79. Ania Loomba, *Colonialism / Postcolonialism*, 176.

80. Alexandra W. Schultheis, "Postcolonial Lack and Aesthetic Promise in *The Moor's Last Sigh*." *Twentieth Century Literature* 47.4 (2001): 570–1.

81. Ibid., 574.

82. Guttman, *Nation of India in Contemporary Indian Literature*, 71–73.

83. Michael Gorra, *After Empire: Scott, Naipaul, Rushdie* (Chicago: University of Chicago Press, 1997), 113.

84. Gonzalez, *Fiction after the Fatwa*, 110.

85. Josna A. Rege, "Victim into Protagonist? Midnight's Children and the Post-Rushdie National Narratives of the Eighties," *Studies in the Novel* 29.3 (1997): 342–75.

86. John Clement Ball, "Acid in the Nation's Bloodstream: Satire, Violence, and the Indian Body Politic in Salman Rushdie's *The Moor's Last Sigh*," *International Fiction Review* 27.1–2 (2000): 37–47.

87. Mona Narain, "Re-imagined Histories: Rewriting the Early Modern in Rushdie's *The Moor's Last Sigh*," *Journal for Early Modern Cultural Studies* 6.2 (Fall/Winter 2006): 55–67. On the contrasting responses of Rushdie and Naipaul to this incident see Nyla Ali Khan, *The Fiction of Nationality in an Era of Transnationalism* (New York: Routledge, 2005), 2–4, 26.

88. See Rebecca L. Walkowitz, "The Location of Literature: The Transnational Book and the Migrant Writer," *Contemporary Literature* 47.4 (Winter 2006): 527–45.

89. Gonzalez, *Fiction after the Fatwa*, 133. On the reception of Rushdie in India see V. Rajakrishnan, "The Land of the Dead in Salman Rushdie's *The Moor's Last Sigh*, and Some Reflections Based on Indian Response to the Theme of Exile," *Indian Literature* 42.3 (1998): 143–54; John Docker, *1492: The Poetics of Diaspora* (London and New York: Continuum, 2001), 216–17.

90. See Gonzalez, *Fiction after the Fatwa*, 165–75.

91. Simon Gikandi, "Globalization and the Claims of Postcoloniality," *South Atlantic Quarterly* 100.3 (2001): 627–58.

92. Greenberg, "'The Base Indian' or 'the Base Judean'?" 94–95; Morton, *Salman Rushdie*, 16–17.

93. Gonzalez, *Fiction after the Fatwa*, 97.

94. Rushdie, *The Enchantress of Florence* (New York: Random House, 2008), 21.

95. Ibid., 19.

96 Hanif Kureishi,"The Rainbow Sign," in idem, *My Beautiful Launderette and The Rainbow Sign* (London: Faber, 1986), 9–38.

97. Kureishi, *My Beautiful Launderette*, 107.

98. Kureishi, "We're Not Jews," *Love in a Blue Time* (London: Faber, 1997), 41–51.

99. Sander Gilman, "'We're not Jews': Imagining Jewish History and Jewish Bodies in Contemporary Multicultural Literature," *Modern Judaism* 23.2 (May 2003): 127–28.

CHAPTER FOUR

The Color of Shylock:
Caryl Phillips

A VIEW FROM THE BLACK ATLANTIC

In *Black Skin, White Masks* (1952), Frantz Fanon diagnosed the perception of Black inferiority as a symptom of White cultural malaise, a sexual fear of the Black male that was also a desire for the worst excesses and perversions. The figure of the Jew has also been stereotyped as a bogey in the Western imagination, a scapegoat on whom the unhealthy instincts of the Whites are projected. In both cases, the alien identity is internalized beneath the mask worn to attain acceptance by White society. In a conscious adoption of the Jew as a mirror image of the victim humanized by resistance to racism, Fanon says he feels responsible in his body for the Jew and regards antisemitism as a personal attack,[1]

> The Jew and I: since I was not satisfied to be racialized, by a lucky turn of fate I was humanized. I joined the Jew, my brother in misery.[2]

This solidarity with the Jew, moreover, invites a sharing of masks and urges a resistance to racialized identity. For both the Negro and the Jew, the "white mask" is a screen for an identity that is mimicked and therefore recognized as fake. The postcolonial figure of the "jew," then, would be a metaphor for the problematics of passing and for the complexities of color and race in social masks. In this analogy, however, the Black is humanized through brotherhood with another victim of racialization, but does not become a "jew."

Caryl Phillips wants above all to understand his identity as a Black man in England, who grew up—after his parents' divorce—among Whites at the time of Enoch Powell's "rivers of blood" speech and who hardly knew the Caribbean island of St Kitts, from which he was taken as a small baby.[3] Phillips states that Caribbean people are born into a region where European nations traditionally exchanged their verdant islands like chess pieces: culture and language were first imported, then imposed, and 'real' history occurred elsewhere."[4] And he has also said that not being born in Britain, yet having no memory of his birthplace, gave him the vantage point to write about the Caribbean diasporic situation and this served as a "safety-valve" for racist views.[5] Growing up on a depressed White working-class estate in Leeds during the 1970s, Caryl Phillips found he lacked any sense of belonging. When his classmates Williams or Goldberg were asked where they came from, the answer was clear—their names declared they were Welsh or Jewish. Phillips, however, was not a name that announced origins, while his skin color stated clearly the impossibility of passing as European and White. Phillips is Black, yet cannot say for certain where he comes from, beyond a mixed Caribbean descent and more distant slave origins in Africa. Inspired by Ralph Ellison's musings on being "invisible" in Salt Lake City, Phillips went to Oxford and began to write, but started to hang out among Blacks in pubs in Ladbroke Grove, an immigrant district in West London.[6] Marked by both class and color, Phillips did not find it easy to be invisible.

American Blacks identified Jews as powerful and wealthy, and in his collection of essays and travelogues, *The European Tribe,* Phillips quotes James Baldwin's declaration that "Negroes are anti-Semitic because they're anti-white."[7] But in Europe the perspective was different, because the Jews, not the Blacks, claimed victim status: "For those on the right (and some in the centre and on the left too) the Jew is still Europe's nigger."[8] Meeting hostility wherever he went in Britain, Phillips found that only the Jews were referred to as a persecuted minority and there was no discussion of Black slavery or the colonization of Africa. As a result, he confesses, he "vicariously chan-neled" part of his "hurt and frustration through the Jewish experience."[9] A crucial turning point was a TV documentary about the Holocaust in the *World at War* series which made the adolescent Phillips wonder whether, if the Europeans could annihilate six million people because they were Jews, Blacks could expect similar treatment.[10] For this reason he came to identify as a Black with Jews as Holocaust victims. *The Nature of Blood* was written in a number of places, including Amsterdam, where Anne Frank's house helped Phillips reconnect vicariously with the figure of a Jewish boy he had once written about in a juvenile story, who jumped from a train on the way to the camps. "That Dutch boy was, of course, me."[11] This was an expression of his own feelings as a West Indian or "Colored" boy who was insulted as a nigger or a "wog," and told to go back to a country different from that on his passport. And, if the identification was not sufficiently clear, Phillips has a poster of Anne Frank hanging over his writing desk.[12] Growing up in England before race consciousness could have given him an identity, he was instinctively drawn to writers who were made to feel they did not belong in the place they called home, among them Frantz Fanon, James Baldwin, John Coetzee, and Anne Frank.[13]

In *The European Tribe* Phillips reads Fanon's identification in *Black Skin, White Masks* of antisemitism as a form of anti-Negroism, which he would later incorporate into his novel *The Nature of Blood*. Fanon writes:

> It was my philosophy professor, a native of the Antilles, who recalled the fact to me one day: "Whenever you hear anyone abuse the Jews, pay attention, because he is talking about you." And I found that he was universally right—by which I meant that I was answerable in my body and in my heart for what was done to my brother. Later I realized that he meant, quite simply, an anti-Semite is inevitably anti-Negro.[14]

Paul Gilroy prefaces his study of racism *Against Race* with this familiar excerpt from Fanon's early work in order to explain his own sense of affinity as a youngster growing up in the sixties in North London with Jews who had recently survived the Holocaust and understood the discrimination suffered by West Indian immigrants:

> some Jewish families had opened their homes to West Indian students who had been shut out from much commercially rented property by the color-bar. I struggled with the realization that their suffering was somehow connected with the ideas of "race" that bounded my own world with the threat of violence.[15]

Gilroy connects his childhood memories of anti-Black violence and, later, of neo-Nazi skinheads with the contradiction of English fascism and the fight against Hitler, alongside segregation and the Ku Klux Klan in America, gradually came to his understanding of the complexities of color and race. Following Hannah Arendt, Gilroy points to European colonialism as the breeding ground of antisemitism; antisemitism emerges from the same theological and philosophical epistemologies which from the sixteenth century inculcated in constructions of knowledge the racial inferiority of Blacks.

It is with this same passage from Fanon in mind that Caryl Phillips looks to recent Jewish history to sort through his confusions about his own personal and cultural identities and refracts it in his writing as a way of giving voice to his own position in Europe in the absence of reference points for talking about slavery, or the Black experience in Britain.[16] The "nature of blood," in his case is most ambiguous (not atypically for many Caribbeans of mixed descent from African slaves, European settlers, and mulattoes); Phillips later discovered he had a Portuguese Jewish grandfather, Emmanuel de Fraites, whose existence was shrouded in silence and never acknowledged.

> I now understood that the cultural hybridity that is the quintessential Carribean condition had certainly marked my person and the quality of the blood that flowed through my veins was doggedly "impure."[17]

Though he does not think his Jewish ancestry is the reason why he wrote *The Nature of Blood,*[18] the empty space in his own story partly explains his concern with the mystery of biological ties, with the disrupted routes that came in place of roots and which could only be tied in writing.[19]

Phillips has traveled, almost compulsively, and commutes between London, St Kitts, and New Haven, which makes him a living embodiment of the disposition that Paul Gilroy termed the "Black Atlantic."[20] His "home" might be said to be somewhere in mid-Atlantic between West Africa, where his ancestors' journey began; Britain, where he was raised; and North America, where he lives most of the time. Phillips has told his lawyer he wants his ashes scattered over the Atlantic Ocean at a point equidistant between the three places.[21] "Migration is not a word" feared by Caribbean people, according to Phillips, for they "are forever moving between versions of 'home' spurred on by the restless confluence of blood in their veins, an impure mixture that suggests transcendence and connectivity."[22] To discover some of his own multiple identities, Phillips has traveled amongst people from whom he is even more different than those amongst whom he grew up. Phillips's novels have been concerned with diverse, displaced African characters in various periods of history. His first novel *Final Passage* (1985) was set in the African diaspora of England and the Caribbean, a diaspora which Stuart Hall has defined as inherently heterogeneous and not bound by one racial or cultural identity.[23] Yet, beginning with *Higher Ground* in 1989, Phillips extended his view to include the Jewish diaspora and the effects of the Holocaust. As Stef Craps notes, this novel uses the Holocaust as a benchmark for global suffering, as when the African-American prisoner calls his cell Belsen and the wardens in the prison "the Gestapo Police." However, each of the three central narrators, the slave trade interpreter, the African-American prisoner, and the Holocaust survivor are given their own narrative space in the novel. None of them and none of their experiences are foils for the others.[24]

After the liberation of the concentration camps, Eva Stern, a Jewish Holocaust survivor in *The Nature of Blood* (1997), who has suffered the extreme results of alienation, hears of other female survivors' passionate plans to reach Palestine and repeats their words: "The journey that we are making across the bones of Europe is a story that will be told in future years by many prophets. After hundreds of years of trying to be with others, of trying to be others, we are now pouring in the direction of home."[25] Yet these dreams are meaningless to Eva without her mother and sister, and reuniting with them is nothing but an illusion. In the first chapter, her uncle Stephan, who has left a wife and child behind in America, is perplexed what to tell the youngster in the British internment camp about the name of the new country, about which he has apprehensions and misgivings. Where "home" is, and what constitutes identity will prove contentious in this novel. Indeed, "home" is a term that begs questions in the novel. The two locations of the first chapter of the novel, the British internment camp in Cyprus and the concentration camp liberated by the English soldiers, are unnatural living spaces that float in the characters' minds somewhere between a lost old country and some undefined and unreal "new country," that represents what they have lost and can never regain. At the conclusion of the novel, Stern recognizes that Malka, the young Ethiopian Jewish immigrant to Israel, "belonged to another land. She might have been happier there."[26] But state policy had "dragged" her people from their home to learn a new language and new ways. Phillips's knowledge of the rescue of Ethiopian Jewry is admittedly limited to a newspaper report in the *International Herald Tribune* that Israeli medical services secretly dumped blood transfusions from Ethiopian immigrants because of the high incidence of AIDS in their country of origin, amid cries of racism in the media. For Phillips this is what clarified the explanation for the racist, practices of Othello's and Shylock's Venice.[27] The "nature of blood" resulted in the antisemitism behind the blood libels at

Portobuffole, the same refusal to accept the blood of Others that present-day immigrants to Europe encounter, and here was the "nature of blood" again in discrimination against Blacks, this time by the Jews![28] In the painful encounter in the novel between the elderly German Jew, Stephan Stern, and Malka, Phillips points to a most ambiguous homecoming based on a failure to transcend the colonial matrix of Black/White bequeathed by the history of European nationalism.[29] This reinterpretation of the story of the rescue of Ethiopian Jewry is consistent with Phillips's postcolonial metamorphosis of the Jew into a metaphor for the complexities of color and race in social masks, a discourse in which the Black is humanized through brotherhood with another victim of racialization.

The novel flits in and out of the consciousness of unrelated protagonists across centuries and cultures in disparate but intense intimate moments detached from history, a telescoping of history that places a blood libel case in Portobuffole, the Holocaust, and the rescue of Ethiopian Jewry in contiguous parallels. The fragmentary incoherence of the non-linear plot reproduces something of the instability Phillips evidently senses in his own cultural and biographical make-up, which prevents him feeling at home, like the Jew, for even when singing *God Save the Queen* at a soccer game with gusto he still cannot relax his vigilance and feel totally at home:

> History has taught me that for people such as myself the rules will change. The goals posts will be moved. A new nationality act will be passed. And another. For people such as myself, the complex troubled history of Britain suggests vigilance. Mercifully, not everybody suffers the same degree of anxiety over this question of belonging. Most people live secure lives in a place they recognize as their own.[30]

Phillips is skeptical whether Britain can ever be a truly multicultural nation, though the presence in Britain of Caribbeans has done much to go beyond racial thinking.[31] In the postmodern transnational condition "we are all unmoored,"[32] in Phillips's pun on what for him expresses the ultimate outsider of the literary imagination and an enduring reference point in his writing, Shakespeare's Moor, Othello, a figure Caryl Phillips reads as his personal history and a key to his subaltern understanding of Shakespeare's play.

OTHELLO, THE MOOR OF VENICE

In *The Nature of Blood,* Phillips presents us with a character we recognize as Othello, yet the role of Othello in this novel is not so simple to understand. What indeed is Phillips doing with Othello and why marry him to an African wife? In order to unravel the plot of the novel and uncover the agenda behind the novel's ending, we must follow Othello into the Jewish Ghetto of Venice—the ultimate site of alienation—and encounter the alien identities which are at the heart of this novel that is so preoccupied with diaspora and the nature of blood.

The character of Othello, as Phillips re-imagines him in *The Nature of Blood,* is primarily concerned with fitting in, becoming one of the Venetians among whom he lives, and his slippery racial and religious identity as a Moor makes this goal at the same time more realizable and more dangerous. In *The European Tribe,* Phillips compares himself to Othello whom he sets up as the representation of the Black man in European society.[33] Othello is for Phillips the "Extravagant Stranger," as in the title of an anthology he compiled of centuries of outsider voices that write from the margin in English literature, the test of any any stable definition of national identity.[34] Race is not an essential sign of difference but rather Othello serves as the archetypal immigrant who must navigate the marginalizing and excluding routes that transverse his life and bring into contact diverse Others in tangential and disjunctive ways, just like the plots of Phillips's novels.[35]

In *The Nature of Blood,* all the characters are Jewish except for the figure of Othello, who is unique among other aliens and who is, in the subtitle of Shakespeare's tragedy, the "Moor of Venice." The Moor's vague and ambiguous—but not hybrid—identity poses a threat to the state; which is thus actually threatened from within much more than from the Turkish fleet. In his commentary on Shakespeare's *Othello,* Stephen Greenblatt remarks that in contrast to the other tragedies, "Little seems at stake." For, according to Greenblatt, the other tragedies "chronicle the fall of kings and princes, connecting familial and psychological concerns to the fate of nations" whereas in this play the threat to the nation, the Turkish armada, is dispatched early on, and the rest of the play is devoted to "domestic concerns seemingly of small consequence for affairs of state."[36] In invoking early modern Italy in the novel, Phillips is surely thinking of Britain, which has no memory of jackboots tramping down their streets:

The British have no memories of the awful mutability of national boundaries, a mutability that can serve seriously to corrode a people's sense of who they are. They have no memory of death camps on their soil, or hands raised in pathetic gesture of defeat. . . . Such a history is dangerous, for it supports myth-making.[37]

But Britain does have a history of antisemitism, including the Jew-badge, judicial executions, and expulsion, and it does have both Shylock and Othello.

Phillips's implicit reading of Shakespeare's play suggests that Othello's attempts to gain acceptance into Venetian society shake the highest echelons of the state. When the wife of Phillips's Othello character is challenged for marrying him, her father says she has betrayed: "her father, her family, and the republic."[38] In Shakespeare's play the very presence of Othello threatens the unity of the brotherhood of Venetians and the essence of the state. His presence forces them to examine how much they are willing to tolerate difference. When Barbanzio interrupts the Duke's discussion of the affairs of state with his personal concerns, he does so with the rationale that to ignore any of his private concerns or Othello's transgressions is to put their entire civilization at stake. Barbanzio addresses them all as a brotherhood, from which Othello is clearly excluded:

. . .The Duke himself,
Or any of my brothers of the state,
Cannot but feel this wrong as t'were their own;
For if such actions may have passage free,
Bondslaves and pagans shall our statesmen be
(*Othello* 1.2, 96–100)[39]

Barbanzio's reference to bondslaves should remind us that:

By Shakespeare's time, people of African descent had become an expected, if numerically small, presence in the metropolis. They were nevertheless perceived as a threat to the state. . . . The authorities, in other words, saw blacks as an anti-social presence, a population that had to be carefully controlled or else eliminated. . . . Shakespeare's *Othello* records anti-black attitudes at a crucial formative moment near the beginning of England's global expansion and commodification of black lives in the slave trade.[40]

What Ashley Dawson alludes to here is essential for an understanding of the flux of identities at the center of Phillips's novel. Whenever the nation state is in a crisis of definition, whether it is Elizabethan England, the Venetian republic, or the Third Reich, colonized subjects or those perceived as racial inferiors will pay the price of the new identity being formed. In "Europe of Strangers," Zygmunt Bauman traces the impact of the ideal of European unity that has led to blaming and excluding the alien for the insecurity felt by the general population:

> That tendency is topped up with another: the well-understandable inclination of political classes to divert the deepest cause of anxiety that is the experience of individual insecurity, to the popular concern with (already misplaced) threats to collective identity. . . . The governments cannot honestly promise its citizens secure existence and certain future; but they may for a time being unload at least part of the accumulated anxiety. . .by demonstrating their energy and determination in the war against foreign job-seekers and other alien gate-crashers, the intruders into once clean and quiet, orderly and familiar, native backyards.[41]

Phillips's postcolonial Othello presages the presence of the formerly colonized subjects in Europe that will be part of the colonization in reverse of the European Union. Despite his anxiety, he believes that he has "moved from the edge of the world to the centre, from the dark margins to a place where even the weakest rays of the evening sun were caught and thrown back in a blaze of glory."[42] Having been born of royal blood, served a mighty warrior and been a slave, he is ready to "stand at the very centre of the empire."[43] According to Clingman, he is a "mimic man," struggling to balance his sense of self with the weightless non-recognition afforded him by Venice.[44]

As the "Moor of Venice," Othello is a particularly useful demonstration of the politicization of the nature of blood and the color of otherness. The term Moor was notoriously indeterminate, as it could refer to the Berber Arab people of North Africa, to Africans generally or Indians, to any darker-skinned peoples, or even to the indigenous inhabitants of the New World.[45]

Those critics as well as audiences of Shakespeare's play who have defended the nobility of Desdemona and Othello have drawn upon the view of "the Moor" as White, European, Oriental, Moroccan, or "a stately Arab of the best caste."[46] In contrast, those who considered Othello and his actions degenerate inveterately saw him as African, primitive, and Black.[47] Until 9/11 at least, a Black Moor would be perceived as less desirable and more inferior than an Arab Moor, and as Shakespeare's play progresses, references to Othello's blackness become more frequent, yet Phillips does not incorporate these scenes of the play in his novel. In fact, he dwells excessively on his character's solitary arrival in Venice, his rambles through the city, his study of its language, manners, and customs, in short his attempts to assimilate. In his desire to be accepted, Othello adopts Venetian dress. However, a Renaissance audience would probably find a more defined "Other" far less threatening to the state. As Lupton writes:

> Whereas for the modern reader or viewer a black Othello is more subversive, "other," or dangerous, in the Renaissance scene a paler Othello more closely resembling the Turks whom he fights might actually challenge more deeply the integrity of the Christian paradigms set up in the play as the measure of humanity.[48]

Certainly, for the English, anxious about forced conversion to Catholicism and wary of the threat of conversion to Islam ("turning Turk"), the figure of the baptized Othello projected fears of both spiritual damnation and sexual transgression.[49]

In *The Nature of Blood,* Phillips is not only concerned with how much difference the state will tolerate, but with how much any given individual is willing to change or must relinquish in order to be accepted by the host society. Phillips does not depict an Othello who is undone by his own jealously or by a villain who hates him for his race. Instead, Phillips ceases to tell Shakespeare's tale at the moment that Othello feels he has most successfully integrated into Venetian society and asks us to consider the price of that success. The Turkish threat has been eliminated; he has a prominent Venetian wife; they are about to celebrate both military and nuptial triumphs; and from what we can see there is no Iago lurking. Rather, Phillips introduces what amounts to a postscript, in the form of an American voice who warns:

And so you shadow her every move, attend to her every whim,
like the black Uncle Tom that you are. Fighting the white man's
war for him. . . . You tuck your black skin away beneath their
epauletted uniform, appropriate their words. . .their manners,. . .
yet you conveniently forget your own family, and thrust your
wife and son to the back of your noble mind. . . . You are lost, a
sad black man, first in a long line of so-called achievers who are
too weak to yoke their past with their present; too naïve to insist
on both; too foolish to realize that to supplant one with the other
can only lead to catastrophe. Go ahead, peer on her alabaster
skin. Go ahead, revel in the delights of her wanton bed, but to
whom will you turn when she, too, is lost and a real storm breaks
about your handkerchiefed head? My friend, the Yoruba have a
saying: the river that does not know its own source will dry up.
You will do well to remember that.[50]

This sarcastic voice "asserts that he is nothing but a white mask, tucking his
black skin away in shame, disregarding his past, language, and family, and
thus forgetting his origins."[51] Nonetheless, as we have seen, *The Nature of
Blood* does not offer an essentialized "return to roots" view of home. Instead,
it evokes a sense of being adrift, of homecomings to promised lands that are
never quite what they were promised to be.[52]

   Even before the dire predictions of this anachronistic voice from an
American future, Phillips's Othello ruminates upon the ramifications of his
isolation. Despite his marriage to Desdemona, on his way to Cyprus, he
reflects:

Alone on these seas, and with none of my kind or complexion for
company, there is nobody with whom I might share memories of
a common past, and nobody with whom I might converse in the
language that sits most easily on my tongue.[53]

In what is truly an innovation on the part of Phillips, his Othello figure has
struggled with the memories not only of his homeland, but (like Stephan) of
the wife and child he left behind. One could hardly imagine Shakespeare
considering the existence of Othello's African wife. The Elizabethan Othello
could have no past and no identity outside the Venetian society to which he
aspired. As Phillips writes in *The European Tribe,* there is no evidence of
Othello having any Black friends, eating any African foods, speaking any

language other than theirs. He makes no reference to any family. From what we are given it is clear that he denied, or at least did not cultivate his past. He relied upon the Venetian system, and ultimately he died a European death—suicide.[54]

This is the "fatal mimicry" described by Fanon which leads the Black man to don a white mask, to deny his roots and assume a European self. Ania Loomba reports that seeing *Othello* performed in one of the cultures of "his" origin in South Africa, where interracial marriages were illegal, reinforced the message that "the play is not just about race in general but about a Black man isolated from other Black people. His loneliness is an integral feature of the play's racial politics. Shakespeare's *Othello* is about the African in Europe and not the African in Africa."[55]

Phillips's dual concern with the exclusion of the outsider, on the one hand, and the migrants' loss of home when they are cut off from their own people, on the other, is brought out most graphically in the curious visit in the novel that Othello pays to the Jewish Ghetto. Most scholars maintain that, though Shakespeare set several of his plays in Venice, he never actually visited the city though some like to speculate that perhaps he did get there during the "lost years" between 1585 and 1592 when we do not know his whereabouts.[56] As for Shakespeare's knowledge of the Jewish Ghetto, scholars have attempted to establish some historicity of the play by pointing to the fact that during those years two of the Christian guards in the Ghetto were named Gobbo.[57] However, readers of *The Nature of Blood* are forced to interrogate what the ghetto is hiding that Othello (unlike Desai and her protagonist Baumgartner, as we saw in the previous chapter) finds but fails to connect to in Venice. For without any precedent at all in the Shakespearean text, Phillips imagines that Othello seeks out a Jewish scribe in the Ghetto to decipher a letter he receives from Desdemona and to write one to her in return, a scene that Clingman has interpreted as one of triangulation, in which the African tries to see beyond the Christian through the Jew, just as in Sartre's *Anti-Semite and Jew* the inauthentic Jew views his fellow Jew through the eyes of the prejudiced Christian.[58]

The Ghetto was first established by the city council in 1516 in the New Foundry (*Ghetto Nuovo*) as both a place of segregation and refuge for Jews who were fleeing violence in the city.[59] This might seem like a workable compromise for the time, though recent research has suggested that the Ghetto was, historically, not a first step in segregation but a further measure in attempting to control Jewish social and commercial contacts with Christians.[60] In fact, though the Venetians fought the Ottoman Empire, there were "Turks" living in Venice and many, especially those from the Balkans and Greece, petitioned the municipality for a separate Ghetto or safe area. In 1621, the Senate granted them an area on the Grand Canal known as the new Fondaca dei Turchi.[61] Phillips's protagonist seems to acknowledge Venetian attitudes towards the Other, but he does not endorse this separatist solution when he tours the Ghetto and concludes:

> Why should they live in this manner defeated my understanding. Surely there was some other land or some other people among whom they might dwell in more tolerable conditions?[62]

As the institution of the ghetto suggests, the city of Venice hides the reality that Othello discovers, their obsession with keeping "the bloodlines pure," and this obsession will lead to the historical reality that scared the fifteen-year-old Caryl Phillips growing up in England who pondered implications of the European Holocaust for Blacks like him. Venice pretends to welcome all cultures, but, in finding the Ghetto, Othello finds Venice's secret: the Ghetto is the proof that Venetians hide those Others who are too different, and ultimately they and the rest of Europe will deport and exterminate them. With the dubious benefit of hindsight we know that in 1943–44, in Venice, two hundred people were deported, and only eight came back from the death camps.[63] At this point, however, Othello does not make a connection between himself and those Others. He uses them to correspond with the woman whom he believes will secure his ties with the Venetian establishment, and when he celebrates his marriage to her he believes he is "entrenched...securely in Venetian society.[64] As Phillips explains in his reading of Shakespeare in *The European Tribe,* when Othello celebrates his marriage to a White Venetian woman, his Desdemona, "It is now that the tragedy commences. But it can only do so because it is precisely at this moment of 'triumph' that Othello begins to forget that he is black."[65] The Othello figure in the novel finds the Ghetto, but he turns his back on it in favor of the middle class suburbs.

A Black Shylock

In his comparison of the Moor of Venice and *The Merchant of Venice,* Michael Neill demonstrates how the Moor and Shylock are both outsiders whose ability to assimilate is paradoxically what the state finds most menacing. According to Neill:

> Of course the particular fear that attaches to the demon-Jew in early modern European culture has to do with his insidious role as the hidden stranger, the alien whose otherness is the more threatening for its guise of semblance. This was a culture whose expansionism, ironically enough, generated fears of hungrily absorptive otherness which were expressing in complementary fantasies of dangerous miscegenation, degeneration and cannibalistic desire; in its fictions the Jew represents the deepest threat of all—that of a *secret* difference masquerading as its likeness.[66]

The proximity or contiguity of "Moor" and "jew" on the stage is not accidental, and indeed, in Imperial literature, there are many ambivalent Jewish characters who take on Negroid characteristics when their authors wish to depict them as depraved or savage. Bryan Cheyette stresses the slipperiness of racial classification which reveals underlying tensions in colonial discourse:

> Jews could be deemed to be black, even in relation to a Judeo-Christian tradition that was apparently at the heart of empire. But one should not, in fact, underestimate the intense arbitrariness of Semitic racial designations in imperial culture.[67]

The trial scene in the novel is a historical blood libel against the Jews, not Shylock's suit for his pound of flesh, and it ends with the public spectacle of their execution in St Mark's Square in Venice. Yet Shylock was for Phillips the hero who dared at his trial to accuse the Venetian Christians of hypocrisy and to defiantly challenge the Venetian colonial system. When the Duke challenges Shylock to say why he should have mercy when he renders none himself, Shylock retorts:

> SHYLOCK: What judgment shall I dread, doing no wrong?
>   You have among you many a purchased slave,
>   Which, like your asses and your dogs and mules,
>   You use in abject and in slavish parts,
>   Because you bought them: shall I say to you,
>   Let them be free, marry them to your heirs?
>   Why sweat they under burthens? Let their beds

Be made as soft as yours and let their palates
Be season'd with such viands?[68]

Of course, Shylock's defense is an ad hominem argument which claims his right to do as he pleases with the human flesh he has so dearly bought. The Christians' disregard for human dignity and freedom under the rules of their society is an instruction he will follow and better, suggesting an interchangeability of Christians, Jews, and Muslims in a Machiavellian marketplace.[69] Nevertheless, this is a significant protest in Othello's city where blackness is "equitable with devil-worship," and most Black Americans, Phillips believes, would readily understand Farah's sympathy for Shylock in Karen Blixen's *Out of Africa*.[70]

It is not, however, Shylock's thirst for revenge or his insistence on the law that inspires Phillips in *The Nature of Blood*. Phillips has Stephan Stern think anxiously in the British internment camp in Cyprus about what these Holocaust orphans might do with guns once recruited by the Hagannah, the Jewish underground army, and Eva too, immediately after liberation, shudders at the revenge killing of a camp guard, sure that "Holy Scriptures" accorded more dignity than this and unable to think of the guards as evil. Rather, Phillips is reading Shylock as the Black man's brother for whom antisemitism is anti-Black; it is the same form of racism. In fact, though Phillips's Othello wanders a lot through Venice, he never meets Shylock, but he does come across the social and sexual segregation of the Jews. It seems that Phillips is reading Shylock as a victim of what the Black man knows all too well to be the dehumanizing effects of racism which must be resisted. In the novel, Eva lets herself be seen naked in public and defiantly refuses to answer questions from the woman officer assigned to process her for transfer to a DP camp because her shame and degradation are part of a knowledge which nobody else could share. She resists an intrusion into her inner self, an abrasive, depersonalizing intrusion that is at the heart of what racism does to human beings of a different color and race. However crazy she might be, she cannot afford to release her grip on what is essentially human and feminine within her, even when people stare at her disfigured body in a public park or children throw stones at her. Eva can thus be seen as a female and Jewish counterpart to Othello, whose experience is mirrored in the novel by the Black Jewish Malka.

Phillips has been criticized for apparently appropriating the Holocaust in *Higher Ground* and *The Nature of Blood* as an equivalent trauma to the suffering of Blacks who were shipped in millions as slaves to the Americas. But Stephen Clingman has demonstrated convincingly that Philips does not establish any such equivalence,[71] and indeed, Stef Craps proposes that Phillips effects in these novels a "management of empathy" that qualifies and checks our emotive responses: for example, after coming to identify with the delirious liberated camp inmate, Eva, the reader finds out that she has served in the *Sonderkommando,* handling the corpses of the victims and thus she is tainted morally by what Primo Levi calls the "gray zone" of Auschwitz. Nevertheless, Craps discerns a cross-cultural communication of trauma, of the kind Cathy Caruth explores in *Unclaimed Experience,* which he sees in the affinity of Eva's experience of deportation to a concentration camp and later of ostracism in Britain as an alien with Malka's experience in Ethiopia being "herded" onto convoys destined for Israel and her reception there.[72]

The attempt in the dedication of Toni Morrison's *Beloved* to "sixty million and more" to shift attention to the passage of Black slaves to America, which would overshadow the Holocaust of European Jewry, has aroused controversy over appropriation of the Nazi genocide as primarily a universal suffering, rather than a state policy directed at the extermination of the Jewish people. Addressing this issue, Walter Benn Michaels has contended that the Holocaust needs to be de-essentialized so that it can pass from race into cultural memory as a "deconstructive performative [which] makes it possible to define the Jew not as someone who has Jewish blood or who believes in Judaism but as someone who, having experienced the Holocaust, can—even if he or she was never there—acknowledge it as part of his or her history."[73] Phillips is not arguing for a "Black Holocaust," or universalizing it in Michaels' sense, but he does form correspondences in *The Nature of Blood* which imply that suffering from racial persecution can be a shared human experience that should not be defined by difference of skin color but can be imagined by those who were not there. For example, in another strand of Phillips's novel, the Jews of Portobuffole are treated as foreigners and will always remain so, forced to practice usury and insisting on living apart. When a blood libel circulates (based on the belief that Jews needed Christian blood to cleanse them of guilt for the killing of Jesus, for which purposes a Christian child was sacrificed, usually at the Passover feast), martyrdom unites them in their ancient faith and tribal identity. Their story is alternated with the story of a young woman in the ghetto and then on the cattle train to the concentration camp (the Eva we have already met in the DP camp), the unnamed Othello's amorous adventures, and, finally, the Ethiopian Malka's alienation in the new country after the Black Exodus to the "promised land."

These are, in Clingman's analysis of the novel, not equivalences but contiguities and metaphorical spaces that dialogize with each other as a Bakhtinian polyphony in a transnational continuum of humanity.[74] If Blacks have found difficulty in articulating a remembrance of their history, partly because of a lack of a common identity and the erasure of African tribal traditions, the Holocaust may serve, as Paul Gilroy has argued in *The Black Atlantic,* as a point of resonance that is neither identification nor an Afrocentric essentialism, which would allow conversation between the histories of Jews and Blacks, whose confrontation with racial violence has, in their different ways, been bound up with modernity.[75] The constellations of experiences of racial violence and discrimination in the novel remind us not of identification, but of the difference which we refuse to recognize in the singularity of the individual that makes up Phillips' version of transnational identity. Clingman writes, "Such a conceptual alignment is itself a syntactic gesture—a mark of contiguity, adjacency, mutual invocation in the realm of identity."[76] This is a metonymic reading of history through what Michael Rothberg has called an "anachronistic aesthetic," which places the Jewish and Black experiences within a postcolonial discourse that summons a "multidirectional" memory of the Holocaust while contesting the racist imaginary and critiquing the minority voices caught up in it.[77] Or, to put it another way, Phillips invites us to engage with issues of "historical distinctiveness," such as the relation of the Holocaust to other histories of racism, and of "national distinctiveness," such as the relation of cultural production to writing identity.[78]

Venice, which has become a familiar locus of the modern imagination, has in effect been rewritten as a site of a timeless diasporic imagining which undoes a Eurocentric view by relating the Afro-Caribbean experience of racism to antisemitism, by relating Othello to Shylock and the Holocaust.[79] What, then, does Shylock look like to the "Moor of Venice" from this postcolonial perspective? We recall, that Shylock is, indeed, dark, as Jews were imagined to be in Elizabethan times, racially equivalent to the Moor.[80] The confusion of race, blood, and color in *The Merchant of Venice* reflects perhaps the confusion of Elizabethan ideas about racial identity—the Prince of Morocco challenges Portia to "cut incision" to see whether his blood is any different from hers—and may result from overlapping of the figure of the theological Jew, who cannot assimilate into the Paulite discourse of nations united in Christ, and the racialized Jew, the crypto-Jews or Marranos in Spain who also reached England and whose identity is unclear and hidden. In any event, Shylock's forced conversion is a device to render the State's "mercy" in confiscating his property, robbing him of the comic villain "jew's" money-lust. The Moor may serve as a comparable example of a demonized stereotype of otherness based on cultural superiority and a muddled idea of national and religious identities that feeds racial and sexual fears. But the differences are significant. Unlike the "jew," whose complexion or outward appearance is deceitful, blackness cannot be washed away, but whether virtue and service to the State of Venice can turn Othello "fair" (as the Duke tells Brabanzio in Act I, scene iii) depends on whether there can be a radical break in the equation of outer appearance and moral or spiritual inner self.[81] Moreover, while Shylock is allowed sufficient humanity to demonstrate the monstrosity of his anti-social behavior, on the early modern stage the Moor "is uniquely poised to negotiate, mediate, even transform the terms of European culture."[82]

Phillips's Othello figure, by contrast, escapes from his fate at the hands of Shakespeare and delivers a lesson that marriage to Desdemona and religious conversion will not bring about the desired social and racial acceptance. Both the Othello figure and Stephan (in his liaison with Malka, the Black Jewess from Ethiopia) find that lying in bed with someone is a displacement of race which prevents them being their true selves. In the novel, Eva Stern suffers the same fate as Shakespeare's Othello, suicide, when she deludes herself into thinking that she could be accepted in England. The nature of blood is innate and immutable; all too human in its ambivalences to assimilation, and it perseveres in a desperate clinging to dignity. It is in this spirit that Phillips' novel writes back to racism and antisemitism, in a new world order that can no longer resist the claims of migrants and refugees, but in which nobody will feel fully at home. Phillips seems closest here to Paul Gilroy's depiction of a diverse Black culture in *The Black Atlantic* with a privileged connection to Africa but not limited to any one nation or ethnic group. This is Phillips's "new world order" in which "there will soon be one global conversation with limited participation open to all, and full participation available to none. In this new world order nobody will feel fully at home."[83]

NOTES

1. Frantz Fanon, *Black Skin, White Masks,* trans. Charles Lam Markmann (London: MacGibbon & Kee, 1968), 160–64.

2. Ibid., 122.

3. Stephen Clingman, *The Grammar of Identity: Transnational Fiction and the Nature of the Boundary* (Oxford: Oxford University Press, 2009), 68.

4. Caryl Phillips, *A New World Order* (New York: Vintage, 2002), 131.

5. Interview with Frank Birbalsingh, "Caryl Phillips: The Legacy of Othello, I," in *Frontiers of Caribbean Literatures in English,* ed. Frank Birbalsingh (New York: St. Martin's, 1996), 185.

6. Caryl Phillips, *The European Tribe* (London: Faber and Faber, 1987).

7. Ibid., 52.

8. Ibid., 53.

9. Ibid., 54.

10. Caryl Phillips,"The Nature of Blood and the Ghost of Anne Frank," *Common Quest* (Summer 1998): 4–7.

11. Ibid., 6; see also idem, *European Tribe,* 52. Clingman, *Grammar of Identity,* 69.

12. See photo in Phillips, "Nature of Blood and the Ghost of Anne Frank," 5.

13. Idem, *New World Order,* 5.

14. Fanon, *Black Skin, White Masks,* 122.

15. Paul Gilroy, *Against Race: Imagining Political Culture Beyond the Color Line* (Cambridge, Mass.: Harvard University Press, 2000), 4.

16. Stephen Clingman, "Forms of History and Identity in *The Nature of Blood,*" *Salmagundi* 143 (Summer 2004): 141–66.

17. Phillips, *A New World Order,* 130.

18. Idem, "Nature of Blood and the Ghost of Anne Frank," 4.

19. Clingman, "Forms of History and Identity," 143–44; idem, *Grammar of Identity,* 72–75.

20. See Paul Gilroy, *The Black Atlantic: Modernity and Double Consciousness* (Cambridge, Mass.: Harvard University Press, 1993).

21. Phillips, *New World Order,* 304.

22. Idem, 131.

23. Stuart Hall, "Cultural Identity and Diaspora," in *Identity: Community, Culture, Difference,* ed. Jonathan Rutherford (London: Lawrence and Wishart, 1990), 222–37.

24. Stef Craps, "Linking Legacies of Loss: Traumatic Histories and Cross-Cultural Empathy in Caryl Phillips's *Higher Ground* and *The Nature of Blood,*" *Studies in the Novel* 40.1–2 (Spring–Summer 2008): 191–202.

25. Caryl Phillips, *The Nature of Blood* (New York: Vintage, 1998), 45.

26. Ibid., 210.

27. Phillips, "Nature of Blood and the Ghost of Anne Frank," 4. Phillips does not identify the concern as AIDS-related and treats the incident as racist. For the factual background to this common view and discussion of alleged racism, see Teshome G. Wagaw, *For Our Soul: Ethiopian Jews in Israel* (Michigan: Wayne State University Press, 1993); Len Lyons, *The Ethiopian Jews of Israel: Personal Stories of Life in the Promised Land* (Vermont: Jewish Lights, 2007); Michael Ashkenazi and Alex Weingrod, eds., *Ethiopian Jews and Israel* (New Brunswick, N.J.: Transaction Books, 1987); Hagar Salomon, *The Hyena People* (Berkeley: University of California Press, 1999).

28. Phillips, "Nature of Blood and the Ghost of Anne Frank," 4–5.

29. Bryan Cheyette, "Venetian Spaces: Old-New Literatures and the Ambivalent Uses of Jewish History," *Essays and Studies* 53 (2000): 65.

30. Phillips, *A New World Order*, 309. See Paul Gilroy, *There Ain't No Black in the Union Jack: The Cultural Politics of Race and Nation* (New York: Routledge, 1992).

31. Phillips, *New World Order*, 295.

32. Phillips in conversation with Frank Birbalsingh, "Caryl Phillips: The Legacy of Othello, II," in *Frontiers of Caribbean Literatures in English,* ed. Frank Birbalsingh. (New York: St. Martin's, 1996), 191. See Phillips, *New World Order,* 6, for another use of this pun when a waiter in West Africa expresses his condolences to Phillips on the death of "his" Princess Diana.

33. Clingman, *Grammar of Identity,* 67.

34. Caryl Phillips, ed., *Extravagant Strangers: A Literature of Belonging* (London: Faber, 1997).

35. Clingman, *Grammar of Identity,*76–77. Rebecca L. Walkowitz relates this to Phillips' transnational status as a writer and the formation of a world literature of migrancy ("The Location of Literature: The Transnational Book and the Migrant Writer," *Contemporary Literature* 47. 4 [Winter 2006]: 537–39).

36. Stephen Greenblatt, ed., *The Norton Shakespeare* (New York: W. W. Norton, 1997), 2091.

37. Phillips, *New World Order,* 295.

38. Idem, *Nature of Blood,* 158.

39. Greenblatt, *Norton Shakespeare,* 2107.

40. Ashley Dawson, "'To Remember too much is indeed a form of madness': Caryl Phillips's *The Nature of Blood* and the Modalities of European Racism," *Postcolonial Studies* 7.1 (2004): 93–94. Ania Loomba, however, warns us against reconstructing Elizabethan attitudes towards Blacks and identifying Othello in terms of contemporary attitudes towards "race" (*Shakespeare, Race, and Colonialism* [Oxford: Oxford University Press, 2002], 1–2, 22–44).

41. Zygmunt Bauman, *Europe of Strangers* (Oxford: ESRC Transnational Communities Programme, 1998), Working Paper no. 3, 10–11; www.transcomm.ox.ac.uk/working%20papers/bauman.pdf.

42. Phillips, *Nature of Blood,* 107.

43. Ibid.

44. Clingman, *Grammar of Idenity,* 85. Clingman is thinking of Fanon's notion of mimicry here, but the mirroring of mimicry in Naipaul or Bhabha (discussed above in chapter three) would seem to be relevant also.

45. Michael Neill, "'Mulattos,' 'Blacks,' and 'Indian Moors': Othello and Early Modern Constructions of Human Difference," *Shakespeare Quarterly* 49.4 (Winter 1998): 364.

46. Greenblatt, *Norton Shakespeare,* 2092.

47. Ibid.

48. Julia Reinhard Lupton, "Othello Circumcised: Shakespeare and the Pauline Discourse of Nations," *Representations* 57 (Winter 1997): 73.

49. Daniel Vitkus, *Turning Turk: English Theater and the Multicultural Mediterranean, 1570–1630* (Houndmills: Palgrave Macmillan, 2008), 77–106.

50. Phillips, *Nature of Blood,* 181.

51. Maurizio Calbi, "'The Ghosts of Strangers': Hospitality, Identity and Temporality in Caryl Phillips's *The Nature of Blood*," *Journal of Early Modern Cultural Studies.* 6. 2 (Fall/Winter 2006): 49.

52. See ibid.; Benedicte Ledent, *Caryl Phillips* (Manchester: Manchester University Press, 2002).

53. Phillips, *Nature of Blood,* 159.

54. Phillips, *European Tribe,* 51.

55. Ania Loomba, "'Local-manufacture made-in-India Othello fellows': Issues of Race, Hybridity and Location in Post-Colonial Shakespeares," in *Post-Colonial Shakespeares,* ed. Ania Loomba and Martin Orkin (New York and London: Routledge, 1998), 148.

56. Shaul Bassi and Alberto Toso Fei, *Shakespeare in Venice* (Treviso: Elzevio, 2007), 11.

57. Ibid., 109.

58. Clingman, "Forms of History and Identity," 156–57.

59. Bassi and Fei, *Shakespeare in Venice,* 152.

60. See Benjamin Ravid, "How 'Other' Really Was the Jewish Other? The Evidence from Venice," in *Acculturation and its Discontents: The Italian Jewish Experience between Exclusion and Inclusion,* ed. David N. Myers et al. (Toronto: University of Toronto Press, 2008), 19–55.

61. Ibid., 124–25.

62. Phillips, *Nature of Blood,* 131.

63. Bassi and Fei, *Shakespeare in Venice,* 152.

64. Phillips, *European Tribe,* 48.

65. Ibid.

66. Neill, "'Mulattos,' 'Black,' and 'Indian Moors,'" 363–64.

67. Bryan Cheyette, "Neither Black Nor White: The Figure of 'the Jew' in Imperial British Literature," in *The Jew in the Text,* ed. Linda Nochlin and Tamar Garb (London: Thames & Hudson, 1995), 39.

68. Greenblatt, *Norton Shakespeare,* 1130.

69. Vitkus, *Turning Turk,* 195.

70. Phillips, *European Tribe,* 55.

71. Clingman, "Forms of History and Identity," 147–48, 159–60.

72. Craps, "Linking Legacies of Loss," 191–202.

73. Walter Benn Michaels, "'You Who Never Was There': Slavery and the New Historicism, Deconstruction and the Holocaust," *Narrative* 4.1 (1996): 13. See on this Emily Budick, "Acknowledging the Holocaust in Contemporary American Fiction and Criticism," in *Breaking Crystal: Writing and Memory after Auschwitz,* ed. Efraim Sicher (Urbana: University of Illinois Press, 1998), 329–43.

74. Clingman, "Forms of History and Identity," 162.

75. Gilroy, *Black Atlantic,* 205–13.

76. Clingman, *Grammar of Identity,* 73. See Clingman's sensitive reading of the multiple constellations in the novel which form a syntactic series of substitutions and alterations of identities between Jew, Venetian, and Black, ibid., 87–92.

77. Michael Rothberg, *Multidirectional Memory: Remembering the Holocaust in the Age of Decolonization* (Stanford: Stanford University Press, 2009), 153–72.

78. Rebecca L. Walkowitz, "Location of Literature," 536–37. Angeles de la Concha, however, sees the collapsing of time in *The Nature of Blood* as a denial of progress in a posthistorical teleology ("The End of History. Or Is It? Circularity versus Progress in Caryl Phillips' *The Nature of Blood*." *Misceaenea* 22 [2000]: 1–19).

79. Cheyette, "Venetian Spaces" 63–65.

80. Janet Adelman, *Blood Relations: Christian and Jew in The Merchant of Venice* (Chicago: Chicago University Press, 2008), 83–85.

81. Loomba, *Shakespeare, Race, and Colonialism,* 58-59.

82. Emily C. Bartels, *Speaking of the Moor: From Alcazar to Othello* (Philadelphia: University of Pennsylvania Press, 2008). 15.

83. Phillips, *New World Order,* 5.

CHAPTER FIVE

Down Cultural Memory Lane:
Ali, Lichtenstein, and Gavron

Place has always been a strong component in our personal identity, as well as in our relation to community and to nation. In Britain, as in ancient Greece and in China under the later Han dynasty, the nostalgia for the countryside has been an urban taste of a privileged elite that has shaped a number of literary conventions in the imagining of a past idyll of social harmony and lost paradises, constructing a binary opposition between the city or wilderness and an ideal space.[1] But in London's East End local memories in the late nineteenth and early twentieth century knew little of the countryside, let alone literature. Slum kids between the wars rarely saw the countryside or the seaside, except on charity outings or on forced evacuation when war came. Yet the East End tenements have often been sentimentalized as a close-knit community characterized in the interwar years by social activism (Trade Unionism and the stand-off with Mosley's fascists in Cable Street) and during the Blitz by steadfast determination.[2] The East End stands for an ethos of what has been lost in most British cities and it has been immortalized with an updated message of multiculturalism and interethnic romance in the television soap opera *EastEnders*. However, the "Cockney spirit" largely represents an imagined community (in many cases a retrospective one) and conceals a less rosy picture in the interwar period. Moreover, a distinction has to be made between the communal "security blanket" of mutual assistance and support, and the larger community which gave a sense of identity that may have differed for ethnic and historical reasons among Jews and non-Jews and may have differing geographical or social boundaries among different groups, though no less inflected with a local territoriality and class solidarity that sometimes ran across ethnic divisions.[3]

Jewish historians and writers who focus on the antisemitism in the interwar East End or its Jewish social and cultural networks have identified it as a Jewish space, when it was just as much English working class, with its distinct and highly conservative mentality and traditional way of life (though some streets were more densely populated by Jews than others).[4] This chapter looks at how a territory of cultural memory that has been populated by successive waves of immigrants (first Huguenots, then Jews, now South Asians) has been occupied by postmodern writers and artists eager to create another twist in the myth of "outcast" London associated with Jack the Ripper, the Siege of Sidney Street, and the Kray twins.[5]

The East End is now up for grabs as a prime property of multiculturalism, but, as a locus of writing, its place in cultural memory may be eclipsing any historical reality. Place here has as much to do with *not* belonging—the archetypal immigrant experience—as with the hazy myths that give us a sense of belonging to a locality or neighborhood.[6] The search for identity that reimagines the East End as a locus of writing is typically undertaken by those who come from comfortable suburbs, from elsewhere, and may result from the fragmentation that is a fall-out of globalizing trends which destabilize constructions of ethnicity in nationhood and in collective identity.

In his review of Monica Ali's *Brick Lane* (2003)[7] which appeared in the *London Review of Books,* Sukhdev Sandhu, a well known scholar of Black and Asian British writing, spends more than half of his review discussing the novel's locale, alternately called Spitalfields, Whitechapel, Tower Hamlets, and Banglatown.[8] When he does introduce the novel it seems that the purpose for this lengthy introduction has been to establish the setting in an area of London that has traditionally been marginal to the city's life, an area with cheap, poor housing in which immigrants who first arrived in London found employment in the garment industry. Yet in this evacuated Jewish space what came before and after the Jewish immigrant experience has shaped the cultural memory into a postmodern palimpsest that has left a multiple impression deep in the popular and literary imagination.

Sandhu is not the only critic of the novel to consider it necessary to provide some background of the history of Brick Lane before discussing the novel that carries the title of the street that rings in the memory of succeeding waves of immigrants. Critics usually include some overview of the Huguenot refugees who came in the eighteenth century to escape religious persecution in France and then the Eastern European Jews who settled in the area "to make what was already a ghetto their own."[9] Moreover, the area has attracted tourists (because of nostalgia hunting) and property speculators (because of the value of eighteenth-century houses and their proximity to the City) at the

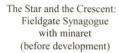

The Star and the Crescent:
Fieldgate Synagogue
with minaret
(before development)

same time that it is still home to the latest group of immigrants, most of them living in poverty.

The underlying reason for the parallel between Jewish and Bangladeshi immigrant experience has to do with a political discourse after 7/7. The Jewish experience of the East End is often cited as evidence that the present-day Muslim inhabitants of the East End are receiving the same treatment as the Jews a hundred years before—suspected as terrorists, shunned as aliens, denied employment.[10] In fact, the Jewish "memory" of the East End has become important for the advocacy in the multicultural debate of an ethnic diversity that would establish a prior heterogeneous cultural identity and undermine any contention that postwar Britain was intrinsically English and White.

The history of the East End is only briefly alluded to at the end of the novel, and there is little evidence of any coexistence of Jews and Muslims: the former Jewish residents do not seem to still live or work in the area or to interact with the current residents. Nonetheless, we know that the earliest Bengali arrivals to the East End worked as assistants to Jewish tailors. By the 1970s, Brick Lane and the surrounding streets had become predominantly South Asian: the Brick Lane Talmud Torah became an Indian cinema; the pupils of a Church of England elementary school, where nuns used to have to learn Yiddish in order to understand the children, are now predominantly Muslim. Street signs have appeared in Bengali. Opposite the Jewish Soup Kitchen, now a historical Listed Building, a wall mural records the Jewish presence in a multicultural mosaic by a local Bengali artist, a statement about an ideal hybridity of the immigrant populations. The Jamme Masjid Mosque, which stands at the corner of Fournier Street and Brick Lane, originally was a Huguenot Church, La Neuve Église, and later the Mahzike Hadath syna-gogue,[11] demonstrating how one immigrant population has replaced another,

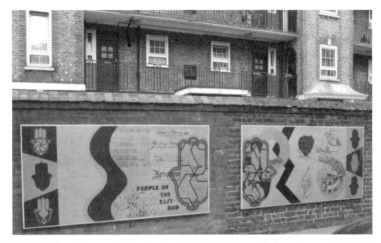

The Multicultural Legacy of Immigration: Murals by Meena Thakor and Kinsi Abdulleh
opposite the Jewish Soup Kitchen, Brune Street, East London

a displacement which records a historical memory in a postmodern palimpsest of signs. This is, however, occupation of a vacated Jewish area, not multicultural hybridity or coexistence. In the streets surrounding Brick Lane, Fournier Street, and Princelet Street, there are food stores and eateries that still bear the names of former Jewish storeowners, such as David Kira, or Kossoff's bakery. But while Hebrew could still be seen in Jewish stores during the first wave of South Asian immigrants, who often worked for Jewish furriers and tailors, most Jewish traders had moved out of the area by the 1980s and the familiar sweatshops had been taken over by South Asian immigrants or their children, occupying such recognizably Jewish spaces as a former synagogue. Wholesalers who had moved to Northwest London still had premises in the East End (as late as 2006), but the visible Jewish presence was now a historical memory.

It is tempting to see in the pattern of immigration by South Asians a repetition of the Jewish experience. Emmanuel Litvinoff, a Jewish journalist and novelist who grew up in the East End, believed that revisiting his childhood memories of the East End could offer lessons to the postwar immigrants.

Brick Lane, 1950s

Clumps of Muslim men stood aimlessly on corners and there was a curious absence of women. Shrill, eerie music wailed in the heat of the afternoon. The odour of spices mingled with the stench of drains. Skinny little girls with enormous, solemn black eyes sat on doorsteps nursing babies. Outside a cinema crudely painted posters of veiled ladies and jeweled rajahs advertised a film from the sub-continent of India.[12]

Yet this history of successful and successful immigrations that passed through and out of the East End does not quite tally with the picture we get of Brick Lane in Monica Ali's novel. Monica Ali claims that in the 1980s, when Nazneen lands in London, the streets of the East End were "truly multi-cultural, Jewish, Bengali and English activities carried out side by side."[13] Actually, the hybridity of the neighborhood comes across only in the historically savvy but deluded character Chanu's preaching about colonialism and nationalism; it becomes significant toward the end of the novel. On the eve of Chanu's departure, Nazneen and Chanu watch a large demonstration outside their window of Muslims and labor activists against the White

New Road Synagogue, 1980s

supremacists. Chanu, finally, now that he has arranged the means for his family to return "home" to Dhaka, ruminates on the immigrants who have preceded them:

> "The young ones," said Chanu, "they'll be the ones to decide. Do you know how many immigrant populations have been here before us? In the eighteenth century the French Protestants fled here, escaping Catholic persecution. They were silk weavers. They made good. One hundred years later, the Jews came. They thrived. At the same time, the Chinese came as merchants. The Chinese are doing very well." Chanu still had hold of her hand. "Which way is it going to go?" (390)

This is a view from the vantage point of failure and departure, and it must call into question ideals of cultural hybridity and successful immigration. Fundamentalism and hybridity are opposed, but the conflict undermines both notions of hybridity and purity. While immigrants from the Commonwealth benefited from the advantages of Britain's welfare state and opportunities for social mobility, their British-born children tend to question assimilatory patterns and integration into Western culture. They may be potential recruits for militant groups and may find resistance movements attractive because they offer a radical ideology and affirmation of ethnic identity. Graduates of the *medresa* are unlikely to achieve economic or social goals and probably have little desire to assimilate to the host society, though the actual terrorist profile is usually well-educated and middle-class. We recall that in Kureishi's "My Son the Fanatic" the boy is unreachable in his rebellion against his father's Western ways; the boy concludes the story on an ironical note when he asks who the real fanatic is after his father beats him up in desperation.

Many of Monica Ali's critics, however, have taken the realism of *Brick Lane* for granted, arguing over the relation of its realistic form with the postcolonial issues of immigration, subaltern voices, and cultural hybridity. Jane Hiddleston maintains that despite its overt realism, the novel draws attention to the artifice associated with its form and to the stereotypes and myths that come in the way of our understanding of the immigrant community.[14] Indeed, residents of Brick Lane have protested that the novel does not fairly represent them. Most of the inhabitants of Brick Lane hail from the Sylhet region of Bangladesh, and the Sylhet Development and Welfare council has condemned Ali's depiction of Bangladeshis as backward and uneducated.[15] Implicit in their criticism is a questioning of Ali's credentials for representing them. The title of Ali's essay on the genesis of the novel, "Where I'm Coming From," makes it clear that, when she is repeatedly asked "What inspired you to write this," she is really being asked a question about her origins. In this essay, Ali describes her history as the child of an English mother and Pakistani father who escaped civil war in East Pakistan with her mother. Her father later joined them, and they settled in an English mill town near Manchester. At first, her parents thought they would return as soon as things settled down "back home," but soon "going home" became a dream. In her attempt to authenticate the connection between her own upbringing and background and that of the Bangladeshis whom she describes in *Brick Lane*, Ali identifies two salient characteristics: one she calls the "Going Home Syndrome," diagnosed by Dr. Azad in the novel, and the other she labels a process of an ongoing "seeking out the periphery." As a writer firmly within the center of the mainstream culture, she claims that finding the periphery is an important part of her journey as a writer and that her hybrid identity and outsider status provide a good place from which to observe the Bangladeshis and the larger Muslim world. However, as Alistair Cormack shows, when Ali depicts Bangladeshis, "realism ceases to be traditional because the form's limits become visible, as do the presumptions by which it works."[16] So, for instance, Chanu, the disappointed immigrant creates a mythic Bangladesh to which he dreams of returning; Karim creates in Nazneen the perfect Bengali village wife, and she imagines him completely at home in the English language.

The setting of Ali's novel is Spitalfields, "a place on the edge."[17] It is a perfect departure point for Ali's journey to the periphery. And if we look at the cultural and social history of the East End we will better understand why Ali's journey takes in not a documentary memory, but an imaginary one. The history of Spitalfields is explicitly evoked twice in the novel: significantly once at the beginning and once in the end. We never see any of the characters of the novel acknowledging the existence or prior existence of other ethnic groups in their neighborhood other than the English. Nonetheless in one of the earliest episodes the Bengali women criticize one of their own who goes to work in a local factory for there she is likely to mix with "all sorts":

> Turkish, English, Jewish. All sorts. . .if you mix with all these people, even if they are good people, you have to give up your culture to accept theirs. That's how it is. (16)

These words, spoken by Mrs. Islam, the eponymous gatekeeper for Bangladeshi culture who is later exposed as a cranky old woman who lends money at interest, explain perhaps why these "others" remain invisible throughout the novel. They represent hybridity, and hybridity contains the threat of cultural annihilation. Mrs. Azad puts it very differently, speaking as her daughter asks for money to go to the pub:

> Fact: we live in a Western society. Fact: our children will act more and more like Westerners. Fact: that's no bad thing. My daughter is free to come and go.[18]

Ironically, hybridity was one of the most threatening aspects of foreign immigration, which threatened the identity and the purity of the body of the nation.[19] Jewish women were maligned not only for taking the jobs of English men and women but because the result would no doubt be a crop of hybrid, weak children.[20] It is the Jews who were blamed for the overcrowding in London and who evoked the most anxiety in the host population, in the years leading to the anti-immigration legislation of 1905 which framed the policing of South Asian immigration in the fifties.[21] Using the same kind of rhetoric that is directed today against the Muslim community, the Jews were urged to cast off their clannish ways and assimilate into English society.[22] In the case of the Bangladeshis, there has been little attempt to use the racism weapon in the same way; they were attacked for exploiting the welfare state but not for polluting the purity of the state. However, recent reports show that the British National Party (BNP), in line with past traditions, is also depicting Moslem men as sexual predators.[23] It is certainly plausible that in Ali's attempt to secure the mystical, as well as monetary, connection between the inhabitants of Spitalfields and Bangladesh, she wanted to duplicate the spiritual links she perceived between Jews and Israel; however, the Bangladeshi diaspora differs from the Huguenot and Jewish enclaves that proceeded them for those groups rarely sought to return to their actual places of origin and were usually unable to do so.

Nazneen, who is trapped in an arranged match in an alienating East London tower-block, falls for Karim, who has been bringing her garments to finish for a sweat-shop (unconsciously following the pattern of Jewish immigrant occupations). At first she sees Karim as someone who has a place in the world, masculine, young, fighting for a cause—later she will come to understand that he is defending his world because he has no place in it. Yet their "un-Islamic" acts of adultery seem to contradict the devout use of Nazneen's prayer-mat. In Nazneen's mind, desire has taken over the Fate which rules her life. Only when she gains a will of her own and a voice, inspired by visions of her dead Amma and memories of her native village, can she see the complex reality in which she lives—the gang fights, the drug dealers, the Hindu restaurants catering to the cosmopolitan tastes of the English for curry and lager.

Early on in Ali's novel, Nazneen awakens to her own body when she watches champion ice skaters on television. In a passage that is similar to the broken idiom of the letters from Nazneen's sister, Hasina, from Bangladesh, Ali draws attention to the difficulty Nazneen has translating what she sees into a familiar context. At the end of the novel her daughters surprise her with a trip to a skating rink near Liverpool Street station. To the objection that you can't skate in a sari, her friend Razia concludes the novel with the words: "This is England. . . . You can do whatever you like" (415). After we have seen the poverty, disenfranchisement, and marginalization of the inhabitants of Tower Hamlets, this closing statement ironically raises the question of translating from one culture to another, with all the ambiguities of hybridity.[24] Nazneen rejects both her Islamist lover Karim and her failed immigrant husband, who returns to Bangladesh to seek his fortune, while she takes an alternative path in a women's dress cooperative, thus asserting her independence as a woman. She can presumably look forward to the possibilities England offers, not of integration but of a vaguer and more ambivalent future in which she may control both her destiny and her body, enjoying a freedom she had not previously conceived possible. Yet, paradoxically, Nazneen has come to this awareness through her memories of her native village, visits by her dead mother's spirit, and a correspondence with her sister Hasina, who has been reduced to prostitution in Dhaka.

Nazneen and her daughters remain in East London, and it is only once both men are gone that Ali has Nazneen notice its multicultural history. She walks through her neighborhood now dominated by Slyheti establishments, past the "faded legend of a time gone by, Schultz Famous Salt Beef. . .past the clothes wholesaler's, up Adler Street and left onto the brief green respite of Altab Ali Park" (393–94). The few remaining Jewish names conjure up the hybridity of the former diasporas that Chanu has turned his back on when he returned to Bangladesh. There he is again trapped in his delusions and dreams, despite his hopes to be free of the dilemmas of hybridity, political extremism, and "ignorant, unrespectable" types: "But when we are back home we won't need to think about these things. Back home we'll really know what's what" (390). Karim, too, has rejected hybridity in favor of radical pan-Islamic nationalism, and, after Nazneen spurns him, apparently also returns "home" to the Bangladesh which he has never seen.

A close reading of Monica Ali's *Brick Lane* suggests that beneath the ideal of multiculturalism lies a more complex reality: disaffected Pakistani youth are drawn to radical Islamist ideas and the victims of racial violence or discrimination sometimes release their frustrations in violence, such as in the 2001 Oldham riots, or the more organized "resistance" of radical Islamist cells. In reality, there have been incidents of violence against the gentrified White neighbors or against local pubs. The multicultural ideal remains just that—an ideal. When Ali concludes with the phrase, "you can do anything in England," therein lay the promise and the danger of multiculturalism. It was after reading this passage and bursting into hysterical laughter, while waiting for a connecting flight at Copenhagen airport, that the Danish literary scholar and Indian novelist Tabish Khair (a Muslim) was informed that he could not enter Britain's multicultural paradise, even as a transit passenger. As he says in his essay on the subject, there are in "multicultural novels" a number of significant gaps.[25]

RACHEL'S ROOM

Like the revival of the Lower East Side in New York, the nostalgia for the Jewish East End of the late twentieth and early twenty-first century was symptomatic of the return of a middle class assimilated generation to their roots in their grandparents' immigrant experience. For American Jews, this was a way of redefining an alternate Jewish identity which sacralized a definitive memory site for the Jewish American experience, for the moment which shaped Jewish American collective memory was the exodus from poverty on the bustling streets of the Lower East Side.[26] The social networks which tied the immigrants to an originary identity in Eastern Europe and bound them within a communal identity were lost with the suburbanization of the Jews. The resulting absence created a forgetting that lay at the heart of memory, while urban renewal erased traces of the former ethnic space (*yeshivot,* stores, slum tenements) that made up the memory map of cultural identity, and the declining neighborhood became a site for a nostalgic return to a "remnant" (in the assimilated affluent Jew's thinking) of a way of life consigned to oblivion.[27] The "Jewishness" of the evacuated space of memory can thus be for assimilated Jews an empty signifier, a sign of an absence of authentic traditions or loss of values, even though those traditions live on in vibrant communities in Crown Heights, Flatbush, Teaneck, or Baltimore, not to mention Mea Shearim and Har Nof in Israel. However, unlike the site-specific return to the Lower East Side, the East End has remained an evacuated space. It is neither a habitable Jewish space nor a site that is exclusively or especially Jewish. It remains empty despite the attempts to "revive" the Jewish East End as a tourist site around Bevis Marks synagogue or through the conscription of religious Jewish commuters working nearby in the City for the few remaining synagogues in the area that were bereft of daily worshippers.[28] Rather, Jewish memory is being located within a wider multicultural territory and within a more metaphysical sense of diaspora in the wake of collective trauma and loss. At the same time, new immigrant settlement that does not always coexist easily with urban renewal and gentrification has inspired solidarity among intellectuals and artists who evidently feel that they are doing something for the underprivileged and socially disadvantaged, as well as reclaiming a bit of London's past from the property developers and speculators.

Though no doubt a sincere and anguished personal odyssey of search for identity, Rachel Lichtenstein's promotion of the discovery of David Rodinsky's sealed room at 19 Princelet Street in London's East End was yet another step in turning an inner city slum with grave social problems into a mythic center of London's urban palimpsest. The synagogue downstairs, found in great disrepair, rain dripping from Torah mantles, had been turned into a museum of immigration, a focal point of East End tours and a location for film crews looking for antiquated period settings. This was a theater of memory in the literal sense, as well as in the sense that Raphael Samuel uses the phrase to describe our understanding of the historical past which "is constructed not so much in the light of the documentary evidence, but rather of the symbolic space or imaginative categories into which representations are fitted."[29] That, argues Samuel, is because images are stronger than reality in the narrative of the past, and in the "retrochic" fad of popular culture in the seventies, first in France, then in Britain, where the revival of period styles fed on the nostalgia generated by the heritage industry and combined with the new technologies of retrieval and recovery of the past.[30] The "living history" movement made the past come alive, but there was also a market for the attraction of repulsion, for Victorian squalor and disease, for the thrill of Jack the Ripper.[31]

Rodinsky's room was opened up in 1980 after being sealed for over a decade, revealing a locked time capsule of a vanished world. Although Rodinsky had long vanished, Lichtenstein took it upon herself to single-handedly rescue Rodinsky's belongings that had been discovered when his room was unsealed, then dismantled and its contents carted off to the Museum of London. She zealously guarded beer bottles and gramophone records, notebooks recording obscure etymologies in ancient languages, shopping lists, and boots that had been thrown out onto the street. Rodinsky disappeared some time in the sixties, probably into a mental health institution, and so left behind the mystery of an individual who could not be pinned down by religious or ethnic classification, or indeed any firm identity. Was he a devout mystic, or an eccentric recluse? An unstable social welfare case or secret Kabbalist?

For Lichtenstein this was an opportunity to create a space for herself in the East End both as an artist—she installed herself in the synagogue building as an artist in residence—and as someone who was descended from East End Jews but married to a man of Pakistani origins from Leeds, who passed for Jewish because of his fair skin (his mother was Irish, his father Muslim) and who even attended synagogue and Zionist youth meetings—a paragon, one might think, of postcolonial hybridity. Lichtenstein herself was technically not Jewish (because her mother was a Gentile) but she could not complete the conversion process and commit to a fully observant Jewish life. What started out as an exploration of her own roots, which she was tracing back to her grandfather Gedaliah Lichtenstein's jewelry shop in the East End, became an obsession with the artifacts of a man who died the year she was born and an exploration beyond his elusive life, to the Whitechapel he knew and the little piece of Eastern Europe that Lichtenstein's ancestors had brought over with them together with actual furnishings of synagogues. If Rodinsky was the caretaker (at least nominally) of the synagogue at 19 Princelet Street, Lichtenstein became the caretaker of the caretaker's lost life. She was thus building her own identity in the past and present, exploring the streets of the East End for some synthesis of the contradictions in her own multiple identities. Her journey took her from her origins to Poland and the Holocaust, as well as to a kabbalistic rabbi in Jerusalem, who advised her to go back and redeem the soul of David Rodinsky. In completing this holy task she frees his wandering spirit and exorcizes herself from the past.

Rodinsky's Room is a narrative in different voices that mounts a rescue of the last remnants of the Jewish East End. It was coauthored with the novelist Iain Sinclair, author of *Downriver* and *Lights Out for the Territory* (explorations of London that incorporate memories of the East End), a collaboration which sets up a complex and sometimes conflicting relationship between these texts.[32] As in W. G. Sebald's *Austerlitz,* the tour of Rodinsky's world proceeds by indirection, through archeological finds, odd and elusive clues to a lost identity and to the enigma of a recluse who taught himself fifteen languages and who seems to have spent much of his time deciphering hieroglyphics or translating from Akkadian and other Semitic languages. Lichtenstein enters 19 Princelet Street as if entering the sacred space of a sepulcher. She seems to be recreating a golem out of the contents of the archival crates she carefully and ritually empties, with sacred reverence and with protectively gloved hands, in the cobwebbed attic of this haunted synagogue. Lichtenstein indeed does become the caretaker herself, fussing over clumsy film crews shooting a film about a golem summoned up by the mystic scholar in the attic. Sinclair plays with the Golem as a metaphor for the mystic encounter with the past that has the power to redeem the present, and the Golem is actually performed in a play in the former synagogue, with built-in special effects provided by the location itself.

The Golem legend is an ancient one, associated with the Maharal of Prague, who is said to have created a creature out of clay that defended the Jews from their enemies. It was kept alive by means of the word *"emet"* (truth) inscribed on its forehead; when it ran amok, like the Sorcerer's Apprentice, one letter was removed to read *"met"* (dead). The Golem's corpse was supposedly kept in the attic of the Old-New Synagogue, in Prague, where it lays still, according to popular belief. The periodic revival of the legend (particularly Yudl Rosenberg's 1909 classic Yiddish reworking and H. Leivick's drama of 1921) responded to new interest in folklore as well as to modern outbursts of antisemitic violence. At the turn of the twentieth century, the leading Yiddish writer Y. L. Peretz, despairing of the lack of spirit which would revive Jewish culture, noted that the Golem was still remembered, but there was no one who knew the incantation that would revive it.[33] He concludes his short story "The Golem" (1893) by assigning the key to continuity of tradition to the realm of the metaphysical:

The *golem*, you see, has not been forgotten. It is still here! But the Name by which it could be called to life in a day of need, the Name has disappeared. And the cobwebs grow and grow, and no one may touch them.

What are we to do?[34]

As assimilation and acculturation in the twentieth century took their toll, the legend moved further from its sources in Talmudic lore and kabbala and became more pliable, like all narratives, to the needs of cultural transformations. After the radical loss of Jewish culture in the Holocaust, there have been attempts in America to revive the Golem, whether as a Superman who would reassert Jewish empowerment, or as a postmodern parody, as in Michael Chabon's *The Amazing Adventures of Kavalier and Clay* (2000), not to mention Cynthia Ozick's female Golem in her 1997 novel *The Puttermesser Papers* (Thane Rosenbaum's post-Holocaust *The Golems of Gotham* is, symptomatically perhaps, really about *dybbuks*). Among the several attempts to summon up the Golem in order to recover a lost Jewish memory and celebrate a Jewish culture that was never personally experienced, Ruth Gilbert cites Lichtenstein's and Sinclair's *Rodinsky's Room*—that is, the intertwined stories of Lichtenstein's search for Rodinsky and Sinclair's invented histories of East London in search of the true Whitechapel. Now Rodinsky may have been a madman in an attic, but he was not himself a golem in the attic, yet what Lichtenstein, in Gilbert's reading, would like to mold out of this cultural clay is a metamorphosed Jewish memory, a "usable past" that would fit a multicultural global identity but also satisfy a growing need to mourn traumatic loss. This suggests that such cultural clay is pliable to individual whims and the "illusion of a shared memory" among Diaspora Jews who wish for some authentic moment wrapped up in mysticism and mystery to bind them together in the diversity of ethnic heterogeneity and in the absence of communal affiliation.[35] It is, nevertheless, an ambivalent figure of "identification representing difference as well as connection."[36] At the same time, the Golem marks an empty space that lures Sinclair's postmodern urban imagination (a retro-gothic horror movie set in slums ripe for development and speculation, like Peter Ackroyd's 1994 novel *Dan Leno and the Limehouse Golem*) and that fuels Lichtenstein's far more driven and urgent—almost frenzied—search for her own Golem (a formless creature with latent powers of redemption that can be remolded at will).

In her search for personal and collective memory, Lichtenstein creates a *"Ner Tamid"* (Eternal Lamp) out of the artifacts from her own family's attic, placing them in the window of Ch. Katz, string manufacturer and wholesaler (one of the last Jewish businesses in the East End besides Elfes the monumental stonemasons, fittingly the last memorial to the departed Jews of the East End).Time is redeemed and sanctified.

> Rodinsky's life was pressed into legend. It belonged at the end of
> an era, before memories became memorial plaques. An
> abandoned room contained all that was left of a man's life and
> Rachel Lichtenstein understood that it was her task, nobody else
> could do it, to live that life again, and to complete it. Find some
> resolution or lose herself in the attempt. That was her joy. That
> was her burden.[37]

So an evacuated Jewish space becomes reinhabited by a *dybbuk* (Sinclair identifies her, in case we had not noticed Lichtenstein's possession by this folklore figure of a wandering spirit). This is a young woman who embodies a memory that has been swept away by the very success of the immigrants who have moved on to greener pastures, an evacuated space blitzed by the Germans and reoccupied by new waves of immigrants from South Asia.

The Kosher Luncheon Club has gone, after its premises were ransacked and daubed by neo-Nazis; the synagogue next door was torched. When Lichtenstein returns to the site on a Friday evening, the Sabbath eve, she walks into a desecration of the Greatorex Street synagogue that is part of a punk rock/art performance.

> Each corner of the *bimah* had a flame-throwing gas torch fixed to
> it, adding to the image of hell. Spaced-out ravers, with
> Technicolor trousers and dreadlocks, frantically waved their arms
> about in the pews. Others sat about stubbing out cigarettes on the
> carpet. The ark had been shut off by a string of cheap flashing
> fairy lights, and from the women's gallery a smoke machine
> billowed obnoxious air to the revelers below.[38]

Meanwhile in the former Kosher Luncheon Club, on a raised stage,

> two women sat dressed in baby pink vinyl, garish make-up
> smeared on their blank faces. They sat behind a large desk piled
> knee-deep in old books. . . . The young ladies were stamping the

books with large rubber implements and then elegantly ripping pages out of them and tossing them on to the floor.[39]

As if the desecration of a holy place on the holy Sabbath were not sufficiently offensive and appalling, the holy books being wantonly destroyed include the community's death register, its *pinkas kehilla,* including a record of the suicide of one Esther Rodinsky. Lichtenstein's hysterical protest brings the performance to a halt, but not before she has become part of the performance and, walking off with the death register, the custodian of memory.

Even Bloom's restaurant, a site of nostalgia for the former immigrants and their children from the North West passage of affluent suburbia, has gone (replaced by a *treyf* burger bar). The East End has come into the hands of property speculators with a greedy eye on restored eighteenth-century facades and lucrative proximity to the City, but its memory is a property left ownerless, claimed by photographers from Bill Brandt to Markéta Luskačová, as well as itinerant artists and writers like Lichtenstein. These have become its tour guides and the memorialists who have detached its memory from the larger metropolis which has swallowed up the East End in post-Thatcherite redevelopment, Jack-the-Ripper tourism, and trendy merchandising of the New Age organic variety. As Sinclair notes, there is no Rodinsky cult that might compete with Anne Frank's house in Amsterdam, no blue plaques (as there are nearby for Miriam Moses, mayor of Stepney, and the artist Mark Gertler). 19 Princelet Street is earmarked as a heritage museum of immigration, the Spitalfields Centre, where, under Susie Symes' stalwart guardianship, visitors are discouraged as would-be trespassers. This site of memory offers a stark and chilling contrast to the alternative reality of Californian Denis Severs' reconstructed eighteenth-century experience in Folgate Street, where the paying visitor is regaled with the sounds, sights, and even smells of a fake past, the "original mystery tour," far more memorable than a museum's period room.[40] In Princelet Street, Rodinsky's spirit is left to roam, free and ripe for fictions.[41]

Daniel Gralton's seductive photograph of Rodinsky's room when it was first opened, with its romantic rearrangement of the disarray, lures Lichtenstein, as in a Vermeer painting, into its interior, although she is only too aware of the trap Sinclair warns about. The creepy damp atmosphere gets too much for her and one day she runs after Rodinsky's apparition in the street, only to discover an old Hasidic gentleman who knew both Rodinsky and Lichtenstein's grandfather; he lets her display her artwork in his shop window, enabling her to return her grandfather's heirlooms to a space that is appropriately commercial and Jewish. The dampness is, in the end, also too much for her asthma, and so she travels to Israel to take up an artist's fellowship in Arad, where the aridity cures her. Here she finds a neutral space where she can recreate Rodinsky at a safe distance but also one that provides her with the raw materials for her memory work, hoards of two-thousand-year-old pottery shards which she uses to refashion old family portraits. But she has been coming to Rodinsky for some time, from her first fascination with the ghostly photographs of child inmates of concentration camps she displayed at art school in Sheffield to her panicky need to reconnect with her grandfather's legacy that is unknown to her, reversing as Ruth Gilbert has noted,[42] the trek of the children of immigrants to suburbia, where many tried to forget their origins and melt invisibly into assimilated Englishness. She reclaims her family's original surname before it was Anglicized to Laurence and, returning from Poland, discerns in the Princelet Street synagogue the same fossilized memories she had encountered in Eastern Europe. Moreover, the front and end pieces of Lichtenstein's guidebook *Rodinsky's Whitechapel* comprise a family photo of, respectively, an East End immigrant family and an assimilated, middle-class suburban Jewish family, thus charting the distance Lichtenstein would like to travel back in time and space through the streets she describes in the intervening pages.

> Lichtenstein was obsessive, ritualistic in her procedures. The quest for an identity, for a family that would confirm her essence and existence, took her on a series of journeys: to Poland, to New York, to Israel—and, inevitably, to Whitechapel. Each exploration—interviews, recordings, buildings and contents listed and photographed—brought her closer to the point of origin. When it was gathered (like the manic accumulations of holy junk in David Rodinsky's Princelet Street attic), she would cancel herself out. She would be free to travel in other dimensions.[43]

This description, from Sinclair's *Lights Out for the Territory,* indicates ways in which Rachel Lichtenstein has herself fused into a mythic memory and become not only the subject of her own work, but also a fellow collector of artifacts of memory—a maker of "re-collections"—which comprise the portable possessions taken from former Jewish territory.

Rodinsky's room, before Lichtenstein came on the scene, was another stop-off in Sinclair's imaginative reclaiming in *Downriver* of people who have become places. Rodinsky enters a gallery of outcasts and tramps who people the pubs and doss-houses of East London, whose voyeuristic view of crime and prostitution is now blocked by "Disneyland" minarets and the recorded voice of the *muezzin*. Tipped off about a mystery that could offer another of his walking stories, Sinclair rushes off in search of the "Vanishing Jew." Describing the heart-arresting moment of turning from Brick Lane with its "fetishist gulch" of commercial competition into Princelet Street, Sinclair speaks of being sucked in "by a vortex of expectation" into the synagogue. Sinclair is a postmodern *flâneur* who stalks London's downtrodden and deteriorating territories in search of hidden clues to the unexplored intimate stories and secret locations of London's violence and poverty that are overwritten by architectural visions and erased from official maps. Sinclair self-consciously intervenes in the metaphorical landscape in order to resist the false, depersonalizing construction of places that have haunted the imagination—above all in his explorations of the East End, where he was once employed as a gardener ("guardian" of public places) and which has also attracted Peter Ackroyd's ghost trawling in his novel *Hawksmoor*.[44] This is part of Sinclair's "psychogeography" of London, which he has devolved from a sort of occult shamanism into a practice of relating subjective feelings and the landscape that resists the neo-Victorian aftermath of Thatcherism by walking London's streets, as Charles Dickens once did so exhaustively and exhaustingly, and re-peopling them with the dead souls of outcast London. As in Will Self's *How the Dead Live* (2000), the ghostwalkers of the invisible city respect no division between the real and the imagined.[45] Peter Ackroyd achieves much the same affect when he ghostwrites (or ghostwalks) Dickens into his postmodern imagination. It is a way of redeeming the lost city by collecting and examining its detritus, just as Walter Benjamin studies material artifacts in *The Arcades Project* in order to reconstruct the history of Second Empire Paris and rescue the artifacts on public display from their commodity value. However, in the twentieth century, when urban life changed so rapidly and commodities were freely available, materialist history has become itself commodified.[46] By turning from historian to autobiographer, in the tradition of the peripatetic memoir, Sinclair is attempting the resurrection of artifacts and the ephemeral traces of Rodinsky's room into the lived life of the East End as an oppositional history that resists the commodification of a privileged site of mythical memory that mummifies and paradoxically suppresses the past.[47]

Here Sinclair struggles with the transformation of Rodinsky's life into a tourist trap that wrenches all the real experience of immigration into a nostalgic Museum of Immigration. But he himself is one of the "ethical Luddites" who have broken into Rodinsky's life in search of a mystery and material for a film:

> There *was* no mystery, except the one we manufactured in our quest for the unknowable: shocking ourselves into a sense of our own human vulnerability. We were a future race of barbarians, too tall for the room in which we were standing. We fell gratefully upon the accumulation of detail: debased agents, resurrectionists with cheap Japanese cameras.[48]

There is no mystery about Rodinsky's disappearance; it is his room which has vanished, replaced by a smokescreen of dubious theatricality inducing spooky hallucinations and mass paranoia.

While Sinclair is concerned with the emptying out of meaning in the guts of London's inner city, Lichtenstein is trying to redeem the presence of the absent Jews in a somatic and historical process that undoes two to four generations of assimilation and confronts traumatic loss in the Holocaust. The East End Jews may have suffered deprivation, but not persecution—the German bombers were indiscriminate during the Blitz. Yet genocide has erased the imagined collective origin of East End Jews in Eastern Europe and with it the cultural space that would constitute material for reinventing postmodern Jewish identity.

The East End, in fact, becomes the focus of a repetition compulsion that pulls Lichtenstein to the uncanny, to the source of repressed identity.[49]

> Whitechapel had to be read like a scriptural roll, an album of unknown relatives. Lichtenstein became a guide, a lecturer, walking the territory so that she could learn by explaining. She would make discoveries by revisiting familiar sites. Talking to herself, she would catch the echoes of immigrant voices.[50]

It is rather like the accidental double exposure of a photograph of Rodinsky's sister, an elusive, unidentifiable face, either man or woman (androgynous like the Golem), that peers elusively, yet also knowingly, from the cover of

Rodinsky's Whitechapel, overprinted with a Hebrew text, and that speaks through voiceless lips. Here we have a personification of postmodern searches for memory that find mysteries in disused synagogues, dilapidated, rotting slums, and dead people. This is not the message of multicultural diversity or the lessons of immigration, but an empty memory that compels Lichtenstein and sucks her in. However much Lichtenstein resists touristic commodification and demands that the memory be filled and mourned, the East End she recreates is as much a simulacrum as Spielberg's Kraków (the "Schindler Tour"), the virtual Jewish space of invented memory which Ruth Gruber describes in her study of the East European tourist itinerary, *Virtually Jewish.*[51] This "klezmer" culture has become a surrogate for the real past of the vanished Jews and serves various local needs, whether political interest in reshaping the national memory (as in Poland), or philosemitic impulses to assuage guilt for the Holocaust and work through the traumatic past. The self-appointed custodians of Jewish monuments and cemeteries are archeologists of the past, but the memory that is constructed may be "Jewish" only in name and may raise issues of whose memory. Gruber points out that the kitschy culture that passes for "Jewish" has become widespread in the West too. David Roskies speaks of a "free market" economy in the postmodern grab for a usable past which can provide a theological or ideological narrative that can recover the past after the radical loss of the Holocaust, and the Holocaust has been the most contested of those narratives.[52] Each generation, Roskies tells us, has told the story of its loss in order to continue the generational chain of transmission, but for all the chronicling of the ghetto diarists and a huge literature of destruction, the present generation, who did not grow up in a Jewish culture, let alone in Yiddish or in Judaism, need to reinvent the past to be able to read its narratives. For Lichtenstein, her story of Rodinsky is just such a dialectic of loss and retrieval, but which she rewrites like some Yiddish folk tale that makes the impossible connection between a vanished past and a fragmented present.[53]

Here art serves as a ritual recital of *kaddish,* the Jewish prayer for the dead incumbent on surviving relatives, for whom Lichtenstein stands proxy. She is saying *kaddish* in her work not only for Rodinsky and the vanished Jewish East End, but for the six million dead of the Holocaust, who have become the "Vanished Jews" of contemporary Poland. On a study trip to Poland, Lichtenstein joins other young Jews in search of their lost ancestors, as well as Poles possessed by a need to know the "Vanished Jews,"[54] and discovers several Rodinsky-like caretakers of derelict abandoned synagogues. Lichtenstein finds the vanished Jewish life in which Rodinsky's family grew up and which was previously unknown to her, there in Poland, a fossilized relic of immigrant origins, rather than the teeming streets of the East End. She also comes across another kind of Vanishing Jew, a director of an art museum who has recently been told she is of Jewish decent—like the other Polish Jews Lichtenstein meets, these are the last Jews of Poland who can say *kaddish* for the dead.[55] It is in Poland that Lichtenstein finally realizes the purpose of her quest—to find Rodinsky's own grave and to say *kaddish* over the tombstone she has erected.

That quest is quite different from Sinclair's purpose, and the tensions between the two authors are worth considering. Lichtenstein is journeying into what Sinclair calls in *Rodinsky's Room* a "lacuna," into a script that was waiting to be written, at the juncture of total dilapidation and dereliction, awaiting a cultural need (one might say a cultic need) to buy into a "usable" past, to forge a sustainable identity out of local legends and to repopulate the East End with a history that was both real and imagined.[56] Sinclair comments,

> The disappearance of the synagogue caretaker, with his presumed cabbalistic practices, was a story fitted to its time. Those with a vested interest in defining Spitalfields as a zone of peculiar and privileged resonance needed a mythology to underwrite the property values. Rodinsky, one erased life, one blank biography among so many, was elected. Essentially the trick of the thing was to strip him of his history and to translate him directly into the substance of the room that had housed him.[57]

In Iain Sinclair's narrative, the self-appointed conservationists of the past are conscripting the ghosts of the Jewish East End to fight their oblivion by the bulldozers, yet we should remember that the gentrification of Georgian properties actually resurrected the weavers' attics and a syncretic architecture that was later obscured by the poverty of inassimilable aliens in overcrowded tenements.[58] In his fiction and in his reading of the fiction of others, Sinclair seizes on Rodinsky as a blank that can be cancelled out and inserted into a gallery of contemporaneous drifters like Davies in Pinter's *The Caretaker* (though that surely was Hackney, not Whitechapel), of girls called Rachel hiding in a wardrobe during the Holocaust, indeed Rachel Lichtenstein herself, caught by the camera as Rodinsky's alter ego reading a book, in a performance of the Vanishing Jew.[59] Thus we have a gallery of intermingling and interchangeable characters whom Sinclair would legitimately press into service as the Golem of the moment.

This is nevertheless a memory of absence, of the "Vanishing Jew," and in her next book, *On Brick Lane* (2007), Lichtenstein attempts to fill that memory. What she inscribes into the streets of Whitechapel is not the Jewish East End as it was or might have been, but the rather unromantic stories of outcasts, market traders, artists, and social workers who inhabit an area that has been reoccupied by Bangladeshi immigrants and their children, as well as by artists (we do not meet the property speculators and the new owners of gentrified eighteenth-century slums that are now worth millions). This is an encounter with marginal identities, individuals who live on boundaries of social, ethnic, and sexual identities. If we had thought the East End was ideally a meeting point of cultures, we find that the different ethnic and religious groups that have moved in to the area have no common ground. As at the time of the mass influx of destitute Jews from the 1880s there is a grinding poverty, violent crime, and attempts to reach out to potentially delinquent youth. What has changed is that there is no cohesive close-knit community; the extended family of the neighborhood has been replaced by fear and despair, though the racist aggression of the eighties has largely subsided. Lichtenstein seeks the common ground, a shared humanity, but she turns her attention to what interests her most—the loners and drop outs, above all the few remaining aging veterans of the East End who have preserved some memory of the past. She greedily devours their stories as the last witnesses of Rodinsky's Whitechapel and bequeaths to us Lichtenstein's pilgrimage, which is all there is to remember in "Banglatown" of the storytellers of the past. She herself creeps gingerly, with permission of the imam, into the interior of the mosque, which is the synagogue where her grandfather used to pray, but the voices of the cantor and the wailing Jews are inaudible. The hushed silence of the prayer hall does not betray its previous occupants, Huguenots, Methodists, and Jews. Overawed, she can barely imagine the Jewish past. Lichtenstein is herself in danger of becoming a Vanishing Jew in the false memories of Sinclair's fictions.

EXCAVATING THE PAST, RECOVERING THE PRESENT

"We excavate the history we need," writes Iain Sinclair in *Rodinsky's Room*, "bend the past to colonize the present."[60] Jeremy Gavron does just this in *An*

Acre of Barren Ground (2005), an imaginative discovery of the story of the houses in Brick Lane, which fleshes out the lives of their inhabitants from Huguenot weavers to Jewish peddlers, from Saxon hunters to English poachers, from South Asian youth to dot.com new arrivals from the City. They act out and speak their stories in their own words (the dot.com section is done as a graphic novel), aided by scraps and diaries.

An Acre of Barren Ground weaves together different and disparate voices that make up the oral history of Brick Lane. Apart from the Jewish grandfather from North London who cannot understand why the slums of the East End could be lucrative to a dot.com executive, there is no trace of nostalgia, only fragments of lives, lived mostly in poverty, despair, madness, and hopelessness. There is something approaching a parallel between the generations of Huguenot, Jewish, and Bangladeshi immigrants, but the East End is never presented as an ethnically determined space. We do not get jostled by the teeming masses of immigrants, we do not see the market crowds in Petticoat Lane ("the Lane"), nor do we hear the singing of the *khazan* or the call of the *muezzin*. No multicultural rainbow here, but lonely voices of obscure individuals ignored by history, among them the prostitutes visited by the famous diarist and confidant of Samuel Johnson, James Boswell.

The primal moment of genesis of Brick Lane comes long before the immigration of the Huguenots or the Jews, long before there were bricks in Brick Lane. In interpolated jungle scenes, Gavron goes back to time immemorial, reminding us that primitive human settlements came after wild boar dropped an acorn on barren ground, leaving unexpected and sometimes illegitimate fruit for future generations. By going back and forth in time, from a Saxon ploughman's lucky find to a modern day convict's spouse, from a devout Huguenot to a corrupt Victorian vestryman, we cannot be assured of any certainty of continuity or community beyond the survival of the species. Gavron's multiple, fragmented portrait of the stories behind the houses on Brick Lane presents a transnational reality—not a "Jewish" story—that brings early hunter societies and primitive agricultural communities into the view of the human struggle to exist in the modern urban jungle.

One of the first shards of memory that Gavron unearths is a scene of an impoverished Jewish immigrant family, who have been tricked out of a passage to America and land unawares in London (a common experience, apparently). The father, a ritual slaughterer by training, is the perennial greenhorn, but when he puts animal organs in his pocket to bring home something for his hungry offspring, he little realizes he is falling into the archetype of the dangerous alien hunted by the police, who have linked the identity of Jack the Ripper with the sinister physiognomy of the "jew," the low-class East European Jew of the East End who in popular imagination butchered his victims, prostitutes, themselves (like the Jew) imagined as polluting outsiders threatening the body of the nation.[61] Gavron does not solve the mystery of the evil monster who cuts out the inner body parts of his victims, and leaves us to ponder the suspicions cast by racial prejudice.

These wheels within wheels of memory fragments, disparate and discordant, somehow ring more truly than the message of integration in Richard Bean's stage comedy *England, Nice People* (2009), which pokes fun at both xenophobia and ethnic insularity, urging us to believe that love between hybrid offspring of different cultures, Muslim, Sikh, and Jewish, will conquer all. By contrast with more realistic accounts such as Parsi Anglo-Indian children's author Farrukh Dhondy's *East End at Your Feet* (1976), the phantasmagoric scene in Salman Rushdie's *Satanic Verses* of Gibreel wreaking apocalyptic retribution in a new Great Fire of London which guts the Shandaar café, an oasis of salvation and resistance, foregrounds the racial tensions in "Brickhall" (a merger of Brixton. Brick Lane, and Southall). police brutality, repression of activists, and racialization of crime in a new Ripper case that shifts the blame onto Muslims rather than Jews. But then Rushdie's postmodern magic realism flits between Bombay and London and is anything but rooted in one place or time, preferring to explore migration between and within East and West, not immigration.[62] Other recent accounts, too, sound false when matched up to the real experience of the East End. For example, Tarquin Hall's *Salaam Brick Lane: A Year in the New East End* (2005) is a story of near-homelessness, depression, criminality, and poverty that is derivative of many East End narratives, but, though it seems to cash in on the success of Monica Ali, it never alludes to *Brick Lane*. It's a rather cliché tale of one year in a rented room above an illegal sweat shop from the privileged view of a journalist returning after many years from abroad with his Indian fiancée. He aspires to White middle-class Englishness, but both sets of parents object to their union, and though they "escape" from Brick Lane they only make it to Hackney (the slummy halfway house to suburban affluence). After living among the South Asian immigrants, old Jewish residents, Afghani refugees, Albanian asylum seekers, and the new yuppie investors of Brick Lane, Tarquin wonders if he will ever be able to relax into a comfortable sense of his "own Englishness."[63]

Place shapes identity, and the virtual community of shared memories, handed down across generations, constructs that identity as a cultural referent. The seduction of place attracts us, sometimes with a knowing falsity, to the lives of those who were reared in intense intellectual communities, raised on values of socialism, and taught to care about their neighbors in an era when nobody cares about ideology or politics. What were, in fact, "ach, horrible times" (as Sarah Kahn corrects Monty when he revisits his old East End friends in Arnold Wesker's *Chicken Soup with Barley*) seem almost paradisiacal from the philistine northern suburbs in which the children and grandchildren of the idealists grew up after the war. The devastating, almost total loss of the centre of diaspora Jewish culture in East Europe was certainly not commensurate with the ten-mile passage to affluent North West London, but the Holocaust did leave a vacuum in ethnic identity at a time when English culture was changing and accepting working class and regional voices; yet the Jewish Angry Young Men defined themselves as English and stood at a critical distance from the Jewish community.[64] For the postwar East End writers, the

> dissolution of the East End was to be a point of departure and a point of return. . . . Personal associations of the East End recur because they are important in tracing what went wrong with the Jewish community, with the revolution, with the world. . . . the East Enders always wanted to leave the ghetto that bore them, but it was never easy to separate from the womb.[65]

The historian David Cesarani compares this progression to the development of the New York intellectuals,[66] but then in England there were no cosmopolitan safety-nets and no comparable Jewish cultural institutions or public figures of the stature of Lionel Trilling and Norman Podhoretz.

Nevertheless, the reinvention of the East End cannot be considered outside the history of its representation since the 1840s when *flâneurs* or armchair tourists explored London's dens of vice. In some accounts, like John Fisher Murray's *The World of London* (1843), the Jewish "ghetto" was represented as an alien country populated by female Hottentots and rapacious Jewish traders who polluted the nation racially and sexually. This was an Orientalizing discourse that related to the East End as an exotic, anachronistic territory of dark barbarism, though Henry Mayhew's ethnographic survey, *London Labour and the London Poor* (1861–62), accorded East End Jews far more respect than the usual caricatures of the tellingly entitled *The Wild Tribes of London* (1855) by Watts Phillips. In the late Victorian period the East End was colonized by upper-class visitors "slumming" among the poor, whose real lives were made public by social investigators Beatrice Webb and Charles Booth or writers Arthur Morrison and Jack London, whose representations of the East End often revealed social tensions and ethnic diversity at the heart of the Empire.[67] But the Anglo-Jewish community paid scant attention to the East End before it was almost too late to save historical and architectural records of the past. At the turn of the twentieth century, the East End was a project for philanthropists, otherwise the poor East European immigrants were largely an embarrassment to the Anglo-Jewish community who celebrated their proud achievements as equal subjects of the British Empire and supported the 1905 Aliens Act, which laid the basis for future immigration control.

Willy Goldman and Simon Blumenthal were among the political activists who emerged from the hard life of the East End between the wars and described ita social reality (Goldman brought out his memoir, *East End, My Cradle* in 1940). Emmanuel Litvinoff's classic *Journey Through a Small Planet* (1972) typically describes just how self-enclosed the world of the Jewish East End was before the Second World War and how few were the opportunities its rough, sordid streets offered to an adolescent weighed down by sexual frustration and a yearning for something better. Antisemitic bullying spurred Litvinoff on to revenge, which he eventually would achieve by becoming accepted as a writer. Yet when we look back at Wesker's *Trilogy* (1960) we can almost pinpoint a time when things were falling apart, after wartime evacuation had torn the children from their homes and upward mobility had facilitated suburbanization, but class solidarity and a cause to fight for were still within living memory. Wesker clings to communal ideals of brotherly love and resistance to fragmentation of home and work that we see also in Wolf Mankowitz's novellas *A Kid for Two Farthings* (1953) and *Make Me an Offer* (1953), and his play *The Bespoke Overcoat* (1956) whose whimsical Jewish humor and homely wisdom seem now too impossibly sentimental. Autobiographical memoirs of the East End such as Bernard Kops' *The World is a Wedding* (1963) and the pictorial album, *Say Goodbye, You May Never See Them Again* (1974) by Arnold Wesker and John Allin, give a child's impressions of family memories and childhood haunts in the Jewish East End before evacuation and the Blitz brought an end to both childhood and community.

However, by 1987, new trends in social history and minority studies, with an emphasis on oral history, encouraged local enthusiasts and amateur historians to launch a celebration of the East End which turned the spotlight on marginalized figures such as prostitutes and anarchists and on the harsh conditions, inadequate social services, and racist violence suffered by the few remaining Jews living in the East End. The roots of racism in antisemitism and discrimination against the new wave of South Asian immigrants then gave a push to such initiatives as the Spitalfields Heritage Center at 19 Princelet Street. The East End was ready for the "heritage industry": "The Jewish East End, now safely re-packaged for most Jews in a world they will never re-enter on a permanent basis, is at particular risk of being distorted..."[68] There is a risk of romanticization, as well as commodification, but the transition has been made from a collective self-definition in terms of middle-class Anglicization that ignored the East End and particularly its Yiddish theatre to awareness of a history of class-struggle, racism, ethnic difference, driven by personal interest in what it was like living among the slums and sweat shops or where exactly immigrant forefathers had lived. This can give new impetus to nostalgic rags to riches memoirs, such as Andrew Miller's *The Earl of Petticoat Lane* (2006), that can still reiterate the benefits of Anglicization, but cultural memories cannot easily be superimposed on the very different realities of the present.

Long known as a crime-ridden socially deprived district outside the powerhouse of the nation's wealth in the City, the East End is now being reclaimed as an integral fiber of the metropolis threatened by globalization and redevelopment. Only in the 1990s a postmodern generation brought up anglicized and distanced from all things Jewish could reinvent themselves in a multicultural discourse that relates them personally to the Jewish immigrant past, whose last living witnesses and memories were fading fast (as in Elliott Tucker's evocation of lost traditions in his 2008 documentary film, *Children of the Ghetto*). This discursive construction stakes a claim for a non-fixed relationship to a larger complex of interethnic and interacial transactions across transnational society.[69] We have come a long way from Israel Zangwill's monumental *Children of the Ghetto* (1892), though Nadia Valman, in a gendered comparison of Zangwill's novel with Monica Ali's

Brick Lane, has suggested that Zangwill's Esther and Ali's Nazneen both emerge from a "ghetto" and claim agency that is not confined by the cultural constraints of a transplanted village from the old country. But for Zangwill the ideal he critiqued was the Anglicized bourgeois gentility of the West End, whereas for Ali the questionable ideal is integration in multiculturalism and feminist liberation.[70] The Brick Lane of Monica Ali, Rachel Lichtenstein, and Jeremy Gavron is perhaps another sign of the times, an attempt to make sense of what happens when memories fade and cultures collide, when the Jew vanishes and is reinvented by postmodernism.

NOTES

1. Yi-Fu Tuan, *Topophilia: A Study of Environmental Perception, Attitudes, and Values* (Englewood Cliffs, N.J.: Prentice-Hall, 1974), 102–12.

2. See William J. Fishman, *East End Jewish Radicals, 1875–1914* (London: Duckworth, 1975).

3. Benjamin J. Lammers, "The Birth of the East Ender: Neighborhood and Local Identity in Interwar East London," *Journal of Social History* (Winter 2005): 331–44.

4. For a study of the extended working-class family in the East End against the background of declining population in the 1950s see Michael Young and Peter Wilmott, *Family and Kinship in East London,* rev. ed. (Harmondsworth: Penguin Books, 1962).

5. See Gareth Stedman Jones, *Outcast London: A Study in the Relationship between Classes in Victorian Society* (Oxford: Clarendon Press, 1971); Geoffrey Alderman and Colin Holmes, eds., *Outsiders & Outcasts: Essays in Honour of William J. Fishman* (London: Duckworth, 1993).

6. Yi-Fu Tuan, *Space and Place: The Perspective of Experience* (Minneapolis: University of Minnesota Press, 1977), 88.

7. Monica Ali, *Brick Lane* (New York: Scribner, 2003). All further references will be to this edition and will be given in parenthesis.

8. Sukhdev Sandhu, "Come hungry, leave edgy," *London Review of Books,* 9 Oct. 2003, http://www.lrb.co.uk/v25/n19/sand01_.html.

9. Ibid.

10. Maleiha Malik, "Muslims are now getting the same treatment Jews had a century ago," *Guardian,* 2 Feb. 2007. See Preface above.

11. Anne J. Kershen, *Strangers, Aliens and Asians: Huguenots, Jews and Bangladeshis in Spitalfields 1660–2000* (London: Routledge, 2005), 68, 85, 87.

12. Emmanuel Litvinoff, *Journey Through a Small Planet* (Harmondsworth: Penguin, 1976), 10.

13. Monica Ali, "Where I'm Coming From," *Guardian,* 17June 2003, http://books
.guardian.co.uk/news/articles/0,,979007,00.html.

14. Jane Hiddleston, "Shapes and Shadows: (Un)veiling the Immigrant in Monica
Ali's *Brick Lane," Journal of Commonwealth Literature* 40.1 (2005): 57–72.

15. Ibid.

16. Alistair Cormack, "Migration and the Politics of Narrative Form: Realism and
Postcolonial Subject in *Brick Lane," Contemporary Literature* 47.4 (2006): 696.

17. Kershen, *Strangers, Aliens and Asians,* 1.

18. Ali, *Brick Lane,* 89.

19. Kershen, *Strangers, Aliens and Asians,* 217.

20. Ibid., 201.

21. Ibid., 8, 59.

22. Ibid., 87.

23. Ibid., 218.

24. See Cormack, "Migration and the Politics of Narrative Form": 696–97, 707–
12.

25. Tabish Khair, "The Death of the Reader," *Wasafiri* 21.3 (2006): 1–5.

26. See Hasia Diner, *Lower East Side Memories: A Jewish Place in America*
(Princeton: Princeton University Press, 2000); and Hasia Diner, Jeffrey Shandler, and
Beth Wenger, eds., *Remembering the Lower East Side* (Bloomington: Indiana
University Press, 2000).

27. Jonathan Boyarin, *Storm from Paradise: The Politics of Jewish Memory*
(Minneapolis: University of Minnesota Press, 1992), 3–4.

28. Sam Brown, "How the East End got cool again," *Jewish Chronicle,* 12 June
2008.

29. See Raphael Samuel, *Theatres of Memory,* vol. 1: *Past and Present in
Contemporary Culture* (London: Verso, 1994), 381-382.

30. Ibid., 85, 190.

31. Ibid., 284; see also David Lowenthal, *The Past is a Foreign Country*
(Cambridge: Cambridge University Press, 1985).

32. Rachel Lichtenstein and Iain Sinclair, *Rodinsky's Room* (London: Granta
Books, 2000). Since this coauthored book and Rachel Lichtenstein's illustrated
guidebook to the East End she imagines Rodinsky would have known, *Rodinsky's
Whitechapel* (London: Artangel, 1999), incorporate Sinclair's work and since Sinclair
incorporates his interpretation of Lichtenstein in his work, we have referred to
Lichtenstein and indicated where she is quoting Sinclair, giving separate citation to
Sinclair's contribution to their coauthored book or to his own work. Sinclair's walks
around Rodinsky's Whitechapel were published as *Dark Lanthorns: David Rodinsky's
A-Z Walked Over by Iain Sinclair* (London: Goldmark Books, 1999).

33. See Ruth Gilbert, "The Golem in the Attic: Rodinsky's Room and Jewish Memory," *Jewish Culture and History* 9.1 (2007): 51–70.

34. I. L Peretz, "The Golem," trans. Irving Howe, in *A Treasury of Yiddish Stories*, ed. Irving Howe and Eliezer Greenberg (New York: Viking, 1965), 246.

35. Gilbert, "Golem in the Attic," 55.

36. Ibid., 55.

37. Iain Sinclair, "Rachel Lichtenstein in Place," in *Rodinsky's Room*, 4–5.

38. Rachel Lichtenstein, "The Princelet Street Synagogue," in *Rodinsky's Room*, 38.

39. Ibid., 38–39.

40. Samuel, *Theatres of Memory*, 1: 114.

41. Sinclair, "Rachel Lichtenstein in Place," 7–11.

42. Gilbert, "Golem in the Attic," 58.

43. Iain Sinclair, *Lights Out for the Territory: 9 Excursions in the Secret History of London* (London: Granta Books, 1998), 232–33, quoted in Lichtenstein, "Princelet Street Synagogue," 56.

44. See Rod Mengham, "The Writing of Iain Sinclair," in *Contemporary British Fiction*, ed. Richard J. Lane, Rod Mengham, and Philip Tew (Cambridge: Polity, 2003), 64–65; Simon Perril, "A Cartography of Absence: The Work of Iain Sinclair," *Comparative Criticism* 19 (1997): 309–39.

45. See "Psychogeography: Will Self and Iain Sinclair in conversation with Kevin Jackson," edited with introduction by Steven Barfield, http://www.literarylondon.org /london-journal/march2008/sinclair-self.html; retrieved 21 Dec. 2009.

46. Alex Murray, "Materialising History: Benjamin, Sinclair and the Paradox of Reading/Writing the Urban Past," *Critical Engagements: A Journal of Criticism and Theory*, 1.1 (2007): 54–74; http://www.3ammagazine.com /3am/materialising-history-benjamin-sinclair-and-the-paradox-of-readingwriting-the-urban-past/ retrieved 21 Dec. 2009.

47. Ibid., 8–10; Christopher C. Gregory-Guider, "Sinclair's *Rodinsky's Room* and the Art of Autobiogeography," http://www.literarylondon.org/london-journal /september2005/guider.html; retrieved 21 Dec. 2009.

48. Iain Sinclair, *Downriver, or, The Vessels of Wrath: A Narrative in Twelve Tales* (London: Paladin, 1992), 136.

49. Gilbert, "Golem in the Attic," 63–65.

50. Sinclair, *Lights Out for the Territory,* 234; quoted in Lichtenstein, *Rodinsky's Whitechapel,* folded inside cover flap.

51. Ruth Ellen Gruber, *Virtually Jewish: Reinventing Jewish Culture in Europe* (Berkeley: University of California Press, 2002). See also chapter six below.

52. David Roskies, *The Jewish Search for a Usable Past* (Bloomington: Indiana University Press, 1999), 14–16.

53. Ruth Gilbert, "The *Frummer* in the Attic: Rachel Lichtenstein and Iain Sinclair's *Rodinsky's Room* and Jewish Memory," *International Fiction Review* 33.1–2 (2006): 27–38. Gilbert reads Lichtenstein's story far less critically than Iain Sinclair and takes no account of Sinclair's own mapping of the absent past, or even the tensions between Lichtenstein's and Sinclair's projects.

54. Les Back cites this as an example of how hybridity and racism can coexist in complex ways ("The Fact of Hybridity: Youth, Ethnicity, and Racism," in *A Companion to Racial and Ethnic Studies,* ed. David Theo Goldberg and John Solomos [Oxford: Blackwell, 2002], 450).

55. What Lichtenstein does not notice is that there are also many Poles discovering their Jewish descent and that Judaism in Poland is far from dead; see Larry N. Mayer and Gary Gelb, *Who Will Say Kaddish?: A Search for Jewish Identity in Contemporary Poland* (Syracuse: Syracuse University Press, 2002).

56. Iain Sinclair, "Witnessing Rodinsky," in *Rodinsky's Room,* 61–67.

57. Ibid., 66–67.

58. Sinclair, "Mobile Invisibility," in *Rodinsky's Room,* 179. The truth is that scandalously little attention has been paid to the conservation of synagogues and other Jewish buildings in the East End. See for a preliminary survey of the destruction and dereliction of East End synagogues, Sharman Kadish, "Squandered Heritage: Jewish Buildings in Britain," in *The Jewish Heritage in British History: Englishness and Jewishness,* ed. Tony Kushner (London: Frank Cass, 1992), 147–65.

59. Sinclair, "Witnessing Rodinsky," 68–77.

60. Sinclair, "Mobile Invisibility," 177.

61. Sander Gilman, *The Jew's Body* (New York: Routledge, 1991), 111–19. In this discussion of the racialization of Jack the Ripper, Gilman points out that the detail that the murderer removed sexual organs from the victims was not known to the general public, but the association would have been made between Jews and prostitutes because of their common association with sexual deviancy and disease.

62. Susheila Nasta, *Home Truths: Fictions of the South Asian Diaspora in Britain* (Houndmills: Palgrave Macmillan, 2002), 70–149.

63. Tarquin Hall, *Salaam Brick Lane: A Year in the New East End* (London: John Murray, 2005), 260.

64. Efraim Sicher, *Beyond Marginality: Anglo-Jewish Literature after the Holocaust* (Albany: New York State University Press, 1985), 25.

65. Ibid., 57.

66. David Cesarani, "Putting London Jewish Intellectuals in Their Place," in *Place and Displacement in Jewish History and Memory: Zakor v'Makor [sic!],* ed. David Cesarani, Tony Kushner, and Milton Shain (London: Vallentine Mitchell, 2009), 143–44, 150.

67. Nils Roemer, "London and the East End as Spectacles of Urban Tourism," *Jewish Quarterly Review* 99. 3 (Summer 2009): 416–34.

68. Tony Kushner, "The End of the 'Anglo-Jewish Progress Show': Representations of the Jewish East End, 1897–1987," in *The Jewish Heritage in British History: Englishness and Jewishness,* ed. Tony Kushner (London: Frank Cass, 1992), 97.

69. For a theoretical consideration of how the inscription of ethnic differentiation is changing in Britain see *Thinking Identities: Ethnicity, Racism, and Culture,* ed. Avtar Brah, Mary J. Hickman, and Máirtin Mac an Ghaill (Houndmills, Basingstoke: Macmillan Press, 1999).

70. Nadia Valman, "The East End Bildungsroman from Israel Zangwill to Monica Ali," *Wasafiri* 24.1 (Mar. 2009): 3–8.

CHAPTER SIX

The Postmodern Jew

POSTMODERN "JEWS"

In the European imaginary, the "jew" has long been a figure for the Other, demonized and later racialized, though in Britain race and skin color have in complex and unstable ways become a matter of class and community. In Kingsley Amis's novel *Stanley and the Women* (1984), an ordinary advertising manager who has married his second wife above his South London lower-class origins displays mundane prejudice against the wealthy "Jewboys" in Bishop's Avenue[1] and "Pakis" (that is, all South Asians). Yet his bantering, casual racism pales next to his ranting misogyny which seems to promote a theory that women are clinically insane and/or malignantly manipulative. Stanley's Irish mistress asks if he is Jewish when she sees his circumcision, but the concern is mainly with social identity and status, all important in a hierarchy that has traditionally been inflected with the nuances of accent, property, and status.[2] By contrast, Stanley is appalled when his son Steve suffers a breakdown and believes the world is threatened by a Jewish conspiracy in a Sci-fi mystical scenario starring the resurrected biblical Joshua.[3]

Such eschatologies typically project racist conspiracies based on the *Protocols of the Elders of Zion,* though Steve's fantasies seem to come out of his own head. Steve offers his secret intelligence to an Arab embassy, whose chief security officer takes him quite seriously before calling the police. Stanley fails to acknowledge his own failings as a father, but he also fails to connect his son's rabid antisemitism with the beliefs of the society around him, just as he dismisses anything outside his comfortable hedonism as abnormal and loony. It does not seem credible to Stanley, and perhaps also to the author, that antisemitism might be characteristic of many sane intelligent people in modern Britain.

As Anthony Julius has concluded, Kingsley Amis' bantering in the novel and in his private life reveals typical social attitudes towards stereotyped Others, a form of "mild" prejudice, but, when questioned by his son, the novelist Martin Amis, he evinces equally typical horror at any programmatic, violent antisemitism.[4] Kingsley Amis, according to Anthony Julius, may evince that English mentality which tolerates prejudice, but not violent hatred.[5] Martin Amis' own novel *Time's Arrow* probes the antisemitic mind and finds that postmodern America resembles Adorno's analysis of the reified society of the Nazi death factories, leading backwards in time, inexorably, to the black hole of Auschwitz. Amis confesses his first love was a Jewess, and his second wife is the glamorous South American Jewish writer, Isabel Fonseca. Amis is proud he has two Jewish daughters, but acknowledges the persistence of English antisemitism based on class prejudice.[6] And yet the eroticized, enigmatic Jewess still captivates Martin Amis's imagination, as if reacting to his father's dislike of Jews with a philosemitic liking for Jews which is equally based on fictitious stereotyping. Zoya in his 2006 novel, *House of Meetings,* for example, who features in a triangular relationship with two brothers, was

> not an acquired taste. Her face was original (more Turkic than Jewish, the nose pointing down, not out, the mouth improbably broad whenever she laughed or wept), but her figure was a platitude—tall and ample and also wasp waisted.[7]

But then Amis' sex-hungry protagonists (for example, John Self in *Money*) do tend to view women pornographically as willing salacious sex machines, who are frequently matched up to various ethnic or sexual stereotypes.

In today's multicultural Britain, skin color and appearance have generally confounded identification, leading to ambiguity and anxiety. Witness the shock, in David Baddiel's film comedy *Infidel* (2010), among his relatives and friends in discovering that Mahmud Nasir, a secular Muslim, was born Solly Shimshillewitz. The ensuing burlesque pokes fun at stereotyping, and the irreverent, comic ridicule questions the prejudices on which religious beliefs and ethnic difference are maintained. Nasir is a Homer Simpson-type Muslim everyman who is plunged into the abyss of identity politics when he discovers his hidden Jewish birth. The post-9/11 situation and the Middle East conflict overdetermine mutual perceptions of Jews and Muslims, and, in order to explain away his *yarmulke* at an anti-Israel demonstration, he publicly burns it, becoming instantly the hero of the radical Islamists. Nasir saves himself from arrest by declaring he is a Jew, much to the shame of his Muslim family and supporters, whom he consoles by saying that at least he is not a fanatic *shi'ite*. Yet the diversity of Muslim identities and of the world-wide Jewish diaspora belie perceptions in terms of colonizers and colonized, revealing deep ambiguities and complexities in any attempt to establish a stable identity. The film therefore places Jew and Muslim in an uneasy duality, as we have seen in Hanif Kureishi's satire of prejudice and fanaticism. "Once again," comments the film's director, "the very malleability of that wandering, spectral identity par excellence—the Jew—seems to attract and function as a barometer for prejudice."[8] The virtual postcolonial or postmodern "jew," however, should not be reduced to a crude universalized metaphor for Otherness, but may be one of several fake and hybrid identities, as we have seen in Salman Rushdie's playful postmodern take on this idea in *The Moor's Last Sigh,* which follows from Rushdie's view that identities are generally false and unstable.

The figure of the "jew" is particularly adaptable to postmodern notions of fluid identity and doubling when things come apart and no center holds in a post-apocalyptic meltdown of history. Julian Barnes' prizewinning *Metroland* (1980) demonstrates how the big events of history are experienced as marginal to the central concerns of life, such as love and the pursuit of happiness. At least Christopher Lloyd and his Jewish friend Toni Barbarowski think they are catching life on the hip as they play the *flâneur* in London's West End, do their best to *épater la bourgeoisie,* and get one-up on other boys, shop assistants, and unsuspecting passers-by, while avoiding being castrated by Nazis or raped by lecherous old men. They must find out what life is all about, especially sex, before adulthood catches up with them and condemns them to a lifetime in suburban Metroland, at the end of the Underground's commuter belt. Christopher's family has little diaspora to offer and his English face cannot match Toni's Mittel Europa features and his cosmopolitan rootlessness:

> Toni far outclassed me in rootlessness. . . . He looked an exile too; swarthy, bulbous nosed, thick-lipped, disarmingly short, energetic and hairy; he even had to shave every day.[9]

Toni has history behind him—Chris imagines his parents must have escaped at the last minute from the Warsaw Ghetto—and thus he comes with several languages and cultures, as well as the "atavistic wrench" of the enormity of the Holocaust, thus outclassing his English friend who feels handicapped by not being Jewish.[10] Toni is the knowable intellectual provocateur who puts

Christopher on the road to knowing what it's all really about. They are self-styled aesthetes after the French intellectual tradition, afraid that "they" (bureaucrats, parents, or the authorities) might somehow put an end to their sensual vision of the world—what if "they" messed around with colors? Christopher's English face feels fairly secure, but Toni's "swarthy, thick-lipped Middle-European features would be completely negrified by sodium."[11] Here, and elsewhere in this novel, an evasive and often self-mocking Englishness is tested and teased out by the ethnicity of the Other.

As an embodiment of inherently ambiguous identity, the "jew" acts as the destabilizing provocative radical whose fundamental ambivalence unsettles Western social norms, the parvenu who is a pariah.[12] When, in *Metroland,* Christopher slips comfortably into the domestic bliss of middle-class marital routine, with its regular mowing of the lawn and chamoising of the car, it is the Jewish intellectual Toni, looking "as swarthy and Jewish and energetic and two-shaves-a-day as ever,"[13] who tries, in vain, to wake him up and remind him of their naïve youthful idealism, their cynical non-conformism, which he has betrayed for an unassuming suburban domesticity and what turns out to be a misguided marital fidelity.

Christopher Lloyd first discovers love and loses his virginity a few streets away from the barricades of the student revolt in Paris in May 1968, an event which passes him by almost unnoticed; love dwarfs the great political struggles around him. Annick, his French lover, is more experienced than he is, and he finds a ready reciprocation of the need for intense emotional openness and intellectual seriousness that the Jew has nurtured in him. But then history is not the dry-as-dust stuff crammed into them at school. Being right there when it happens makes no impression on the young man losing his virginity and falling in love for the first time. It is history that is marginal and incidental in the lives of individuals. Chris drifts apart from Toni and finds that the long awaited Future has arrived without fanfare. He suddenly discovers that his acceptance of the everyday has proved a bar to what used to bind his friendship with Toni, the constant outcast who despises all pretensions and institutions, including the value of art and poetry, and cannot understand why Chris is faithful to his wife Marion, despite his disbelief in "Judeo-Christianity" and in moral philosophy. The "jew," then, is marginal because radical politically and radically different, therefore subversive: the skeptical disbeliever, the tempter into rationalism, who shuns the old boys'

.

network of school friends, and scorns, instead of parodying, cozy suburban Metroland.

This is an account of acne-spotted adolescence and first love embarrassingly weighed down with fears of faux pas, but also inflected with consciousness of cultural difference; Christopher is totally unconvincing when he tries to pass as French and is easily recognized as a "Brit" by fellow English students. The "jew" here is the measure of cultural difference, just as in *Arthur and George* (2005), Barnes' historical fiction about a real life mystery involving Sir Arthur Conan Doyle (the "Great Wyrley Outrages"), George Edalji functions as the Other (with a hybrid Scottish-Indian pedigree), falsely convicted of livestock mutilations. The overtones of ritual slaughter and prejudiced response may say something about the quiet, almost discreet nature of English racism that rarely raises a fuss (a policeman castigates Edalji as a half caste Parsi, one of the "Jews of Bombay,"[14] and an anonymous letter writer tells Doyle after Edalji's release that he should have been kept in prison along with "black and yellow faced Jews").[15] However, this, unlike the Dreyfus case, according to Edalji, is largely undeserving of a great struggle of good and evil.[16]

Another story of a pair of school friends in which the soul mate is also a Jew, Nigel Williams' novel *Star Turn* (1985), demonstrates not only the fluidity of all identities, but also the unreliability of any narrative or autobiography. Here it is not so much that Isaac Rabinowitz ("Zak"), the smart Jew on the streets of the poverty-stricken East End of London in the early twentieth century, has a history and a belonging that is envied by the English boy who lacks any identity, but that all identities are fake and history is largely a construction that does not withstand the test of either credibility or verification. Who we are essentially amounts to the stories we invent about ourselves. Writing his life in 1945, the narrator (whose name we can never be sure of) finds he cannot remember what he needs to know in order to know what he is. As a writer of propaganda in Britain's wartime Ministry of Information, he could invent the facts, and it would be impossible to ascertain the truth. If, for example, he insists he has read a book called *The Playground,* but its author Harris insists it is called *The Basement,* this is not just a Pinteresque party scene of language games and innuendoes, like several literary parodies in the novel, but it demonstrates the inability to establish any "real" state of affairs. Certainly, historians are not to be trusted, and Williams' novel depicts a series of familiar historical events and a gallery of historical personages, from Ramsay Macdonald and D. H. Lawrence to Freud and Goebbels, which play out Monty Pythonesque scenes of satirical absurdity that debunk history. As in *Metroland,* history looks quite incidental when viewed through personal experience. There is, in fact, no such thing as history, shouts Isaac's father, as he throws Spencer, Macaulay, and Marx off the shelves of his bookstore and into the dustbin of history, "just a mad succession of names and dates and places, all of them lies."[17] The only duty is to tell the truth, a duty that the narrator finds impossible to fulfill because nobody can agree on the truth; it is merely a "convenient fiction that we use to measure conduct."[18]

Mr. Rabinowitz's bookstore initiates the working-class narrator into the world of the intellect and into communism, as well as into acquaintance with Tessa, the daughter of a suburban English dentist, with whom Zak has a fateful relationship. Zak rebels against his father's atheism because he wants to be part of history, but he cannot find a belief that can hold him, whether it is synagogue attendance or Nature, Marxism or the Labour Party. Zak, it turns out, is a mirror-image of his opposites, including the leader of the British Fascist Party, Oswald Mosley, who hires him as his bodyguard (as he did hire Ted "Kid" Lewis, a Jewish prize boxer from the East End).[19] The new Jewish muscularity and fascism mirror each other and Isaac's impersonation of Mosley becomes an acting out of the fake double for the weak fake that Mosley really is. The "jew" has become his enemy and reveals much in common with him, as if one were the doppelganger of the other, thus making good and evil, victim and perpetrator, not opposites but merely relativistic terms.

Similarly, a schizophrenic Goebbels is discovered doing impersonations of a Bronx cab driver in an American Jewish stand-up comedy routine. History is not just debunked, it is deflated. All the famous names, in fact, who made history turn out to be pathetic and ridiculous. Ramsay MacDonald is exposed as a transvestite. Williams has a drunken Churchill do a brilliant travesty of one of his most famous war speeches at a party before he slides to the floor. History is lived as an erotic fantasy, beginning with the Western Front, where the two friends have run away from home and find a real war zone that looks like a dream landscape. The relationship of the individual and history is never credible; it is never happening to anyone except in personal memory, which is totally unreliable. History is not what is lived but remembered, and what is remembered can only be imagined. That could say something serious about the relativity of historical truths, but when it comes to the Holocaust it is difficult to believe that concentration camps are less real than the scripted scenarios which the narrator helps create for propaganda films. As we will see again further on, the disbelief in the Nazi atrocities that the British government fostered in its policy of disinformation does make it easy to dismiss the Jews' stories about mass killings, but then what is the "real" once one has removed conventions of veracity? Is the narrator's boss Alan Brown really a Jewish refugee from Germany whose real name was Braunstein and who speaks perfect English to disguise his foreign identity? What is the narrator's real name—Henry Swansea, the name he writes and works under, or the "unconvincing" Amos Barking (which could be either a canine call for attention or a London suburb downriver)? Can any story ever be told, least of all one of unimagined traumatic horror such as the Holocaust? Alan tells Amos that his problem believing stories of the Final Solution, when news reaches the British government through "reliable sources" via a contact in Switzerland, is that he can't tell truth from fiction.[20]

Zak's Jewishness, the narrator claims, was of no relevance to their friendship, yet nevertheless he idly wonders whether, if he made Zak a little less Jewish, more a strong, blonde, perfect hero, he might be a useful image for Allied propaganda. But the Jewishness of the Jew makes this impossible. Like Zak, Amos is a misfit, secretly opposed to the war, and unable to face the task of defending the indefensible (which cannot be sold to the public as Nazi-style total war, or a warning to stop antisemitism, only as revenge for the bombing of Coventry). Alan, who has none of Amos's Anglo-Saxon compunction or hypocrisy and all of Zak's intensity, makes him join the fire bombing raids of Dresden to show him that mass killing is not a dream, and to force him to choose between his scruples and what has to be done to win the war against the Nazis. In the end, Amos must conform and win Tessa's love or lose his job. Paradoxically, he must lie and forfeit his rationale as the narrator of his own story or stop writing. The two Jews in his life have used their sharp intellect to remove his cover, leaving him exposed to the unrelenting fire of the "real." In the novels by Barnes and Williams, a familiar postmodern take on history renders the figure of the "jew" all the more ambiguous and paradoxical, as a vehicle to deconstruct the very idea of history and unmask complicity with defending the indefensible (both Toni and Zak offer a tempting and nihilistic skepticism toward English complacency and suburban comfort), yet it draws on the Jews' surfeit of historical memory and stereotyping to do this.

Postmodern constructions of identity tend to discard mononuclear and homogenous categories in favor of multiple versions of alternative ethnic, gender, spiritual, or sexual self-identification and affiliation. With the collapse of the nuclear family, the breakdown of master-narratives of nationhood, and the spread of a multiethnic and multicultural society, the "Other" has come to the fore as a subject of racial, ethnic, religious, and ideological tensions, while the "self" has become marginalized and fragmented. James Joyce's Leopold Bloom, in *Ulysses,* was the quintessential everyman, an epitome of modernist dissolution of identity, but he was also the Wandering Jew and an embodiment of Christian antisemitism from the blood libel to the Ballad of Little Hugh of Lincoln, which Stephen Dedalus rehearses for Bloom as they compare notes on Irish and Jewish national destiny in the middle of the night in Bloom's kitchen. In Will Self's *How the Dead Live* (2000), true to Joyce's ecumenical baptized Jew, the dead Lily Bloom wanders the city and explores its netherworld, while obscenely mouthing the American Jewish slang of her origins and the crude patois of West End brothels. Aspiring to a secular Jewish *Finnegan's Wake* set in a Dantean purgatory, but not really getting beyond that aspiration, *How the Dead Live* parades an endless parody of well-known literary passages. Yet the word play never amounts to more than an extended joke in which the ever-pessimistic self-pitying Lily clings to life like a vengeful howling animal thirsting (even in posthumous disembodiment) for more sex.[21] The overwrought monologue of an overweight dead woman recollecting her dying never achieves the ecstatic life-affirming climax of Molly Bloom (in the last lines of *Ulysses*), and, instead, her own meditation on living death and life as death in the suburbs of North London indulges in a torrent of abuse (as vicious as it is often viscous) thrown at anyone and anything in sight.

Lily Bloom is unloving and unloved, admitting no commitment or identity, a convinced atheist who practices "Jewish" cynicism, a materialist incurably angry for her losses and suffering. The punning "d'jew" (and even "mindjew" and "wouldjew") teases us about ethnic associations. The dying Lily Bloom denies she is Jewish when offered religious salvation by a Black hospital nurse. We are treated to a self-mocking parody of "Jewish Antisemitism" as Lily recollects how embarrassing authentic Jews looked to self-hating Jews of North-West London, embarrassing because they remind Lily of her own Jewish upbringing and demonstrate to her just how much her integration into the neighborhood has left her, looking back from her dying, with nothing to show in the way of identity. She finds most hateful successful Jewish celebrities, such as Yehudi Menuhin, the "ultimate effete, artistic Jew" cosseted in his gilded Highgate cage, [22] who will outlive her (he actually died in 1999 at the age of eighty-three, suffering from no more than bronchitis). No Jew who makes no pretence of his identity can deserve such longevity!

Lily, like most self-haters, has internalized hostile stereotypes of the Jews as loud, vulgar *nouveau-riches* whose plump wives drive expensive Mercedes down Golders Green Road to stock up on more calories at the kosher bakery, an excessive and tasteless display of conspicuous consumption too soon after the Holocaust, when Jews were being "*slimmed down* for the ovens."[23] Lily "always hated Golders Green" and if she had to take her children, the offspring of a mixed marriage (her "mongrel kids"), to the cinema there, she couldn't hide her "racial self-disgust": she hated the "press of Jewry, all munching and gabbing and shmoozing their way through the ads"—it was like being in synagogue![24] Swearing never to go there again, she is nevertheless drawn back to this Jewish space when driving home from shopping to the "anemia" of her "goyish" husband and stops off at Bloom's take away to savor "exotic" Jewish food, proudly hobnobbing with wayward smart Jews.[25]

This love-hate relationship with her Jewishness drives the malicious animus of Lily's black humor. For example, Lewis and Mary Rubens are Lily's neighbors in Hendon and own a dry goods store that, even when it is taken over by Elvers' *Waste of Paper* chain, becomes known in the family as "Jewmar" (a jocular nickname based on an acronym of the couple's combined first names, Lew-mar).

> Here, strained through net curtains, rustling about in a nylon,
> gingham-patterned house dress, and dumped down on a velour-
> covered three-piece suite, was all the sour affected, sub-gentility
> of my own lower-middle-class, Jewish upbringing. The
> Rubenses' place smelt of gefilte fish and matzo balls—despite

the fact that Mary Rubens cleaned relentlessly; she was a laving engine.[26]

The Rubens' obsessive cleaning, which can only keep stereotypical smells of Jewishness in, not eradicate them, reminds Lily uncomfortably of the shabby English gentility into which she has married, standards she had to *fail* to maintain. This is at one with the general disparaging of everyone and everything, but Jewish self-hatred has acquired its own status, something to be proud of, that is, until Israel drew fire for "behaving like an honest-to-God gang of .99 calibre fascist assholes."[27]

Nowadays, Lily tells us, Jewish antisemitism received little attention when antisemitism was no longer the prerogative of "awkward convocations" receiving silent assent,[28] or the subtle bigotry of English gentility, like her in-laws the Yaws who did not hate Jews, Blacks, or women, only disliked them for themselves alone and incidentally hated their Jewishness, blackness, or femininity.[29] Musing on Jewish antisemitism, Lily thinks of Groucho Marx in *Horse Feathers* as equivalent to Hitler's demagogy and her own father's quick-fire delivery of gags; only Jews could hate Jews so intensely (which is probably why Lily chose her first husband Dave Kaplan who jokes he was a goy passing as a Jew).[30] But then, as has commonly been observed, self-hatred is the stuff of Jewish humor. In *Jokes and their Relation to the Unconscious,* Freud thought that Jews were unusual in their penchant for the self-ironic "Jewish joke," which articulated the psychopathology of everyday life; Homi Bhabha explains this as a self-critical minority community's attempt to regulate hostile stereotypes and attain self-knowledge.[31] In Self's postmodern take on the "jew," self-hatred is a Jewish joke that parodies inassimilable Jewish difference, as in "Jew jokes" told by Jews in Germany since the Enlightenment which made fun of Jews' anxiety about their inability to efface their difference of physiognomy or language and become "civilized."[32]

In America, Lily could pass as the proverbial "*shiksa*"—blond and buxom—a "big thing" in the forties. She was brought up to regard Blacks as Other, as untouchable, a prejudice she cannot get out of her system, and she never forgives herself for her part in the death of her son David when he was playing the "nigger" game. Yet Lily's daughters, who spend much time firing ironically witty barbs at each other, reflect her own split non-identity: one daughter, the "*shiksa*" Charlotte, has taken on the facial mask and surname of her English father, and the other, Natasha the messed-up junkie, admits to having Jewish blood, as if she were some kind of vampire, or, if pressed, will say she is "half-Jewish—I get all of the guilt and none of the community."[33] Dark, olive complexioned Natasha Bloom is hooked up with similarly dark-skinned Russell, her drug pusher and a nasty criminal gang figure before becoming a disrespectable estate agent and failed property speculator, whom Lily at least admires for being an uncompromising East End Jew:

> Russell's family never moved beyond the pale, never went for the colourless indifference of the northern 'burbs. They stuck it out down the Mile End Road, shneidering out of premises in Whitechapel, attending services with the congregation at shul, going for the occasional shmeiss at the steam baths in Hackney. They kept faith with their Cockney patter—the word of God the costermonger—and have spawned another generation of chancers like Russell, living off his wits, winging it, like a dark angel passing over the feast of commerce.[34]

This image of procreative promiscuity and Semitic philandering stands in stark contrast to the infertile Charlotte and Richard Elvers who spend a fortune on consultations with the specialist Lord Churchill (whose paternal grandfather was a Jacob Rotblatt and whose name leaves open speculation ranging from his honorific title to charlatanry).

In this suburban Book of the Dead (a shorter earlier version was entitled *The North London Book of the Dead*) everyone achieves a popular New Age version of karma. The dead have to carry around the results of their desires and deeds in their former lives, whether it is the fat that they gained in eating and lost in dieting or the babies that did not survive—Lily is lumbered with a lithopedion, as well as the nine-year-old killed in a traffic accident. Death merely replicates the effects of life, and so what goes around, comes around. Lily ought to come to some knowledge of self, except that Self is her creator, who has imbued her with some of the self-destructive urges and addictions that he went through in reaction to his privileged upbringing in North-West London. She never learns anything from her Aboriginal death guide, Phar Lap Jones, who hints mysteriously that she should rid herself of the phantasms she (like the other dead) has herself created in her subconscious.

The Holocaust is here determinant as death factor/factory. Before she is turned into ashes in the "Dachau-brick" Golders Green Crematorium, the terminally ill Lily hallucinates a vision of New York and joins a Harlem funeral as Gershwin's blues fill her head with "Yid slickery" jazz and Hitler gives her the kiss of death—Kurt Waldheim's rehabilitation seems to contribute to the lie of the Holocaust being over and finished with.[35] Self (whose American Jewish mother's family had some connection to the Holocaust) seems to be saying that death, which to Lily seems like a release from the "living death" of Hendon and no more bothersome than her previous relocation from "Jewmerica,"[36] is present all the time in our lives, a banal inversion, perhaps, of Leopold Bloom's celebratory exploration of Dublin's netherworld, also the vantage point of the universal figure of the Wandering Jew. Here Death is merely a mirror of life, located in an alternate inner city slum area, Dulston, an even duller shadow-district than the real Dalston, its "cystrict," or sister neighborhood cistern, a barely visible cyst in the obscenely gangrenous skin of London.

History itself sheds any pretense at linear progression and offers a post-apocalyptic spectacle to those hysterical old women at the end of Yeats' "Lapus Lazuli" whose private pain and hysterectomies become public property in a Stoppardian inversion of the world as stage: "History is never in the round, —it's always on the stage, and while the curtain may be death, why is it then that so many scrutinizing eyes stud the proscenium, peering into the dimness of the stalls? Are they tragic or comedic masks—or not masks at all?"[37] But then history looks even more ironic and often irrelevant when you're more dead than the living zombies of London's dull suburbs (such as "Dulburb") and the random, arbitrary violent events in the outside world effect little change in the lives of the living dead or the dead living. Indeed, excessive violence, especially when visited on Jews or by Jews (such as Baruch Goldstein or Yigal Amir), helps vent the anger that, besides jealousy and proud shame at being Jewish, wards off the loss and suffering Lily must relive unremittingly in traumatizing replay. Lily manages to enter Natasha's psychotic visions, before being reincarnated in her womb as her own granddaughter (this time with a snub nose, as she may possibly have been sired by the non-Jewish Miles whom Natasha seduced into adulterous sex). It seems that in the end, Lily will have to relive as an abused child the empty story she has told in the necropolis that is Self's imagined London. In this postmodern version of history, personal experience is a ghostly reliving of a transhistorical nightmare as only a post-Holocaust Jew could imagine it.

Denial of being a Jew has particular nuances peculiar to England, where the old public school traditions of cricket fields and noble ancestry force the eponymous anti-hero of Giles Coren's sexual comedy novel, *Winkler* (2005), to shamefully hide any traces of his Jewishness, particularly his circumcision, which prevents him exposing himself in locker-rooms and delays sexual relations for some years. When his Irish girlfriend subjects it to a painful inspection (in a rehash of the similar scene in Kingsley Amis's *Stanley's Women*), she is shocked to discover he is a Jew, but then she had never seen Blacks before either. At one point Winkler thinks that if he had grown up among Jews, his penis would have made no difference; his difference derives from his denial of who he is. It is in Freudian terms a displacement for castration inflicted by the father (who in this case has betrayed his family and his Jewish identity) and, as Jon Stratton suggests, may be a fetishized symbol of deeply ambivalent feelings about assimilation.[38] Winkler, a self-loathing and lethargic office drone who seems to bear no other name (like Wee Little Winkle in the Scots nursery rhyme), though he is sometimes addressed familiarly or affectionately as "Wink," externalizes Jewish stereotypes, regarding all Jews as dirty or tainted with criminality (everything in his family seems to be "stolen"). His greatest shame of discovery came at the school Fathers' Match, since his father had run away with a *shiksa* and he could produce only a dodgy uncle who nevertheless carries the day.

Unlike Martin Amis's *The Rachel Papers,* the release comes not with conversion from idealism, but with a realization of his fantasies when an aged neighbor, Wallerstein, reveals his Holocaust story. Wallerstein, whose penis is not just circumcised but deformed, a double mutilation that erases the shameful and potentially lethal sign of sexual difference, tells Winkler the story of how he survived by passing as a Pole when he lost his family in the bombing of the Blitzkrieg, then escaping from the Warsaw Ghetto to join the partisans in the forest. Wallerstein relates how he would avenge himself on German soldiers by turning them into "jews": he circumcises them, cuts out their tongues, and sets them free to be killed by Polish villagers as "jews." Winkler identifies with the old man's tales of the partisan band and discovers this erotically arouses him. What he perceived as his mark of shame is transformed into a weapon. In his mental "cinema," he transposes his own sexuality to the Holocaust victim who murders German prisoners, even when the war is almost over, because that is the only way to respond to antisemitism. Winkler wonders how he himself would have passed as an Aryan. He has indeed been passing as Gentile all these years:

Were Winkler's looks "good"? Certainly he was in no danger of being taken for a Swede or a Pole or a German. . . . His nose was relatively small and very straight. His ears were sleek and well-fitted. He did not gesticulate too much when he spoke and he rarely suffered from sinus trouble. This was all thanks to mongrelisation of the blood; he was a robust cross-breed rather than a frail thoroughbred.[39]

But his name gives him away and so does the physical mark of difference, his circumcision.

Winkler listens to the old man, stops acting the schlemiel, and in an *acte gratuite* becomes a murderer. The physical mark of his Jewish identity is no longer a handicap. He joins the drug scene and enjoys kinky sex with a voluptuous long-legged Australian dancer called Albuquerque, whose abuse of his body re-inscribes his penis as a viral, volatile projectile. Now he is able to declare himself as a Jew for the first time "proactively," amazed to find out that two other members of the gang, Baz and Jason, "do" the Jewish Sabbath thing on Friday nights to please their parents; now, he has "no secrets."[40] Happy, living life to the full, there is no barrier to his freedom as a post-modern punk Raskolnikov. Until, that is, Inspector Porfiry (presumably the Metropolitan Police have borrowed him from Dostoevsky) and Sergeant Tolkien (an alias of a Jew called Arnold Finkel who appropriately names himself after a literary fantasist) turn up on the doorstep when he is undressed and stoned. The liberated Winkler has rescued a blind young woman from an attacker, but then he realizes an old fantasy, to push a fat lady under a train. Winkler is wanted for the wrong murder, the depraved abuse and killing of the blind woman, but little do the police realize how close their suspicions are to Winkler's secret fantasies and sex life.

Winkler has freed himself from his inhibitions, from his self-conscious anxiety about adopting correct attitudes (especially regarding Muslims). He lets go and adopts the postmodern mindset, according to which (to paraphrase *The Brothers Karamazov*), once God is denied and boring old "Judeo-Christian" morality trashed, all is permitted. Normality, in which sick brutality is a joke and mass murder of children a cause for journalists to celebrate, looks no more attractive than Winkler's heartless adolescent nihilism. In neither state is truth discernible from lies. It looks as if Winkler has put behind him the cynical incredulity that typically meets Jewish stories of atrocity, whether Holocaust deniers, indifferent colleagues in the office preoccupied with their own egos, or the Foreign Office during the Second World War who could have saved Jews; even his insensitive grandfather echoes the general disbelief almost word for word.

Once liberated, however, Winkler is in danger of losing all control over his desires as fantasy floods into the real world and his empathic over-identification with the victim turns out to be the flip side of the mind of a sado-masochistic perpetrator. Truth and falsehood appear to be interchangeable, as Holocaust nightmares fill his head and paranoiac hallucinations of being scapegoated as a "jew" by English antisemites grip him with constant fear. In Winkler's deranged mind, the myth of the "jew" becomes something approaching wish-fulfillment that projects Winkler's own guilt, both misplaced and well-founded.

However, there is a twist in this story. Wallerstein, as we suspect, turns out to be a Pole fleeing a guilty past who has been passing as a "jew," another "Wilkomirski" who believes in the stories he has concocted out of a soup of Holocaust survivors' testimony. It also turns out that, as a result of acts of adultery and miscegenation, Winkler's grandfather is not really his grandfather, and Winkler is not by Jewish law a Jew. However, Winkler has learned what it is to be a "jew." He has learned that a Jew can play cricket, but cannot be an Englishman playing cricket. Identity is invented, yet it is all he has at the end of the day to make his name mean something to someone. Uncle Bill the convict reassures Winkler, "We are whatever they say we are. If we weren't, then why would they say we were? What we think we are is meaningless. To them you're a Jew. So be a Jew. What does it matter? It's easier once you've made a decision."[41] His Christian friends are no more authentic, Winkler concludes, than Jews without knowledge of their heritage; what matters is belonging.

WRITING BACK TO ANTISEMITISM: JEREMY GAVRON AND DAVID BADDIEL

When the empire "writes back" in the work of postcolonial minorities, contradictions and comic misunderstandings highlight the fragmentation of all identities, as can be seen in Zadie Smith's *White Teeth* and Jeremy Gavron's *Book of Israel* (2002). Gavron's novel writes back to antisemitism by telling the story of Lithuanian Jewish immigrants in Leeds, Johannesburg, and, finally, middle-class London suburbia. Israel, now Jack, Dunn comes up to Oxford in the late forties and confronts antisemitic stereotypes, but is not quite au fait with the etiquette of the elitist English world he enters. The typically naive Jewish newcomer to English upper-class snobbism is asked whether he is Orthodox and fails to understand he is being questioned about his rowing preferences, not his synagogue affiliation![42] Jack shuns the university Jewish Society, but he is no more accepted by his carousing, promiscuous fellow students than his Catholic girlfriend.

Antisemitic stereotypes, we come to learn, are deeply embedded in English culture, whether it is the filthy Jews overcrowding Leeds tenements and squeezing out English workers, or the stingy rich "jew" who will always be an intrusive alien in decent society. Gavron pieces together the story of a Jewish family from Lithuania that immigrates to England and then disperses over the next generations throughout England, Israel, and South Africa. The last descendants of the Dunsky clan can barely recall their Jewish heritage and binge on Palwin kosher wine at the Passover feast while trying to recreate something of the ritual *seder,* though it ends more like a trendy party.

Gavron's oral history technique not only disarms any judgmental view and exposes prejudiced stereotype, it strips history of any authority over the official story which suppresses the truth about antisemitism. Writing back to antisemitism revises history particularly when the genteel English antisemitism described so deftly by George Orwell is silenced in official accounts of the Second World War. True, Britain did admit several thousand refugees from Nazi Germany, many of them prominent scientists or artists, and the ten thousand children brought to England on the *Kindertransport* in 1938–39 owe their lives to England's desire to show some measure of compassion (but not to adults who might compete for jobs or try to enter Palestine), as well as to the efforts of dedicated and forgotten individuals such as Nicholas Winton.

However, in *The Secret Purposes* (2004), David Baddiel subverts both the official discourse and Jewish collective memory. Significantly, Baddiel's exploration of his Jerwish origins and Holocaust past was facilitated by a BBC TV series *Who Do You Think You Are?* (2004), which capitalized on the boom in family history against the background of search for identity in a multicultural society and the easy solidarity with the suffering of migrants affected by colonialism, slavery, and genocide (the show featured a number of celebrities, including several Jews). The installment featuring Baddiel's story typically emphasized religious difference, as well as the mystery and silences of the past with which a multiethnic audience could empathize and which characterize the generation after the Holocaust.[43] *The Secret Purposes* tells the story of a German Jewish refugee and his Aryan wife, and it exposes underlying prejudiced attitudes of government and the general population. It takes some time for Isaac Fabian to get the nuances of working-class banter, and with difficulty he understands why Jimmy, his "mate" in the college kitchen (where he might otherwise have been studying or lecturing), listens to Lord Haw-Haw (the pro-Nazi English broadcaster) on the radio. Yet, however misinformed and ignorant he is, the English working man is sympathetic to the suffering of Jews at the hands of the Nazis. But that is not a story that is allowed to circulate in public. The government does not want atrocity stories to spread about Jews, who are regarded as somehow less than innocent. Additionally, according too much attention to stories of concentration camps (which were held to be unreliable if they came from exclusively Jewish sources) would boost Nazi propaganda claims that Britain was fighting the Jews' war. It is something that is thought liable to anta-gonize public opinion which, it is claimed on the basis of Mass Observation reports, regards Jews as too prominent and too pushy. Hitler may have gone too far, but the Jews were to be seen as being at fault for taking more than their fair share of the nation's wealth and leading positions; indeed, antagonism in certain quarters towards refugees stemmed from the feeling that Jews brought antisemitism on themselves, or that giving too much attention to persecution of Jews would increase antisemitism at home.[44] The wartime attitudes toward refugees (especially popular approval for internment of aliens after the fall of France) and lack of sympathy for the plight of the Jews may explain a neglected domestic root of present-day British unwillingness to come to terms with its own history of racism.[45] In 1945, George Orwell stated there was no "Jewish Problem" in Britain, yet

> it is generally admitted that anti-Semitism is on the increase, that
> it has been greatly exacerbated by the war, and that humane and
> enlightened people are not immune to it. It does not take violent
> forms (English people are almost invariably gentle and law-
> abiding), but it is ill-natured enough, and in favourable
> circumstances it could have political results.[46]

In reporting widespread antisemitic remarks from people of different classes and professions (including one woman who asked not to be told about German atrocities against the Jews, because it would make her hate them all the more), Orwell comes to two conclusions:

One—which is very important and which I must return to in a moment—is that above a certain intellectual level people are ashamed of being anti-Semitic and are careful to draw a distinction between "anti-Semitism" and "disliking Jews". The other is that anti-Semitism is an irrational thing. The Jews are accused of specific offences (for instance, bad behaviour in food queues) which the person speaking feels strongly about, but it is obvious that these accusations merely rationalise some deep-rooted prejudice.[47]

For Orwell, antisemitism was a form of nationalism and might indeed gain a foothold, though not in the form of mass violence or anti-Jewish legislation. Baddiel, writing against the background of an intellectual "new antisemitism," has a good sense of such "reflexive" antisemitism. One German Jewish refugee in the novel comments, "I've heard more thoughtless anti-Jew comments here than I ever did in Germany. The only difference is that, here, they come wrapped in a gentlemanly distaste for doing anything about it."[48]

Like Orwell before him, and very much in line with his conclusions, Baddiel penetrates the English antisemitic mentality through the device of an unlikely private investigation by a young Englishwoman. June Murray, a translator from German at the Ministry of Information, who is increasingly upset by the reports of what is happening to Jews in Nazi-occupied Europe and cannot accept the memorandum prohibiting their being made public. The stories of murder of Jews are dismissed as not credible or at least not verifiable. When Isaac and other Jews over sixteen are interned on the Isle of Man, along with Jew-hating Nazis, she makes it her business, using a forged letter of introduction, to find out the truth for herself by interviewing interned refugees.[49] Yet even on the way there she is made to realize that other stories have also been distorted or covered up, such as the truth about the retreat from Dunkirk, an alternative version of which figures in Ian McEwan's postmodern novel *Atonement*. How can the truth be told if there is no way of countering official versions of History? As we already saw in *Star Turn* and as we can see in another British postmodern novel about the unreliability of history, Rachel Seiffert's *The Dark Room* (2001), it is not so easy to develop a reliable or accurate picture even when there is testimony.[50] Most of the internees are still not fully aware of the larger events that have engulfed them and destroyed their families, nor were those who got out in time able to say what happened after Hitler's invasion of Poland. Worse, they do not trust June, a government official, and are fearful for their own safety should the Germans invade Britain. None of what June hears is quite horrific enough to sufficiently impress her superiors and convince them to change policy, although an interview with the wife of a German embassy worker reveals just how much the Germans hate the Jews and hold them responsible for the "injustice" done to the master race.

There is no need for Baddiel to tell us that in the 1930s such views of the Jews were also prevalent on the right in Britain. It is enough to show the thinking behind classification of refugees (those with communist sympathies being classed as less reliable) and to have the officials emphasize the need for affidavits from persons who are "*straightforwardly* British"[51] (that is, not from Jews). The inference is that the Jews are not quite to be trusted, though nobody actually says they are in themselves a risk to the security of the nation. By fictionalizing history (rather than historicizing fiction), Baddiel is taking a calculated risk with the credibility of the authentic documents he does present, but in this way unspoken truths are exposed about the "jew" in English culture in the period following *Kristallnacht,* which was a rehearsal for the deportation of Jews, and before the Wannsee conference which decided on the Final Solution. Britain stood by unmoved at the Evian conference, in 1938, unwilling to offer admittance of any significant number of refugees at a time when the Jews of Germany could have been saved.

The news of the sinking by U-boats on 2 July 1940 of the *Arandora Star,* with its load of "enemy aliens" being shipped out to Canada, brings home to June how futile her report is, if only because the British could not understand the Jews were sworn enemies of Hitler and the victims of what was becoming apparent as a deliberate state policy to exterminate Europe's Jews. The British may be humane and have a wonderful sense of humor, but the general indifference to the fate of the Jews remains an unspoken response to what was already emerging as unimaginable horror. Isaac's fabricated story, the one June has been looking for, is in fact a distorted version of his friend Waldstein's untold and untellable story of incarceration in the Sachsenhausen concentration camp. Only years later, in his old age, visiting Auschwitz for the first time, does Isaac realize how incriminating that interview would now be in an age of Holocaust denial, how contaminated it was with the deceits and betrayals of his intimate relationship with June, whose own "secret purposes" become confused and entangled.

It may never be possible to establish an objective truth. But the children of Holocaust survivors and their contemporaries no longer feel constrained to maintain the silence enforced by the Anglo-Jewish community or by their doting parents who were only too grateful for Britain's refuge and protection and who did not want to risk their hard-won safety by drawing attention to themselves or voicing any resentment at signs of renewed antisemitism. Their children, however, did not need to comply with the "low profile" of a community with which they no longer have any affiliation, and they were not under social pressure to integrate into an Englishness that had been swept away by multiculturalism and a multiethnic society based on the second generation of a new wave of refugees, South Asians and Afro-Caribbeans, who changed the meanings of diaspora and ethnicity:[52] unlike their parents, as Caryl Phillips tells us, who "could sustain themselves with the dream of one day 'going home,'" they were already at home, with nowhere else to go, and "needed to tell British society this."[53] The new freedoms of the sexual and feminist revolutions, moreover, encouraged contemporary Jewish writers and artists to give voice to their own multiple identities, but also to resist the antisemitism institutionalized in race discourse, to speak radically as Jews.

NOTES

1. Kingsley Amis, *Stanley and the Women* (London: Hutchinson, 1984), 33.

2. Ibid., 236.

3. Ibid., 40–42.

4. Anthony Julius, *The Trials of the Diaspora: A History of Anti-Semitism in England* (Oxford: Oxford University Press, 2010), 357–58.

5. Ibid., 358.

6. Interview with Maya Sel'a, "Lo sofer afekhad," (in Hebrew), *Haaretz,* 12 Nov. 2010, *Galleriya* supplement, 2.

7. Martin Amis, *House of Meetings* (New York: Vintage Books, 2008), 38.

8. Josh Appignanesi, "Unothering the Other: *Ajami / The Infidel*," *Jewish Quarterly* 215 (Summer 2010): 50.

9. Julian Barnes, *Metroland* (London: Pan Books, 1990), 32.

10. Ibid.

11. Ibid., 15.

12. Zygmunt Bauman, "Allosemitism: Premodern, Modern, Postmodern," in *Modernity, Culture, and 'the Jew,'* ed. Bryan Cheyette and Laura Marcus (Cambridge: Polity Press, 1998), 143–57.

13. Barnes, *Metroland,* 143.

14. Julian Barnes, *Arthur and George* (New York: Knopf, 2006), 296.

15. Ibid., 306–7. The racialization of Edlaji emphasized by Conan Doyle in the novel does not seem to have been of significance in the real-life case.

16. Ibid., 325–26.

17. Nigel Williams, *Star Turn* (London: Faber, 1986), 45.

18. Ibid.

19. When the "Kid" (born in 1893 as Gershon Mendeloff) discovered Mosley's true ideology of antisemitism, he knocked out Mosley's bodyguards in a bloody punch-up as the fascist leader looked on helplessly; Morton Lewis, *Ted Kid Lewis: His Life and Times* (London: Robson Books, 1992), 227–28.

20. Williams, *Star Turn*, 60.

21. The joke is hardly original. In the title story of Alvin Greenberg's 1998 short story collection, also titled *How the Dead Live*, a ghostly mugger refuses to take a Rolex because there is no concept of time in the hereafter.

22. Will Self, *How the Dead Live* (New York: Grove Press, 2000), 83.

23. Ibid., 212, emphasis in the original.

24. Ibid., 212–13.

25. Ibid., 213.

26. Ibid., 54.

27. Ibid., 352.

28. Ibid.

29. Ibid., 184.

30. Ibid., 78.

31. Homi K. Bhabha, "Foreword: Joking Aside: The Idea of a Self-Critical Community," in *Modernity, Culture, and 'the Jew,'* ed. Bryan Cheyette and Laura Marcus (Cambridge: Polity Press, 1998), xv–xx.

32. See S. L. Gilman, "Jewish Jokes: Sigmund Freud and the Hidden Language of the Jew," *Psychoanalysis and Contemporary Thought* 7 (1984): 591–614.

33. Self, *How the Dead Live*, 353.

34. Ibid., 357.

35. Ibid., 118–19.

36. Ibid., 185–86. Self's mother similarly married out twice in a bid for assimilation, which Self has offered as the explanation for her hatred of other Jews (rather than hatred of self), in particular the "colorless" Anglo-Jewish community, whom he holds responsible for the polarization of identities (interview with Jason Solomons, "Sounds Jewish Special: Jewish Book Week," 3 Mar. 2010, http://www.guardian.co.uk/commentisfree/belief/audio/2010/mar/03/jewish-book-week-sounds-jewish).

37. Ibid., 2–3.

38. Jon Stratton, *Coming Out Jewish: Constructing Ambivalent Identities* (London: Routledge, 2000), 65. See also Sander Gilman, *The Jew's Body* (New York: Routledge, 1991), 90–96, 150–55; and Jay Geller, *On Freud's Jewish Body: Mitigating Circumcisions* (New York: Fordham University Press, 2007).

39. Giles Coren, *Winkler* (London: Vintage Books, 2006), 149–50.

40. Ibid., 273.

41. Ibid., 369.

42. Jeremy Gavron, *The Book of Israel* (London: Scribner's, 2002), 201.

43. Gemma Romain, "Who Do You Think You Are?: Journeys and Jewish Identity in the Televisual Narrative of David Baddiel," *Jewish Culture and History* 11 (2009): 283–96.

44. For a detailed account of public opinion on Jewish refugees and their internment, as well the Nazi treatment of Jews, see Tony Kushner, *The Persistence of Prejudice: Antisemitism in British Society during the Second World War* (Manchester: Manchester University Press, 1989), 142–57.

45. The historian Tony Kushner has argued that the long-term domestic history of racism and wartime antagonism towards Jews as victims of Nazism should be taken into account in understanding present-day discrimination against immigrants ("Remembering to Forget: Racism and anti-Racism in Postwar Britain," in *Modernity, Culture, and 'the Jew,'* ed. Cheyette and Marcus, 226–41).

46. George Orwell, "Antisemitism in Britain," in *The Collected Essays, Journalism and Letters of George Orwell: As I Please, 1943–1945* (New York: Harcourt, Brace and World, 1968), 333.

47. Ibid., 334.

48. David Baddiel, *The Secret Purposes* (New York: Harper, 2006), 153.

49. The story of the Jewish refugees interned by the British has not often been told from their point of view. A few accounts appeared during and immedfiately after the war, but only forty years later did researched studies and memoirs appear. See Peter and Leni Gillman, *Collar the Lot! How Britain Interned & Expelled its Wartime Refugees* (London: Quartet Books, 1980); Miriam Kochan, *Britain's Internees in the Second World War* (London: Macmillan, 1983); Connery Chappell, *Island of Barbed Wire: The Remarkable Story of World War Two Internment on the Isle of Man* (London: Robert Hunt, 2005); David Cesarani and Tony Kushner, *The Internment of Aliens in Twentieth Century Britain* (London: Frank Cass, 1993). An incomplete novel by an inmate has been published posthumously—Ruth Borchard, *We are Strangers here: An "Enemy Alien" in Prison in 1940* (London: Vallentine Mitchell, 2008). As in Baddiel's novel, the interned Jewish refugee's wife is Aryan but here she is herself interned; her semi-fictional account gives the British credit for decency and incidences of kindness, yet also tells of suspicion and insensitivity to the refugees'

suffering. See also Marion Berghahn, *Continental Britons: German-Jewish Refugees from Nazi Germany* (Oxford: Berg, 1984).

50. See Efraim Sicher, *The Holocaust Novel* (New York: Routledge, 2005), 195–96.

51. Baddiel, *Secret Purposes,* 103. Emphasis in the original.

52. Victor Seidler, "Modernity, Jewishness, and 'Being English,'" in *The Revision of Englishness,* ed. David Rogers and John McLeod (Manchester: Manchester University Press, 2004), 15–29; see also Victor Seidler, *Shadows of the Shoah: Jewish Identity and Belonging* (Oxford: Berg, 2000); Anne Karpf, *The War After: Living with the Holocaust* (London: Minerva, 1997).

53. Caryl Phillips, *A New World Order* (New York: Vintage, 2002), 242.

CHAPTER SEVEN

Radically Jewish

DIASPORA JEWS, DIASPORA BLUES

The appropriation of the figure of the "jew" in postcolonial and postmodernist discourse may partly be explained by the tendency to legitimize a new diasporic situation, but, more significantly, the transnational migrancy of the human condition has created fundamental ambiguities in identity for which Jewish diasporic wandering across languages, borders, and cultures might seem an inviting paradigm. In his essay "The Postcolonial and the Postmodern," Homi Bhabha discusses the complex ways in which social and political boundaries have changed. Cultural value is now located in what Bhabha calls the "transnational as translational."[1] Bhabha is convinced that postcolonial discourse has anticipated the problematics of the postmodern challenge to linear narratives, agency, discursive closure, and determinacy of meaning.

In a series of staged or exoticized photographs of Jews that represent them as diverse portraits of hybrid identities spanning continents and cultures across the world Frederic Brenner's project *Diaspora: Homelands in Exile,* for example, looks at the imminent loss of diaspora communities which have preserved Jewish historical memory through customs and ritual practices, yet concludes that there is an "irreducible" exile in homeland, even in Israel.[2] Daniel and Jonathan Boyarin go back to Paul's discourse of "nation," which was intended to complete the notion of Jewishness in order to understand the later downgrading of Jewish ethnic and theological difference into a sign of disorder and discord in a universal Christian polity. The "jew" becomes the sign for difference, but, the Boyarins argue, the diaspora experience "constrained Jews to create forms of community that do not rely on one of the most potent and dangerous myths—the myth of autochthony." In other words, while antisemites (Gentile and Jewish) malign Judaism as racist, Jewish nationalism is (from an anti-Zionist ultra-Orthodox position) dispensable to rabbinical theology.[3] The legacy of that radical Jew, Paul, however, has had disastrous effects on the fate of Diaspora Jews over the ages who were rejected by the "universalistic" Christian nation for being exclusivist and for not redeeming themselves by disappearing into Christianity.

Diaspora, which was once a term unique to the Jews' exilic situation, is now a term applied to ethnic minorities who are not at home in their host society, and so it has come to include Jews only in as much as they cling to a universal condition of rootlessness, in a de-essentialized sense that denies them exclusive rights to an ancestral homeland.[4] Diaspora has not replaced the nation-state, but certainly periphery has moved towards the cultural center, transforming traditional models of identity and challenging globalization, while reimagining Europe as a site for hybridity, with all the ironies of thinking of Britain as a cultural "home," a term loaded with clichés and ambivalences as immigrants discover their identities in the "motherland" that rejects them but also redefine the host society.[5] Diasporism has won a new legitimacy as a de-essentialized transnational or pan-European identity in postcolonial critics' recognition that the axis has shifted from "home" and "colony" to a swinging pendulum of displacement and resettlement.[6] Against this background, the metaphorical representation of the ultimate migrant across cultures and continents and refugee from persecution everywhere, the "jew," has gained a new lease of life as the boundaries blur not just between nations but also between the fantastic and the real, the historical and the imagined.

Before moving on to consider what real Jews do with the postcolonial discourses about the "jew," it is worthwhile recalling that the "turn to diasporism"[7] does not necessarily operate on a bipolar axis of Israel/exile or take for granted the centrality of Israel to Jewish life. Israeli law on immigration and marriage has at times alienated some secular Diaspora Jews who saw it as exclusivist and compromised by a religion which did not play any role in their identity make-up, while more right-wing ultra-Orthodox Jews found the secular character of Israeli society unacceptable. But something had changed in Israeli identity by the twenty-first century that made the diaspora past far more important than previously, while government policy took on the responsibility of fostering Israel's central position in Jewish life and of the security concerns of Jewish communities threatened by antisemitism and Islamist terror. Diaspora Jewish leaders, on the other hand, sensed that the need for continuity required redirection of resources to communal growth and away from support for Israeli causes, while a growing number of secular Jews no longer felt they could support Israel's policies without question and that they had the right to criticize Israel. Tainted by insinuations of double loyalties and global conspiracies, Diaspora Jews find themselves on the defensive, especially in the wake of real espionage cases, such as the Pollard affair, and may resent Israeli attempts to muster political and financial support among Diaspora Jews or persuade them to leave comfortable homes in the West and return to their ancestral homeland.[8] Expansion of the European Union seemed to offer new possibilities for a secular Jewish cultural identity that would suit a supranational or transnational ethnic diversity, not tied to religion or community, and different from the Judaism practiced in America or Israel. Meanwhile, while ethno-national diasporas are hardly recent and relations with the host society and distant homelands have never been simple, new concepts of diaspora gained ground globally in the 1990s and early twenty-first century, enabling Diaspora Jews to see themselves alongside other ethnic minorities in a pluralist and global culture and no longer pressured into full assimilation.[9]

Diasporism seeks alternate models of "being" or "doing" Jewish that look to initiatives in the American Jewish community which have taken critical views of both Israel and traditional Judaism, while opening up to variant Jewish sexual and gender identities. Although it rests on the case of the Jewish exile for its deconstruction of the nation-state, the "new Diasporism" is not a uniquely Jewish phenomenon in its claim to an imaginary trans-national community. The self-styled programmatic "Diasporism" formulated by the painter R. B. Kitaj nevertheless sees in the two-thousand-year exile (dispersion in Greek) "a way of life (and death), consonant with Jewishness itself, even though Israel is reborn."[10] Kitaj is one of many Diaspora Jews who could say that Hitler made him a Jew, not just in his growing preoccupation with Jewishness in his art, but also in the consciousness that chance saved him from the fate Hitler intended for him. He sees his art as a mandatory testimony, inspired by the diasporism of the historian Simon Dubnow, whose last words when the Nazis shot him were allegedly "Shreib un farshreib!" (write and write it down). Cynthia Ozick, on the other hand, has vigorously opposed the assumption in George Steiner's definition of Jewish identity as extraterritorial and based on a portable culture, or in the parodic diasporism in Philip Roth's *Operation Shylock,* that the diaspora is intrinsic to a sense of Jewishness and to a writing self. Ozick has argued instead for a viable Jewish culture in English, a new Yavneh, rather than an Athens, to match Jerusalem.[11]

The establishment of the State of Israel was supposed to spell the end of exile, and if Diaspora Jews do not feel that Israel is the center of their lives or feel no commitment to the Jewish State, which they may never have visited, then diaspora has to be redefined in terms of modes of Jewish life that are rooted in America or Europe and do not necessarily evolve out of fear of persecution.[12] Some, such as Antony Lerner (former head of the Jewish Policy Research Institute in London), speak of a revival in European Jewry that could sustain an independent, self-sufficient community and culture, but others are more pessimistic and see little future for a viable Jewish life outside Israel or outside the ultra-Orthodox community. Without those nuclei of identification, many young Jews drift away from Jewish culture and community, and with a zero population growth together with rampant exogamy (currently running at around sixty per cent), there seem little grounds for optimism for growth and expansion. Yet, in the gentile perception of their dual loyalties, Jews are collectively expected to take a stand that is critical of Israel and not to "automatically" defend what is seen as "their" country.[13]

Whereas postwar Jewish authors went "beyond marginality" to write about the Jewish community they knew so well, whether critically or nostalgically, from within contemporary British drama and prose, they did so with a keen sense that their difference had been assimilated within a pluralistic and more open society and that they were a generation removed from the marginalized status of Jews in England.[14] But Jonathan Wilson may not have been alone in finding he could only become a *Jewish* writer in the seventies when he moved to America, where there was a vibrant tradition of Jewish writing within a cosmopolitan American culture.[15] Postmodernism has nevertheless dissolved boundaries of rigid social and ethnic categories, and a new generation of Jews "with attitude" has challenged the long-standing apologetic position of the Anglo-Jewish establishment. Clive Sinclair and Howard Jacobson, for example, have brought back the ugly "jew" with a vengeance, acting out the stereotype in parodies of the Jew who has internalized racialized typecasting, yet masochistically wishes to be part of an "Englishness" that defines itself as excluding Jews.[16] Postmodern Jewish writers have a far more complex relationship with their Jewishness, which becomes an "ineffable and usable" identity[17] that negotiates the contradictions and absurdities of dual loyalty to Britain and Israel, or satirizes the secular identity expressed in the obsessive addiction to Jewish food and traditions without any religious affiliation. This is as much a counter-narrative that resists integration as a protest against the complacency and bourgeois philistinism of a community that, until the nineties, remained indifferent to antisemitism and was largely silent about the Holocaust. The burden of collective memory of persecution, above all the radical marker of difference, the Holocaust, brands them, in body and mind, as "jews." Their re-imagining of European modernity is necessarily a confrontation with modern antisemitism.

The Holocaust, Albert Memmi once said, has inaugurated "a new era in the history of Jewish literature," as it has in the writing of the ex-colonials.[18] This suggests Jewish writers have been "liberated" and can review European history from the viewpoint of the former victims of persecution and genocide. Post-Holocaust Jewish literature could thus be seen as parallel to postcolonial writing in the way it takes a new view also of present ethnic relations, Writing back to antisemitism like Gavron and Baddiel, Clive Sinclair takes a particularly diasporic posture in his comic play with Jewish internalization of persecution, but in the cognizance that, however domesticated and safe English hedgerows and mowed lawns seem, the worst fears of anti-Jewish hostility have not so long ago been a reality in Europe. *Blood Libels* (1985) is a fantasy exorcism of the *dybbuk* or phantom of the Holocaust which haunts the narrator, as well as an explicitly indecent exposure of Jewish middle class hypocrisy, a favorite subject of Anglo-Jewish comic novels. Racked by insomnia, the narrator searches the obsessive memory of Jewish catastrophe for some clue to the workings of history and comes up with a psychosomatic theory of Jewish history. In a capricious postmodern vein, Sinclair would have us believe that no higher authority than immediate causes link his Jewish destiny with his own psychosomatic "Scriptophobia."

The personal displaces the historical in a way that disrupts any fixed identity which might determine Jewish history. The immediate cause in this case is Jake Silkstone's discovery of his rabbi in a compromising position with the family's au pair Helga during his Bar Mitzvah celebrations. Helga is, in fact, from Germany, though the family pretends she is Swiss, in keeping with the taboo on all things German, and the narrator has blackmailed her into complying with his sexual fantasies under threat of revealing she has been feeding the family non-kosher pork. "Rabbi Nathan's Folly," as the incident comes to be called and as Jake Silkstone names his first novel, releases the *Daughter of Germany* of any need to feel guilty about the Holocaust.[19] However, history itself switches with fantasy in an alternate reality in a way that satirizes Jewish paranoia, but also says something about a demented mind persecuted by history. In the mundane setting of St Albans (the Roman Verulamium) antisemitic pogroms are carried out by the fascist Children of Albion, and the fictional tales about the "jew" become true, as blood libels recirculate in England and Jake's son falls victim to a local pogrom against the Jews.

Sinclair's narrator acts out the wild and pornographic fantasies that lie just below the surface of his subconscious. In fact, in the eighties, just after the Israeli invasion of Lebanon and the Sabra and Shatilla massacres, the fantasies are about to come above the surface: a right-wing British nationalist teams up with PLO terrorists (on the rationale of "my enemy's enemy is my friend"); hostility toward Jews emerges from Sinclair's vision of a New Age neo-Blakean cultism and is ready to erupt into actual violence; a military takeover in Israel meets no resistance. Jake's secret erotic life in England with its sadomasochistic fantasies of flagellation and abuse is mirrored by the grotesque fantasy of the real events in Israel where Jake goes to research the life of Orde Wingate, the British officer and English friend of the Jews who helped them resist the British. Jake goes to Israel also in order to enact his love-hate relationship with the Jewish State by having anal sex with a Peace Now activist's wife who hosts him for the Passover *seder*, thus following Orde Wingate in a symbolic proof of his manhood, which in England Jews can only perform on the football pitch in an amateur club named for the legendary hero. Just as in Israel the hardliners led (at that time) by Arik (Ariel) Sharon (who makes a brief appearance in the novel) have proved Jews to be as equally violent and unscrupulous as other nations, the writer finds his own masculinity being tested not just in bed, but also when faced with the possibility of revenge.[20] Philip Roth (under the guise of "Jerry Ungar") evidently inspires Silkstone, who apes Roth's meta-fictional alter ego Zuckerman in his agony over whether his psychosomatic ills and diaspora *angst* can be cured by adulterous adventures or whether the moral price of Jewish national survival is too high. As Bryan Cheyette has remarked, in *Blood Libels* and in *Cosmetic Effects* (1989), Sinclair has erased the boundary between body and nation, so that the inscription of identity on the writer's body becomes a fluid and delirious fantasy that displaces the poles of England and Israel into a postulated extraterritorial diaspora identity.[21]

This is not a programmatic diasporism (as in Kitaj's *Diaspora Manifestos*) so much as an aesthetics of dissolution of body and self which acknowledges that Israel is too rooted in its soil and demands an excessive commitment to national ideals, making it difficult to easily absorb the diaspora artist's need to carry within him centuries of persecution and wandering. Jake's enthusiastic support for the Wingate Football Club could be taken as a British Jewish identification with the muscular Jewish body, especially after the Six Day War, which was seen as a source of pride in the strong heroic soldiers who had—this time—saved the Jews from destruction.[22] In Israel, the land of proud conquerors and macho pride, where, it will be remembered, Portnoy failed to prove his manhood, Jake makes it but is horrified by the consequences. In England, medieval antisemitism raises its head again, yet it is the Diaspora Jew who, obsessed by antisemitic conspiracies and with his wife's marital infidelities, triggers off the latent belief in the guilt of the Jews and sparks off atrocities in Golders Green and Hendon, a realization of the myth that Jews are themselves responsible for antisemitism. If one could make sense of Jake's delirious mind-wanderings and confused anorectic neuroses, it might seem that he is caught in the vice of assimilationist self-eradication, on the one hand, and dangerous identification as a proud Jew, on the other. But the punch line awards irony to any Jewish clinging to ancient tribalism: at the end of the novel, Jake discovers he was adopted and might not be Jewish after all!

One might say that the establishment of the State of Israel has forced the issue of double loyalty and challenged the identity of Diaspora Jews, even if the "negation of diaspora" is no longer official policy in Israel. The dream of Zion has become a reality that is not only not utopian but has again brought down the wrath of the nations on the Jews, while diaspora history has turned into a nightmare of genocide and renewed persecution, yet also offers a fantastic dreamscape where escape from history might be possible. For this reason, perhaps, Sinclair prefers to wander through the imagination, especially the imagination of the Singer brothers, reinventing "Ashkenazia" (as in his story of that name), or to follow the footsteps of his favorite Yiddish poet, Melekh Ravich, who, in the 1930s, sought an alternate Jewish homeland among the Aborigines in Kimberley, a region in Western Australia named for the famous South African gold fields, reconstructed in the fantastic art of Ravich's son, the painter Yosl Bergner.[23] The "Diaspora Imaginary" (to use Vijay Mishra's term modeled on Benedict Anderson's "imagined communities") is such a dream landscape where ethnicity negotiates a space within multiculturalism for an identity that resists essentialism and can claim a shared sense of *not* belonging, especially when exile or migration no longer means a state of homelessness but of dislocation.[24] "Diaspora Blues" (to borrow the title of Sinclair's 1987 book about his trip to Israel) seem pandemic in Britain. Sinclair sees the Diaspora Jewish writer as a parvenu and an exile, sharing Kafka's existential dis-ease and spiritual inner exile (another Kafka's curse, this time evident in psychosomatic symptoms of chronic eczema). Sinclair's writing is "a search for a place in which I feel at home, where my literacy will not be in question."[25] But, since he knows little Yiddish and no Hebrew, he cannot find that place, and that is what his writing is about. He admits to dual loyalty, but the split is between his history and his culture, and he describes being pulled in opposite directions by the "Flavius syndrome" of betrayal and the "Bar-Kochba syndrome" of militant messianism.

WRITING JEWISH: HOWARD JACOBSON'S FANTASIES

The British Jewish comic novelist Howard Jacobson likewise writes out of a diasporic condition. In fact, Jacobson revels in *not* belonging, and what he enjoys most is annoying the general public by waving his obnoxious Jewishness in front of their English sensibilities: stereotypically loud, vulgar, abusive, and rude. This performance is consciously "hyper-Jewish" in his comic novel, *Kalooki Nights* (2006), which, if we accept Jacobson's bragging, is the most Jewish novel ever written.[26] The narrator, Max Glickman, grows up in suburban Manchester in rebellion against his proud atheist father who turned his back on the stinking *shtetl* past and who despised "frummies" (religiously observant Jews). Max has managed to procure a copy of *Scourge of the Swastika: A Short History of Nazi War Crimes* by Lord Russell of Liverpool (1954), an exposé based on the Nuremburg Trials of the atrocities committed by the Third Reich—whose cover illustration of victims cowering beneath a pair of jackboots Max reinterprets as showing the eternally persecuted Jewish people. Later Max will lose his virgin innocence when shown, in a revelation of obscene photographs of Nazi atrocities, what should not be shown to anyone and certainly not to pubescent boys: the titillating image of naked Jewish women being selected for death. Max obsesses about the Holocaust, drawn, like Sinclair's Jake Silkstone, from Thanatos to Eros, and acts out the role of victim of Hitler, of Germany, of all antisemitic Gentiles everywhere. He responds with rage whenever anyone suggests he should put it behind him, turn the other cheek, or stop bringing it into everything. At the same time, Jacobson deliberately offends Jewish readerships because he does not respect taboos, most of all not the taboo on Holocaust jokes. Jacobson believes that since the Holocaust was the most obscene event imaginable, there should be nothing wrong with dirty jokes about it.[27]

As a child, returning by train from a seaside outing with his extended family, Max sits on his mother's lap and says, "Jew Jew, Jew Jew, Jew Jew." His family attempts to pretend he is imitating the train's steam engine, but cannot stop the child's ranting, "Jew Jew," I said, clamping my teeth around the J's. "Jew Jew, Jew Jew. . . ."[28] His father blames his mother, quite irrationally, for being preoccupied with Kalooki, a weekly social gathering to play a game that seems to have involved more shouting and heated arguments than the dealing of cards. The boy grows up with the J-word on his mind at every step and suffers from an Auschwitz syndrome that he carries around his neck (in his comparison) like Coleridge's albatross.

He relieves his stress by becoming a cartoonist who specializes in obscenity—breaking a taboo on things Jews don't do. As in the Lennie Bruce joke so beloved of Alex-Li Tandem, the world is divided into "Jewish" and "Goyish," and loose trousers with a double pleat are Jewish, bulging denim pants are, inevitably, goyish, which only seems to exacerbate his phallic anxieties. Of his choice of career he remarks,

> It relieved some of the stress I was under. The stress of a failed marriage and a failing career—the usual—but also the stress of coming from an ethno-religious minority, or whatever you call us, whose genius doesn't extend to irresponsible recreation.[29]

Jacobson defines Jews as disputatious; a Jew will answer a question with a question.[30] Max makes the point, "we are a dialectical people".[31] Along with the J-word comes the incessant Jewish "why? why? why?" that is so intolerable to Max's Gentile wife, Chloë. He appears to have married her precisely because she hates Jews and because they feed on each other's contempt for each other, perhaps also because of her deluded hope of redeeming the Jew (she kneels in prayer for him, naked save for a silver cross) and of changing him (she wants him to get a nose job). He is the exotic Other, whom she Orientalizes, photographing him as an Arab sheikh, and he begins to act and talk in the image in which he has been made by her (another example of the mimicry we saw in chapter four). She is the proverbial Other of the Jewish imagination, the alluring *shiksa,* a pejorative Yiddish term that has passed into American popular culture for the maligned Gentile slut, whore, and prostitute (Max wants us to know Jews can also be racist). Max finds her desirable for her symmetrical Aryan body, desirable because prohibited, his Buchenwald *Schicksal* (destiny or fate), as he puns, thinking of the black humor of concentration camps. Max "marries out," motivated by a mixture of Jewish self-hatred and pity for the rejected *shiksa,* but then, provoked by his mother-in-law's genteel English antisemitism, he gets into a rage—the pattern of a classic misogynist (a theme of a previous novel, *No More Mister Nice Guy*). Jacobson's fictional persona plays the "bad" (inassimilable) Jew to the hilt, hypersensitive to the point of boiling over at every imagined reminder of who he is—the quintessential "jew." Like Philip Roth and the German Jewish humorist Max Biller, Jacobson plays the *enfant terrible* writing back to stereotypes of the Jew as crucifier, the lecherous pervert and insatiable sexual predator, too much brain and not enough body, with a "Jewish" nose that interferes with marital relations. Max is unmanned not because he cannot control his wild imagination, but because he is the lover taken as the "jew" yet rejected for being *too* Jewish.

Max's father is a boxing fan (the new muscular, non-Jewish Jew) and he has driven into his son his contempt for "medieval Jewishry," the traditional Jews, who, to his way of thinking, tread in fear of pogroms. Yet Max, quite treacherously, betrays a sneaking envy for his Orthodox friend's family, the Washinskys, who are purposeful and serious in their synagogue worship and enjoy a homely family togetherness missing in his own rowdy and godless household. Max's father insists that only assimilation will save Jews from persecution, yet, as his son notes, he mixes in an intellectual ghetto exclusively with like-minded Jewish communists who can only express themselves with Yiddish words and phrases. The magic appeal of a warm *Shabbes* table lures Max to the notion that is so central to Judaism and so hateful to assimilationists like his father: separation. Separation is symbolized by the Havdalah ceremony at the termination of the Sabbath, when the Jew takes leave of the Sabbath angels with a lit candle and a reviving whiff of aromatic spices, thanking the Creator for dividing the sacred from the profane, light from darkness, and (though Jacobson omits these words of the Havdalah prayer) Israel from the other nations.[32]

The beautiful idea of separation that makes a Jew Jewish in body and soul is, of course, the opposite of integration. It is, ideally, a separation into the moral strictures of Hebraism, not some superior and condescending status of Chosenness but a serious state of holiness (as Jacobson cites Maimonides' *Guide to the Perplexed*).[33] Multiculturalism supposedly respects difference, but in fact the Jew's difference is a division that sets up a physical, sexual, and religious barrier which protects the Jewish household from assimilation, exogamy, and blasphemy. Perhaps for this reason, Max explodes the myth of the ideal Jewish family when, in his cartoonist's cynical imagination that is fed by gossip and insinuation, he mentally depicts his friend Manny's brother Asher sleeping with the daughter of the Gentile woman who tends the fire on the holy Sabbath, the daughter of a German father no less. Manny himself ends up gassing his parents in a macabre and symbolic double murder that reenacts Nazi euthanasia. Separation, it seems to Max, is not an ideal condition, not so much because it exacerbated antisemitism, as in his father's view, but because separation, "keeping apart what didn't belong together, the great act of discrimination at the center of Jewish thought as well as Jewish diet," is debilitating and prevents Mrs. Washinsky from lifting a finger to keep her house in order.[34] In particular, the modesty of the Jewish woman drives him to immodest thoughts, because it entices him with thoughts of the forbidden—he even draws lewd cartoons of *haredi* (ultra-Orthodox) women in Stamford Hill (Jacobson makes a similar comment in his non-fictional critique of the Jewish community, *Roots Schmoots* [1993]). Naively, Max believed that separation was also the essence of art, but learns that art, or rather his secular and blasphemous form of it, is unacceptable in the traditional Jewish world. Nevertheless, he respects the idea of separation as a Jewish aesthetic, because it represents the ability of discernment in monotheism, which defends itself from the hedonistic paganism with which he has become besotted. So Max turns to a self-hatred that realizes the Gentile's fantasies and myths of the "jew," which wins him neither success nor happiness, only further contempt. His hand craved to draw, beginning with a putative juvenile graphic novel, *Five Thousand Years of Bitterness*, which drew inspiration from *Scourge of the Swastika,* and he depicts a world full of Hitlers, following the Jewish tradition that every generation has its Amaleq trying to destroy the Jews. Yet at the same time, the self-hating Jew has an anarchic hand that works against his more sensible impulses and plunges his ventures into disaster.

Max makes his fantasies come true, particularly the pornographic scenarios of Jew-hating sadistic Germans. If the world wants the Jew to stop whining about being a Holocaust victim, Max is there to remind them that it happened, and it happened to him. This leads to some zany comic episodes, in which he tries to persuade his German second wife Zoë to take part in sexual depravity and act the prostitute in Berlin, but Max becomes disillusioned when it turns out Germans are into infantile regression and are only interested in monotonous demonstrations of defecation. At one point, he allows a German male student to kiss him in a Prague beer hall, only to find himself being begged for forgiveness for what the Germans did to the Jews. These are the "Auschwitz Germans" who need the "Holocaust Jew" to satisfy their need for forgiveness. Max is himself locked in a Holocaust syndrome and imagines a prisoner being forced to strip naked and draw for the infamous Ilse Koch, the sadistic Witch of Buchenwald ("Die Hexe von Buchenwald," also known as the "Bitch of Buchenwald"), who was accused of making lampshades and other ornaments out of prisoners' skin, though the legends of depraved sexual acts into which she forced inmates probably owe more to movies made about her, such as *Ilsa, She-Wolf of Buchenwald* (a movie that Max happens to view in a possibly fantasized wife swapping scene with his sex-mad friend Errol).

Alongside Dorothea Binz (a sadistic SS overseer at Ravensbrück) and Myra Hindley (a notorious British multiple murderess, whose iconic portrait by Marcus Harvey raised much controversy), Ilse Koch takes center stage in Max's fetishization of women as depraved sadists. He imagines her humiliating Jewish men at the place of their covenantal sign of racial difference from other men, their bond to the God of Israel and their sign of imagined castration. It is not that Max is insensitive to sexual abuse of women in the camps.

> It was simply that there was a terrible inversion of the nature of things in the idea of a woman beating a man, of power and cruelty being deflected so perversely from their usual course.[35]

Max finds these sadomasochistic scenes arousing for they assert Jewish virility and acquiescence as interdependent in sexual exploitation, joining Jew and German as partners in a sick game of power relations. At the same time, he also feels empowered as an imagined victim who wreaks revenge for all Jews and all men. The Shylock who has proved his humanity by being pricked and spat upon now has his revenge by inhabiting the minds of antisemites and Holocaust deniers, by being their living hell. Ilse Koch, as his Uncle Ike reminds the family, is the antithesis of his father's belief that modernity would bring assimilation. Revenge comes in the form of mischievous, self-mocking satire that holds nothing sacred, including and particularly the Holocaust.

Max Glickson's comic art, like Jacobson's, aspires to English humor, unfathomable, he thinks, to Americans, whose taste for comics is exuberantly expressed in the *Zap!* and *Whamm!* of Superman's efforts to save the world—a project thought up by a Jewish artist called Jerry Siegel whom Jacobson quotes as saying that he was inspired by overwhelming pity for the downtrodden of the world and the desire to save them. Jacobson's own comic art is more nuanced, in the satirical fashion of such eighteenth-century classic cartoonists as Thomas Rowlandson, who was himself prone to stereotyping Jews as filthy alien peddlers and usurers (as were several famous English caricaturists in the age of popular prints, before the advent of newspaper cartoons). Max prefers self-denigration and lampooning the Jewish community rather than imagining saving the world, in contrast, for example, to the heroes of Michael Chabon's postmodern fantasy novel, *The Amazing Adventures of Kavalier and Clay,* who do attempt to rescue Holocaust victims and escape history through fantasy by bringing back the Golem. Exceptionally, Max identifies with Bernie Krigstein (1919–1990), who drew a comic *Master Race* (1955) in which a Holocaust survivor pursues the camp Commandant to his death under a New York subway train, a scene Max reenacts with the figure of his nemesis, Ilse Koch, on the London Underground.[36]

Max is like the humpback in Sir Isaiah Berlin's parable who pretends the hump is not there, ignores it, or deals with his hump by proudly showing it to everyone.[37] Or rather, in the Groucho Marx joke Jacobson tells in the epigraph to *Kalooki Nights,* he is the humpback who trumps the assimilated Jew when he retorts to the wealthy man's saying, "I used to be a Jew," with the punch line: "Really? I used to be a hunchback."[38] This is doubtlessly why Max cannot but see the tailor Selick Washinsky as a hunchback in his front window, a display of racial stereotypes, at least as his father's "commie cronies" (the new muscular Jews) have taught him to see the monstrous creature whom Hitler wished to destroy.

THE POSTMODERN RETURN OF THE "JEW"

The "jew" now appears as the return of the repressed, the fear of the inassimilable, who has become in French psychoanalysis a trope for "the destabilized, decentered postmodern subject in a theoretical system that persists in defining (or 'fetishizing') them from without"—a post-Holocaust privileging of the stereotyped "jew" which antisemitism immortalized as a figure of hatred.[39] This *revenant* postmodern "jew" now stands at the center of a Holocaust discourse which sees "Auschwitz" as the rupture or caesura between modernism and postmodernism, a European disaster that is also, in Blanchot's terms, a "disastered" writing, a writing of disaster.[40] If for Lyotard, in *Heidegger and the "jews,"* "Auschwitz" was a synecdoche for the transgressive rupture of the project of modernity that inaugurated postmodernity, then the "jews" of his title are the figurative victims among the surviving generations of Europeans who come after. They are the silenced presence within Western culture, its "forgotten," who form part of its representational systems. Unlike xenophobia, the antisemitism of the West

> is one of the means of the apparatus of its culture to bind and represent as much as possible—to protect against—the originary terror, actively to forget it. It is the defensive side of its attack mechanisms—Greek science, Roman law and politics, Christian spirituality, and the Enlightenment, the "underside" of knowledge, of having, of wanting, of hope.[41]

The "jews" are held hostage by the West; they are the "irremissible in the West's movement of remission and pardon."[42] Converted, expelled, and exterminated, the "jews" never go away and remain inseparable from the Western imagination: the return of the repressed. As Hannah Arendt put it in her study of Rahel Varnhagen, there was no escaping identification as a Jew:

> In a society on the whole hostile to the Jews—and that situation obtained in all countries in which Jews lived, down to the twentieth century—it is possible to assimilate only by assimilating to anti-Semitism also.[43]

Both Christianity and antisemitism were integrating components of the society of the time to which Arendt refers and had to be accepted as a condition of assimilation.

Removed or distanced from an authentic Jewish tradition, postmodern Jews infract this sense of being unable to be other than Other, and therefore are liable to think of themselves in some figurative sense as guilty survivors, guilty, at least in Jacobson's distorted and perverse parody, because the "bad" Jews incited genocide. Resistance to annihilation throws them back to the Jewish past and the traditions their forefathers had abandoned in order to assimilate. They weave and reweave the myths of a vanished Yiddish-speaking world into a "usable past," an imagined common origin in some Jewish Eastern Europe, or more generally Russia, where Jewish martyrdom in the pogroms and the Holocaust has created an invented community of the "*shtetl*," first in America, then elsewhere, in musicals like *Fiddler on the Roof* and popular fiction.[44]

The responsibility to "remember" the past weighs heavily on the assimilated generation that has little or no knowledge of their heritage and who think of post-Holocaust Jewish existence as precarious and threatened. In the fiction, poetry, and translation work of the British Jewish writer Elaine Feinstein, such an imagined "Russian" past can merge with a Russian poetic tradition in which the poet is, in Marina Tsvetaeva's famous phrase, always a *zhid*—"a jew." Feinstein's novella, *The Border* (1984), sets up a classic scenario of the European Jewish intellectual, Hans Wendler, paralyzed by persecution yet unable to wrench himself away from his native Austria and his mistress. An associate of Walter Benjamin, whose intellectual work, legendary flight to France, and suicide on the Spanish border serve as a codex and repeated reference in this narrative, Wendler is an assimilated Jew who cannot easily contemplate life as a writer in exile, even after an invitation from a Paris theater company. This is a story of sexual and political betrayal, emotional blackmail, divided loyalties, and conflicted selves at the "border" of both fidelity and history. The improvident, self-deluded writer acts as a salutary lesson of Jewish fate during the Holocaust, but also as a plea for the value of art and love to be held up, against all odds, over national and religious ties. Feinstein has more recently shifted the Jewish cultural itinerary to the martyred Jews of Spain. In her poem "Scattering," which understands diaspora to be just that, a dispersal, not an exile, she looks to a new diaspora of Israeli Jews in London's Belsize Park and California's Beverly Hills,

awaiting the next Armageddon of the Middle East, while the construct of "Sepharad" revives an idyllic symbiosis of Arab and Jew in a postcolonial solidarity of the oppressed (a political trope that has been quite fashionable and politically correct in post-Zionist rhetoric).[45]

HISTORY, MEMORY, IDENTITY: FROM IMMIGRATION TO ACTIVISM

The sexual and gender choices for postmodernist Jewish writers also changed radically because of the women's liberation movement and the involvement in it in the 1970s of many Jewish feminists who were faced with what were ultimately unsatisfactory choices: a career and independence which rejected the Jewish family, and universal campaigns which often ignored Jewish issues and antisemitism. Yet feminism gave Jewish writers a particular radical view of the historical memory of Jewish victimhood and, of most relevance to multicultural Britain, the Jewish immigrant experience. At first glance, the role of the memory carrier of the Jewish immigrant experience should be an advantage in multicultural Britain and in a globalized transnational transit of economic, political, and ethnic refugees. It should offer poignant lessons when Britain does not always welcome migrants and asylum seekers or tolerate fully society's sexual and gendered Others. *Guardian* columnist and novelist Linda Grant has explored the tenuous links between the legacy of her family's immigrant experience and her personal identity in *Remind Me Who I am, Again* (1998), a painful memoir of her mother Rose who suffered from a form of Alzheimer's disease in which memory rapidly deteriorated. This memoir, written in the genre of the literary confession, is basically a narrative about identity, as well as about both human and Jewish memory. It asks what identity is when the mind is damaged beyond repair. What then does it mean to be Jewish and to be human? Apart from the mother's short-term memory loss, it turns out that the entire family has prevaricated the truth—they are all liars, and are covering up the dirty little secrets of the Jewish family which contribute to the lie of an ideal patriarchal harmony. It proves impossible to recover the family story with any certainty. Postmodern writers usually delight in the uncertainty of the past as a questionable foundation of a personal or collective past, but for Jews memory is everything; it is survival and knowing why you are different. It is, as Linda Grant reiterates, a matter of life and death—quite literally when the body forgets to control its muscles.

Grant may originally have been Ginsberg, but even that is not certain in the absence of documents and with only conflicting stories, fading photographs, and anecdotes to go on. What is clear, from a threatening letter penned by an anonymous Mosleyite, is that the Ginsbergs renamed themselves Grant in the 1930s to avoid the violent antisemitism in England, coming mainly from Mosley's British Union of Fascists. Memory of pogroms and persecution, and, later, the fate of European Jewry in the Holocaust were lessons well learnt in acquiring social masks, but not in acquiring the English manner of knuckling under or polite self-denial. Avoidance of conscription or black-marketeering (stereotypical "Jewish" behavior during the war) was for Linda's father nothing to be ashamed of—on the contrary, these stereotypical attributes showed business acumen and the knack of legitimate money-making.

Linda grew up among loud-mouthed Jews who showed off their newly acquired wealth because they remembered that poverty, pogroms, and persecution had been the norm, so that to brag about possessions was to be proud of survival.

> That history breathed down our necks as we were growing up, a constant reminder that where there were suburbs and houses and trees and allotments and W. H. Smith and Tesco and Marks and Spencer, a kind of mental chasm yawned beneath our feet into which we were always fearful that we could fall. It was a habit of thinking, a trick of being in two places and realities at once, which conditioned the way we saw the world, hell-bent on shops and cinemas and walking in public parks in our finery, but acknowledging that there was more to life than this, that there was a darkness in us we couldn't be rid of.[46]

The maternal grandparents came from Kiev, Yiddish-speaking pious Jews—Grant calls them "peasants"—who were probably given the name Haft by a careless immigration officer. Linda Grant's mother, Rose, rebelled against her parents' old-fashioned *shtetl* ways, and restricted her Judaism to the traditional East European dishes in the kitchen and the annual Passover feast, a purely culinary religion, apart from annual synagogue attendance on the Day of Atonement and celebration of Christmas as an excuse for shopping expeditions and partying. The family has distanced itself from the Jewish community, so that the generational transmission of Jewish tradition is all the more disrupted when Rose is put into care in north London in a Jewish home where the staff is non-Jewish (mainly Black) and attach no meaning to the rituals they help the residents perform (and which the residents themselves are beyond relating to). Grant notes, "The link has been broken with the past. . . . It forces me to wonder what it means to be Jewish."[47] Certainly, looking in the mirror, she thinks she is more likely to be Slav than to have come out of Egypt with the Jewish people, and she feels like an "antisemite" among the Jews of Golders Green, with their beards and wigs, the unassimilated "bad" Jews who represent what her mother rejected.[48] Yet when two gentiles are given a role at her nephew's bar mitzvah in a Liberal synagogue service, the long-awaited moment of confirmation in religious and family bonding, there is a *frisson* of indignation, despite Grant's insistence on tolerance that overrules tribal identity and on the characteristically English adage, "live and let live," including marriage with non-Jewish partners, one of the last prohibitions that has kept her family Jewish.[49]

Successful integration comes at the cost of rebellion by the next generation of British-born Jews. Linda's parents showered her with luxury, nothing was too good for their two daughters, but she resented her mother's lack of tender care and came to detest her portly, materialistic father. Her parents had no time for such English values as "[d]iscipline, self-restraint, modesty, respect for authority, introspection, and even artistic values" (the values of the world outside the front door), and so Linda despised her parents as outdated dinosaurs, while secretly imitating "them"—the English.[50] The Beatles emerged nearby, on Merseyside, and experimentation with sex and drugs promised a new freedom outside the confining bourgeois comfort of the home that her father's success in his hairdressing accessories business had bought and decorated, in the style of "Jewish rococo," with handcrafted reproduction eighteenth-century furniture. Now that her mother, the last one of the family alive to tell the family story, is losing her memory, Linda Grant regrets missing the opportunity to listen to her family's stories and has to piece together her divided self through conjecture and gossip.

Here is a typical pattern among immigrant families, as Grant reminds us, struggling to fit in and integrate with modernity and Englishness, but pulled by their parents' traditions which separate them from society. At the time, as a teenager, she regarded her parents as hypocrites; in mid-life she realizes how ridiculous that divide seems compared with the huge chasm between her parents and the immigrant generation, for whom they served as cultural interpreters.[51] Now she is caught out by her mother's inability to tell her where they come from and who they are. The images of the vanished East End shown in the old age home are not much help for someone from Liverpool who wishes to reclaim a sense of belonging to time and place.

However, Linda herself wonders if she too has not adopted her mother's secretive habits and led a double life. She has chosen the path of militant feminism and her mother holds it against her that she never came back from college or gave her grandchildren, as she expected. How much, Linda Grant wonders, of her mother's increasingly erratic and irrational behavior, her childish tantrums, and repetitive questions can be explained by her illness, and how much by her personality? "And my own self, the one that grew out of my relationship with my parents—was it partly formed out of the slow composition of blood that ceased to be liquid and flowing but clumped itself into clots which made their silent way into her head?"[52] How much of her own identity derives from the history of the dysfunctional family? Linda finds herself mothering her mother, who becomes the totally dependent child, manipulatively controlling her and making her feel guilty for choosing her freedom and career over caring for her mother.

In this memoir, as in Grant's novel *Still Here* (2002), a middle-aged woman who survived the sexual revolution must face the flawed choices made long ago and the resulting emptiness. In *Still Here*, Alix asks what remains of the shipwreck of her life:

> The phallic right, the phallic entitlement to which everyone else must submit—brutal, simple, magnificent—this is what thirty years of feminism had battled to overthrow, and where had it got us, the generation that took to the streets? What did we wind up with? Empty cunts. What's the resolution? The resolution is that there is no resolution, no catharsis, no release. Submission and acceptance, or refusal to submit and accept. Both ways are intolerable.[53]

An architect, Alix sets out, in obedience to her mother's will, to redeem the family property lost in the Holocaust, as well as restoring converted synagogues. She takes on the burden of personal and historical responsibility and plays along with the stereotypes of the wealthy, powerful "jews" to do so (otherwise the Jews might well find themselves again in the gas chambers). But it is Joseph Shields, a Chicago Jew who married a convert and went to live in Israel, who must bear the burden of guilt for what he did during the Yom Kippur War. Alix does what Joseph's estranged wife Erica could never do—take on moral agency and sentence him "to life"—then allows him, in the closing scene, to silence her with his Jewish penis (the sign of his identity) in her Jewish mouth (the stereotype of the loud, erotic, thick-lipped Jewish female) and satisfy her lust.[54] Alix, the would-be Augie March, gets what she wants, but knows there can be no resolution and the alternative to submission to the Jewish phallus is empty loneliness.

Like Evelyn Sert in an earlier novel, *When I Lived in Modern Times* (2000), Vivien Kovaks in Grant's *The Clothes on their Backs* (2008) grows up in a vacuum of knowing very little about her family's origins in Hungary or why they changed their name from Kovács. Like the author, Vivien breaks from her stifling refugee home where nothing has changed and goes to college, where she experiments with sex and drugs, later enjoying the thrilling freefall of amphetamines and sex with an Underground train guard who has no history and is attracted to the powerful sign of the swastika, much to her horror after she joins the anti-Nazi League, distributing leaflets (rather ineffectively) against John Tyndall's National Front.

Vivien likes to play out other identities, which is one way not to face her own, and to renegotiate the assumed "invisibility" of British Jews, who are outwardly integrated but whose ethnicity and history were effectively erased from the national narrative and from the literary imaginary before postcoloniality came along. Under the alias of Miranda Collins she penetrates the trust of a renegade uncle, Sándor Kovács, modeled on the notorious slum landlord Peter Rachman, a Holocaust survivor who spent years in Siberian labor camps. Uncle Sándor survived the Hungarian forced labor units and after the war carried on his successful career as a pimp and property racketeer, before fleeing for England during the 1956 uprising. What Vivien finds attractive in this unscrupulous evil man is his lust for life, which he lives with a passion even after his release from jail. He holds the key to the secrets to her past before the Holocaust and offers an alternative to her parents' paranoia which keeps them trembling before the authorities—they have made sure she even had a baptismal certificate so she should be a "proper person." Sándor had a penchant for Black women and hoped to marry his Jamaican-born lover Eunice, who identified with him as someone who also had come out of Egyptian slavery. But after Vivien's intrusion into their lives everything goes terribly wrong. Vivien comes back to her uncle's house after she has been assaulted by neo-Nazi skinheads who recognize her in the street as a Jewess, but stifles her pain and goes to sleep, only to be awakened by murderous screams—Sándor has tried to murder her boyfriend, a tenant in the house. Holding the bloody serrated knife which had cut her birthday cake, she cannot reconcile herself to the hatred she has experienced and has herself unleashed, just as she previously failed to reconcile her father with her uncle. She awakens to the banality of life and comes to what might be considered as a similarly banal conclusion: that clothes are what make new lives, as they did for her refugee parents before her, who came with only the proverbial clothes on their backs. At the end she is left, besides two daughters, with two dead husbands (both of whom, rather incredibly, perished in restaurants) and a neglected middle-aged body, with little to look forward to other than the freedom of an unknown future and endless window shopping. The alternate responses to racism and antisemitism, of paranoia and amorality, are surely not appetizing or satisfactory.

Feminism has dictated the choice of freedom and a career over a traditional Jewish family and its patriarchal structure. As the British Jewish feminist dramatist Michelene Wandor puts it, there's a "mythic duality" in "the dichotomy of the patriarchal Jewish father figure on the one hand, and the dominant Jewish mother figure on the other." As opposed to secular liberalism which views these two as equal or complementary, in Judaism "this creates a peculiar love-hate ambivalence and fear in each sex for the strength of the other." In order to redress this gender divide and overcome the stereotypical portrayal of Jewish gender relations, Wandor urges us to acknowledge vulnerabilities in both sexes and value interdependence in order to bridge this "destructive" gender gap.[55] It was, nevertheless, the Jewish experience of antisemitism that pushed feminist Jews into the fight against racism and into identifying in the 1980s as Jewish feminists.[56] Grant's first book was *Sexing the Millennium* (1993), a seminal feminist text, and the threat of antisemitism comes to bear on collective as well as personal identity in *Remind Me Who I Am, Again*. The avowal of who she is makes a defining statement about her writing self as a feminist who grew up against the background of the Jewish immigrant experience that is fired by the Jewish moral imperative to social action, but who rebels against the erasure of memory resulting from the parents' failure to pass on to their children a clear sense of their history and origins.[57]

For Elena Lappin, too, the Jewish experience of immigration is very important for her writing, except that in her case, as for Eva Hoffman, she feels exile is part of her sense of self and her diaspora identity because of the loss of language.[58] Lappin (born in Moscow, 1954), the sister of Max Biller, the provocative German Jewish satirist, fled Czechoslovakia after the Soviet invasion and has explored comic situations of women who come as outsiders to marriage and to Anglo-Jewry. In the title piece of her short story collection, *Foreign Brides* (1999), an Israeli woman vents her frustration at her football-crazy, outwardly religious husband by feeding the family non-kosher meat and getting the pork butcher into bed.

Lappin joins Michelene Wandor and Charlotte Mendelson as "bad Jewish girls" who have shirked the sentimental family sagas that were the traditional fare of the Anglo-Jewish novel in order to reject the role of Jewish Princess. Instead, they blast the illusionary stability and security of the Jewish family. Charlotte Mendelson's *When We Were Bad* (2007) shows a Reform woman rabbi's family spinning out of control as one sexual scandal follows another. The opening scene scripts the scenario for the most public exposure of shame: a bridegroom steps down from the wedding canopy in a synagogue to avow his devoted love to a married woman. Another insider's view is a prize-winning first novel by Naomi Alderman, *Disobedience* (2006), about a lesbian daughter of a rabbi in the North London suburb of Hendon. Both Jacobson and Alderman write Jewish, that is, they use unashamedly Jewish language and situations without glossary and their voices blend into the multiethnic diversity of postmodern British fiction. Indeed, the preoccupation with sexual, spiritual, and personal identity in these novels is shared with a number of contemporary Jewish American authors. Jews were to be seen as no less wayward and humanly corrupt than anyone else in the permissive, promiscuous West. Jay Rayner's novel *Day of Atonement* (1998) explores the Jewish underworld of sexually obsessed con-men and convicts who inhabit the gray zone of Jewish suburbia and who could be associates of the shady characters in Pinter's *The Homecoming*. Nor does Giles Coren's *Winkler* spare any sacred cows left over from the Anglo-Jewish comic novel tradition about growing up Jewish in Britain any more than Howard Jacobson's *The Mighty Walzer* (1999) and his *Kalooki Nights*. There are always the perennial suburban Jewish family sagas that boast a pedigree of survival of persecution suitably tarnished by scandal for avid readers, as well as memoirs that look back nostalgically to a time when Jews were striving to dress in English clothes and act more English than the English. However, it seems that the search for a secular diaspora Jewish identity in multicultural Britain of the early twenty-first century was unlikely to produce a Chaim Potok or Cynthia Ozick, but British Jewish fiction was teeming with Alex Portnoys and Duddy Kravitzes.[59]

RADICAL DIASPORISM

We should not mistake postmodern explorations of "Jewishness" for commitment to the beliefs of Judaism, but instead recognize a tendency to mix and match a *bricolage* of ethnic, gender, or sexual identities, a counter-discursive cut-and-paste that expresses difference as individuals, rather than as members of a religion or ethnic group. This is the postmodern Jewish answer to the great question Mitchell Cohen asked of American Jewry, to engage with the world or to turn inward, "Shaatnez or monism."[60] As Jill Robbins reminds us in her discussion of Derrida's autobiographical *Circonfession,* the Jewish encounter with modernity has in fact often entailed a turning back from Christianity (as in the case of Rosenzweig), or Greek philosophy and Enlightenment values (as in Levinas' return to Jewish sources), a turning that imbibes of what it is rejecting, which, for the secular Jew is mostly unknown and unintelligible (Hebrew being an unknown native tongue).[61] Circumscribing the self is an inscribing of self that writes back to what defines self as Other. Perhaps this might partly explain why Rosenzweig, Buber, Arendt, even Kafka and Gershon Scholem, as well as Levinas and Derrida, hold such fascination for the post-Holocaust generation, because they write out of a cultural premise and a way of thinking or language which have hosted them, yet which both tempted them and denied them a place.

The Holocaust was the primal scene of the traumatic disillusion with modernity, but the British Jewish philosopher Gillian Rose has warned about the dangers of the ruins of Auschwitz or the restored Jerusalem becoming new centers of Jewish thought. In *Mourning Becomes the Law* she subjected Derrida and Levinas to close scrutiny and criticism, concluding that a hermeneutics that was preoccupied with loss and mourning did not facilitate political action, while postmodernism and an uncritical multiculturalism that overthrew tradition would not allow the reconstruction of law based on reason.

I resist equally the super-eminence conferred on "the Holocaust" as the logical outcome of Western metaphysical reason, and the unique status bestowed on Judaism as providing the communitarian and ethical integrity which otherwise lies in ruins in the "post-modern world." Instead I argue that reinvigorated, open-hearted reason can discern a third city buried alive beneath the unequivocal opposition of degraded power and exalted ethics, [of] Athens and Jerusalem. . . . Postmodernism in its renunciation of reason, power, and truth identifies itself as a process of endless mourning, lamenting the loss of securities, which, on its own argument, were none such. Yet this everlasting melancholia accurately monitors the refusal to let go. . . .[62]

Convinced that the opposition between liberal individualism and cultural pluralism was invalid, Gillian Rose sought to negotiate a new polity that would also find space for women within Jewish law.

Postmodernism has seen a return that is both a turning back and around, as well as a turning inwards, that nevertheless embraces alterity as an ethical command to others, but also as a self recognition. As with "cultural Judaism" in America,[63] the "post-denominational" forms of identification of "serious Jews" have attracted young adults in search of an alternative style of community that espouses egalitarian values, social commitment, and outreach beyond the conventional boundaries of synagogue membership.[64] Certainly, there has been a polarization in Jewish religious affiliation and identification in Britain since the 1990s, with a swing from a discourse of complacent security to concern for continuity and a discourse of insecurity in the wake of 9/11 and the backlash against multiculturalism.[65] Many Jews may redefine themselves in ways that are not "essentially" or even "authentically" Jewish. In his conversations with Jewish secular intellectuals, Nick Lambert found that in Britain, Holland, and Italy there was an alienation from organized Jewish religion, as well as a repulsion from the internal bickering of communal politics and the divisiveness of a largely unrepresentative communal leadership. Few of Lambert's interviewees felt any strong bond with other Jews, and he questioned whether, from a sociological standpoint, Jews were a nation or shared any ties and allegiance.[66]

For Hannah Arendt, Jews were the ultimate Europeans, enjoying a pariah status which gave them mobility, and intellectuals from Czech writer Milan Kundera to George Steiner think of Jews as Europe's essential cosmopolitans, embodying the spirit of Europe and ensuring its unity. Today, that nostalgic ideal, largely remembered through Stefan Zweig's remembrances of turn of the century Vienna, are likely to be met with some skepticism.[67] As in America, the identification of "Mittel Europa" and Ashkenazi Hampstead liberals with the "real" Jews has been challenged by the growing awareness of the Sephardic heritage and contact with non-European Jews in India or even the Caribbean, as well as encounters with Jews of color or with cultural hybridity in Israel and elsewhere. Being Black and Jewish is "cool." This is partly because being multi-racially Jewish overrides the notorious ambiguity of the Jews' "whiteness," to which suburban Jews strived after the Second World War.[68] In particular, the question of "who is a Jew?" has burst the bounds of biological definitions in the embracing of Judaism by others, as well as the rediscovery of some of the ten lost tribes, descendants of Marranos, and the return of "hidden Jews" in South America and Poland. By contrast, New Age concepts of multi-faith "spirituality" (including, incidentally, a popularized kabbalah marketed by devotees of the pop star Madonna), alongside attempts to construct a "postmodern" Judaism or a non-religious Judaism, make speaking of any "original" sense of the Jewish faith quite impossible.[69]

Multiculturalism, too, has helped to make the Jewish "thing" hip. The revival of klezmer has spread a pseudo "East European Jewish" culture around Europe and America along with a *Fiddler on the Roof* nostalgia, but it has also injected new life into Jewish popular culture. As with "ethnic" food, Jewish music has become part of the global fusion cuisine of culture, but has also brought non-European and non-mainstream elements back into the expression of Jewishness. Since Rabbi Shlomo Carlebach took his guitar to California in the 1960s and danced with the hippies, Jewish music and Jewish culture in general have not been the same. The South American beat mixes soul and Hasidic; Jewish rap merges the traditional with African American rhythm. But then in previous generations profane Western music was often sacralized in cantorial settings and East European folksong found its way into Hasidic melodies. What an experimental klezmer band like the British *Oi Va Voi* has done (clearly under the influence of the American *Klezmatics*) is to dust off cantorial, Yiddish, and Ladino traditions and set them to modern lyrics, combining East European and gypsy motifs, performed by a trans-cultural ensemble (one of the soloists is a soprano born in Ghana; none of the band speaks Yiddish). Josh Breslau, drummer and cofounder, says it's a voyage of discovery, making contemporary music out of old songs.[70] One of their lyrics explains what it's about:

> *It's all about identity*
> *A retrospective odyssey*
> *But where I live and who I meet*
> *Are stronger in defining me.*

One of the band's founders, virtuoso violinist Sophie Solomon (born in 1978 of a Christian mother and Jewish father), has gone her own way, joining up with Canadian DJ Josh Doiglin, a.k.a. Socalled, in a performance of "Hiphopkhasene"[71] to go beyond fantasies of East European *shtetls* and explore postmodern questions of authenticity in music.[72] Authenticity may be a moot point, especially when the audience responds to the music in order to negotiate their own positions regarding the Holocaust past and imagined perception of the "jew." In this revival of "Yiddishland," an inclusive term that takes in the lost sounds of Eastern Europe before and during the Holocaust "klezmer" music, with its eclectic and accrued jazz elements, has acquired a life of its own as a definition of secular diaspora Jewish culture which looks back with mixed irony and longing for a cultural identity that was lost two or three generations previously.[73] This is American playwright Tony Kushner's response to klezmer music as an agnostic who wishes to believe, a supporter of Israel who thinks the founding of the Jewish state was a calamity:

> Hebrew- and Yiddish-illiterate, I barely know how to pray; riddled with ambivalence, child of Marx, Freud, Mahler, Benjamin, Kafka, Goldman, Luxemburg, Trotsky, An-ski, Schoenberg, mongrel product of Judaism's and of Jewish exteriority, of its ghetto-hungry curiosity, of its assimilationist genius, I now approach Judaism as Jews once approached the splendid strangeness of the Goyishe Velt: I am shall we say deeply confused, but not complacent. And this I think of course is profoundly Jewish.[74]

There could perhaps be no better phrasing of the ironic and distanced stance of the diaspora identity of many assimilated Jews for whom hip-hop blends into a multiethnic scene where they can experiment with different cultural identities, while identifying with a "radical Jewishness" that serves as a wedge against the materialist Jewish establishment, perceived as dictating norms for communal affiliation, but that can also open up to rediscovery of Jewish roots and traditional Judaism or Hasidism. In radical fringe groups such as Jewdas (inspired by the American Jewish magazine *Heeb*), re-identification often displays parodied antisemitic images and tropes, as if taking on stereotypes as the "Jewish thing"; to be rootless, cosmopolitan, and subversive is to plug into the multicultural transgression of ethnic, sexual, and gender boundaries in an oppositional stance to essentialized identities.[75]

SPEAKING AS A JEW...

Radical political activism draws on Jewish ethics in order to declare solidarity with anti-Zionist campaigns for "Palestine." It becomes a rallying call for a new "diasporism," that is, a Jewish identity freed from definition by affinity to religion or Israel.[76] What distinguishes this kind of activism from the Jewish liberation movement of the seventies in America, which brought together the militant Jewish Defense League, left Zionists, the newly religious *havura,* and feminists,[77] is that there is no Jewish revolution happening in middle-aged middle-class suburbia and there are no longer Jewish causes, such as the campaign to free Soviet Jewry, nor a Vietnam war to motivate solidarity between different political groupings. The activists have moved on from the Civil Rights movement and global radical caucuses tend to be hostile to Israel and "Zionist" causes.

Meanwhile, rampant assimilation has eroded any power the religious and communal establishment might have had. Moreover, there has been a generational shift, and the dissenters of yesteryear are now themselves parents of rebellious adolescents. Marginalized Jews from comfortable middle-class professional backgrounds who express their Jewishness by identifying with disadvantaged ethnic groups in poor income groups have been dubbed by Naomi Seidman "vicarious Jews," a term Karen Brodkin has picked up to describe the way in which narratives of discrimination and exploitation have been retold among American Jewish feminists.[78] The phenomenon can be explained by the way ethnicity in America is equated with racial divisions in identity politics and falls into a tradition of disavowal or reluctance in declaring a Jewish subject position when identifying as Jews with radical causes. However, we will argue that in Britain, where Jews could be proud of a history of social activism in the garment industry in the East End and in leftist politics, the activities of "vicarious" Jews: have been stimulated as much by defensive moves to disidentify from "bad" religious and Zionist Jews.

We have seen the aversion to "frummers" in the writing of Will Self, Howard Jacobson, and Linda Grant as black-cloaked specters who embarrass "modern" Jews. *Guardian* columnist Jonathan Freedland mocks the absurd stringencies of Jewish law that seem to him to make Jewish rabbis look ridiculous in public. And yet liberal intellectuals' critique of the Jewish state has reached such a pitch that Jewish intellectuals on the left like Freedland feel obliged to defend their own sense of belonging to a Jewish collective, while at the same time he is torn between loyalty to Israel, which alienates foes, and honest criticism, which alienates friends. This is a dilemma which has a history, and one that Freedland chronicles in his own family in his memoir *Jacob's Gift* (2005) in the case of his uncle, Nat Mindel, an immigration official in British Mandate Palestine and an ardent Zionist, as well as another uncle, Mick Mindel, a passionate Communist and trade union activist who (like Sarah Kahn in Wesker's *Trilogy*) did not leave the Party even after Stalin's crimes were revealed (including the murder of Mikhoels and the execution of Yiddish writers) and the Red Army repressed the workers' uprising in Hungary. Freedland is aware of their blind delusions in maintaining a schizophrenic duality but he opts for what he calls "bothness" in embracing a mild form of Judaism and dedication to a socialist vision of Britain, hopping from an interview at 10 Downing Street to an elderly aunt in the East End. Thinking through the identity which he is bequeathing to his newborn son Jacob, the heritage of the Biblical patriarch of that name, Freedland defends a collective Jewish identity against liberal criticism which claims that it is inseparable from nationalism, on the grounds that it is a legitimate human impulse to be part of a nation, far deeper than the togetherness of football team supporters. To mitigate the common denigration of a Jewish collective, Freedland issues the caveat that "Jews and Zionists" be ever vigilant that their national identity should never lead to oppression. To be part of the Jewish people is no mere tribalism in an age of globalization when an individual's place in the world is being whittled away; it gives a personal place in a long history that goes back to Abraham.[79]

Part of the discomfort felt by Jews in Britain is explained by the assumption in the public mind that all Jews feel the same way about Israel. This, as Linda Grant is at pains to point out, is far from being the case, whether we are talking about typically suburban middle-class Jews who send their son or daughter to Israel to strengthen their Jewish identity, or ultra-Orthodox rabbis in Stamford Hill for whom the Zionist state is anathema; certainly, the Board of Deputies does not speak in unison when it comes to Israeli government polices.[80] Something of the hopes British Jews had invested in the idealism of Israel's founding fathers and the disillusion they experienced is conveyed in Mike Leigh's play *Two Thousand Years* (2005), but then neither the fix Josh seeks in religion, nor his sister's waving of a Venezuelan flag, lead them out of their syndrome of not being able to change the world or themselves. Indeed, among liberally minded secular Jews there has been a distancing from Israel's policies. British Jewry is divided, and not just on the issue of Israel's policies: while the more affluent and religiously observant may tend to vote Conservative, social cleavages cut across ethnic voting patterns.[81]

Groups such as "Independent Jewish Voices" or "Jews for Justice" speak "as Jews," but the "Jewishness" from which they speak is very often what left-feminist Lynne Segal (speaking of her rather neglected Australian childhood) calls an "empty category," which represses what little remains of Jewish memory or traditions.[82] The radical diasporism of "vicarious Jews" such as Segal, a professor of gender studies at Birkbeck College, London University, serves as a legitimizing platform to criticize Israel and gain acceptance in social and political discourse.[83] Mary-Kay Wilmers, who runs the virulently anti-Zionist and anti-American *London Review of Books* and boasts among her ancestors Stalin's chief henchman and a psychoanalyst associated with Freud, similarly defines her "Jewishness" in bitter criticism of Israel: "My people. . .have a responsibility," she declares, explaining that, "I feel a particular right to speak out on this because of my background."[84] Citing Jewish experience of the Holocaust, Jewish bloggers, signatories of petitions, letter writers to liberal or left-wing newspapers, and authors of autobiographies present themselves as "non-Jewish Jews" (in Isaac Deutscher's memorable phrase) aligned with politically correct positions (though Deutscher himself admitted that, while the nation-state was deplorable, the Holocaust had made Israel a necessity and not a single other country had successfully divested itself of nationalism in the name of international solidarity).[85]

Such "disidentification" may, in psychoanalytical terms, affirm identity, while leaving the postcolonial Jew unmarked as a "jew" and providing a strategy to publicly criticize Israel, whose existence and raison d'être challenge diasporism and embarrass those who do not wish to be identified as Jews with the Jewish State.[86] In *The Question of Zion* (2005), a title that invokes Edward Said, Jacqueline Rose protests against unspecified and unnamed crimes committed on a "daily basis" by the Israeli state "in the name of the Jewish people"[87] (notwithstanding the Road Map peace plan and Sharon's pullout from Gaza). Rose places herself in the dichotomy posited by Tom Paulin—you are either a Zionist or an anti-Zionist—from which she seeks to extricate herself by distinguishing between anti-Zionists who are opposed to the state of Israel as a colonialist venture and left-Zionists who are opposed to the post-1967 occupation of "Palestine."

The distinction between anti-Zionism and antisemitism, a questionable one when it comes to the right of a Jewish nation to self-determination and self-defense,[88] is one held tenaciously by prominent Jewish intellectuals. What David Hirsh has dubbed the "Livingstone formulation"[89] is often employed by self-styled "independent Jewish voices," or "antiracist" Jews, such as Brian Klug, who speaks of Jewish values, not Jewish ethnicity. Klug has cordoned off anti-Zionism from antisemitism on the grounds that there is no Jewish collective which wishes to be represented by Israel or the Zionist movement and therefore any charge of antisemitism leveled against critics of Israel must itself be a defamation of Jews! Moreover, Klug argues, in Theodor Herzl's vision, the Jewish state was meant to put an end to antisemitism, which arose only because the Jews had no state of their own, so antisemitism can only be an invention of the opponents of criticism of Israel.[90] Such circular logic, however, can be challenged by the fact that antisemitism still exists around the world and is directed against both Israel's existence and Jews of other countries regardless of whether they hold any loyalty to Israel or agree with its policies. The sociologist Robert Fine has tried to break down the dualist stand-off between "alarmist" commentators on the "New Antisemitism" and their critics or "deniers" by looking at the way the unnatural polarization of the two camps pathologizes the discourse. Each camp presents rhetorical positions that, as it were, call their enemy into existence, detracting from any examination of real-world antisemitism. The problem is that the claim to "universalism" by the critics of the theory of the New Antisemitism rests on their opposition to the "privileging" of the Holocaust as a Jewish suffering and the claim that antisemitism (whether real or imagined) creates a "smokescreen" to detract from criticism of Israel or draw attention away from real racism such as the rise of Islamophobia.[91]

They would have us believe that levels of antisemitism are blown out of proportion and are being used to bolster Zionist rhetoric or an unrepresentative community leadership.[92] In his novel, *The Finkler Question* (2010), which won the prestigious Booker Man prize, Howard Jacobson mocked such types and fantasized an anti-Zionist organization of "ASHamed" Jews, who proudly assert their shame at Israel's policies from a high moral ground "as Jews," but are shown to be self-seeking opportunists whose arguments are absurd, illogical, and hypocritical.[93] The parodies of real positions and statements of "alarmists" and "deniers" are more sad than funny, and the plot is left unresolved and incomplete, as if the quarrels over religion and politics will go on forever, and Jews are fated to live out the stereotypes affixed to them, always blaming themselves or each other for the persecution and mockery they suffer.

In American playwright David Mamet's critique, self-hating Jews, like the wicked son of the Passover Haggadah, reject any identification with the Jewish community and, in response to antisemitism, relieve their guilt and anxiety, and gain social approval for their defamation of Israel and Judaism.[94] Actually, the *epikoros* type goes back two thousand years to Elisha ben Abbuya, known as Akher (the "Other"), who lived in the first century CE, and who is depicted in rabbinic literature as the archetypal *epikoros* (from the Greek Επίκουρος but not necessarily connected to the teachings of the Greek philosopher).[95] The *epikoros* strays from Torah observance to Hellenistic ways, but should be distinguished from the sectarian and heretic (*min*) or the apostate (*mumar*);[96] rather, this was someone with great knowledge of Jewish law who rebelled within the Jewish community. Mamet's postmodern *epikoros,* by contrast, has little or no knowledge of Jewish traditions and history, abjures any affiliation with the Jewish community and Jewish cultural organizations, yet delights in a smattering of Yiddish expressions and is proud to be not a "Jew" but "Jew-ish." The "Jew-ish" are not exactly self-haters, though they write off the "kosher laws" as a fanatic one-upmanship of antiquated regulations that have no place in "modern" life, thus replicating middle-class liberal English prejudice against Jewish difference and against Judaism per se (as we would expect from a rationalistic discourse curiously in line with Christian theological views based on the Pauline dispensation). The "Jew-ish" journalist Jonathan Margolis proudly eats a bagel with bacon to demonstrate his disdain for "*frummers*" and his refusal to join the Jewish community; his model is the Larry David type, or Jonathan Miller's "amphibious" Jew, half-in and half-out, who denounces antisemitism but is thoroughly ambivalent about Israel, is not bothered by intermarriage, yet would never deny being a Jew.[97] As for Heine, the Jewish religion is a misfortune, an embarrassment, but the Final Solution has shown the impossibility of being a Jew not only on the street, but also in one's own home. Jewish identity has therefore become largely imaginary, ascribed to others by armchair post-Zionists or neurotic Portnoys, who are proud to be ashamed to be Jews.[98]

Not all radical and progressive Jews should be dismissed as self-haters. On the contrary, if we recall that Judaism teaches the ethical duty of social activism known as *tikkun olam* ("mending the world") and is dedicated to the social justice that is identified with the radical left, we may find that such labels blur the real differences between Jews and reduce the debate into a binary opposition of rhetorical constructs.[99] Among "radical Orthodox" and anti-Zionist Jews, exasperation with Israel's "intransigence" is expressed in concerns for repercussions for Diaspora Jews who do not take a stand on Israeli policies,[100] a fear that Israel's actions and the failure to criticize Israel fuel antisemitism. "Antisemitism" has become a red flag with which left and right wing Jews routinely attack each other (as in the row on the pages of the British media that broke out in fall 2009 over Conservative Party courting of Polish and Lithuanian politicians who had been associated with antisemitic views). The search advocated by Robert Fine for a "cosmopolitan" space that would free secular diaspora Jews from the impasse of the exclusive binary oppositions in such rhetorical constructions is nothing new.[101] Albert Memmi, whose faith in universalism was shattered by the Holocaust and France's own collaboration in deportation of the Jews, searched in vain for an alternative to the Zionist "solution" of the "Jewish problem." When Zionism was excluded from postcolonial discourse as a colonizing force, Memmi, a supporter of the Tunisian liberation movement, was forced to look for "Jewish" solutions to universal issues, rather than universal solutions to the "Jewish problem."[102]

EPILOGUE: OUR BORATS, OUR SELVES

In arguing in *After Empire: Melancholia or Convivial Culture?* (2004) for a humanist global culture that focuses on conviviality rather than identity, Paul Gilroy has addressed the dangers arising from multiculturalism and sought assets to be gained from an immigrant population in terms of homogeneity, not diversity. Only by facing the colonial past, he contends, can community relations be debated, but the discourse of race must also be confronted and interpreted. One of Gilroy's examples is the comedian Sacha Baron Cohen's performance of characters Ali G. and the "Kazakhstani" Borat to elicit racist and antisemitic stereotypes from unwitting interviewees and to expose indifference toward the Holocaust in much the same way Montesquieu satirized the gender and ethnic hierarchy in *Lettres Persanes*. Both Cohen and Montesquieu use the guise of alienated "disloyal" characters who perform a fake identity in order to act out covert judgments on the social order or to project prejudiced views of aliens; both enjoy an ironic freedom that has been circumvented by a globalized culture of consumer capitalism and domination that places its obligations on its would-be citizens.[103] In the comedy aimed at middlebrow America, real live yokels become objects of a commodifying globalization.[104] When confronted by a real Kazakhstan, "Borat" taunted the authorities to sue the Jew Cohen, in effect inviting them to enact the stereotyping mentality which he parodied. There was certainly sufficient bigotry and prejudice for Cohen to exploit amid charges that multiculturalism led to division rather than diversity.[105] However, it was not widely noticed that Cohen was reviving a long tradition of minstrelsy from the beginning of the twentieth century. Known as "Jewface," singers would don Jew-noses and perform antisemitic ditties, a genre that has been revived by disaffected Jews in a provocative adoption of a hostile self-image.[106]

By definition, "internationalist" or "transnational" identities ought to dissolve national and geographical, as well as gender and sexual, borders. Alisa Lebow's study of Jewish ethno-autobiographic film, *First Person Jewish,* as well as her own film *Treyf* (with Cynthia Madansky, 1998), brings out her sensibilities as a lesbian New Yorker, British university lecturer, and film theorist/maker working between genders and among immigrant groups, committed to political activism in Turkey and elsewhere. Her discussion of autobiographic filmmaking that engages with the parallel "visibility" of Jewishness/queerness/queer Jewishness forces a redefinition of "Jewish" identity because it transgresses normative Jewish modes of family and heterosexual marriage. *Treyf* presents the male Jewish-accented voice that lays down the law as "out of place" (the sound is not synchronized, and particularly not with the *treyf* food and *treyf* relationships depicted in the film). The paradox is that the filmmakers' performance of assimilated White American voices represses a "Jewish" voice in speaking for dissent that abrogates patriarchal authority and has to go out of the community, beyond the pale, in order to achieve dialog.[107] In a British context, Ruth Novaczek's experimental film *Rootless Cosmopolitans* (1990), whose title alludes to antisemitic stereotypes of the Jews as aliens, a label which became quite sinister under Stalin, takes a humorous look at London's Jewish community through the eyes of two women, Estelle and Lily. They do not want the Jewish Princess package with a family and a kosher home, where "anglified" assimilation is the supreme test of social acceptance, yet their identities are formed out of stereotypical perceptions they have grown up with, name-calling, and ostracism. Because the film is shot in black and white, using an out of sync voice over, our assumptions about color and race are skewed because we cannot easily match the color/race of the speakers, one of whom appears to have "African" hair and physical features, thus bringing into question the "whiteness" of the Jews. The voice-over tells us of often being taken for foreigners or Blacks. Indeed, they feel more affinity for Blacks, who sometimes express empathy with the People of the Bible, yet the virulent antisemitism of Louis Farrakhan tells a different story about Black hostility. The physiological signs of Jewishness (Jewish "looks") cannot be denied, nor can elocution lessons wipe out the mother's immigrant accent, so the best thing, Estelle tells us against the background of a shopping street in Stamford Hill, a racially mixed space that markets Jewish food, is to make the best of it and choose what parts of Judaism to celebrate.[108]

The evident disavowal of whiteness at work here is strikingly similar to a phenomenon in the United States which subverts the construct of whiteness as a measure of social acceptance, often conflated with a racial marker of difference. This performance of Jewish blackness seems to reverse Fanon's response to Sartre's conviction in *Anti-Semite and Jew* that "Jewish conduct is overdetermined from the inside," that the Jew is seen as a White and not given away so easily by visibility like the Black:

> Simple enough, one has only not to be a nigger. Granted, the Jews are harassed—what am I thinking of? They are hunted down, exterminated, cremated. But these are little family quarrels. The Jew is disliked from the moment he is tracked down. But in my case everything takes on a *new* guise. I am given no chance.[109]

Bryan Cheyette, in his thorough and thoughtful critique of this passage, questions the essentialist bifurcation apparent in Fanon, arguing that it is precisely the ambiguity of the "jew's" skin color, the "unstable" and "promiscuous" identities of the "jew" in the European imagination, that get lost, preventing a historical understanding of Jewish victimhood.[110] Unlike the "black-face" performance of, say, Al Jolson in *The Jazz Singer,* Novaczek is not presenting a minstrelsy black mask which accentuated the Jew's white skin, but is attempting to redefine the "color" of Jewishness in a multicultural agenda that posits identity beyond fixed categories of race and color, gender and sexuality.[111]

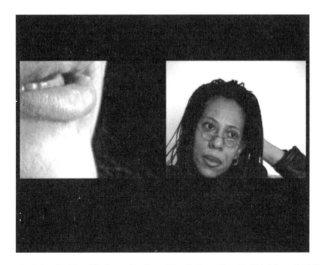

Rachel Garfield, still from *So You Think You Can Tell* (video, 2000)

Here, too, the twin "vices" of "jew" and "homosexual," so common in fin-de-siècle European cultural discourse, highlight the difficulties of putting Jewish and lesbian identities together. Nevertheless, the "mosaic" of broken parts in *Rootless Cosmopolitans* breaks the Anglo-Jewish community's pact of silence and uses stereotypes of the Jewish body to express pride in racial difference.[112] The foregrounding of stereotypes as a way of demonstrating the ambiguity of the Jew's racial difference, as well as the persistence of prejudices, is found also in the work of Rachel Garfield, an artist based in London, for example in her video installation, *So You Think You Can Tell* (2000). Garfield's interviews test color lines that run across community boundaries and elicit responses to racial stereotypes, much as does Sacha Baron Cohen in his conceit of Ali G., a fictional persona who tricks unsuspecting victims to voice hidden prejudice. Garfield also looks to London-based Israeli performance artist Oreet Ashery, whose impersonation of a Hasid, Marcus Fisher, tests "norms" by engaging viewers interactively with the transgression of gender and sexuality in a "male" Jewish world but also inverting in a surrealist performance Marcel Duchamp's transvestite persona.[113] What these artists are doing in their performance of cultural resistance is to inscribe themselves as women in a history of feminization of the "jew" that goes back to Otto Weininger's *Sex and Character* and racial antisemitism, thus placing the representation of the Jewish body at the interstice of sexual/gender politics with race discourse.[114] But it is also an intervention in sexual politics that introduces Cixous' "jewoman" (*juifemme*)[115] into postmodern play with the boundaries of identities and (in Ashery's case) with the surrealist fantasy of desire generating reality, thus positioning the "jew" as a transgressive figure that splits cultural legacy and subject position across an ethnic-sexual axis.[116]

Clearly, playing with stereotypes also works through anxieties about one's own identities and sets them in relation to other ethnic minorities in multicultural Britain, but it eventually destabilizes all identities and demonstrates the complexities of passing or of crossing boundaries. These are attempts to forge multiple identities in a world-wide diaspora which has become, in a postmodern and postcolonial view, the naturalized condition of the Jewish people, with no respect for frontiers in a nominally unified Europe or a transnational globalized world. In a postcolonial world, social masks, which are constantly in flux, can be explored and also resisted, while, as we have seen, marginalized voices of women and Jews become privileged. The sexual revolution and the permissive society have eroded the Jewish communal demand to procreate and put down roots. Generational continuity is displaced by postponement of childbearing, an abdication of parenthood that rejects Fackenheim's "614th commandment" not to hand Hitler a posthumous victory. Instead, an all-embracing spirituality independent of moral agency or militant agnosticism appeal to autonomous sovereignty, while experimentation with alternate gender/sexual identities tests the permeability of social boundaries. It could be objected that "universalism" is paradoxically a form of particularism that calls on a superior Jewish ethical code or moral vision, and indeed, the tensions between universalism and particularism are very much at the core of the multicultural debate. In *Cartographies of Diaspora: Contesting Identities*, Avtar Brah suggests that one way of working through the problem of conflict between universalism and difference is through "diaspora space," "where difference and commonality are figured in non-reductive relationality. Here, axes of differentiation and division such as class, gender, and sexuality articulate a myriad of economic, political and cultural practices through which power is exercised. Each axis signifies *a specific modality of power relation*. What is of interest is how these fields of power collide, enmesh, reconfigure *and with what effects*."[117] Far from a model of integration or a multicultural free for all, Brah tells us that "diaspora space" operates with its own inclusions and exclusions, producing various subject positions, and generating a large degree of ambivalence.[118]

A constant reinvention of identities that align themselves with globalized concepts of cosmopolitanism, exile, and diaspora must be problematic if they are meant to constitute a deterritorialized, non-essentialized Jewish space, for collective memory will always return to haunt the Diaspora Jew as a subject facing the destruction in the storm of history as in Walter Benjamin's trope of the Angelus Novus,[119] just as Elaine Feinstein pictures it in the scene of Benjamin's suicide in *The Border*. In particular, the resurgence of antisemitism as a physical threat and the hostile environment in which tropes of the "jew" circulate in mainstream public discourse reintroduce the Holocaust as a historically determined sign of difference, returning the "jew" to Sartre's definition in *Anti-Semite and Jew* as one who is identified by others as a Jew. The various perceptions of being a Jew and constructions of the "jew" in the West determine Jewish identity as post-genocidal. Jean Amery helped define the "Holocaust Jew" caught between the impossibility and necessity of being a Jew. Having thrown off his Austrian clothing, he is racialized as a Jew destined for death, although he cannot identify with Jewish life.[120] "The Holocaust has become the key site, not bounded by the Jewish community's self-regulating definitions, of identification as a Jew."[121] In fact, the "Holocaust Jew" became an archetypal figure for all Jewish experience during the Holocaust, when poets and witnesses could find nothing comparable in their collective memory, and afterwards became universalized into an archetype for all suffering,[122] a point of solidarity but also appropriation.

In a previous chapter, we saw how the Vanishing Jew emerged out of erasure in the genocide of the Holocaust and in the demographic shifts that brought to an end the vibrant Jewish life associated with London's East End. The recovery of an imagined past in the case of Rachel Lichtenstein was typical of the rediscovery not of a nostalgic immigrant experience but of an abandoned family, the Rodinskys, who rejected the path to affluence in the suburbs. The return of the repressed past of the children of assimilated Jews, paradigmatic for Jon Stratton, forces a negotiation of Jewish memory, in which cultural texts are unearthed and reevaluated, adapted and rewritten for postmodern conditions of hybridity and transformation, but never fully restored.[123]

The Postmodern Jew in effect displaces tropes of the "jew," but also acts out the self-image of "Jewishness" itself, caught in the hall of mirrors of representation and enthralled by an ethnic origin in *thanatos*. In order to exit this paranoiac impasse, the Postmodern Jew must transform the trope of "jew" into a meaningful experience that evades the binarism of "essentialism" versus "anti-essentialism," neo-tribalism versus anarchic nomadism. This would mean, Max Silverman writes of French postmodernism, abolishing the figure of the "jew" and transforming it from a trope into "a site for negotiation beyond the dichotomies of sameness and difference, universalism and particularism, reason and anti-reason, essentialism and relativism. It would imply defetishizing 'the Jew,' conceiving of 'the Jew' neither simply as an open-ended signifier nor as an unproblematic signifier, but as a real hybrid between the two, a 'Jew' in inverted commas but with an upper-case 'J'."[124] Instead of looking for a linear passage of antisemitic narratives, which could lead to an almost paranoiac search for symptoms of antisemitism everywhere, we should see the circulation of the figure of the "jew" as a complex development within cultural production that has a fascinating and complex history, both as an archetypal Other and as politicized discourse.

In his final act of self mockery in Jacobson's *Kalooki Nights,* Max finally marries a Jewish woman from his native Manchester suburb of Crumpsall, and umlauted to boot, like all the non-Jewish women in his life. Alÿs, despite her heavy Jewish depression and affinities with the ghetto that he has escaped, is a sandal-buckled parody of the Postmodern/Postcolonial Jew who persuades Max to abandon the public dirtying of Jewish laundry and get on the train of trendy causes, to write the kind of gendered narratives people will read. But nothing can be more unbearable than a ride on the "Wonderment Express" with an archetypal Holocaust Jewess. Alÿs, heavy with Jewish sorrow, takes Max on the "Jew-Jew" train to the "heartlands of our bad conscience,"[125] but he draws the line at "Palestine." Although his internationalist father thought the Jewish state should never have existed, Max considers this the final betrayal that symbolized the ultimate anti-Jewish Jewishness of the politically correct Postmodern Jew who cites Jewish historical experience in an act of self-denial by supporting the destruction of Israel. Alÿs has to go, but, when she does, Max behaves as if he has killed her, just like a Nazi, together with his own chance of freedom from his Jewish neuroses and complexities. There is, Jacobson seems to insinuate, no escape, only endless guilt.

NOTES

1. Homi K. Bhabha, *The Location of Culture* (London: Routledge, 1994), 171–97.

2. Frederic Brenner, *Diaspora: Homelands in Exile* (New York: HarperCollins, 2003), *ix*. See on this Shaul Bassi, "'Funny, You Don't Look Hybrid': Jewish Memory Revisualized," in *Postcolonial Studies: Changing Perceptions,* ed. Oriana Palusci (Trent: Dipartmento di Studi Litterari, Linguistici e Filologici, 2006), 339–53. Reliance on visual representation alone may, of course, invite a fallacy that Jews should look alike, without regard to cultural memory and practice that may transcend local ties and bind Jews globally in complex ways.

3. Jonathan and Daniel Boyarin, "Diaspora: Generation and the Ground of Jewish Identity," *Critical Inquiry* 19.4 (Summer 1993): 699. See Arnold Band's response, "The New Diasporism and the Old Diaspora," *Israel Studies* 1.1 (1996): 323–31.

4. This postcolonial rhetoric of diaspora that emerges from rejection of Jewish "racist" aspirations to a "fictive" homeland and territorial sovereignty is rehearsed from an Indian diasporic perspective, in a Freudian and Lacanian analysis in Vijay Mishra, *The Literature of the Indian Diaspora: Theorizing the Diasporic Imaginary* (London: Routledge, 2007), 12–14, 19–20. See William Safran, "The Jewish Diaspora in a Comparative and Theoretical Perspective," *Israel Studies* 10. 1 (2005): 36–60.

5. See Jopi Nyman, *Home, Identity, and Mobility in Contemporary Diasporic Fiction* (Amsterdam: Rodopi, 2009), 9–27; Susheila Nasta, *Home Truths: Fictions of the South Asian Diaspora in Britain* (Houndmills: Palgrave Macmillan, 2002), 1–8. See the discussion of Andrea Levy in chapter three above and the ambivalence of "home" in the writing of Caryl Phillips, discussed in chapter four.

6. Nasta, *Home Truths,* 7, 32.

7. Bryan Cheyette, "'Ineffable and Usable': Towards a Diasporic British-Jewish Writing," *Textual Practice* 10 (Spring 1996): 295–313.

8. Gabriel Sheffer, *Diaspora Politics: At Home Abroad* (Cambridge: Cambridge University Press, 2003), 232–36.

9. See the conclusions in ibid., 246–58.

10. R. B. Kitaj, *The First Diasporist Manifesto* (New York: Thames and Hudson, 1989), 30. See Sander Gilman, "R. B. Kitaj's 'Good Bad' Disposition and the Body in American Jewish Postmodern Art," in his *Love+Marriage=Death, and Other Essays on Representing Difference* (Stanford: Stanford University Press, 1998), 136–83.

11. Cynthia Ozick, "America: Toward Yavneh," *Judaism* 19 (Summer 1970): 264–82. For a detailed critique of American Jewry's "exceptional" diasporism and its parody in Roth's novel see Michael Galchinsky, "Scattered Seeds: A Dialogue of Diasporas" in *Insider/Outsider: American Jews and Multiculturalism,* ed. David Biale, Michael Galchinsky, and Susannah Heschel (Berkeley: University of California Press, 1998), 185–211.

12. Caryn Aviv and David Shneer, *New Jews: The End of the Jewish Diaspora* (New York: New York University Press, 2005), 1–25. See Keith Kahn-Harris and Ben Gidley, *Turbulent Times: The British Jewish Community Today* (London and New York: Continuum, 2010).

13. Op-Ed, "Second Thoughts about the Promised Land," *Economist,* 11 Jan. 2007, 53–56; http://www.acbp.net/About/PDF/ARTICLESecond %20thoughts %20about%20the%20Promised%20Land.pdf.

14. Efraim Sicher, *Beyond Marginality: Anglo-Jewish Writing after the Holocaust* (Albany: State University of New York Press, 1985).

15. Jonathan Wilson, "How I Became a Jewish Writer in America," in *Who We Are: On Being (and not Being) a Jewish American Writer,* ed. Derek Rubin (New York: Schocken, 2005), 157.

16. Bryan Cheyette, "Imagined Communities: Contemporary Jewish Writing in Great Britain," in *Contemporary Jewish Writing in Europe: A Guide,* ed. Vivian Liska and Thomas Nolden (Bloomington: Indiana University Press, 2008), 94–98, 105–7.

17. Cheyette, "'Ineffable and Usable.'"

18. Albert Memmi, *The Liberation of the Jew* (New York: Orion Press, 1966), 180.

19. On the "Daughter of Germany" see Efraim Sicher, "The Burden of Memory: The Writing of the Post-Holocaust Generation," in *Breaking Crystal: Writing and Memory after Auschwitz,* ed. Efraim Sicher (Urbana: University of Illinois Press, 1998), 60–65.

20. For a discussion of modern Jewish literary tropes of masculinity, see Warren Rosenberg, *Legacy of Rage* (Amherst: University of Massachusetts Press, 2001).

21. See Bryan Cheyette, "Diasporas of the Mind: British-Jewish Writing Beyond Multiculturalism," in *Diaspora and Multiculturalism: Common Traditions and New*

Developments, ed. Monica Flundernik (Amsterdam and New York: Rodopi, 2003), 73–76.

22. For a reading of Sinclair's short story "Wingate Football Club" as an example of liberation of the Jewish body and a remedy for Portnoy's "complaint," see Melvyn Konner, *The Jewish Body* (New York: Schocken, 2009), 203–6.

23. Clive Sinclair, "The Kimberley Fantasy: An Alternative Zion," *Wasafiri* 57 (Spring 2009): 33–43.

24. Vijay Mishra, *The Literature of the Indian Diaspora: Theorizing the Diasporic Imaginary* (London: Routledge, 2007), 1–21. See Monika Flundernik, "The Diasporic Imaginary: Postcolonial Reconfigurations in the Context of Multiculturalism," in *Diaspora and Multiculturalism: Common Traditions and New Developments,* ed. Monica Fludernik (Amsterdam: Rodopi, 2003), *xi–xxxvi.*

25. Clive Sinclair, *Diaspora Blues: A View of Israel* (London: Heinemann, 1987), 51.

26. Ruth Gilbert, "Contemporary British-Jewish Writing: From Apology to Attitude," *Literature Compass* 5.2 (2008): 396.

27. Jacobson, speaking at a reading of *Kalooki Nights,* Jewish Community Centre for London, Hampstead, London, July 2007.

28. Howard Jacobson, *Kalooki Nights* (New York: Simon & Schuster, 2007), 15.

29. Ibid., 3–4.

30. Jacobson, speaking at a reading of *Kalooki Nights,* Jewish Community Centre for London, Hampstead, London, July 2007.

31.Jacobson, *Kalooki Nights,* 237.

32. Ibid., 36–7.

33. Ibid., 359.

34. Ibid., 186.

35. Ibid., 99.

36. Ibid., 226–27. Apart from Bernie Krigstein and a briefly-mentioned Harvey Kurtzman (creator of *Mad* comics), Jacobson ignores a long line of American Jewish cartoonists who similarly looked into the mirror and laughed at the distorted image; in particular, one might mention Will Eisner, the pioneer of the graphic novel, who depicted the urban poverty he knew as a child. Art Spiegelman, who used the genre to draw the story of his father's Holocaust trauma, is only quoted in the epigraph to one chapter of Jacobson's novel as saying that maybe everyone has to feel guilt after the Holocaust. See George M. Goodwin, "More than a Laughing Matter: Cartoons and Jews," *Modern Judaism* 21 (2001): 146–74. See also Art Spiegelman, "Bernard Krigstein's Life Between the Panels," *New Yorker,* 22 July 2002: http://www.newyorker.com/critics/books/?020722crbo_books; accessed 23 July 2009.

37. Isaiah Berlin, "Jewish Slavery and Emancipation" (1951), in *The Power of Ideas,* ed. Henry Hardy (London: Chatto & Windus, 2000), 162–85.

38. Jacobson, *Kalooki Nights,* frontispiece.

39. Elizabeth Bellamy, *Affective Genealogies: Psychoanalysis, Postmodernism, and the 'Jewish Question' after Auschwitz* (Lincoln: Univ. of Nebraska Press, 1997), 31.

40. Maurice Blanchot, *L'écriture du désastre* (Paris: Gallimard, 1980).

41. Jean-François Lyotard, *Heidegger and "the jews,"* 23.

42. Ibid., 22.

43. Hannah Arendt, *Rahel Varnhagen: The Life of a Jewess,* trans. Richard and Clara Winston (Baltimore: Johns Hopkins University Press, 1997), 256; see also Elisabeth Young-Bruehl, *Hannah Arendt: For Love of the World* (New Haven: Yale University Press, 1982), 92.

44. See David Roskies, *The Jewish Search for a Usable Past* (Bloomington: Indiana University Press, 1999), 57.

45. Elaine Feinstein, *Talking to the Dead* (Manchester: Carcanet, 2008), 50–53. See Efraim Sicher, "Sir Salman Rushdie Sails for Spain and Rediscovers India: Postmodern Constructions of Sepharad," in *Sephardism: Spanish Jewish History in the Modern Literary Imagination,* ed. Yael Wise-Halevi (Stanford: Stanford University Press, 2012), 256–73.

46. Linda Grant, *Remind Me Who I Am, Again* (London: Granta Books, 1998), 33.

47. Ibid., 223.

48. Ibid., 262–63.

49. Ibid., 259.

50. Ibid., 71.

51. Ibid., 47.

52. Ibid., 104.

53. Linda Grant, *Still Here* (London: Little, Brown, 2002), 342.

54. Ibid., 370–73.

55. Michelene.Wandor, "The Sex Divide in Jewish Culture: A Meditation on Jewishness and Gender," *Jewish Quarterly* (Spring 1997): 12–13.

56. See Jenny Bourne, "Homelands of the Mind: Jewish Feminism and Identity Politics," *Race & Class* 29 (1987*)*: 1–24.

57. See Oliver Groß, "Second-Generation Authors in Britain," in *Anglophone Jewish Literatures,* ed. Alex Stähler (London: Routledge, 2007), 133–40.

58. Elena Lappin, "At Home in Exile: A Conversation between Eva Hoffman and Elena Lappin," *Jewish Quarterly* (Winter 1995): 11–14.

59. Jonathan Wilson, who moved from England to America after an idealistic stint in Israel, admits to hero-worship of Saul Bellow and identification with Portnoy in his own relationship with his mother ("How I Became a Jewish Writer in America," 152–53).

60. Mitchell Cohen, "In Defense of Shaatnez: A Politics for Jews in a Multicultural America," in *Insider/Outsider,* 36.

61. Jill Robbins, "Circumcising Confession: Derrida, Autobiography, Judaism," *Diacritics* 25.4 (Winter, 1995): 20–24.

62. Gillian Rose, *Mourning Becomes the Law* (Cambridge: Cambridge University Press, 1996), 11; see Arnold Jacob Wolf, "The Tragedy of Gillian Rose—Jewish Social Critic," *Judaism* 46.4 (Fall 1997): 481–89.

63. See Judith Seid, *God-Optional Judaism: Alternatives for Cultural Jews Who Love Their History, Heritage, and Community* (New York: Citadel Press, 2001).

64. Shoshana Boyd Gelfand, "Post-denominational Communities: Finding a Home for Serious Jews," in *New Conceptions of Community,* ed. Jonathan Boyd (London: Jewish Policy Research, 2010), 8–10; Joseph Finlay, "Towards an open community," in ibid., 17–19.

65. Kahn-Harris and Gidley, *Turbulent Times.*

66. Nick Lambert, *Jews and Europe in the Twenty-First Century: Thinking Jewish* (London: Vallentine Mitchell, 2008).

67. Ibid., 118–34.

68. See Alex Kasriel "Being a Black Jew Means Ordered Spontaneity," *Jewish Chronicle,* 8 May 2008. Not all the examples are of happy harmony. See also Rebecca Walker, *Black, White and Jewish: Autobiography of a Shifting Self* (New York: Berkley Publishing Group, 2001). For more on Rebecca Walker, the daughter of Alice Walker (author of *The Color Purple*), and the Black-Jewish imaginary see Melanie Kaye/Kantrowitz, *The Colors of Jews: Racial Politics and Radical Diasporism* (Bloomington: Indiana University Press, 2007), 33–65.

69. See Steven Kepnes, ed., *Interpreting Judaism in a Postmodern Age* (New York: New York University Press, 1996); Steven Kepnes, Peter Ochs, and Robert Gibbs, *Reasoning after Revelation: Dialogues in Postmodern Jewish Philosophy* (Boulder, Colo.: Westview Press, 1998); S. Daniel Breslauer, *Creating a Judaism without Religion: A Postmodern Jewish Possibility* (Lanham Md.: University Press of America, 2001). For a counter-response by Chief Rabbi Lord Jonathan Sacks see his *Future Tense: A Vision for Jews and Judaism in the Global Culture* (London: Hodder & Stoughton, 2009).

70. Interview, Reshet Moreshet Israel State Radio, 19 Jan. 2010, 1700.

71. Piranha CD-PIRI1789, released 2003.

72. Sophie Solomon, interview, "World on Your Street: Global Music," BBC 3 http://www.bbc.co.uk/radio3/world/onyourstreet/mssophie3.shtml. See Abigail Wood, "(De)constructing Yiddishland: Solomon and SoCalled's HipHopKhasene," *Ethnomusicology Forum,* 16.2 (2007): 243–70.

73. Jonathan Freedman, *Klezmer America: Jewishness, Ethnicity, Modernity* (New York: Columbia University Press, 2008); Ruth Ellen Gruber, *Virtually Jewish:*

Reinventing Jewish Culture in Europe (Berkeley: University of California Press, 2002); Magdalena Waligórska, "A Goy Fiddler on the Roof. How the Non Jewish Participants of the Klezmer Revival in Kraków Negotiate Their Polish Identity in a Confrontation with Jews," *Polish Sociological Review* 4.152 (2005): 367–82. See chapter five, above.

74. Tony Kushner, "Commentary on the Klezmatic's CD, *Possessed,*" http://inyomind.net/Chatterbox/possessed%20notes.

75. Kristy Warren, "Twenty-First Century Jewish Journeys in Music," *Jewish Culture and History* 11 (2009): 172–83; Dani Kranz, "Living Local: Some Remarks on the Creation of Social Groups of Young Jews in Present-Day London," *European Review of History* 18.1 (2011): 79–88.

76. This is the rationale offered by radical Jews who define themselves as universalists; see Julius, *Trials of Diaspora,* 544–60. See a definitive statement in Melanie Kaye/Kantrowitz, *Colors of Jews, xi–xii.*

77. See Jack Nusan Porter and Peter Dreier, eds., *Jewish Radicalism: A Selected Anthology* (New York: Grove Press, 1973).

78. Naomi Seidman, "Fag-Hags and Bu-Jews: Towards a Politics of Vicarious (Jewish) Identity," in *Insider/Outsider,* 254–69; Karen Brodkin, "On the Politics of Being Jewish in a Multiracial State," *Anthropologia* 45 (2003): 59–68.

79. Jonathan Freedland, *Jacob's Gift: A Journey into the Heart of Belonging* (London: Hamish Hamilton, 2005), 373–76. In a blog, Jonathan Freedland deplored the silence of liberal opinion when criticism of Israel was being translated into attacks on Jews and synagogues. He also protested the division into "good and bad" Jews depending on a statement of condemnation of Israel; such a statement should not be necessary, he felt, but he made it nevertheless ("As British Jews come under attack, the liberal left must not remain silent," *Guardian,* 4 Feb. 2009).

80. Linda Grant, "What British Jews think of Israel," *Independent,* 13 May 2007. See also Natan Aridan, *Britain, Israel and Anglo-Jewry: 1949–1957* (London: Frank Cass, 2004); Danny Ben-Moshe and Zohar Segev, eds., *Israel, the Diaspora, and Jewish Identity* (Brighton: Sussex Academic Press, 2007).

81. Laurence Kotler-Berkowitz, "Social Cleavages and Political Divisions: A Comparative Analysis of British, American and South African Jews in the 1990s," *Journal of Modern Jewish Studies* 1.2 (2002): 204–33.

82. Lynne Segal, *Making Trouble: Life and Politics* (London: Serpent's Tail, 2007), 21. Anthony Julius brings evidence that such groups are ineffective and marginal to the larger Jewish community (*Trials of Diaspora,* 544–60), but he fails to notice that these individuals and groups offer an alternative to Jewish communal identification which may be attractive and also unquantifiable.

83. Howard Wollman, "'As a jew. . .'": Identity Claims and the Critique of Israel," unpublished paper, 9th European Sociology Association convention, Lisbon, Portugal, Sept. 2009.

84. Anne McElvoy, "Mary-Kay Wilmers: Queen of Plots," *Sunday Times,* 18 Oct. 2009.

85. Isaac Deutscher, *The Non-Jewish Jew and Other Essays* (London: Oxford University Press, 1968), 111–13.

86. Ibid. Anthony Julius distinguishes oppositional Jews, whether converted or assimilationist, from opportunistic Jews, who use their disidentification from other Jews to give substance to or even support antisemitic defamations of Israel or Judaism, *Trials of the Diaspora,* 28–38. In either case, Jewish antisemitism does not always spring from self-hatred.

87. Jacqueline Rose, *The Question of Zion* (Princeton: Princeton University Press, 2005), 11.

88. Ibid., 13–14.

89. See the Introduction, above.

90. Bruce Klug, "The Myth of the New Anti-Semitism," *The Nation* (Feb. 2004), www.thenation.com/doc/20040202/klug; accessed 18 Jan 2008; idem, "The Collective Jew," 1–19; see also Klug's statement on behalf of Independent Jewish Voices, "No one has the right to speak for British Jews on Israel and Zionism," *Guardian,* 5 Feb. 2007, http://www.guardian.co.uk/world/2007/feb/05/comment.israelandthepalestinians; accessed online; and Anne Karpf, Brian Klug, Jacqueline Rose, and Barbara Rosenbaum, eds., *A Time To Speak Out: Independent Jewish Voices on Israel, Zionism and Jewish Identity* (London: Verso, 2008).

91. Robert Fine, "Fighting with Phantoms: A Contribution to the Debate on Antisemitism in Europe," *Patterns of Prejudice* 43.5 (2009): 259–79.

92. Kahn-Harris and Gidley, *Turbulent Times,* 143–59.

93. The name "ASHamed Jews" ironically risks confusion with both the anti-smoking campaign Action on Smoking and Health and the Torah outreach network AISH (*The Finkler Question* [London: Bloomsbury, 2010], 266); it was apparently inspired by the actress Miriam Margolyes, who once described herself on BBC Radio Four's program *Desert Island Discs* as "a proud Jew. . .but an ashamed Jew" (quoted http://thetanjara.blogspot.com/2008_10_01_archive.html; accessed 17 Oct. 2010). In the novel, Finkler uses a similar phrase when he is invited to appear on the same long-running radio show. A public debate convened at Hampstead Town Hall in October 2010, featuring Howard Jacobson and Brian Klug, as well as Melanie Phillips, seemed to realize the real existence of "Ashamed Jews" in its title "Are Jews Ashamed of being Jewish?," or at least assumed it was a legitimate question.

94. David Mamet, *The Wicked Son: Anti-Semitism, Self Hatred, and the Jews* (New York: Schocken, 2006).

95. For a renewed discussion of rabbinic sources see Alon Goshen-Gottstein, *The Sinner and the Amnesiac: The Rabbinic Invention of Elisha ben Abuya and Eleazar ben Arach* (Stanford: Stanford University Press, 2000). In the Talmud, *epikoros* is a term applied to anyone disrespectful towards the Rabbis or who mocks the Torah (Sanhedrin 99b–100a); see also Ethics of the Fathers 2:14.

96. For a definition of these terms see Talmud Tractate Horayot 11a, Khulin 10a.

97. Jonathan Margolis, "Not Jewish but Jew-ish," *Guardian*, 30 Nov. 2009, http://www.guardian.co.uk/world/2009/nov/30/jewish-judaism-jonathan-margolis.

98. Alain Finkielkraut, *The Imaginary Jew*, trans. Kevin O'Neill and David Suchoff (Lincoln: University of Nebraska Press, 1994), 117–20.

99. Dan Rickman, "Being a Left-wing Orthodox Jew," http://www.ynetnews.com /articles/0,7340,L-3786910,00.html; accessed 10 Oct. 2009.

100. Tony Klug, "Are Israeli policies entrenching antisemitism worldwide?" unpublished paper, Limmud conference, 30 Dec. 2009.

101. Fine, "Fighting with Phantoms."

102. Albert Memmi, *Portrait of a Jew*, trans. Elisabeth Abbott (New York: Orion Press, 1962), 3–8.

103. *After Empire*, 79.

104. Elliot Borenstein, "Our Borats, Our Selves: Yokels and Cosmopolitans on the Global Stage," *Slavic Review* 67.1 (2008): 1–8.

105. A survey showed Britain to be among the most bigoted and xenophobic of Western nations: Olga Wojtas, "Brits are not the most tolerant neighbours," *Times Higher Education Supplement*, 2 Feb. 2007; http://www.timeshighereducation.co.uk /story.asp?storyCode=207668&sectioncode=26.

106. See Robert A. Saunders, *The Many Faces of Sacha Baron Cohen: Politics, Parody, and the Battle over Borat* (Lanham, Md.: Lexington Books, 2008), 17, 45. Saunders points out, however, that Cohen is not alienated from his British Jewish identity

107. Alisa Lebow, *First Person Jewish* (Minneapolis: University of Minnesota Press, 2008), 103–4; see Jonathan C. Friedman, *Rainbow Jews: Jewish and Gay Identity in the Performing Arts* (Lanham, Md.: Lexington Books, 2007).

108. Ruth Novaczek, *Rootless Cosmopolitans*, http://www.luxonline.org.uk /artists/ruth_novaczek/rootless_cosmopolitans.html.

109. Frantz Fanon, *Black Skin, White Masks* (London: MacGibbon & Kee, 1968), 115–16. See Matthew Frye Jacobson, *Whiteness of a Different Color: European Immigrants and the Alchemy of Race* (Cambridge Mass.: Harvard University Press, 1998), 171–99.

110. Bryan Cheyette, "White Skin, Black Masks: Jews and Jewishness in the Writings of George Eliot and Frantz Fanon," in *Cultural Readings of Imperialism: Edward Said and the Gravity of History*, ed. Keith Ansell-Pearson, Benita Parry, and

Judith Squires (London: Lawrence & Wishart, 1997), 121–25; "Frantz Fanon and the Black-Jewish Imaginary," in *Frantz Fanon's 'Black Skin, White Masks,'* ed. Maxim Silverman (Manchester: Manchester University Press, 2005), 74–99.

111. See on this point Seidman, "Fag-Hags and Bu-Jews," 260. For consideration of Jolson's use of black-face and the amibiguity of Jewish racial identity in Hollywood, see Michael Rogin, *Black Face, White Noise* (Berkeley: University of California Press, 1996).

112. Lebow, *First Person Jewish*, 132–37.

113. Rachel Garfield, "Ali G: Just Who Does He Think He Is," *Jewish Quarterly*180 (Winter 2000): 69–72; idem, "Transgressing the Sacred: The Art of Oreet Ashery," *Jewish Quarterly* (Summer 2002): 11–13. Ashery's transgressive antics on stage seem to be closer to the burlesque entertainment of *Nice Jewish Girls Gone Bad* than Garfield's description of "therapy."

114. See Ann Pellegrini, "Whiteface Performance: 'Race,' Gender, and Jewish Bodies," in *Jews and Other Differences: The New Jewish Cultural Studies,* ed. Jonathan and Daniel Boyarin (Minneapolis: University of Minnesota Press, 1997), 108–49.

115. Hélène Cixous, "Sorties," in *The Newly Born Woman,* by Hélène Cixous and Catherine Clement (London: I. B. Tauris, 1996), 101. See also Elaine Marks, "Juifemme," in *People of the Book: Thirty Scholars Reflect on their Jewish Identity,* ed. Jeffrey Rubin Dorsky and Shelley Fisher Fishkin (Madison: University of Wisconsin Press, 1996), 343–56.

116. For a discussion of such postmodern play with desire that characterizes feminist ethnoautobiography see Susan Rubin Suleiman, *Risking Who One is: Encounters with Contemporary Art and Literature* (Cambridge, Mass.: Harvard University Press, 1994); Suleiman, *Subversive Intent: Gender, Politics, and the Avant-Garde* (Cambridge Mass.: Harvard University Press, 1990). Jewish feminist artists in America, by contrast, who negotiate the unstable categories of "whiteness" and ethnicity express rather different generational fault lines in their reconfiguration of stereotypes of the Jewish American Princess and the self-hating Jew; see Lisa E. Bloom, *Jewish Identities in American Feminist Art: Ghosts of Ethnicity* (New York: Routledge, 2006).

117. Avtar Brah, *Cartographies of Diaspora: Contesting Identities* (London: Routledge 1996), 244.

118. Ibid., 245.

119. See the attempt to square a living practice of being Jewish with feminist and postcolonial theory in Jonathan Boyarin, *Storm from Paradise: The Politics of Jewish Memory* (Minneapolis: University of Minnesota Press, 1992), *xiii–xviii.*

120. Jean Amery, *At the Mind's Limits* (Bloomington: Indiana University Press, 1980).

121. Jon Stratton, *Coming Out Jewish: Constructing Ambivalent Identities* (London: Routledge, 2000), 241.

122. See on this figure in American literature, James E. Young, *Writing and Rewriting the Holocaust: Narrative and the Consequences of Interpretation* (Bloomington: Indiana University Press, 1988), 99–116; for German examples of the tortured identity of the "Holocaust Jew" see Michael André Bernstein, "Unrepresentable Identities: The Jew in Postwar European Literature," in *Thinking About the Holocaust after Half a Century,* ed. Alvin Rosenfeld (Bloomington: Indiana University Press, 1997), 18–37.

123. Stratton, *Coming Out Jewish,* 68–83; Ruth Gilbert, "The Frummer in the Attic: Rachel Lichtenstein and Iain Sinclair's *Rodinsky's Room* and Jewish Memory," *International Fiction Review* 33.1–2 (2006): 27–38. See chapter five, above.

124. Max Silverman, "Re-Figuring 'the Jew' in France," in *Modernity, Culture, and 'the Jew,'* 205.

125. Jacobson, *Kalooki Nights,* 377.

Bibliography

1. PRIMARY TEXTS

Ali, Monica. *Brick Lane*. London: Doubleday, and New York: Scribner, 2003.

Amis, Kingsley. *Stanley and the Women*. London: Hutchinson, 1984.

Amis, Martin. *House of Meetings*. New York: Vintage Books, 2008.

Baddiel, David. *The Secret Purposes*. New York: Harper, 2006.

Barnes, Julian. *Arthur and George*. New York: Knopf, 2006.

———. *Metroland*. London: Jonathan Cape, 1980.

Carey, Peter. *My Life as a Fake*. London: Faber, 2003.

Churchill, Caryl. *Seven Jewish Children: A Play for Gaza*. London: Nick Hern Books, 2009.

Coren, Giles. *Winkler*. London: Vintage Books, 2006.

Desai, Anita. *Baumgartner's Bombay*. New York: Houghton, 2000.

———. *Zigzag*. Boston: Houghton, 2004.

———. "Footsteps on Water." *Wasafiri* 24.1 (2009): 54–56.

Feinstein, Elaine. *The Border*. London: Hutchinson, 1984.

———. *Talking to the Dead*. Manchester: Carcanet, 2008.

Gavron, Jeremy. *An Acre of Barren Ground*. London: Scribner, 2005.

———. *The Book of Israel*. London: Scribner, 2003.

Gordimer, Nadine. "My Father Leaves Home." *New Yorker*. 7 May 1990. 42.

Grant, Linda. *Remind Me Who I Am, Again*. London: Granta Books, 1998.

———. *Still Here*. London: Little Brown, 2002.

———. *The People on the Streets: A Writer's View of Israel*. London: Virago, 2006.

———. *The Clothes on their Backs*. New York: Scribner, 2008.

Hall, Tarquin. *Salaam Brick Lane: A Year in the New East End*. London: John Murray, 2005.

Hare, David. *Via Dolorosa and When Shall We Live?*. London: Faber, 1998.

Jacobson, Howard. *Kalooki Nights*. New York: Simon & Schuster, 2007.

———. *The Finkler Question*. London: Bloomsbury, 2010.

Kureishi, Hanif. "The Rainbow Sign." In *My Beautiful Launderette and the Rainbow Sign*. London: Faber, 1986. 1–38.

———. "We're Not Jews." In *Love in a Blue Time*. London: Faber, 1997. 41–51.

Lessing, Doris. *Landlocked*. New York: New American Library, 1958.

———. *Martha Quest*. New York: New American Library, 1952.

———. *A Ripple from the Storm*. New York: New American Library, 1958.

———. *Under My Skin: Volume One of My Autobiography to 1949*. New York: Harper, 1994.

———. *Walking in the Shade*. New York: Harper Collins, 1997.

Levy, Andrea. *Every Light in the House Burnin'*. London: Headline, 1994.

———. *Fruit of the Lemon*. London: Headline, 1999.

———. *Small Island*. New York: Picador, 2004.

Lichtenstein, Rachel. *On Brick Lane*. London: Hamish Hamilton, 2007.

———. *Rodinsky's Whitechapel*. London: Artangel, 1999.

Lichtenstein, Rachel, and Iain Sinclair. *Rodinsky's Room*. London: Granta, 1999. Reprinted, London: Granta, 2000.

Naipaul, V. S. *The Mimic Man*. New York: Viking, 2001.

Phillips, Caryl. *The European Tribe*. London: Faber and Faber, 1987.

———. *Higher Ground*. New York: Viking Press, 1989.

———. *The Nature of Blood*. New York: Vintage, 1998.

———. "The Nature of Blood and the Ghost of Anne Frank." *Common Quest* (Summer 1998): 4–7.

———. *A New World Order*. New York: Vintage, 2002.

Rushdie, Salman. *The Enchantress of Florence*. New York: Random House, 2008.

———. *Imaginary Homelands: Essays and Criticism, 1981–1991*. London: Granta Books and New York: Viking, 1991.

———. *The Moor's Last Sigh*. London: Vintage, 1996.

———. *The Satanic Verses*. London: Viking, 1988.

———. *Shalimar the Clown*. London: Vintage, 2006.

Self, Will. *How the Dead Live*. London: Bloomsbury, 2000.

Seth, Vikram. *Two Lives: A Memoir*. New York: HarperCollins, 2006.

Sinclair, Iain. *Dark Lanthorns: David Rodinsky's A-Z Walked Over by Iain Sinclair*. London: Goldmark Books, 1999.

———. *Downriver, or, The Vessels of Wrath: A Narrative in Twelve Tales*. London: Paladin, 1992.

———. *Lights out for the Territory: 9 Excursions in the Secret History of London.* With illustrations by Marc Atkins. London: Granta Books, 1998.

Smith, Zadie. *The Autograph Man.* London: Penguin, 2002.

———. *White Teeth.* London: Penguin, 2000.

Williams, Nigel. *Star Turn.* London and Boston: Faber and Faber, 1985.

2. SECONDARY SOURCES

Ahmad, Dohra. "'This fundo stuff is really something new': Fundamentalism and Hybridity in *The Moor's Last Sigh.*" *Yale Journal of Criticism* 18.1 (2005): 1–20.

Alexander, Edward. "Multiculturalism's Jewish Problem.*"* *Academic Questions* 5.4 (1992): 63–68.

Amery, Jean. *At the Mind's Limits.* Bloomington: Indiana University Press, 1980.

Anidjar, Gil. *The Jew, the Arab: A History of the Enemy.* Stanford, Calif.: Stanford University Press, 2003.

Anderson, Benedict R. *Imagined Communities: Reflections on the Origin and Spread of Nationalism.* Rev. ed. London: Verso, 1991.

Arendt, Hannah. *Rahel Varnhagen: The Life of a Jewess.* Trans. Richard and Clara Winston. Baltimore: Johns Hopkins University Press, 1997.

Ashcroft, Bill, Gareth Griffiths, and Helen Tiffin, eds. *The Empire Writes Back: Theory and Practice in Post-Colonial Literatures.* 2nd ed. London: Routledge, 2002.

Aviv, Caryn and David Shneer. *New Jews: The End of the Jewish Diaspora.* New York: New York University Press, 2005.

Back, Les, and John Solomos. *Theories of Race and Racism: A Reader.* London: Routledge, 2000.

Baker, Stephen. "'You must remember this': Salman Rushdie's *The Moor's Last Sigh.*" *Journal of Commonwealth Literature* 35.1 (2000): 43–54.

Bale, Anthony. *The Jew in the Medieval Book: English Antisemitisms 1350–1500.* Cambridge: Cambridge University Press, 2006.

Ball, John Clement. "Acid in the Nation's Bloodstream: Satire, Violence, and the Indian Body Politic in Salman Rushdie's *The Moor's Last Sigh.*" *International Fiction Review* 27.1–2 (2000): 37–47.

Bande, Usha. "Baumgartner's Bombay: An Assessment." *Punjab University Research Bulletin* 20.2 (1989): 131–33.

Baram, Daphna. *Disenchantment: The Guardian and Israel.* London: Guardian Books, 2004.

Barker, Hulme, et al., eds. *Europe and its Others.* Colchester: Essex University, 1985.

Bassi, Shaul. "'Funny, You don't Look Hybrid!': Jewish Memory Revisualized." In *Postcolonial Studies: Changing Perceptions.* Ed. Oriana Palusci. Trent: Dipartimento di Studi Litterari, Linguistici e Filologici, 2006. 239–53.

———— and Alberto Toso Fei. *Shakespeare in Venice.* Treviso: Elzevio, 2007.

Bauman, Zygmunt. "Allosemitism: Premodern, Modern, Postmodern." In *Modernity, Culture, and 'the Jew.'* Ed. Bryan Cheyette and Laura Marcus. Cambridge: Polity Press, 1998. 143–56.

Bellamy, Elizabeth J. *Affective Genealogies: Psychoanalysis, Postmodernism, and the 'Jewish Question' after Auschwitz.* Lincoln, Neb.: University of Nebraska Press, 1997.

Beller, Steven. *Antisemitism: A Very Short Introduction.* Oxford: Oxford University Press, 2007.

Berek, Peter. "The Jew as Renaissance Man." *Renaissance Quarterly* 51.1 (1998): 128–62.

Berkowitz, Michael. *The Jewish Self-Image: American and British Perspectives, 1881–1939.* London: Reaktion Press, 2000.

————. "Rags and Riches, or Bogeymen of the Bourse: Antisemitism and the Abstract Economy in England, the United States, France and Central Europe, 1720–1900." In *Inclusion and Exclusion: Perspectives on Jews from the Enlightenment to the Dreyfus Affair.* Ed. Sam W. Bloom and Ilana Y. Zinguer. Leiden: E. J. Brill, 2003. 267–74.

Berlin, Isaiah. "Jewish Slavery and Emancipation" (1951). In *The Power of Ideas.* Ed. Henry Hardy, London: Chatto & Windus, 2000. 162–185.

Bethlehem, Louise. "Membership, Dismemberment and the Boundaries of the Nation—Manfred Nathan's *Sarie Marais: A Romance of the Anglo-Boer War.*" *African Studies* 63.1 (2004): 95–117.

Bhabha, Homi K. "Foreword: Joking Aside: The Idea of a Self-Critical Community." In *Modernity, Culture, and 'the Jew.'* Eds. Bryan Cheyette and Laura Marcus. Cambridge: Polity Press, 1998. *xv–xx.*

————. *The Location of Culture.* London: Routledge, 1994.

————, ed. *Nation and Narration.* London: Routledge, 1990.

Birbalsingh, Frank. "Caryl Phillips: The Legacy of Othello, I." In *Frontiers of Caribbean Literatures in English*. Ed. Frank Birbalsingh. New York: St. Martin's, 1996. 183–90.

———. "Caryl Phillips: The Legacy of Othello, II." In *Frontiers of Caribbean Literatures in English*. Ed. Frank Birbalsingh. New York: St. Martin's, 1996. 191–97.

Blanchot, Maurice. *L'écriture du désastre*. Paris: Gallimard, 1980.

Bloch, Alice and John Solomos, eds., *Race and Ethnicity in the 21st Century*. Houndmills and New York: Palgrave Macmillan, 2010.

Bliss, Corinne Demas. "Against the Current; A Conversation with Anita Desai." *The Massachusetts Review* 29.3 (1988): 522.

Bourne, Jenny. "Homelands of the Mind: Jewish Feminism and Identity Politics." *Race & Class* 29 (1987): 1–24.

Boyarin, Jonathan. *Storm from Paradise: The Politics of Jewish Memory*. Minneapolis: University of Minnesota Press, 1992.

——— and Daniel Boyarin. "Diaspora: Generation and the Ground of Jewish Identity." *Critical Inquiry* 19.4 (Summer, 1993): 693–725.

———. *Powers of Diaspora: Two Essays on the Relevance of Jewish Culture*. Minnesota: University of Minnesota Press, 2002.

Brah, Avtar. *Cartographies of Diaspora: Contesting Identities*. London: Routledge 1996.

Brah, Avtar, and Annie E. Coombes, eds. *Hybridity and its Discontents: Politics, Science, Culture*. London: Routledge, 2000.

Brenner, Michael and Gideon Reuveni, eds. *Emancipation through Muscles: Jews and Sports in Europe*. Lincoln, Neb.: University of Nebraska Press, 2006.

Brook, Stephen. *The Club: The Jews of Modern Britain*. Rev. ed. London: Constable, 1996.

Budick, Emily Miller. "Acknowledging the Holocaust in Contemporary American Fiction and Criticism." In *Breaking Crystal: Writing and Memory after Auschwitz*. Ed. Efraim Sicher. Urbana: University of Illinois Press, 1998. 329–43.

Calbi, Maurizio. "'The Ghosts of Strangers': Hospitality, Identity and Temporality in Caryl Phillips's *The Nature of Blood*." *Journal for Early Modern Cultural Studies* 6. 2 (Fall/Winter 2006): 38–54.

Canovan, Margaret. "'Breathes there the man, with soul so dead...': Reflections on patriotic poetry and liberal principles." In *Literature and the Political Imagination*. Ed. John Horton and Andrea T. Baumeister. London: Routledge, 1996. 170–97.

Cantor, Paul A. "Tales of the Alhambra: Rushdie's Use of Spanish History in *The Moor's Last Sigh.*" *Studies in the Novel* 29.3 (1997): 323–75.

Cardús, Salvador. "New Ways of Thinking About Identity in Europe." In *Ethnic Europe: Mobility, Identity, and Conflict in a Globalized World*. Ed. Roland Hsu. Stanford: Stanford University Press, 2010. 63–79.

Carroll, David. "Foreword: The Memory of Devastation and the Responsibilities of Thought: 'And let's not talk about that.'" In *Heidegger and "the jews."* Ed. Jean-François Lyotard. Trans. Andreas Michel and Mark S. Roberts. Minneapolis: Minnesota University Press, 1988. *vii–xxix*.

Cesarani, David. "Putting London Jewish Intellectuals in Their Place." In *Place and Displacement in Jewish History and Memory: Zakor v'Makor* [*sic*!]. Ed. David Cesarani, Tony Kushner, and Milton Shain. London: Vallentine Mitchell, 2009. 141–53.

——, ed. *The Making of Modern Anglo-Jewry*. Oxford: Blackwell, 1990.

Cheah, Pheng. *Inhuman Conditions: On Cosmopolitanism and Human Rights*. Cambridge, Mass.: Harvard University Press, 2006.

Chesler, Phyllis. *The New Anti-Semitism: The Current Crisis and What We Must Do About It*. San Francisco: Jossey-Bass, 2003.

Cheyette, Bryan. *Constructions of "the Jew" in English Literature and Society: Racial Representations, 1875–1945*. Cambridge: Cambridge University Press, 1993.

——. "Diasporas of the Mind: British-Jewish Writing Beyond Multiculturalism." In *Diaspora and Multiculturalism: Common Traditions and New Developments*. Ed. Monica Flundernik. Amsterdam: Rodopi, 2003. 45–82.

——. "Frantz Fanon and the Black-Jewish Imaginary." In *Frantz Fanon's 'Black Skin, White Masks*. Ed. Maxim Silverman. Manchester: Manchester University Press, 2005. 74–99.

——. "Imagined Communities: Contemporary Jewish Writing in Great Britain." In *Contemporary Jewish Writing in Europe: A Guide*. Ed. Vivian Liska and Thomas Nolden. Bloomington: Indiana University Press, 2008. 90–115.

——. "'Ineffable and Usable': Towards a Diasporic British-Jewish Writing." *Textual Practice* 10 (Spring 1996): 295–313.

————. "Liberal Anti-Judaism and the Victims of Modernity," *American Literary History* (2001): 540–43.

————. "Neither Black nor White: The Figure of the Jew in Imperial British Literature." In *The Jew in the Text*. Ed. Tamar Garb and Linda Nochlin. London: Thames & Hudson, 1995. 31–41.

————. "Neither Excuse nor Accuse: T. S. Eliot's Semitic Discourse," *Modernism/modernity* 10.3 (2003): 431–37.

————."Venetian Spaces: Old-New Literatures and the Ambivalent Uses of Jewish History." *Essays and Studies* 53 (2000): 53–72.

————. "White Skin, Black Masks: Jews and Jewishness in the Writings of George Eliot and Frantz Fanon." In *Cultural Readings of Imperialism: Edward Said and the Gravity of History*. Ed. Keith Ansell-Pearson, Benita Parry, and Judith Squires. London: Lawrence & Wishart, 1997. 106–26.

————, ed. *Between "Race" and Culture: Representations of "the Jew" in English and American Literature*. Stanford, Calif.: Stanford University Press, 1996.

————, and Laura Marcus, eds. *Modernity, Culture, and 'the Jew.'* Cambridge: Polity Press, 1998.

Christie, Clive J. *Race and Nation: A Reader*. London: I. B. Tauris, 1998.

Cixous, Hélène, and Catherine Clement. *The Newly Born Woman*. London: I. B. Tauris, 1996.

Clingman, Paul. *The Moon Can Wait: A Biography of the Hon AE Abrahamson*. London: Penguin Books, 2004.

Clingman, Stephen. "Forms of History and Identity in *The Nature of Blood*." *Salmagundi* 143 (Summer 2004): 141–66.

————. "Other Voices: An Interview with Caryl Phillips." *Salmagundi* 143 (2004): 112–40.

————. *The Grammar of Identity: Transnational Fiction and the Nature of the Boundary*. Oxford: Oxford University Press, 2009.

Cohen, Mitchell. "In Defense of Shaatnez: A Politics for Jews in a Multicultural America." In *Insider/Outsider: American Jews and Multiculturalism*. Ed. David Biale, Michael Galchinsky, and Susannah Heschel. Berkeley: University of California Press, 1998. 34–53.

Concha, Angeles de la. "The End of History. Or Is It? Circularity versus Progress in Caryl Phillips' *The Nature of Blood*." *Misceaenea: A Journal of English and American Studies* 22 (2000): 1–19.

Cormack, Alistair. "Migration and the Politics of Narrative Form: Realism and the Postcolonial Subject in *Brick Lane*." *Contemporary Literature* 47.4 (2006): 695–721.

Craps, Stef. "Linking Legacies of Loss: Traumatic Histories and Cross-Cultural Empathy in Caryl Phillips's *Higher Ground* and *The Nature of Blood*." *Studies in the Novel* 40.1–2 (Spring-Summer 2008): 191–202.

Crick, Bernard, ed. *National Identities: The Constitution of the United Kingdom*. Oxford: Blackwell, 1991.

Dabydeen, David. *The Black Presence in English Literature*. Manchester: Manchester University Press, 1986.

Da Silva, Tony Simoes. "Whose Bombay is it Anyway? Anita Desai's *Baumgartner's Bombay*." *Ariel* 28.3 (1997): 63–77.

Davison, Neil. *Jewishness and Masculinity from the Modern to the Postmodern*. New York: Routledge, 2011.

Dawson, Ashley. "'To Remember Too Much Is Indeed a Form of Madness': Caryl Phillips's *The Nature of Blood* and the Modalities of European Racism." *Postcolonial Studies* 7.1 (2004): 83–101.

Defoe, Daniel. *Miscellaneous Works*. London: George Bell & Sons, 1888.

Delany, Sheila, ed. *Chaucer and the Jews: Sources, Contexts, Meanings*. New York: Routledge, 2002.

Deutscher, Isaac. *The Non-Jewish Jew and Other Essays*. London: Oxford University Press, 1968.

De Voogd, Peter. "Anita Desai's Baumgartner." In *Shades of Empire in Colonial and Postcolonial Literaures*. Eds. C. C. Barfoot and Theo D'haen. Atlanta: Rodopi, 1993. 33–89.

Dickens, Charles. *The Letters of Charles Dickens, 1862–1864*. Vol. 10. Oxford: Oxford University Press, 2002.

Diner, Hasia. *Lower East Side Memories: A Jewish Place in America*. Princeton: Princeton University Press, 2000.

———, Jeffrey Shandler, and Beth Wenger, eds. *Remembering the Lower East Side*. Bloomington: Indiana University Press, 2000.

Docker, John. *1492: The Poetics of Diaspora*. London and New York: Continuum, 2001.

Eaglestone, Robert. "'You Would Not Add to My Suffering If you Knew What I have Seen': Holocaust Testimony and Contemporary African Trauma Literature." *Studies in the Novel* 40.1–2 (2008): 72–85.

Easthope, Antony. *Englishness and National Culture*. London: Routledge, 1999.

Eggerz, Solveig. "The German-Jewish Epoch of 1743–1933: Tragedy or Success Story?" (2007). http: www.acjna.org/acjna/articles_detail.aspx ?id

Fanon, Frantz. *Black Skin, White Masks*. Trans. Charles Lam Markman. London: MacGibbon & Kee, 1968.

Featherstone, Mike. *Undoing Culture: Globalization, Postmodernism and Identity*. London: Sage, 1995.

Feryn, Lies. "Entangled Memories of the Holocaust and Partition in Anita Desai's *Baumgartner's Bombay*." Master's Thesis. University of Ghent, May 2009; http://lib.ugent.be/fulltxt/RUG01/001/414/388/RUG01-001414388_2010_0001_AC.pdf.

Finkielkraut, Alain. *The Imaginary Jew*. Trans. Kevin O'Neill and David Suchoff. Lincoln, Neb.: Nebraska University Press, 1994.

Fine, Robert. "Fighting with Phantoms: A Contribution to the Debate on Antisemitism in Europe." *Patterns of Prejudice* 43.5 (2009): 259–79.

Fisch, Harold. *The Dual Image: The Jew in English and American Literature*. London: World Jewish Library, 1970.

Flundernik, Monika. "The Diasporic Imaginary: Postcolonial Reconfigurations in the Context of Multiculturalism." In *Diaspora and Multiculturalism: Common Traditions and New Developments*. Ed. Monica Fludernik. Amsterdam: Rodopi, 2003. *xi–xxxvi.*

Foot, Paul. *Immigration and Race in British Politics*. Harmondsworth: Penguin Books, 1965.

Foxman, Abraham H. *Never Again?: The Threat of the New Anti-Semitism*. San Francisco: HarperSanFrancisco, 2003.

Freedland, Jonathan. *Jacob's Gift: A Journey into the Heart of Belonging*. London: Hamish Hamilton, 2005.

Freedman, Jonathan. *Klezmer America: Jewishness, Ethnicity, Modernity*. New York: Columbia University Press, 2008.

———. *The Temple of Culture: Assimilation and Anti-Semitism in Literary Anglo-America*. New York: Oxford University Press, 2000.

Furman, Andrew. "The Jewishness of the Contemporary Gentile Writer: Zadie Smith's *The Autograph Man.*" *MELUS* 30.1 (2005): 3–17.

Galchinsky, Michael. "Scattered Seeds: A Dialogue of Diasporas." In *Insider/Outsider: American Jews and Multiculturalism*. Ed. David Biale,

Michael Galchinsky, and Susannah Heschel. Berkeley: University of California Press, 1998. 185–211.

Galvin, Fernando. "The Search for a Cultural Transformation: Caryl Phillips as a Case Study." *REAL: The Yearbook of Research in English and American Literature* 20 (2004): 245–62.

Garfield, Rachel. "Ali G: Just Who Does He Think He Is?" *Jewish Quarterly* 180 (Winter 2000): 69–72.

———. "Transgressing the Sacred: The Art of Oreet Ashery." *Jewish Quarterly* (Summer 2002): 11–13.

Gates, Henry L., ed. *"Race," Writing and Difference*. Chicago: Chicago University Press, 1985.

Gelber, Mark. "What is Literary Anti-Semitism?" *Jewish Social Studies* 47.1 (1985): 1–20.

Geller, Jay. *On Freud's Jewish Body: Mitigating Circumcisions*. New York: Fordham University Press, 2007.

Gikandi, Simon. "Globalization and the Claims of Postcoloniality." *South Atlantic Quarterly* 100.3 (2001): 627–58.

Gilbert, Ruth. "Contemporary British-Jewish Writing: From Apology to Attitude." *Literature Compass* 5.2 (2008): 394–406.

———. "The Frummer in the Attic: Rachel Lichtenstein and Iain Sinclair's *Rodinsky's Room* and Jewish Memory." *International Fiction Review* 33.1-2 (2006): 27–38.

———. "The Golem in the Attic: Rodinsky's Room and Jewish Memory." *Jewish Culture and History* 9.1 (2007): 51–70.

Gilman, Sander L. *Difference and Pathology: Stereotypes of Sexuality, Race, and Madness*. Ithaca, N.Y: Cornell University Press, 1985.

———. *The Jew's Body*. New York: Routledge, 1991.

———. *Jewish Frontiers: Essays on Bodies, Histories, and Identities*. London: Palgrave Macmillan, 2003.

———. *Jewish Self-Hatred: Anti-Semitism and the Hidden Language of the Jews*. Baltimore: Johns Hopkins University Press, 1986.

———. *Multiculturalism and the Jews*. New York: Routledge, 2006.

———. *Smart Jews: The Construction of the Image of Jewish Superior Intelligence*. Lincoln, Neb.: University of Nebraska Press, 1997.

———. "'We're Not Jews'": Imagining Jewish History and Jewish Bodies in Contemporary Multicultural Literature." *Modern Judaism* 23.2 (2003): 126–55.

Gilroy, Paul *.After Empire: Melancholia or Convivial Culture?*. London: Routledge, 2004.

———. *Against Race: Imagining Political Culture Beyond the Color Line*. Cambridge, Mass.: Harvard University Press, 2000.

———. *The Black Atlantic: Modernity and Double Consciousness*. Cambridge, Mass.: Harvard University Press, 1993.

———. *There Ain't No Black in the Union Jack: The Cultural Politics of Race and Nation*. London: Routledge, 1992.

Ginsberg, Elaine K., ed. *Passing and the Fictions of Identity*. Durham, N.C.: Duke University Press, 1996.

Goldberg, David Theo, and John Solomos. *A Companion to Ethnic and Racial Studies*. Oxford: Blackwell, 2002.

Gonzalez, Madelena. *Fiction after the Fatwa: Salman Rushdie and the Charm of Catastrophe*. Amsterdam: Rodopi, 2005.

———. "*The Moor's Last Sigh*: Marginal Alternatives, the Reconstruction of Identity through the Carnival of Indetermination." In *Subverting Masculinity: Hegemonic and Alternative Versions of Masculinity in Contemporary Culture*. Eds. Russell West and Frank Lay. Amsterdam: Rodopi, 2000. 128–43.

———. "'New Ways to Be Beautiful': The Search to Escape Identity in *The Moor's Last Sigh*." In *Flight from Certainty: The Dilemma of Identity and Exile*. Eds. Anne Luyat and Francine Tolron. Amsterdam: Rodopi, 2001. 100–11.

Gorra, Michael. *After Empire: Scott, Naipaul, Rushdie*. Chicago: University of Chicago Press, 1997.

Greenblatt, Stephen, ed. *The Norton Shakespeare*. New York: W. W. Norton, 1997.

Greenberg, Jonathan. "The Base Indian or the Base Judean? Othello and the Metaphor of the Palimpsest in Salman Rushdie's *The Moor's Last Sigh*." *Modern Language Studies* 29.2 (1999): 93–107.

Greene, Sue. "Use of the Jew in West Indian Novels." *World Literature Written in English* 26.1 (1986): 150–69.

Groß, Oliver. "Second-Generation Authors in Britain." In *Anglophone Jewish Literatures*. Ed. Axel Stähler. London and New York: Routledge, 2007. 133–40.

Gruber, Ruth Ellen. *Virtually Jewish: Reinventing Jewish Culture in Europe*. Berkeley: University of California Press, 2002.

Guttman, Anna. "Marketing the Figure of the Jew: Writing South Asia, Reading America." In *The Global Literary Field*. Eds. Anna Guttman, Michel Hockx, and George Paizis. Newcastle-upon-Tyne: Cambridge Scholars Press, 2006. 60–79.

————. *The Nation of India in Contemporary Indian Literature*. New York and Houndmills, Basingstoke: Palgrave Macmillan, 2007.

————. "The Jew in the Archive: Textualizations of (Jewish?) History in Contemporary South Asian Literature." *Contemporary Literature* 51,3 (2010): 503–31.

Halkin, Hillel. "Salman Rushdie Surrenders." *Commentary* (July 1996): 55–59.

Hall, Stuart. "Cultural Identity and Diaspora." In *Identity: Community, Culture, Difference*. Ed. Jonathan Rutherford. London: Lawrence and Wishart, 1990. 222-37. Reprinted in *Colonial Discourse and Post-colonial Theory: A Reader*. Ed. Patrick Williams and Laura Chrisman. London: Harvester, 1993. 392–403.

————, ed. *Representation: Cultural Representation and Signifying Practices*. London: Sage, 1997.

Hammerschlag, Sarah. *The Figural Jew: Politics and Identity in Postwar French Thought*. Chicago: University of Chicago Press, 2010.

Harrar, Heinrich. *Seven Years in Tibet*. New York: Tarcher, 1997.

Harrison, Bernard. *The Resurgence of Antisemitism: Jews, Israel, and Liberal Opinion*. Boston: Rowman & Littlefield, 2006.

Hayes, Peter, ed. *Lessons and Legacies: The Meaning of the Holocaust in a Changing World*. Evanston, Ill.: Northwestern University Press, 1991.

Head, Dominic. *Cambridge Introduction to Modern British Fiction, 1950–2000*. Cambridge and New York: Cambridge University Press, 2002.

————. "Zadie Smith's *White Teeth*: Multiculturalism for the Millennium." In *Contemporary British Fiction*. Eds. Richard J. Lane, Rod Mengham, and Philip Tew. 106–19. Cambridge: Polity, 2003.

Hess, Jonathan. "Sugar Island Jews? Jewish Colonialism and the Rhetoric of 'Civic Improvement' in Eighteenth Century Germany." *Eighteenth Century Studies* 32.1 (1998): 92–100.

Hiddleston, Jane. "Shapes and Shadows: (Un)veiling the Immigrant in Monica Ali's *Brick Lane*." *Journal of Commonwealth Literature* 40.1 (2005): 57–72.

————. *Understanding Postcolonialism*. Stocksfield: Acumen, 2009.

Hirsch, Marianne. *Family Frames: Photography, Narrative and Postmemory*. Cambridge, Mass.: Harvard University Press, l997.

———. "The Generation of Postmemory." *Poetics Today* 29.1 (2008): 103–28.

Hirsh, David. "Anti-Zionism and Antisemitism: Cosmopolitan Reflections." Yale Initiative for the Interdisciplinary Study of Antisemitism Working Paper Series #1, 2007. http://www.yale.edu/yiisa/working paper/hirsh/David%20Hirsh%20YIISA%20Working%20Paper.pdf.

———. "Accusations of Malicious Intent in Debates about the Palestine-Israel Conflict and about Anti-Semitism: The Livingstone Formulation, 'Playing the antisemitism card' and Contesting the Boundaries of Antiracist Discourse," *Transversal* 1 (2010): 42–77.

Hitler, Adolf. *Mein Kampf.* Trans. Ralph Manheim. Boston: Houghton Mifflin, 1943.

Ho, Elaine Y. L. "The Languages of Identity in Anita Desai's *Baumgartner's Bombay.*" *World Literature Written in English* 32.1 (1992): 96–106.

Husain, Ed. *The Islamist: Why I Joined Radical Islam in Britain, What I Saw Inside and Why I Left.* London: Penguin Books, 2007.

Hutnyk, John. *The Rumor of Calcutta: Tourism, Charity, and the Poverty of Representation.* London: Zed Books, 1996.

———, Virinder S. Kalra, and Raminder Kaur, eds. *Diaspora & Hybridity.* London: SAGE, 2005.

Iganski, Paul and Barry Kosmin, eds. *A New Anti-Semitism?: Debating Judeophobia in 21st Century Britain.* London: Profile Books, 2003.

———. *The New European Extremism: Hating America, Israel and the Jews.* London: Profile Books, 2006.

Jacobson, Matthew F. *Whiteness of a Different Color: European Immigrants and the Alchemy of Race.* Cambridge, Mass.: Harvard University Press, 1998.

Jaspers, Karl. *The Question of German Guilt.* New York: Fordham University Press, 2000.

Joppke, Christian. "Limits of Integration Policy: Britain and her Muslims." *Journal of Migration and Ethnic Studies* 35.3 (2009): 453–72.

Judaken, Jonathan. "So What's New? Rethinking the 'New Antisemitism' in a Global Age." *Patterns of Prejudice* 42.4–5 (2008): 531–60.

Julius, Anthony. *Trials of the Diaspora*: *A History of English Anti-Semitism.* Oxford: Oxford University Press, 2010.

Jussawalla, Feroza and Reed Way Dasenbrock, eds. *Interviews with Writers of the Post Colonial World.* Jackson: University Press of Mississsippi, 1992.

Kadish, Sharman. "Squandered Heritage: Jewish Buildings in Britain." In *The Jewish Heritage in British History: Englishness and Jewishness.* Ed. Tony Kushner. London: Frank Cass, 1992. 147–65.

Kahn-Harris, Keith and Ben Gidley. *Turbulent Times: The British Jewish Community Today.* London and New York: Continuum, 2010.

Kalmar, Ivan Davidson, and Derek J. Penslar, eds. *Orientalism and the Jews.* Waltham, Mass.: Brandeis University Press and Hanover: University Press of New England, 2005.

Karpf, Anne. *The War After: Living with the Holocaust.* London: Minerva, 1997.

Katz, Jacob. "The Jewish Diaspora: Minority Position and Majority Aspirations." *Jerusalem Quarterly* 25 (Fall 1982): 68–78.

Katznelson, Ira. "'To Give Counsel and to Consent': Why the King (Edward I) Expelled His Jews (in 1290)." In *Preferences and Situations: Points of Intersection Between Historical and Rational Choice Institutionalism.* Eds. Ira Katznelson and Barry Weingas. New York: Russell Sage Foundation, 2005. 88–126.

Kershen, Anne. *Strangers, Aliens and Asians: Huguenots, Jews and Bangladeshis in Spitalfields 1660–2000.* London: Routledge, 2005.

Kertzer, David I., ed. *Old Demons, New Debates: Anti-Semitism in the West.* New York: Holmes & Meier, 2005.

Khair, Tabish. "The Death of the Reader." *Wasafiri* 21.3 (2006): 1–5.

Khan, Nyla Ali. *The Fiction of Nationality in an Era of Transnationalism.* New York: Routledge, 2005.

Kitaj, R. B. *The First Diasporist Manifesto.* New York: Thames and Hudson, 1989.

Klug, Bruce. "The Collective Jew: Israel and the New Antisemitism." *Patterns of Prejudice* 37.2 (2003): 117–38.

———. "The Myth of the New Anti-Semitism." *The Nation.* Foreign Affairs section. 2 Feb. 2004. http://www.thenation.com/doc/20040202/klug

Kosmin, Barry Alexander. *Majuta: A History of the Jewish Community of Zimbabwe.* Salisbury: Mambo Press, 1980.

Kotler-Berkowitz, Laurence. "Social Cleavages and Political Divisions: A Comparative Analysis of British, American and South African Jews in the 1990s." *Journal of Modern Jewish Studies* 1.2 (2002): 204–33.

Kral, Françoise. "Shaky Ground and New Territorialities in *Brick Lane* by Monica Ali and *The Namesake* by Jhumpa Lahiri." *Journal of Postcolonial Writing* 43.1 (2007): 65–76.

Kushner, Tony. "The End of the 'Anglo-Jewish Progress Show': Representations of the Jewish East End, 1897–1987." In *The Jewish Heritage in British History: Englishness and Jewishness*. Ed. Tony Kushner. London: Frank Cass, 1992, 78–105.

———. *Anglo-Jewry since 1066: Place, Locality and Memory*. Manchester: Manchester University Press, 2009.

Lambert, Nick. *Jews and Europe in the Twenty-First Century: Thinking Jewish*. London: Vallentine Mitchell, 2008.

Lampert, Lisa. *Gender and Jewish Difference from Paul to Shakespeare*. Philadelphia: University of Pennsylvania Press, 2004.

Lane, Richard J., Rod Mengham, and Philip Tew, eds. *Contemporary British Fiction*. Cambridge, UK: Polity Press, 2002.

Langmuir, Gavin. *Toward a Definition of Antisemitism*. Berkeley: University of California Press, 1990.

Lappin, Elena. "At Home in Exile: A Conversation between Eva Hoffman and Elena Lappin." *Jewish Quarterly* (Winter 1995): 11–14.

Lassner, Phyllis. *Colonial Strangers: Women Writing the End of the British Empire*. New Brunswick, N.J.: Rutgers University Press, 2004.

Lassner, Phyllis, and Lara Trubowitz, eds. *Antisemitism and Philosemitism in the Twentieth and Twenty-first Centuries: Representing Jews, Jewishness, and Modern Culture*. Newark: University of Delaware Press, 2008.

Laqueur, Walter. *The Changing Face of Anti-Semitism: From Ancient Times to the Present Day*. Oxford: Oxford University Press, 2008.

Ledent, Benedicte. *Caryl Phillips*. Manchester: Manchester University Press, 2002.

Lee, Robert A., ed. *Other Britain, Other British: Contemporary Multicultural Fiction*. London: Pluto, 1995.

Lebow, Alisa S. *First Person Jewish*. Minneapolis: University of Minneapolis Press, 2008.

Leveson, Marcia. *People of the Book: Images of the Jew in South African English Fiction 1880–1992*. Johannesburg: Witwatersrand University Press, 1996.

Levine, Gary M. *The Merchant of Modernism: The Economic Jew in Anglo-American Literature, 1864–1939*. New York: Routledge, 2003.

Lewis, Bernard, Edmund Leites, and Margaret Case, eds. *As Others See Us: Mutual Perceptions, East and West*. New York: International Society for the Comparative Study of Civilizations, 1985.

Liotard, Corinne. "Otherness in Anita Desai's *Baumgartner's Bombay*." In *Flight From Certainty: The Dilemma of Identity and Exile*. Eds. Anne Luyat and Francine Tolron. New York: Rodopi, 2001. 112–24.

Loomba, Ania. *Colonialism-Postcolonialism*. 2nd ed. London: Routledge, 2005.

———. "'Local-Manufacture Made-in-India Othello Fellows': Issues of Race, Hybridity and Location in Post-Colonial Shakespeares." In *Post-Colonial Shakespeares*. Eds. Ania Loomba and Martin Orkin. New York and London: Routledge, 1998. 143–63.

———. *Shakespeare, Race, and Colonialism*. Oxford: Oxford University Press, 2002.

López, Alfred J. "'Everybody else just living their lives': 9/11, Race and the New Postglobal Literature." *Patterns of Prejudice* 42.4–5 (2008): 509–29.

Lowe, Jan. "No More Lonely Londoners." *Small Axe* 9 (2001): 166–80.

Lowenthal, David. *The Past is a Foreign Country*. Cambridge: Cambridge University Press, 1985.

Lupton, Julia Reinhard. "Othello Circumcised: Shakespeare and the Pauline Discourse of Nations." *Representations* 57 (Winter, 1997): 73–89.

Lyotard, Jean-François. *Heidegger and the "jews"*. Trans. Andreas Michel and Mark S, Roberts. Minneapolis: University of Minnesota Press, 1991.

Maccoby, Hyam. *Antisemitism and Modernity*. London: Routledge, 2006.

MacKenzie, John M. *Orientalism: History, Theory, and the Arts*. Manchester: Manchester University Press, 1995.

MacShane, Denis. *Globalising Hatred: The New Antisemitism*. London: Weidenfeld and Nicolson, 2008.

Malieckal, Bindu. "Shakespeare's Shylock, Rushdie's Abraham Zogoiby and the Jewish Pepper Merchants of Precolonial India." *Upstart Crow* 21 (2001): 154–69.

Mamet, David. *The Wicked Son: Anti-Semitism, Self Hatred, and the Jews.* New York: Schocken, 2006.

Marks, Elaine. "Juifemme." In *People of the Book: Thirty Scholars Reflect on their Jewish Identity.* Eds. Jeffrey Rubin Dorsky and Shelley Fisher Fishkin. Madison: University of Wisconsin Press, 1996.

Mayer, Larry N. and Gary Gelb. *Who Will Say Kaddish?: A Search for Jewish Identity in Contemporary Poland.* Syracuse: Syracuse University Press, 2002.

McLeod, John. *Postcolonial London: Rewriting the Metropolis.* London: Routledge, 2004.

Mearsheimer, John J., and Stephen M. Walt. *The Israel Lobby and US Foreign Policy.* New York: Farrar, Straus, and Giroux, 2006.

Meer, Nasar and Tehseen Noorani. "A Sociological Comparison of anti-Semitism and anti-Muslim Sentiment in Britain." *Sociological Review* 56.2 (2008): 195–218.

Memmi, Albert. *The Liberation of the Jew.* New York: Orion Press, 1966.

———. *Portrait of a Jew.* Trans. Elisabeth Abbott. New York: Orion Press, 1962.

Mengham. Rod. "The Writing of Iain Sinclair." In *Contemporary British Fiction.* Eds. Richard J. Lane, Rod Mengham, and Philip Tew. Cambridge: Polity, 2003. 56–67.

Michaels, Walter Benn. *The Trouble with Diversity: How We Learned to Love Identity and Ignore Inequality.* New York: Metropolitan Books, 2006.

———. "'You Who Never Was There': Slavery and the New Historicism, Deconstruction and the Holocaust." *Narrative* 4.1 (1996): 1–16.

Mishra, Vijay. *The Literature of the Indian Diaspora: Theorizing the Diasporic Imaginary.* London: Routledge, 2007.

Modood, Tariq. *Multiculturalism: A Civic Idea.* Cambridge: Polity, 2007.

Morton, Stephen. *Salman Rushdie: Fictions of Postcolonial Modernity.* Basingstoke: Palgrave Macmillan, 2008.

Moss, Laura. "The Politics of Everyday Hybridity: Zadie Smith's *White Teeth.*" *Wasafiri* 39 (2003): 11–17.

Mufti, Aamir R. *Enlightenment in the Colony: The Jewish Question and the Crisis of Postcolonial Culture.* Princeton: Princeton University Press, 2007.

Mundill, Robin R. *England's Jewish Solution: Experiment and Expulsion, 1262–1290*. Cambridge: Cambridge University Press, 1998.

———. *The King's Jews: Money, Massacre and Exodus in Medieval England*. London: Continuum, 2010.

Nairn, Tom. *The Break-Up of Britain: Crisis and Neo-Nationalism*. London: New Left Library, 1977.

Narain, Mona. "Re-imagined Histories: Rewriting the Early Modern in Rushdie's *The Moor's Last Sigh*." *Journal for Early Modern Cultural Studies* 6.2 (Fall/Winter 2006): 55–67.

Nasta, Susheila. *Home Truths: Fictions of the South Asian Diaspora in Britain*. Houndmills: Palgrave Macmillan, 2002.

Nayak, P. M., and S. P. Swain. "The Outsider in Desai's *Baumgartner's Bombay*." *Commonwealth Novel in English* 6.1–2 (1993): 112–20.

Neill, Michael. "'Mulattos,' 'Blacks,' and 'Indian Moors': Othello and Early Modern Constructions of Human Difference." *Shakespeare Quarterly* 49.4 (Winter 1998): 361–74.

Newman, Judie. *The Ballistic Bard: Postcolonial Fictions*. London: Arnold, 1995.

Nochlin, Linda, and Tamar Garb, eds. *The Jew in the Text: Modernity and the Construction of Identity*. London: Thames and Hudson, 1991.

Nyman, Jopi. *Home, Identity, and Mobility in Contemporary Diasporic Fiction*. Amsterdam: Rodopi, 2009.

Omer-Sherman, Ranen. "Introduction: The Cultural and Historical Stabilities and Instabilities of Jewish Orientalism." *Shofar: An Interdiscipinary Journal of Jewish Studies* 24.2 (2006): 1–10.

Orwell, George. "Antisemitism in Britain." In *The Collected Essays, Journalism and Letters of George Orwell: As I Please, 1943–1945*. New York: Harcourt, Brace and World, 1968. 332–41.

Ozick, Cynthia. "America: Toward Yavneh." *Judaism* 19 (Summer 1970): 264–82.

Pandit, Lalita. "A Sense of Detail and A Sense of Order: Anita Desai Interviewed by Lalita Pandit." In *Literary India: Comparative Studies in Aesthetics, Colonialism and Culture*. Ed. Patrick Colm Hogan and Lalita Pandit. Albany: State University of New York Press, 1995. 153–74.

Parekh, Bhikhu. *Rethinking Multiculturalism: Cultural Diversity and Political Theory*. Basingstoke: Macmillan Press, 2000.

Penslar, Derek. *Shylock's Children: Economics and Jewish Identity in Modern Europe.* Berkeley: University of California Press, 2001.

Perfect, Michael. "The Multicultural Bildungsroman: Stereotypes in Monica Ali's *Brick Lane.*" *Journal of Commonwealth Literature* 43.3 (2008): 109–20.

Perril, Simon. "A Cartography of Absence: The Work of Iain Sinclair," *Comparative Criticism.* 19 (1997): 309–39.

Phillips, Melanie. *Londonistan: How Britain is Creating a Terror State Within.* London: Gibson Square, 2006.

Pick, Daniel. *Svengali's Web: The Alien Enchanter in Modern Culture.* New Haven: Yale University Press, 2000.

Pickering, Michael. *Stereotyping: The Politics of Representation.* Basingstoke: Palgrave, 2001.

Plantenga, Bart. *Yodel-Ay-Ee-0000.* New York: Routledge, 2004.

Pulzer, Peter. "Emancipation & its Discontents: The German-Jewish Dilemma." Research Paper No. 1. Brighten: Center for German-Jewish Studies, University of Sussex, 1997.

Ragussis, Michael. *Figures of Conversion: "The Jewish Question" & English National Identity.* Durham, N.C.: Duke University Press, 1995.

Rajakrishnan, V. "The Land of the Dead in Salman Rushdie's *The Moor's Last Sigh,* and Some Reflections Based on Indian Response to the Theme of Exile." *Indian Literature* 42.3 (1998): 143–54.

Ravid, Benjamin. "How 'Other' Really Was the Jewish Other? The Evidence from Venice." In *Acculturation and its Discontents: The Italian Jewish Experience between Exclusion and Inclusion.* Eds. David N. Myers et al. Toronto: University of Toronto Press, 2008. 19–55.

Rege, Josna A. "Victim into Protagonist? Midnight's Children and the Post-Rushdie National Narratives of the Eighties." *Studies in the Novel* 29.3 (1997): 342–75.

Roberts, Ronald Suresh. *No Cold Kitchen.* Johannesburg: STE, 2005.

Robbins, Jill. "Circumcising Confession: Derrida, Autobiography, Judaism." *Diacritics* 25, 4 (Winter, 1995): 20–38.

Rogers, David and John McLeod, eds. *The Revision of Englishness.* Manchester: Manchester University Press, 2004.

Romain, Gemma. "Who Do You Think You Are?': Journeys and Jewish Identity in the Televisual Narrative of David Baddiel," *Jewish Culture and History* 11 (2009): 283–96. Reprinted in *Jewish Journeys: From Philo to*

Hip Hop. Ed. James Jordon, Tony Kushner, and Sarah Pearce. London: Vallentine Mitchell, 2010. 332–48.

Rose, Gillian. *Mourning Becomes the Law*. Cambridge: Cambridge University Press, 1996.

Rose, Jacqueline. *States of Fantasy*. Oxford: Oxford University Press, 1996.

———. *The Question of Zion*. Princeton: Princeton University Press, 2005.

Rosenfeld, Alvin H. *Anti-Zionism in Great Britain and Beyond: A "Respectable" Anti-Semitism?*. New York: American Jewish Committee, 2004. www.ajc.org/atf/cf/%7B42D75369-D582-4380-8395-D25925B85E AF%7D/AntiZionism.pdf.

Roskies, David G. *The Jewish Search for a Usable Past*. Bloomington: Indiana University Press, 1999.

Ross, Michael. *Race Riots: Comedy and Ethnicity in Modern British Fiction*. Montreal: McGill Queen's University Press, 2006.

Roth, Philip. *The Human Stain*. Boston: Houghton Mifflin, 2000.

Rothberg, Michael, *Multidirectional Memory: Remembering the Holocaust in the Age of Decolonization*. Stanford: Stanford University Press, 2009.

Rozmovits, Linda. "'Now you see 'em, now you don't': Jewish visibility and the problem of citizenship in the British Telecom 'Beattie' campaign." *Media Culture Society* 22. 6 (2000): 707–22.

Runnymede Trust. *A Very Light Sleeper: The Persistence and Dangers of Anti-Semitism*. London: Runneymede Trust, 1994.

Sacks, Jonathan. *The Dignity of Difference: How to Avoid the Clash of Civilizations*. Rev. ed. London: Continuum, 2003.

———. *The Home We Build Together: Moving Beyond Multiculturalism*. London: Continuum, 2007.

———. *Radical Then, Radical Now*. London: Continuum 2000.

Said, Edward W. *Culture and Imperialism*. New York: Knopf, 1994.

———. *Orientalism*. New York: Pantheon Books, 1978.

———. *Out of Place: A Memoir*. London: Granta Books, 1999.

Samuel, Raphael. *Theatres of Memory*. Vol. 1: *Past and Present in Contemporary Culture*. London: Verso, 1994.

———. *Theatres of Memory*. Vol. 2: *Island Stories—Unravelling Britain*. Eds. Alison Light, Sally Alexander, and Gareth Stedman Jones. London: Verso, 1998.

Sandhu, Sukhdev. "The Pornography of Fame: Zadie Smith, *The Autograph Man*." *Wasafiri* 39 (2003): 64–67.

————. "Come hungry, leave edgy." *London Review of Books.* 9 Oct. 2003. http://www.lrb.co.uk/v25/n19/sand01_.html.

Saunders, Robert A. *The Many Faces of Sacha Baron Cohen: Politics, Parody, and the Battle over Borat.* Lanham, Md.: Lexington Books, 2008.

Schechter, Ronald. "Rationalizing the Enlightenment: Postmodernism and Theories of Anti-Semitism." *Historical Reflections/Réflexions Historiques* 25.2 (1999): 279–306.

Schoenfeld, Gabriel. *The Return of Anti-Semitism.* San Francisco: Encounter Books, 2004.

Schultheis, Alexandra W. "Postcolonial Lack and Aesthetic Promise in *The Moor's Last Sigh*." *Twentieth Century Literature* 47.4 (2001): 569–96.

Scott, Joan Wallach. *The Politics of the Veil.* Princeton: Princeton University Press, 2007.

Selengut, Charles, ed. *Jewish Identity in the Postmodern Age: Scholarly and Personal Reflections.* St Paul, Minn.: Paragon House, 1999.

Seidler, Victor. *Shadows of the Shoah: Jewish Identity and Belonging.* Oxford: Berg, 2000.

Sell, Jonathan P. A. "Chance and Gesture in Zadie Smith's *White Teeth* and *The Autograph Man*: A Model for Multicultural Identity?" *Journal of Commonwealth Literature* 41.3 (2006): 27–44.

Shapiro, James. *Shakespeare and the Jews.* New York: Columbia University Press, 1995.

Shain, Milton. *The Roots of Antisemitism in South Africa.* Charlottesville: University Press of Virginia, 1994.

Sheffer, Gabriel. *Diaspora Politics: At Home Abroad.* Cambridge: Cambridge University Press, 2003.

Shepherd, Robin. *A State Beyond the Pale: Europe's Problem With Israel.* London: Weidenfeld & Nicolson, 2009.

Shepherd, Ronald. *Ruth Prawer Jhabvala in India: The Jewish Connection.* Delhi: Chanakyu Publications, 1994.

Shimoni, Gideon. *Community and Conscience: The Jews in Apartheid South Africa.* Waltham, Mass.: Brandeis University Press, 2003.

————. *Jews and Zionism: The South African Experience, 1910–1967.* Cape Town: Oxford University Press, 1980.

Shindler, Colin. "Reading *The Guardian*: Jews, Israel-Palestine and the Origins of Irritation." In *Jews, Muslims and Mass Media.* Ed. T. Parfitt, and Y. Egorova. London: Routledge Curzon, 2003. 157–77.

———. "The Reflection of Israel within British Jewry." In *Israel, the Diaspora and Jewish Identity.* Ed. Danny Ben-Moshe and Zohar Segev. London: Sussex Academic Press, 2007. 227–34.

Sicher, Efraim. *Beyond Marginality: Anglo-Jewish Literature after the Holocaust.* Albany, N.Y.: New York State University Press, 1985.

———. "Imagining the 'jew': Dickens' Romantic Heritage." In *British Romanticism and the Jews.* Ed. Sheila A. Spector. London and New York: Palgrave, 2002. 139–55.

———. *Antisemitism, Multiculturalism, Globalization: The British Case.* Analysis of Current Trends in Antisemitism, no. 32. Jerusalem: Vidal Sassoon Center for the Study of Antisemitism, Hebrew University of Jerusalem, 2009.

———. "Sir Salman Rushdie Sails for India and Rediscovers Spain: Postmodern Constructions of Sepharad." In *Sephardism: Spanish Jewish History in the Modern Literary Imagination.* Ed. Yael Wise-Halevi. Stanford: Stanford University Press, 2012. 256–73.

Silverman, Max. "Re-Figuring 'the Jew' in France." In *Modernity, Culture, and 'the Jew.'* Ed. Bryan Cheyette and Laura Marcus, 197–207.

Silverstein, Paul. "Immigrant Racialization and the New Savage Slot: Race, Migration, and Immigration in the New Europe." *Annual Review of Anthropology* 34 (2005): 363–84.

Sinclair, Clive. "The Kimberley Fantasy: An Alternative Zion." *Wasafiri* 57 (Spring 2009): 33–43.

Smith, Katharine Capshaw. "Narrating History: The Reality of the Internment Camps in Anita Desai's *Baumgartner's Bombay.*" *Ariel* 28.2 (1997): 141–57.

Solanki, Mrinalini. "Baumgartner's Bombay: An Attempt to Survive." *Indian Women Novelists.* Vol. 2. Ed. R. K. Dhawan. New Delhi: Prestige Books, 1995. 1–13.

Spivak, Gayatri Chakravorty. "Can the Subaltern Speak." In *A Critique of Postcolonial Reason.* Cambridge, Mass.: Harvard University Press, 1999.

———. *The Spivak Reader: Selected Works of Gayatri Chakravorty Spivak.* Eds. Donna Landry and Gerald MacLean. New York: Routledge, 1996.

Stähler, Axel. "The Holocaust in the Nursery: Anita Desai's *Baumgartner's Bombay.*" *Journal of Postcolonial Writing* 46. 1 (2010): 76–88.

Stein, Rebecca. "The Ballad of the Sad Cafés: Israeli Leisure, Palestinian Terror, and the Post/colonial Question." In *Postcolonial Studies and*

Beyond. Eds. Ania Loomba et al., 317–36. Durham: Duke University Press, 2005.

Stoetzler, Marcel. "Cultural Difference in the National State: From Trouser-Selling Jews to Unbridled Multiculturalism." *Patterns of Prejudice* 42.3 (2008): 245–79.

Storry, Mike, and Peter Childs, eds. *British Cultural Identities*. London: Routledge, 1996.

Stratton, John. *Coming Out Jewish: Constructing Ambivalent Identities*. London: Routledge, 2000.

Su, Jung. "Inscribing the Palimpsest: Politics of Hybridity in *The Moor's Sigh*." *Concentric* 29.1 (2003): 199–226.

Taneja, G. R. "*Baumgartner's Bombay*: A Note." In *Indian Women Novelists* Set I. Vol. 4. Ed. R. K. Dhawan. New Delhi: Prestige Books, 1993. 163–73.

Teverson, Andrew. *Salman Rushdie*. Manchester: Manchester University Press, 2007.

Tew, Philip. *The Contemporary British Novel*. 2nd ed. London: Continuum, 2007.

Taguieff, Pierre-André. *La nouvelle judeophobie*. Paris: Mille et Une Nuits, 2002.

Tournay, Petra. "Challenging Shakespeare: Strategies of Writing Back in Zadie Smith's *White Teeth* and Caryl Phillips' *The Nature of Blood*." In *Refracting the Canon in Contemporary British Literature and Film*. Eds. Susana Onega and Christian Gutleben. Amsterdam: Rodopi, 2004. 207–29.

Travis, Madelyn. "'Heritage Anti-Semitism' in Modern Times?: Representations of Jews and Judaism in Twenty-First-Century British Historical Fiction for Children." *European Judaism* 43.1 (Spring 2010): 78–92.

Trousdale, Rachel. "'City of mongrel joy': Bombay and the Shiv Sena in *Midnight's Children* and *The Moor's Last Sigh*." *Journal of Commonwealth Literature* 39.2 (2004): 95–110.

Trumpener, Katie. *Bardic Nationalism: The Romantic Novel and the British Empire*. Princeton: Princeton University Press, 1997.

Tylee, Claire, ed. *"In the open": Jewish Women Writers and British Culture*. Newark: University of Delaware Press, 2006.

Upstone, Sara. "Same Old, Same Old." *Journal of Postcolonial Writing* 43.3 (2007): 336–49.

Valman, Nadia. "The East End Bildungsroman from Israel Zangwill to Monica Ali." *Wasafiri* 24.1 (March 2009): 3–8.

Van Onselen, Charles. "Randlords and Rotgut 1886–1903." *History Workshop Journal* 2.1 (1976): 33–89.

Vitkus, Daniel. *Turning Turk: English Theater and the Multicultural Mediterranean, 1570–1630.* Houndmills and New York: Palgrave Macmillan, 2008.

Waligórska, Magdalena. "A Goy Fiddler on the Roof. How the NonJewish Participants of the Klezmer Revival in Kraków Negotiate Their Polish Identity in a Confrontation with Jews," *Polish Sociological Review* 4.152 (2005): 367–82.

Walkowitz, Rebecca L. "The Location of Literature: The Transnational Book and the Migrant Writer." *Contemporary Literature* 47.4 (Winter 2006): 527–45.

Wandor, Michelene. "The Sex Divide in Jewish Culture: A Meditation on Jewishness and Gender." *Jewish Quarterly* (Spring 1997): 12–13.

Warren, Kristy. "Twenty-First Century Jewish Journeys in Music." *Jewish Culture and History* 11 (2009): 172–83. Reprinted in *Jewish Journeys: From Philo to Hip Hop.* ed. James Jordan, Tony Kushner, and Sarah Pearce. London: Vallentine Mitchell, 2010. 202–15.

Weinhouse, Linda. "Faith and Fantasy: The Texts of the Jews." *Medieval Encounters* 5.3 (1999): 391–408.

Weiss, Timothy. *Translating Orients: Between Ideology and Utopia.* Toronto: University of Toronto Press, 2004.

Werbner, Pnina. "The Limits of Cultural Hybridity: On Ritual Monsters, Poetic License, and Contested Postcolonial Purifications." *Journal of the Royal Anthropology Institute* 7.1 (2001): 133–52.

———. "Theorizing Complex Diasporas: Purity and Hybridity in the South Asian Public Sphere in Britain." *Journal of Ethnic and Migration Studies* 30.5 (2004): 895–911.

Williams, Patrick, and Laura Chrisman, eds. *Colonial Discourse and Post-Colonial Theory.* New York: Columbia University Press, 1994.

Wilson, Jonathan. "How I Became a Jewish Writer in America." In *Who We Are: On Being (and not Being) a Jewish American Writer.* Ed. Derek Rubin. New York: Schocken, 2005. 151–68.

Wisse, Ruth R. *Jews and Power.* New York: Schocken, 2007.

Wistrich, Robert. *Antisemitism: The Longest Hatred.* London: Thames Methuen, 1991.

———. *Anti-Semitism and Multiculturalism: The Uneasy Connection.* Jerusalem: Vidal Sassoon International Center for the Study of Antisemitism, 2007.

———. *Antisemitism in Western Europe at the Turn of the 21st Century.* Jerusalem: World Jewish Congress, 2005.

———. *Between Redemption and Perdition: Modern Antisemitism and Jewish Identity.* London: Routledge, 1990.

———. *A Lethal Obsession: Anti-Semitism from Antiquity to the Global Jihad.* New York: Random House, 2010.

———, ed. *Demonizing the Other: Antisemitism, Racism, and Xenophobia.* Amsterdam: Harwood Academic Publishers, 1999.

Wood, Abigail. "(De)constructing Yiddishland: Solomon and SoCalled's *HipHopKhasene*." *Ethnomusicology Forum*, 16.2 (2007): 243–70.

Worthington, Kim L. *Self as Narrative: Subjectivity and Community in Contemporary Fiction.* Oxford: Clarendon Press, 1996.

Yao, Steve. "Towards a Taxonomy of Hybridity." *Wasafiri* 38 (2003): 30–35.

Young, Robert James Craig. *Colonial Desire: Hybridity in Theory, Culture, and Race.* London: Routledge, 1995.

———. "Hybridism and the Ethnicity of the English." In *Cultural Readings of Imperialism: Edward Said and the Gravity of History*. Eds. Keith Ansell-Pearson, Benita Parry and Benita Parry. London: Lawrence & Wishart, 1997, 127–50.

———. *Postcolonialism: An Historical Introduction.* Oxford: Blackwell, 2001.

———. *Postcolonialism: A Very Short Introduction.* Oxford: Oxford University Press, 2002.

Zierler, Wendy. "'My Holocaust Is Not Your Holocaust': 'Facing' Black and Jewish Experience in *The Pawnbroker, Higher Ground*, and *The Nature of Blood*." *Holocaust and Genocide Studies* 18.1 (2004): 46–67.

Index

Efraim Sicher teaches English and Comparative Literature at Ben-Gurion University of the Negev, Beer-Sheva, Israel, and has published widely on the British nineteenth-century novel, dystopia, and modern Jewish culture. His most recent books are *The Holocaust Novel* (2005) and *Rereading the City/Rereading Dickens* (2nd revised edition, 2012). He is the editor of a forthcoming volume of essays, *Jews Color Race*.

Linda Weinhouse is Professor of English and Women's Studies at the Community College of Baltimore County. She has published articles on Doris Lessing, Alice Munro, Nadine Gordimer, Cynthia Ozick, and Anita Desai.